Advancing Human Development

Advancing Human Development

Theory and Practice

Frances Stewart, Gustav Ranis,
and Emma Samman

OXFORD
UNIVERSITY PRESS

OXFORD
UNIVERSITY PRESS

Great Clarendon Street, Oxford, OX2 6DP,
United Kingdom

Oxford University Press is a department of the University of Oxford.
It furthers the University's objective of excellence in research, scholarship, and education by publishing worldwide. Oxford is a registered trade mark of Oxford University Press in the UK and in certain other countries

First Edition published in 2018

Published in the United States of America by Oxford University Press
198 Madison Avenue, New York, NY 10016, United States of America

British Library Cataloguing in Publication Data
Data available

Library of Congress Control Number: 2017955563

ISBN 978–0–19–879445–5

Preface

This book represents the authors' work on human development (HD) which started in the 1980s with a series of North–South roundtables organized by Mahbub ul Haq, Khadija Haq, and Üner Kirdar. These roundtable discussions formed the origins of the UNDP's *Human Development Report* which was first published in 1990. The team responsible for that *Report* was led by the brilliant Mahbub ul Haq. Gustav Ranis and I were part of the team of consultants. We were inspired by discussions conducted by the preparatory team, including prominently Amartya Sen, whose conceptualization of the capability approach underlies many of the ideas of HD. From then we produced a series of papers on HD. This book includes some of these papers, substantially revised and updated, as well as additional work.

Chapter 1 builds on Stewart (2006) 'The Evolution of Economic Ideas: From Import Substitution to Human Development'; Chapter 2 contains material from Stewart (2014) 'Against Happiness: A Critical Appraisal of the Use of Measures of Happiness for Evaluating Progress in Development'; Chapter 3 draws on and updates Ranis et al. (2000) 'Economic Growth and Human Development' and Suri et al. (2011) 'Paths to Success: The Relationship between Human Development and Economic Growth'; Chapter 4 is a substantially revised version of Ranis and Stewart (2012) 'Success and Failure on Human Development, 1970–2007'; Chapter 6 is a revised version of Ranis et al. (2006) 'Human Development: Beyond the Human Development Index'; and Chapter 7 is a revised version of Stewart (2013b) 'Capabilities and Human Development: Beyond the Individual. The Critical Role of Social Institutions and Social Competencies'.

Work conducted over many decades, of course, owes a great deal to numerous people who have stimulated and critiqued many of the ideas contained here. I am particularly indebted to successive directors of the UNDP's Human Development Report Office—above all, Mahbub ul Haq, who led the initial teams with wisdom, enthusiasm, commitment, and fun. Richard Jolly, Sakiko Fukuda Parr, Kevin Watkins, Jeni Klugman, Khalid Malik, and Selim Jahan carried the work forward in the same spirit with great skill and enthusiasm. I would also like especially to acknowledge the contributions of co-authors of the works listed above, including Alexandro Ramirez, Tavneet

Suri, Michael Boozer, and Yilli Dong, and to thank them for permitting us to draw on the work here. Among the contributions of many former students, I would particularly like to thank Sabina Alkire, Severine Deneulin, and Arnim Langer whose ideas made a substantial contribution to parts of the analysis in this book. Emma and I are grateful to Vidya Diwakar for her contribution to Chapter 3, of which she is a co-author, and to Michelle Chew for her contributions to copy-editing the book.

My biggest debt is to the late Gustav Ranis who was a wonderful collaborator and friend for almost forty years.

Frances Stewart

Contents

List of Figures ix
List of Tables xi
List of Abbreviations xiii

1. The Evolution of Development Thought: From Growth to Human Development 1
2. Should Happiness or Human Development be the Main Development Objective? 26
3. The Relationship between Human Development and Economic Growth 45
4. Success and Failure in Human Development, 1980–2014 74
5. Successful Transition Towards a Virtuous Cycle of Human Development and Economic Growth: Country Studies 94
6. Human Development: Beyond the HDI 123
7. Capabilities and Human Development: Beyond the Individual—The Critical Role of Social Institutions and Social Capabilities 158
8. The Politics of Progress in Human Development 184
9. Achievements, Challenges, and the Way Forward 205

References 237
Index of Names 267
Index of Subjects 273

List of Figures

1.1.	Ideas and development: a diagrammatic representation	4
1.2.	Gross capital formation as % of GDP, 1960–2014	9
1.3.	Industry value-added as % of GDP, 1960–2014	9
1.4.	Under-five mortality by region, 1960–2014	10
1.5.	Gross primary school enrolment rate, 1970–2014	10
1.6.	Gross secondary school enrolment rate, 1970–2014	11
1.7.	Average annual growth in GDP per decade, 1961–2010	11
1.8.	Aid to social sectors as % of total Development Assistance Committee aid, 1970–2010	16
1.9.	Government expenditure on education as % of GDP, 1980–2010	23
2.1.	Scatter of happiness score and HDI, latest year available	36
3.1.	The relationship between HD and GNP	46
3.2.	Classification of country performance, 1970–2014	65
A.3.1.	HD and economic growth by region, initial values and change, 1970–2014	68
4.1.	Change in HDI by region, 1980–2013, % p.a.	75
4.2.	Education expenditure as % of GDP, 1980s and 2000s	79
4.3.	Public expenditure on health as % of GDP, 1995 and 2014	80
4.4.	Gross secondary enrolment ratio, % of age group, 1980s and 2000s	80
4.5.	Female % in total secondary enrolment 1980s and 2000s	81
4.6.	Income per capita, 1980, in US$	82
4.7.	Annual growth in GDP, 1980–2014	82
4.8.	Inequality in the 1980s and 2000s	83
4.9.	% of population in poverty, most recent date	84
4.10.	Political freedom index (polity2), 1980s and 2000s	86
4.11.	Gender Inequality Index (GII), average 2005, 2010, and 2013	87
4.12.	Intentional homicides per 100,000 people, average 2000–14	88
4.13.	No. of years in intense conflict, 1980–2014	89
4.14.	Environmental Progress Index (EPI) and ten-year change, 1996–2016	90
4.15.	CO_2 emissions per capita, 1980–2013, average	91

5.1. Positive transitions to be explored, 1970s–2000s 95
5.2. Negative transitions to be explored, 1970s–2000s 95
5.3. Annual growth in Ethiopia, 2000–14 108
5.4. Net annual aid to Ethiopia, 1970s–2014 108
5.5. Under-five mortality in Ethiopia, 1970–2014 109
5.6. Mozambique: food production index, 1970–2012 111
5.7. Mozambique: % change per annum in exports and GNI per capita, 1981–2014 111
5.8. Peru: GDP per capita and food production indices, 1970–2012 116
5.9. Average annual % growth in GDP, weak performers, 1970s–2000s 120
5.10. Gross capital formation as % of GDP, weak performers, 1970–2013 120
7.1. The relationship between social institutions and individual capabilities 172
7.2. Social cohesion triangle 178
7.3. High and low social cohesion 178
8.1. Progress in life expectancy, literacy, and living standards in thirteen Latin American countries, 1900–2000 192
9.1. Proportion of countries classified as 'free', 1980–2015 212
9.2. Unemployment as % of labour force, 1991–2014 219
9.3. Labour's share of corporate income by skill level, 1995–2009 220
9.4. Mobile phones per 100 people, 2000–14 221
9.5. % of population with electricity, 1990–2012 222
9.6. % of population with access to internet, 2001 and 2014 222
9.7. Violent conflicts in the world, 1989–2016 223
9.8. Refugees and internally displaced, 1980–2015, millions 224
9.9. A measure of economic insecurity, 1980–2014 225
9.10. Material footprint by region, 1990–2008 227
9.11. CO_2 emissions by region, 1980–2011 227

List of Tables

1.1. The stages of evolution of thought 5
2.1. Correlations between happiness score and HDI and components, around 2015 35
2.2. Correlation between happiness score and HDI, by level of HDI, around 2015 35
2.3. Some correlates with happiness measures across individuals, various years 38
2.4. Elements of Bhutan's Gross National Happiness Index 42
A.3.1. From economic growth to the change in life expectancy, 1970–2014 69
A.3.2. From economic growth to the change in HD (measured by education and IMR change, 1970–2014) 70
A.3.3. From HD to change in economic growth (dependent variable is GDP per capita growth, 1970–2014) 71
A.3.4. Country classification by decade, 1970s to 2000s 72
4.1. Countries with successful basic HD experiences, 1970s to 2000s 77
4.2. Countries with particularly weak basic HD performance, 1970s to 2000s 77
6.1. Requirements for human flourishing 125
6.2. Dimensions and indicators 131
6.3. Mental well-being indicators 133
6.4. Empowerment indicators 134
6.5. Political freedom indicators 135
6.6. Social relations indicators 136
6.7. Community well-being indicators 137
6.8. Inequality indicators 140
6.9. Work conditions indicators 140
6.10. Leisure conditions indicators 141
6.11. Economic insecurity 142
6.12. Political stability indicators 143
6.13. Correlations between retained indicators and HDI 144

6.14. The relationship of indicators to the core measures 145
6.15. Correlation among basic indicators of HD 146
B.6.1. Summary of indicators and sources 149
B.6.2. Correlations between retained indicators and per capita income 156
B.6.3. Selected indicators for OECD countries, and relationship to HDI 157
7.1. Role of social institutions in affecting major capabilities 163
7.2. The domains of social cohesion 176
C.7.1. Classification of countries according to HD, economic, political, and social performance 182

List of Abbreviations

BRAC	Building Resources across Communities
EG	economic growth
EPI	Environmental Progress Index
FRELIMO	*Frente de Libertação de Moçambique*
GDI	Gender Development Index
GDP	gross domestic product
GEM	Gender Empowerment Measure
GII	Gender Inequality Index
GNI	gross national income
GNP	gross national product
GSER	Gross Secondary Educational Enrolment, % of age-group
GSERF	Gross Secondary Educational Enrolment of Females, % of age-group
GSERMF	Gross Secondary Educational Enrolment, male to female ratio
HD	human development
HDI	Human Development Index
HDIF	human development improvement function
HDRO	Human Development Report Office
HI	horizontal inequality
HPI	Human Poverty Index
HR	human rights
IFIs	international financial institutions
ILO	International Labour Organization
IMF	International Monetary Fund
IMR	infant mortality rate per 1,000 live births
INSCR	Integrated Network for Societal Conflict Research
ISI	import-substituting industrialization
LAC	Latin America and the Caribbean
LE	Life Expectancy at birth

MDGs	Millennium Development Goals
MF	material footprint
MPI	Multidimensional Poverty Index
MST	*Movimento Sem Terra*
NGO	non-governmental organization
NIEO	New International Economic Order
OECD	Organisation for Economic Co-operation and Development
OPEC	Organization of the Petroleum Exporting Countries
PPP	purchasing power parity
PQLI	Physical Quality of Life Index
PSNP	Productive Safety Net Programme
PT	*Partido dos Trabalhadores*
R&D	research and development
RENAMO	*Resistência Nacional Moçambicana*
SDGs	Sustainable Development Goals
SMCs	socially mobilized communities
TRT	Thai Rak Thai Party
UDHR	Universal Declaration of Human Rights
UN	United Nations
UNDP	United Nations Development Programme
UNHCR	The Office of the United Nations High Commissioner for Refugees
UNICEF	United Nations Children's Fund
WAVES	Wealth Accounting and the Valuation of Ecosystem Services
WDI	World Development Indicators
WHO	World Health Organization

1

The Evolution of Development Thought

From Growth to Human Development

> The basic objective of development is to create an enabling environment for people to live long, healthy and creative lives... Human development is a process of enlarging people's choices. The most critical ones are to lead a long and healthy life, to be educated and to enjoy a decent standard of living. Additional choices include political freedom, guaranteed human rights and self-respect.
>
> United Nations Development Programme (UNDP),
> *Human Development Report 1990*

1.1. Introduction

The human development (HD) approach was initiated in 1990 with the first *Human Development Report*. It represents a major change from the widely accepted views of development of post-colonial decision-makers and advisers in the 1950s and 1960s, which put growth in per capita incomes as the central objective of development. However, the approach did not represent a complete break from previous thinking. Rather it was the outcome of a long evolution in ideas, policies, and outcomes. This chapter traces this movement of thought about development, broadly from growth to HD, with some digressions en route. It thus provides the historical context for the ideas developed in this book.

In the forty-year span, from the 1950s to the 1990s, there were many changes in the way development was viewed—both in terms of objectives and the mechanisms thought to be optimal to achieve these objectives. Views of the appropriate aims of development and how to achieve them emerged in response to a number of factors. These include: changing conditions in developing countries and the global economy, evolving theories partly in response to these changes on the ground, and policy changes which in turn affected conditions and outcomes. The policies introduced were formulated under the influence of prevailing ideas as well as varying pressures from the interest groups and populations affected. Each set of policies contributed to further changes in socio-economic conditions giving rise to new problems and opportunities, new thinking, and further changes in policy. This chapter explores this evolving logic, which ultimately led to HD becoming a central objective.

Section 1.2 sketches a framework for considering the evolution of thought about development. Section 1.3 provides a brief overview of the major changes that occurred. More detailed analysis of the evolution is provided in Section 1.4. Section 1.5 briefly takes the story beyond the introduction of the HD concept in the 1990s, to consider the impact it has had, some limitations to date, and new challenges to the concept.

1.2. A Framework for Considering the Evolution of Development Strategies

The evolution of development strategies is a complex, organic, and cumulative process. It involves the interaction of development outcomes (or events in the world), ideas, policymaking, and the consequences of those policies, which in turn affect the way the world is perceived, leading to a new cycle of thought/policy/events. Each of these stages is influenced by political pressures and interest groups.

Ideas do not come out of the blue but are heavily influenced by two types of context, both historically formed: on the one hand, the intellectual context; and on the other, the socio-economic context. The intellectual context is invariably multifaceted. There tends to be a prevailing view—sometimes known, critically, as 'conventional wisdom'—although there are always dissenting voices. In order to trace the evolution of ideas, here we generally take an oversimplified view, attributing to each era a particular set of prevalent ideas (or conventional wisdom), but pointing also to some alternative strands of thinking. For developing countries, especially in the immediate aftermath of colonialism, ideas from developed countries dominated; even though some challenged developed country perspectives, it was virtually impossible to ignore them altogether. As a result, ideas that were prevalent about what to do in developing countries frequently reflected the views of economists (and to a lesser extent others) in and about developed countries. This initial hegemony of ideas was enforced by the international financial institutions (IFIs) which have been, and remain, a dominant source of influence over thinking, largely reflecting developed country views. However, over time, a richer and more varied intellectual context has developed, with many ideas contributed locally.

The other important contextual element is the prevailing socio-economic situation: the state of the economy (income levels, economic structure, investment rates, employment, etc.) and the state of the people (poverty rates, education, health, sanitation, etc.). Policies are formulated to deal with the prevailing socio-economic situation, in the context of the intellectual heritage which determines the range of policies considered appropriate and feasible. Although contemporary socio-economic conditions are highly relevant to policy choice, ideas tend to limit decision-makers' (and advisers') perceptions of these conditions, so there is a tendency to continue to adopt an accepted position long after clear failures are (or should be) apparent. International actors tend to be heavily influenced by developments in their own countries and their ideological and intellectual presuppositions. As Dudley Seers (1962, 329) pointed out in an aptly titled article ('Why Visiting Economists Fail'), 'what usually happens is that the model the economist consciously or unconsciously uses turns out to be the sort of model suitable for a developed country'.

Socio-economic conditions change over time. Old problems may be solved and new ones emerge in both developed and developing countries. Policy choices have consequences—foreseen and unforeseen—i.e. they lead to a new 'reality'. Where the policy choices lead to unforeseen and undesired consequences, they can cause a revision in development thinking—for example, if a growth-promoting policy has the consequence of an unsustainable level of debt, new thinking evolves to deal with the debt situation. Consequently, after a time lag, new objectives may be adopted and new policies selected in line with the new thinking, again subject to evolving political power and interests.

We thus observe a cyclical process, as the new policies in turn influence socio-economic conditions, create new problems and opportunities, stimulate new ideas, and eventually foster policy change. Further complications to this cyclical process arise from two sources. First, there may be world events, such as global recession, which constrain a country's options. Second, interest groups play a major role in shaping thought and influencing policy. For example, those gaining by an import-substitution strategy may oppose import liberalization, or the financial sector may support capital market liberalization and oppose domestic capital controls.

The cyclical process briefly summarized above is illustrated in Figure 1.1. The evolution of development thinking in the last half of the twentieth century, with the movement from a focus on growth in the 1950s to HD in the 1990s and beyond, broadly follows such a cyclical process. The rest of this chapter aims to show how the process worked in practice over this period, and in so doing, trace the origins of the idea of HD.

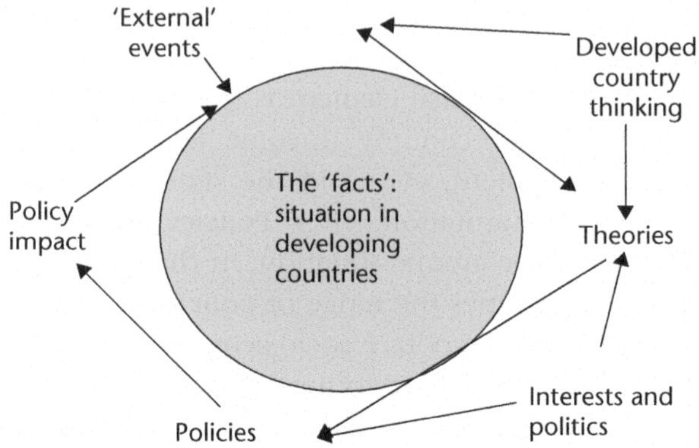

Figure 1.1. Ideas and development: a diagrammatic representation

1.3. An Overview of the Major Changes in Thought

We need to differentiate two types of change: first, changing *objectives*; and second, changes in views about the best *processes*, or mechanisms, needed to achieve the objectives. There have been major changes in both since the 1950s. With respect to objectives, the change has been from economic growth to human-centred objectives; and in terms of process, there has been a switch from a state-oriented approach to reliance on the market, both in ownership and allocation of resources. For both types of change, the speed (and even the direction) of change has varied among institutions, across countries, and over time. In general, while the acceptance of human-centred objectives has been extensive and sustained,[1] in principle at least, changes in process have been more controversial.

There are links between mechanisms and objectives. Some 'mechanisms' (e.g. the market system) constitute important objectives for some players,[2] while the mechanisms adopted generate interest groups which can influence objectives. There is also an ideological connection between objectives and mechanisms—a strong market orientation in relation to mechanisms is associated with placing a high value on market outcomes and market values, and consequently monetary incomes as a measure of achievement. Conversely, human-centred objectives encourage more scepticism about market mechanisms.

[1] The chief economist of the World Bank, Kaushik Basu, was reported as stating that 'the Human Development Reports permanently changed global development discourse by putting people rather than GDP growth at the center of their analysis' (unpublished report on a World Bank Forum on the *2013 Human Development Report*, 22 May 2013). (An abbreviated account is given in Jackson-Han 2013.)

[2] For example, George W. Bush has stated: 'The case for trade is not just monetary, but moral' (Bush 1999).

Table 1.1. The stages of evolution of thought

Timeframe	Socio-economic context	Dominant strands in developed country thinking	Dominant thinking about development
1950s	Low incomes; post-colonialism	Keynesianism	**Growth**, planning, and industrialization (Rostow, Lewis, Nurkse)
1960s	Desire to develop		
1970s	Growth, but high poverty and unemployment	A. Keynesianism	A. **Employment** (Seers) **Redistribution with growth** (Chenery, Singer) **Basic Needs** (ILO, Streeten, Ranis, Stewart, Haq) **PQLI** (Morris)
		B. Marxism	B. Dependency (*dependencia*) (Frank, Furtado)
		C. Neoclassical revival	C. Prices/market (Little, Scott, Scitovsky)
1980s	Acute balance of payments and debt problems	Monetarists' counter-revolution	Pro-market and anti-state; monetarism in macro policy (Friedman, Balassa, World Bank) New political economy (Krueger, Bhagwati)
Late 1980s to mid-1990s	Negative/weak growth, high poverty, high debt of 1980s	New theories of growth and trade; informational asymmetries; alternative motivations; institutions	The move towards human-oriented objectives: **Poverty reduction** **Capabilities** **Human Development** **MDGs** (Sen, Haq, Ranis, Stewart, Streeten)

Table 1.1 provides an overview of the developments we explore in this chapter. The changes have been divided into decades, which provides a convenient oversimplification. Ideas take time to change and are by no means simultaneously or universally accepted, nor do they fit neatly into decades. In many decades, more than one school of thought is present. The second column indicates the changing socio-economic context, with a very brief summary of the major problems confronting decision-makers at the beginning of each decade. We can see from this that there were big changes over time. The third column indicates dominant thinking about the economy in developed countries, and the fourth column shows how thinking about development changed, including both objectives and mechanisms. The names of some of the people particularly closely associated with each category of thought are also included—although the list of names is by no means complete. The objectives are picked out in bold, while the other elements consist largely of changing thought about mechanisms rather than objectives. The table ends in 2000, with the Millennium Development Goals (MDGs), which in some ways

epitomize the switch to HD; they contain only 'human'-oriented goals, with no mention of the economy, and were subscribed to by every major institution and government, North and South. Development in the subsequent decade, culminating in the global agreement on the Sustainable Development Goals (SDGs) in 2015, is discussed at the end of this chapter.

Section 1.4 now provides a more detailed discussion of the evolution summarized in Table 1.1.

1.4. The Evolution of Ideas from the 1950s to the 1990s: Planning, Growth, and Basic Needs

At the beginning of the 1950s, most developing countries found themselves in a situation of profound underdevelopment and dependency, characterized by low incomes, a predominantly agrarian structure with a large subsistence subsector, and heavy dependence on the advanced countries for technology, management, and capital goods. Under colonialism, economic development was directed mainly towards the production of primary products, owned and controlled by settlers or colonialists. The rest of the economy, which typically accounted for the majority of the population, remained outside the small 'modern' enclave. For the most part, the education and health levels of the majority of the population were very poor. Latin America was somewhat of an exception, most countries having become independent in the nineteenth century, but their trade sector too was dominated by primary product exports, and while levels of incomes, health, and education were higher than in most other developing regions, they were substantially worse than in developed countries. The majority of developing countries had a life expectancy of below fifty years and quite a few below forty years, while illiteracy rates of over 50 per cent were common. This was the socio-economic reality confronting policymakers in the early 1950s. To combat this situation, thinkers and policymakers in developing countries gave primacy to economic growth as their overriding economic objective, with industrialization seen as the most effective way of achieving higher incomes, following the trajectory of the more developed countries.

Developed countries, too, recognized the need for a new growth-centred approach to the former colonial territories. President Truman (1949) famously declared that:

> We must embark on a bold new program for making the benefits of our scientific advances and industrial progress available for the improvement and growth of underdeveloped areas.... The old imperialism is dead—exploitation for foreign profit has no place in our plans.

Among developed countries, as a result of the long depression experienced between the two world wars followed by wartime experience of planning and controls, Keynesian views of policymaking were generally accepted, and a quite strongly interventionist economic philosophy prevailed. In countries such as the UK and France, basic industries were taken into public ownership. This was also the era of apparently thriving socialism in the Russian empire. Consequently, a statist interventionist philosophy came from advisers in developed countries, which resonated with the objectives, politics, and philosophy of newly independent countries.

All agreed that the dominant objective of economic policy in developing countries was to increase economic growth: it was assumed that if growth were achieved, other objectives would also be met, including employment expansion and poverty reduction, through what came to be known as a 'trickle-down' process. Economists' advice on how to achieve the growth objective had three main prongs:

- that industrialization was an essential element in the process of catching up with developed countries (Prebisch 1950, Singer 1950, Mahalanobis 1953, Lewis 1954, Rostow 1960);
- that surplus labour in agriculture provided a major potential resource (Nurkse 1953, Lewis 1954, Fei and Ranis 1964); and
- that government intervention of various kinds was needed to tap this potential and promote industrialization, including support for investment and protection against industrial imports (Rosenstein-Rodan 1943, Hirschman 1958).

Economists from both North and South accepted this pro-government, pro-intervention, and pro-industrialization stance, as well as the associated planning and import controls. Prebisch, Mahalanobis, and Lewis were the intellectual giants behind the strategy from the South. From the North, Nurkse, Rostow, Rosenstein-Rodan, and Myrdal were prominent.[3]

These policies had the support of interest groups in both the North and the South. In the South, the elites saw opportunities for profits and power in developing industry and workers stood to gain from industrial expansion, while the poor in agriculture—most likely to lose from the policies—were generally not organized for political or economic lobbying. In the North, support

[3] Economists differed in their emphasis. The Lewis/Ranis-Fei model incorporated two key ideas: the potential use of surplus labour in agriculture and the role of industrialization in growth; Prebisch and Singer were strong proponents of the need for industrialization to counter deteriorating terms of trade for primary products; while Rosenstein-Rodan, drawing from Eastern European experience, emphasized the need for government intervention to overcome externalities; this was supported by Hirschman making the case for 'unbalanced' growth.

for development offered both economic and political benefits—markets for their products, a role for their companies, and a weapon in the Cold War.

1.4.1. *Policies in the 1950s and 1960s*

'The need for development planning is well recognised' (Fei and Ranis 1964, 199). Plans (typically five-year plans) were introduced almost everywhere: for example, by Mahalanobis in India, Prebisch in Latin America, and Seers and Lewis in many African economies (see e.g. Killick 1976). The state was given a major role in determining economic priorities via price and import controls, investment planning, and sometimes as a producer. Policies promoted investment through direct investment by the state, especially in underdeveloped infrastructure, and foreign investment was encouraged with a variety of tax incentives. Import-substituting industrialization (ISI) was adopted based on high tariffs and quantitative import restrictions. Although the focus was on economic growth based on industrialization, policies were also introduced to accelerate the development of the social sectors.

1.4.2. *Consequences of the Pro-Planning Pro-Industrialization Policies*

The policies adopted were in some ways remarkably successful. Savings and investment rates rose substantially (see Figure 1.2), industry grew, most countries saw sustained growth (see Figures 1.3 and 1.7), and a few countries, notably Taiwan and the Republic of Korea, experienced spectacular growth rates. Social indicators, such as under-five mortality and school enrolment rates, also improved (see Figures 1.4, 1.5, and 1.6). But other developments were less welcome. Population growth accelerated and growth in employment, especially in the industrial sector, lagged behind output. Unemployment and underemployment emerged as serious problems, partly as a consequence of the very success of policies in expanding output and employment in the industrial sector. The growth of employment opportunities together with a rise in real wages in this sector (partly due to the widespread introduction of minimum wages) increased job-seeking. As opportunities and real wages in the modern sector expanded, rural–urban migration increased, as did open urban unemployment and the urban informal sector.[4] Moreover, the incidence of poverty remained very high as a proportion of the population in most developing countries, while the absolute numbers of people falling below a given poverty line increased.

[4] The Harris–Todaro model formalized this relationship (though omitting the informal sector) (see Harris and Todaro 1970).

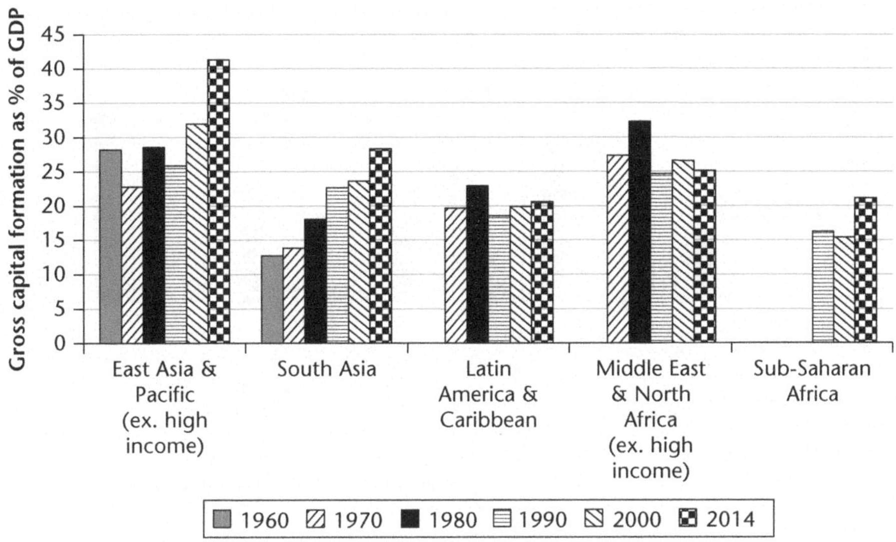

Figure 1.2. Gross capital formation as % of GDP, 1960–2014
Source: World Bank (n.d.)

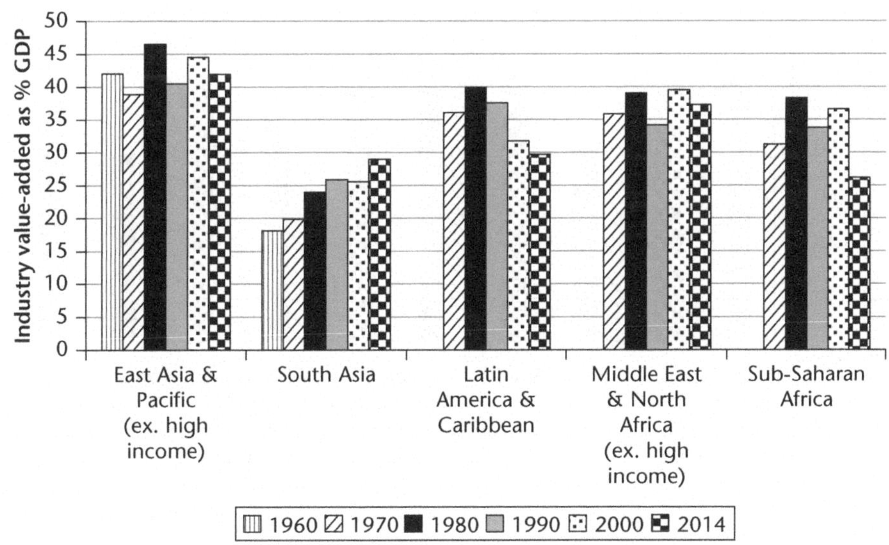

Figure 1.3. Industry value-added as % of GDP, 1960–2014
Source: World Bank (n.d.)

A dualistic pattern of development resulted, with a small, relatively privileged modern sector leaving the rest of the economy with low incomes and investment. The International Labour Organization (ILO 1976, 15) summarized the position: 'it has become increasingly evident, particularly from the

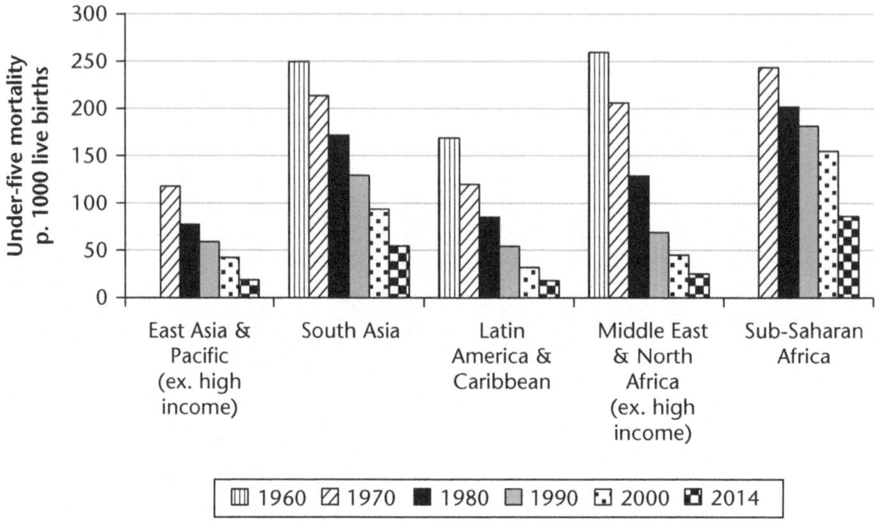

Figure 1.4. Under-five mortality by region, 1960–2014
Source: World Bank (n.d.)

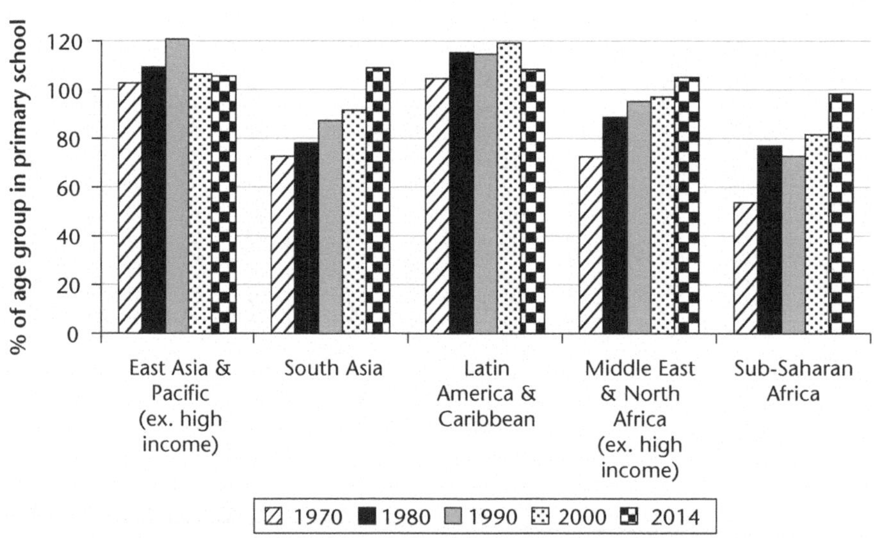

Figure 1.5. Gross primary school enrolment rate, 1970–2014
Source: World Bank (n.d.)

experience of the developing countries, that rapid growth at the national level does not automatically reduce poverty or inequality or provide sufficient productive employment'. Put briefly, trickle-down from economic growth had been insufficient. Moreover, the economic independence sought was

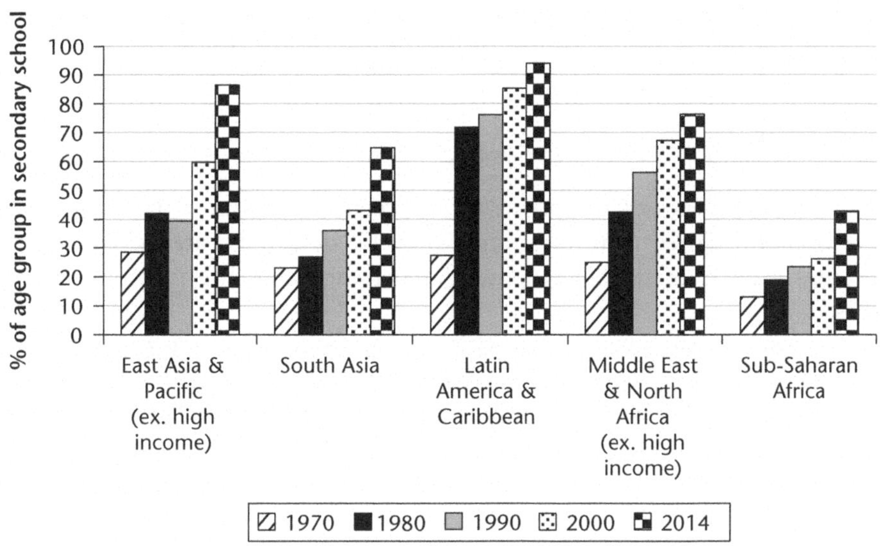

Figure 1.6. Gross secondary school enrolment rate, 1970–2014
Source: World Bank (n.d.)

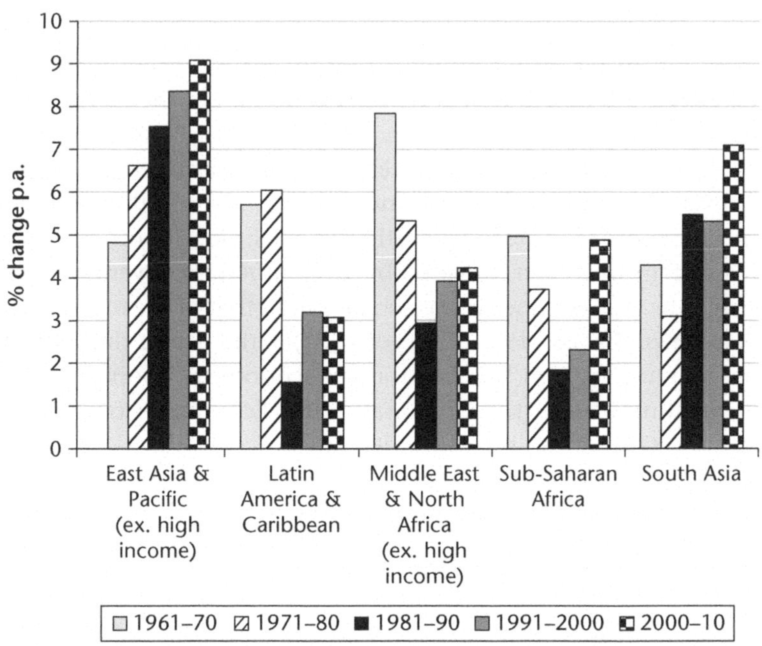

Figure 1.7. Average annual growth in GDP per decade, 1961–2010
Source: World Bank (n.d.)

elusive, as heavy dependence on developed countries for capital and technology remained.

1.4.3. *Thinking in the Late 1960s and 1970s*

These consequences of the pro-state ISI policies led to new thinking about development. Three distinct strands may be detected, each a reaction to different aspects of the development experience over the previous twenty years.

First, some became concerned with the failure to achieve economic independence. This gave rise to the dependency school of thought, both Marxist and structuralist, by writers mostly from the South, such as Furtado, Sunkel, Amin, and Frank—the last an American but working in Latin America (Frank 1969, Sunkel 1969, Amin 1974, Furtado 1985). They focused on the problems arising from the heavy dependence on developed countries in peripheral economies—for markets, technology, finance, and managers—and argued for reduced links between rich and poor countries, although there were major differences within the dependency school (see reviews by Palma 1978 and Oman and Wignaraja 1991, ch. 5).[5] The dependency school was dominated by scholars from the South, and its views were in no way shared by the donor community.

A second reaction to the events of the 1950s and 1960s, initiated in the 1970s but only becoming dominant in the 1980s, reflected the growing influence of monetarism and neoclassical economics in the North. The rapid and fairly egalitarian growth experienced in East Asia, which was argued to have adopted a neoclassical free market approach, was contrasted with what was claimed to be a capital-intensive and elite-dominated pattern of growth in many other countries. It was argued that in most developing countries, the incentive system had been distorted by government interventions, and the role of (imperfect) governments was too large and that of the market too small (Little et al. 1970, Balassa 1971, Krueger 1974). Criticism of the statist model came almost entirely from Western-trained economists, sponsored by major Western institutions (e.g. the Organisation for Economic Co-operation and Development (OECD) and the World Bank).

The third reaction to developments in the 1950s and 1960s saw the beginnings of a more human-centred approach to development, and it is this which lay the foundations for the HD approach. In the light of the rising poverty and

[5] Some believed that the North–South relationship could be controlled by active policies; some felt that this was impossible because of the political consequences of dependency (e.g. Leys 1975); while some thought that the North–South connection was ultimately progressive and would eventually lead to the emergence of a proletariat and revolution (Warren 1980).

unemployment that had become evident in the 1960s, it was argued that countries had been pursuing the *wrong objective*. Seers pointed to the need to 'dethrone GNP' (gross national product): '[the] questions to ask about a country's development are therefore: what has been happening to poverty? What has been happening to unemployment? What has been happening to inequality?' (Seers 1972, 24). Broadly following these questions, candidates put forward for replacing GNP as the main economic objective were, successively, employment, redistribution with growth, and the fulfilment of basic needs. This rejection of growth as the major objective came primarily from developed countries and international institutions. It was viewed less favourably by developing country governments.

The idea of making employment the major objective of development was initiated by Seers working with the ILO.[6] However, deeper analysis of the role of employment suggested that employment is generally not wanted in itself (indeed, traditionally economics has regarded employment as involving *disutility* not *utility*), but rather for the various benefits it confers, including income-generation and recognition (Sen 1975). Consequently, types of employment which generated only very low incomes and little respect did not constitute an appropriate objective. Hence, a second major ILO Employment Mission (to Kenya, led by Hans Singer and Richard Jolly) concentrated on *productive employment*, focusing on raising productivity and the incomes of those already working (often in the informal sector) as much as providing new employment for the unemployed (ILO 1972).[7] Drawing on the *Kenya Report*, Chenery and others advocated *redistribution with growth* as the prime objective of development (Chenery et al. 1979). This proposed giving priority to the incomes of the poor, by weighting them more heavily in measurement of incomes, and to achieve redistribution by siphoning off the fruits of growth in the form of investment resources for the poor, thereby permitting continued growth while gradually increasing the incomes of the poor as they acquired additional assets.

Yet are incomes, even incomes of the poor, an adequate objective? Incomes, it was argued, were not wanted for themselves but for the way of life they made possible. The poor had basic needs that should be met; income was a means rather than an end, and often not a very efficient means since some basic needs, goods or services were best provided by the public sector. Hence a

[6] Seers led an ILO Employment Mission to Colombia that made full employment its central objective and did not even include GNP projections in the main body of the ILO report, though ironically an appendix showed that achievement of the full employment objective involved a substantial acceleration in growth of GNP (ILO 1970).

[7] This approach was revived by the ILO in the 2000s, also in reaction to unsatisfactory employment growth, as a need for 'decent' employment (ILO 2000).

basic needs approach to development emerged, first in the ILO, then taken up by the World Bank (see ILO 1976, Streeten et al. 1981, Stewart 1985).

A parallel development was an increasing emphasis on human rights (HR). The 1948 Universal Declaration of Human Rights (UDHR) declared that everyone had 'economic, social and cultural rights indispensable for his [*sic*] dignity and the free development of his personality' (Article 22). Elaborating on this, Article 25 stated that everyone had a right to a 'standard of living adequate for the health and well-being of himself and his family, including food, clothing, housing and medical care and necessary social services and the right to security in the event of unemployment, sickness, disability', while Article 26 declared that everyone had a right to education 'directed to the full development of the human personality'. This remarkable document covers very much the same ground as the basic needs approach. The HR approach was given renewed focus in the International Covenant on Economic, Social and Cultural Rights (1966), which entered into force in 1976 and has been ratified by the vast majority of countries. The economic and social rights embodied in the Covenant are very similar to those advocated by the basic needs approach.[8] In principle the two approaches are complementary, and adopting an rights approach could be an effective way of advancing basic needs, and, equally, meeting basic needs would contribute to realizing these human rights. In practice, however, the early attempts to enforce the Covenant were not effective, with the main responsibility for supervision allotted to a working group of government representatives and experts which did little to define the requirements for realizing particular rights, or to secure effective supervision (Westerveen 1984, Alston 1987).

Each of these approaches was a reaction to the consequences of the previous growth-focused development strategy. The dependency approach responded to the evident failure of developing countries to become economically independent or to achieve favourable terms of trade, market, and technology access, despite industrialization and economic growth. The anti-planning reaction responded to the perceived inefficiencies of the growth strategy. And the nexus of the employment/redistribution/basic needs approaches responded to the failure of the growth strategy to deliver in terms of human needs and distribution.

1.4.4. *Policies in the 1970s*

The dependency (*dependencia*) approach had most influence on policies in the 1970s, though its effects were short-lived. The neoliberal philosophy only

[8] For a comparison see Stewart (1989).

began to influence policymaking significantly in the 1980s; the import-substitution and planning policies continued to work quite well in the 1970s, sustained by international borrowing and with support from powerful local interest groups. Most developing countries continued their previous inward-looking, macroeconomic, and interventionist policies over this period. The basic needs approach had a strong, but short-lived, influence on *donor* philosophy, but limited impact on developing country policy, while the International Covenant on Economic, Social and Cultural Rights appeared to have had very limited influence over policymaking.

The underlying belief of the dependency school was of gross unfairness in the world's economy, with a bias against the South: this formed the background to the Organization of the Petroleum Exporting Countries (OPEC) as well as to the claims for a New International Economic Order (NIEO) put forward by the G77 in 1974, which contained demands for improved terms for developing countries, including on market access, trade, technology transfer, and aid. Besides OPEC activities, other policy manifestations of the dependency approach were restrictions on foreign direct investment and controls over technology transfer, adopted most comprehensively by the Andean Pact countries and India.

Neither the employment objective nor redistribution with growth significantly affected policy, the latter perhaps because of a basic political flaw in its reasoning: that once elites have secured large benefits from growth they were unlikely to allow these benefits to be taken away and redistributed to the less well-off as required by the strategy. The basic needs approach was widely adopted by the international community, first by the ILO, then by the World Bank under McNamara as well as by major bilateral aid agencies and some of the specialised agencies of the United Nations, which introduced a series of basic needs-style targets, such as Universal Primary Healthcare and Universal Primary Education. But developing country governments were in general more impressed by the conclusions of the dependency school, and viewed the basic needs approach as an excuse by the developed countries to avoid their demands for an NIEO. There was a large shift in aid towards the social sectors, and away from support to industry (see Figure 1.8). Although few developing countries accepted the approach fully, the evidence shows continued improvements in human indicators over the 1970s (see Figures 1.4 and 1.5).

1.4.5 *Consequences of OPEC Actions*

It was the *dependencia* thinking that had the largest impact on immediate events and policymaking. In the sellers' market created by high world demand, the belligerent attitude of the oil producers led to a major oil price

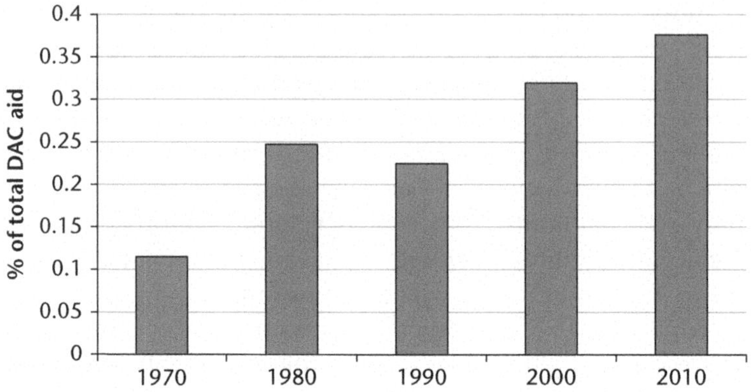

Figure 1.8. Aid to social sectors as % of total Development Assistance Committee aid, 1970–2010

Source: Development Assistance Committee statistics

rise in 1972–3,[9] creating large imbalances in the world economy and inflationary pressures in developed countries. Most oil-importing developing countries borrowed to finance the resulting trade deficits, eventually leading to a massive accumulation of debt as well as rising budgetary and trade imbalances, made worse by a further increase in oil prices in 1978–9. In developed countries, inflation rates accelerated, reaching unprecedented levels. These changes were influential in generating a major turnaround in thinking in dominant developed countries in the early 1980s, and subsequently in developing countries.

1.4.6. *Development Thought in the 1980s: The Dominance of Neoliberalism*

The first revolution in thinking occurred in developed countries. With a radical change in the political complexion of governments in the US and UK, partly due to the electorates' response to rampant inflation, economic philosophy changed too. Milton Friedman (1969) replaced Keynes. Reagan and Thatcher espoused monetary policies, abandoning Keynesianism, in principle if not always in practice.[10] This had the immediate effect of raising world interest rates, ushering in world recession, and causing a downward movement in commodity prices. The resulting rise in interest rates and worsening

[9] Crude oil prices rose fourfold in 1972–3, and more than doubled in 1978–9.

[10] Thatcher did succeed in slowing down the growth in the money supply and securing a budgetary balance. Reagan pursued monetary policies to the point of generating high interest rates. But budgetary and trade imbalances exploded in a most Keynesian way.

terms of trade meant that many developing countries could no long afford to service their debts and had to turn to the IFIs—the International Monetary Fund (IMF) and World Bank—for assistance. Latin America and sub-Saharan Africa were affected most. Asia generally had avoided a debt accumulation in the 1970s and countries there were able to retain more autonomy.

The view that the state in developing countries had overreached itself had already been argued by a succession of pro-market analysts in the early 1970s. The discrediting of what came to be termed 'dirigisme', with the view that government failures usually outweighed market failures, was carried further in the early 1980s (Little 1982, Lal 1983). A monetarist, anti-government, pro-market *laissez-faire* philosophy became generally accepted in major developed countries, permeating aid agencies and educational establishments and, as a consequence, the 'technocrats' in developing countries who were mainly educated in these establishments.

1.4.7. *Policy Consequences of Neoliberalism*

By 1980, the anti-state, pro-market philosophy had been adopted by the World Bank and IMF, whose power over policymaking in developing countries greatly increased in this decade. The onset of an acute debt crisis in the early 1980s, as a result of the debt accumulated in the 1970s and the rise in interest rates when developed countries switched to monetary policies, gave both the World Bank and the IMF much greater power over developing country policymaking. The World Bank initiated structural adjustment loans, which were conditional on the deregulation of markets, reduced price controls, subsidies, and tariffs, and the elimination of restrictions on imports and foreign direct investment. IMF loans were conditional on the acceptance of monetarism—the reduction and eventual elimination of budgetary and trade imbalances through tight controls over the budget and money supply. The IMF and World Bank policies taken together were conveniently labelled by Williamson (1989) as 'the Washington consensus'. Considerations of poverty reduction or basic needs virtually disappeared from these institutions. The IFIs' growing control over policymaking in developing countries led to the adoption of monetarist policies and deregulation in the majority of developing countries over the course of the 1980s. There was a massive switch in policies, including by some countries which adopted Washington consensus policies independently of the IFIs.[11]

[11] See, e.g. Williamson (1990), World Bank and UNDP (1989), and Dean et al. (1994) for evidence of the advance of these policies in Latin America and Africa.

1.4.8. *Consequences of Stabilization and Adjustment Policies in the 1980s*

For the regions most subject to Washington tutelage—Africa and Latin America—the stabilization and adjustment policies were accompanied by falling gross domestic product (GDP) per capita for much of the 1980s, worsening income distribution, falling real expenditure per head on the social services, and, in many countries, by a quite sharp rise in both private and social poverty (Cornia et al. 1986). There was evidence of rising malnutrition in many African countries. Educational enrolments and achievements fell, as did investment rates, in a number of Latin American and African countries. Yet despite strong efforts, the macro imbalances were mostly not eliminated, as falling commodity prices and continued accumulation of debt made the situation more challenging. Both 'adjusting' and 'non-adjusting' countries did poorly.[12] The large and widespread rise in absolute poverty in Latin America and Africa gave a major impetus to the recognition of the need for a change in both objectives and mechanisms.

1.4.9. *New Thinking in Response to the Adjustment Era*

As with the 1970s, we can detect three different types of response to the stabilization era: one was increasing recognition of the deficiencies of the rather simplistic neoclassical model underlying the Washington consensus policies; the second was acceptance of the need for a much greater focus on poverty reduction; and the third was advocacy of a major change in development objectives, once more away from incomes, but this time towards HD and the expansion of capabilities.

1.4.9.1. THEORETICAL CRITIQUES OF THE MODEL

Over this period, there were a large number of criticisms of the validity of the neoclassical model—from both an empirical and a theoretical perspective. One criticism of the model was its failure to capture essential elements of the successful East Asian cases.[13] In both Taiwan and the Republic of Korea,

[12] Kakwani (1995) found that countries with adjustment programmes made less progress on social indicators than countries without such programmes; but see also Sahn et al. (1997) who argue, for Africa, that adjustment programmes tend to benefit the poor. For criticisms of the latter's model, see De Maio et al. (1999). Numerous studies of the macro-effects of stabilization and adjustment policies, by the IFIs themselves and by academics, have come to mixed conclusions on their effects. Assessments of IMF programmes tend to suggest somewhat negative effects on growth, while those of the World Bank indicate slight positive effects compared with an estimated 'counterfactual'. Effects on investment were negative. See, e.g. Khan and Knight (1985), Khan (1990), Killick and Malik (1995), and Mosley et al. (1991). Most studies have been unable to find significant positive effects in Africa.

[13] For example, see Wade (1990), Pack and Westphal (1986), Amsden (1989), and Lall (1994).

the governments were shown to have played a much more active role than allowed for in the market model, while high savings and investment—public as well as private—and high levels of human resources were also demonstrated to have been an essential feature. Moreover, the relatively weak economic performance of many of the 'adjusting' countries also led to doubts about its validity. The initial premise was that growth and equity would improve in a liberalized economy (e.g. Little et al. 1970). But macro performance did not live up to the promise of the neoclassical critique. There was a fall in investment rates and per capita output in 'adjusting' regions during the 1980s. Economic growth in the 1980s in Africa and Latin America was very low, and despite some recovery in the 1990s still did not attain the rates of the 1960s and 1970s (see Figure 1.7). Moreover, Asian countries, not subject to stabilization and adjustment programmes, did much better and showed accelerated growth. Destabilizing fluctuations in private capital flows in the 1990s—notably in Mexico and East Asia—following the liberalization of capital markets also led to widespread questioning of this aspect of the model, and the advocacy of capital controls and/or a tax on international capital transactions (Haq et al. 1996, FitzGerald 1999, Caprio et al. 2001).

There were also critiques of the theoretical structure underlying the neoliberal model. One concerned the premise that economic agents were exclusively short-term maximizers: long-term self-interest, altruism, and a sense of identity and community were also shown to influence behaviour.[14] The model's assumptions about information were also shown to be deficient (Stiglitz and Weiss 1981, Stiglitz 1994). New developments in theories of growth and trade emphasized the importance of learning, economies of scale, oligopoly, and externalities (e.g. Helpman and Krugman 1986, Roemer 1986, Lucas 1988). The major policy thrust of these theoretical criticisms is the need for a more active role by the state than contained in the neoclassical prescriptions. These theoretical developments generally concerned mechanisms rather than objectives, mainly accepting economic growth as the basic objective. Their criticism of the model was in large part from the perspective of *efficiency*. However, they did put strong emphasis on human capabilities as a *source* of economic growth. This is most clear in the 'new growth theories', where technical change broadly depends on human capacities.

1.4.9.2. A RENEWED FOCUS ON POVERTY REDUCTION

The stabilization and adjustment policies of the 1980s were heavily criticized for the rise in poverty that accompanied them (Cornia et al. 1986), and from

[14] For an overview, see Alkire and Deneulin (2002). Recent developments in behavioural economics endorse the view that most people are not short-term maximizers (see World Bank 2015).

1990 poverty reduction became a central objective of the World Bank, starting with the 1990 poverty-focused *World Development Report.* World Bank President Lewis Preston (1992) declared that '[p]overty reduction must be the benchmark against which our performance as a development institution is judged. If we are not helping to reduce poverty, we are not doing our job.' Similar changes occurred at the IMF. In 1990, Michel Camdessus, managing director of the IMF, acknowledged that 'macroeconomic policies can have strong effects on the distribution of income and on social equity and welfare. A responsible adjustment programme must take these effects into account, particularly as they impinge on the most vulnerable or disadvantaged groups in society' (Camdessus 1990). Each IMF country Mission was required to report on the poverty implications of country programmes. Williamson, who devised the term Washington consensus, himself revised the proposed content of this consensus to include poverty reduction and investment in human resources (Williamson 1997). Despite this important shift in focus, the IFIs continued to define poverty in monetary terms, the World Bank (1990) introducing the dollar a day poverty line.

In parallel, the UN added to its Human Rights Covenants, with 'The Right to Development' in 1986 and the Convention on the Rights of the Child in 1989. Monitoring of social and economic human rights was improved with the establishment of the Independent Committee of Experts on Economic, Social and Cultural Rights in 1986.

1.4.9.3. CHANGING THE MEASURE OF PROGRESS: CAPABILITIES AND HUMAN DEVELOPMENT

A much more radical change—which echoes some of Seers' much earlier writings, the ideas behind basic needs, and the proposal of Morris (1977) to measure progress by a Physical Quality of Life Index (PQLI)—was to reassess the metric by which progress is measured. For humans to flourish, money incomes—even incomes of the poor—are a highly deficient indicator. There are multiple dimensions to living flourishing lives; and consequently, in assessing well-being or deprivation, a much richer multidimensional set of indicators is needed than simply incomes. Sen powerfully argued that a flourishing life requires an expansion of capabilities—what people can be or do (Sen 1980, Sen 1999a); similarly, the basic needs authors proposed that the development of a 'full life' involved multiple dimensions (ILO 1976, Streeten et al. 1981, Stewart 1985). To achieve conditions which promote human flourishing, '[i]ncome is a means not an end' (UNDP 1990, 10). Income is needed to buy essential commodities, but so is an effective state providing comprehensive basic services and social institutions which support a well-functioning society in which humans can flourish in multiple ways (Fei et al. 1985, Stewart 2013b).

The *Human Development Report*, first published in 1990, combined Sen's capability approach and the basic needs focus on the needs of the most deprived. As noted at the outset of this chapter, the first report stated: 'The basic objective of development is to create an enabling environment for people to live long, healthy and creative lives' (UNDP 1990, 9). The view that HD consisted in the expansion of the choices people have to do and be a variety of things was derived from Sen's capability approach. The strong focus on the need to give priority to improving the conditions of the poor, and a concentration on goods and services for the poor, reflects the basic needs approach. Or, in capability terms, the focus is on the failure of some basic capability to function, where basic capabilities (very similar to basic needs) are 'intended to separate out the ability to satisfy certain elementary and crucially important functionings' (Sen 1992, 45). In other words, a basic capability could entail the opportunity to become literate—which is, in turn, a critically important functioning.

Perhaps the most important contribution of the HD approach, as embodied in successive Human Development Reports, has been to achieve growing acceptance that monetary income and GNP per capita are inadequate as the exclusive way of assessing outcomes, even when income is adjusted to allow for its distribution and measures of income poverty are included. The first report introduced the multidimensional Human Development Index (HDI) as a rough measure of HD across countries. Though it is agreed by all, including its initiators, to be a very imperfect measure of HD, the HDI has come nearest to achieving Seer's objective of dethroning GNP, while the Multidimensional Poverty Index (MPI) has done the same for the measurement of poverty (Alkire and Foster 2009). While neither the HDI nor the MPI has as yet displaced monetary measures, they are increasingly presented alongside them, and thereby given parallel significance. Taking HD as the paramount objective does not mean that monetary incomes and GNP should be ignored—economic resources provide a fundamental means to achieve HD, while HD in turn feeds into higher growth (see Chapter 3). But it does mean that well-being assessments should give priority to what happens to human lives, rather than what happens to the economy, and this has important implications for policy choice and sequencing.

1.5. Developments since the 1990s: Towards a Greater Emphasis on HD

HD and poverty reduction have gained a central role in policy since 1990. These objectives secured global acceptance with the MDGs agreed in 2000, and the SDGs adopted in 2015. The MDGs included halving income poverty by 2015 as well as a number of other specific goals which would contribute to HD, such as improvements in maternal mortality, education, and so on. The MDGs do not refer to income per capita, indicating a displacement of income by human-centred objectives. The SDGs, in turn, have a continued central focus on multidimensional human objectives and on deprivation, while they include 'inclusive' growth as one of the principles (United Nations 2015).

As an indication of the increasing acceptance of HD, many countries produced national Human Development Reports, and measures of MPI are increasingly being adopted alongside (and sometimes instead of) income poverty measures. This does not mean that GNP has been altogether displaced—indeed, it continues to be dominant in political discourse—but it is increasingly seen as a means to achieve human-centred objectives rather than an end in itself, among developed as well as developing countries. For example, a commission on the measurement of economic performance and social progress, instituted by French President Nicolas Sarkozy, entitled its final report *Mismeasuring our Lives: Why GDP doesn't Add Up* (Stiglitz et al. 2010). Among developed countries, increasing attention is being given to subjective measures of well-being (measures of 'happiness' or 'life satisfaction'), and it is argued that these should supplement if not supplant income as a measure (Easterlin 2001, Layard 2011). Chapter 2 analyses the relationship between HD and 'happiness' as predominant societal objectives, and argues that HD, or the advance of capabilities, should be the dominant objective of development policy, although considerations of how development affects perceived well-being should be an important additional consideration.

At the same time, growing environmental pressures have led to the idea that any measure of progress, whether incomes, HD, or happiness, must be 'sustainable'. The Sarkozy Commission report includes all three elements—capabilities, environmental sustainability, and subjective well-being—without reconciling them. The new set of global goals are called SDGs to reflect the importance given to environmental issues, and of the seventeen goals, four include the word 'sustainable' in relation to economic or social goals, while four are exclusively related to the environment.

As far as HD is concerned, three reports have been devoted to environmental issues, one on the global water crisis (UNDP 2006), one on fighting climate change (UNDP 2007), and one on sustainability and equity (UNDP 2011). Increasingly 'Sustainable Human Development' rather than 'Human Development' is advocated as the objective. Yet there has not been a true attempt to integrate sustainability and HD. Measures of HD reflect current achievements. Yet a proper perspective on HD would relate not just to current achievements but to likely HD over future decades. These will be affected by environmental developments, especially climate change. Indeed, advancing

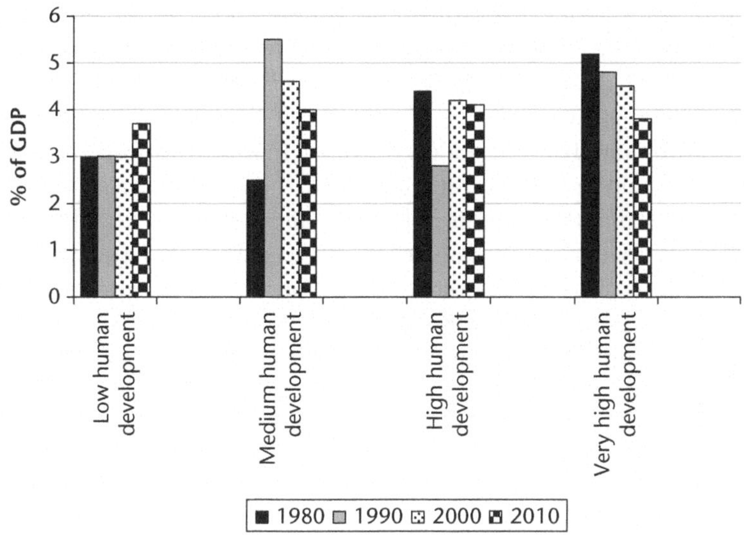

Figure 1.9. Government expenditure on education as % of GDP, 1980–2010
Source: UNDP, HDRO statistics

current achievements on HD may be at the expense of future trajectories, unless the current performance is based on sustainable resource use. This means that the environment should not be an add-on to the HD approach but integrated into it, both in measurement and in policy. In measurement, several approaches are possible: one would try to assess the trajectory of HD over several decades, aggregating this into a single measure using some discount rate. But this is complex and unappealing intuitively. Another approach would be to deduct environmental costs likely to affect future HD adversely in estimating current HD. This too is complex. Thirdly, the income element of the HDI could be 'greened'—work is underway on this, for example in the 'waves' partnership.[15] Or a sustainability measure could be included as a fourth element in the HDI. The simplest approach (albeit the crudest) would be to measure the ratio of the HDI to carbon use involved in achieving the HDI, and rank countries accordingly. We return to this issue in Chapter 9.

However, while there has been much progress in terms of changing development objectives, there has been less in changing policy. The most important concrete achievements of the HD approach are a rise in the proportion of resources low-HD countries (but not others) and donors devote to social expenditures (see Figures 1.8 and 1.9). The extensive introduction of cash transfers and other social protection programmes can also be seen as a response

[15] See <http://www.wavespartnership.org/>.

to the emphasis on HD (Barrientos and Hulme 2008). In general, there was progress in meeting MDGs, although not all targets were met (Fukuda-Parr 2014, World Bank 2016). Yet, there has been very little change in the thrust of *economic* policy—either in terms of the role of the market, or in relation to macroeconomic stabilization policies. Indeed, in many respects the role of the market is being enlarged, without regard to the consequences for HD. One reason for this is that the analysis of HD has rarely explored what the approach means for macroeconomic management, incentives and the allocation of resources, or the role of the market. In addition, of course, interest groups are particularly powerful in these areas, which would make any challenge to conventional pro-market thinking especially difficult to achieve. Nonetheless, the financial crisis of the 2000s showed that developing countries were more expansionary and protected their social expenditures to a greater extent than in the debt crisis of the 1980s (Stewart 2012b, Martorano et al. 2013).

1.6. Conclusion

This chapter has traced the source and development of ideas of HD over half a century, showing how they emerged as a result of problems arising from previous approaches to development as well as intellectual advances. History continues to evolve and so do ideas. Today the biggest challenges to the approach are twofold. First, to identify human-friendly economics, as achievements are being threatened by conventional austerity and market economics; and second, to incorporate ideas of sustainability into the approach, since environmental pressures, especially arising from global warming, represent the greatest threat to HD.

Although the idea of HD has gained widespread acceptance, major progress faces several constraints. First, most economic policy continues to be market-dominated, often leading to worsening income distribution (see e.g. Morley 2000, Cornia 2004, Ball et al. 2013, Piketty 2014, Hardoon et al. 2016). At a macro-policy level, countries continue to be encouraged to adopt familiar 'austerity' programmes in the face of economic fluctuations and crises. Second, exogenous or near-exogenous developments—notably HIV/AIDS, natural disasters, and civil war—are having a seriously deleterious impact on HD. Their incidence is worsened by rising inequality and adverse environmental effects.

The donor community is thus giving mixed messages on HD and poverty. On the one hand, the general idea that HD should be promoted and poverty reduced is broadly agreed, and numerous programmes that promote HD receive support at a micro level. But on the other hand, the pressures for more liberalization in the economy and for orthodox macro-adjustment have continued unabated; these are not supportive of HD and can indeed threaten progress. Ironically, competitive pressures from the global economy have the same effect: there is downward pressure on taxation and expenditure so that economies remain competitive in the short term, yet in the longer run promoting human capacities through investment in education and health are essential for sustaining growth, as well as HD.

Developing countries themselves, of course, filter these contradictory messages though their own political systems. All are being pushed in a similar liberalizing direction, but the pace of change varies, and some countries with progressive governments and strong traditions of supporting human investments succeed better than others in promoting HD, as shown in later chapters. In Latin America, a number of countries saw improved income distribution and social achievements in the 2000s (Cornia 2011), in part owing to political shifts. Political factors are discussed in Chapter 8.

Nonetheless, a major challenge for the HD approach is to change the *process* of development in an HD-supporting direction, as well as the objective. This requires more radical rethinking of economic models, and more substantial changes in the economic system than have been achieved hitherto. We return to these issues in Chapter 9.

2

Should Happiness or Human Development be the Main Development Objective?

> *Happiness* is the meaning and the purpose of life, the whole aim and end of human existence.
>
> Aristotle, *Nichomachean Ethics*, Book 1, 1095a
>
> The utilitarian doctrine is that *happiness* is desirable, and the only thing desirable, as an end; all other things being only desirable as means to that end.
>
> J.S. Mill, *Utilitarianism*, 95.
>
> It is thus self-evident that the best society is the *happiest*.
>
> Richard Layard, *Happiness*, 224.

The idea that measures of happiness, or subjective well-being, should be used as the sole (or a dominant) measure of country progress has been advocated by a number of scholars over the past decades (Easterlin 2001, Kahneman 2003, Graham 2011, Layard 2011, Helliwell et al. 2012, 2013).[1] It has also been taken up officially—for example, by the Sarkozy Commission (Stiglitz et al. 2010); and most famously by the Bhutan government, which has replaced GNP as the measure of the country's progress by a measure of Gross National Happiness. In the light of these views, which are gaining increasing adherence, this chapter considers whether 'happiness' should replace HD as the overriding development objective. Much of the motivation behind the happiness agenda is to argue that subjective measures of well-being are superior to GNP, and those who advocate this approach do not explicitly contrast the happiness goal with HD. As should be clear from Chapter 1, we also have many criticisms

[1] Material for this chapter was drawn from Stewart (2014). We are grateful for permission to reuse it here (copyright © United Nations Development Programme, reprinted by permission of Taylor & Francis Ltd, <http://www.tandfonline.com>, on behalf of the United Nations Development Programme).

of GNP as a measure of progress. However, in this chapter we analyse and critique the displacement of GNP by happiness as the overriding goal and argue that subjective measures of happiness should *not* displace objective measures, such as those embodied in the HD approach, in which progress is assessed as the expansion of capabilities or freedoms (UNDP 1990, Sen 1999a), or in an HR approach, which gives precedence to the realization of universal human rights.

The chapter is organized as follows: we start in Section 2.1 with an account of the origins, evolution, and motivations of the happiness approach, going back to nineteenth-century utilitarians, and then discuss modern happiness gurus, whom we call 'neo-utilitarians'. A critical question that inevitably arises in discussing happiness as an objective is how it is to be defined and measured. Section 2.2 reviews some definitions that have been suggested and ways it has been measured. Section 2.3 briefly discusses some alternative 'objective' measures of development progress and how these differ from subjective approaches. Section 2.4 goes on to discuss a number of problems with the happiness approach if used as the exclusive goal of development, particularly in contrast to the HD or capabilities approach and that of HR. Section 2.5 considers policy implications of the happiness approach and argues that these policies can be perverse from several perspectives. Section 2.6 considers whether there is any role for subjective measures in assessments of development progress, and if so, what. Finally, Section 2.7 concludes.

2.1. Who Favours Happiness?

2.1.1. *Classical Utilitarians*

Aristotle is foundational in his conceptualization of and focus on happiness.[2] His views are embodied in the statement that 'happiness is the meaning and purpose of life'. Yet, as we shall see, his views can be interpreted as the foundation of the capability approach as much as of the subjective measures of happiness that form the focus of the happiness approach today. For many centuries, the human-centred approach of Aristotle and other Greeks was largely displaced by religious views about the meaning and purpose of existence. However, in the eighteenth century a new humanism emerged, and the pursuit of happiness was recognized by Thomas Jefferson as a fundamental human right and objective (along with others, including life and liberty), a view which was embodied in the US Constitution. However, given that

[2] Precursors include hedonists such as Aristippus and Epicurus.

Jefferson (and the US Constitution) included multiple rights, in this context a simple measure of happiness would not be sufficient to assess national progress.

In contrast to this pluralistic approach, Jeremy Bentham (following Hutcheson 1726), who introduced the phrase 'the greatest good for the greatest number' as the way to assess morality of actions, and Gay,[3] Hume, and Priestley (Hume 1751, Priestley 1768), proposed that 'it is the greatest happiness of the greatest number that is the measure of right and wrong' (Bentham 1776, Preface, second para.; in some places he replaces this phrase with 'the greatest total sum of happiness'). Bentham followed this up with detailed recommendations for a 'felicific calculus' and his philosophy became the basis for progressive reforms, for example of sanitation by Chadwick in England in the early nineteenth century. Adopted (with some qualifications) by John Stuart Mill and Edgeworth, Sidgwick, and others, the approach provided the foundations for welfare economics. For each person, it was assumed that welfare maximization would be achieved by individual consumer choice, in which the 'rational' individual would equate her marginal utility from the purchase of any good with that obtained by buying any other good. Hence prices were equated with the marginal utility every consumer got from every good, so prices multiplied by quantities consumed could be assumed to represent a measure of welfare. Adding up all purchases in the economy one arrives at national income, and thus the initial utilitarian ethics provides the foundation for regarding national income as a measure of national well-being.

There are, however, many heroic assumptions behind this simple argument. First is the issue of the distribution of income or utility. If we assume there is diminishing marginal utility to extra consumption (or income), then the marginal utility of richer individuals, for any given additional income, will be less than for poorer individuals, and utility maximization would require redistribution of income. Without such redistribution, maximizing national income would not maximize national utility. This was the conclusion of Bentham, Mill (to some extent), and Pigou. For example, Bentham stated: 'But the quantity of happiness will not go on increasing in anything near the same proportion as the quantity of wealth.... The effect of wealth in the production of happiness goes on diminishing as the quantity by which the wealth of one man exceeds that of another goes on increasing' (Bentham and Bowring 1838, 229).[4] The implication of this is that GNP as such cannot be

[3] In 1731, Gay argued that 'happiness, private happiness, is the proper or ultimate end of all our actions...' (Gay 1731, 'A Dissertation Concerning the Fundamental Principle and Immediate Criterion of Virtue, etc.', cited in Schneewind 2003, 404).

[4] According to Pigou (1932, chapter 8, para. 3): 'it is evident that any transference of income from a relatively rich man to a relatively poor man of similar temperament, since it enables more intense wants to be satisfied at the expense of less intense wants, must increase the aggregate sum

interpreted as a measure of societal utility, but it must be weighted according to the level of income of the recipients (as proposed by Chenery et al. 1979). But this assumes that one can compare utility across individuals. Robbins denied this was so, stating: 'in our hearts we do not regard different men's satisfactions from similar means as equally valuable' (Robbins 1945, 140–1). Once it was accepted that interpersonal comparisons of utility were not valid, economists could say nothing about distributional issues, and were left arguing that maximizing national income—the efficiency maximum—by reaching a Pareto optimal position would maximize welfare, and any redistribution from this income could then be brought about through political decisions.

There are other powerful objections to the view that national income is a measure of national well-being, including the existence of externalities, social interactions and values (such as that people value other people's well-being), a neglect of people's actual physical (or mental) condition, and a consequential assumption—that all that matters are outcomes and not how one gets there. These objections have been powerfully articulated by Sen (1977) and formed the major impetus behind his development of the capability approach, as shown in Chapter 1. GNP may increase while income distribution is worsening, maternal mortality and child malnutrition are high and show no improvement, the government is repressive, and human rights are being violated. Despite these powerful objections to GNP as the measure of progress, it remains the dominant way in which economic development is assessed, although alternatives have been suggested and are gaining ground—for example, the HDI. It is in this context that the neo-utilitarians developed the case for happiness as an alternative to income in assessing progress.

2.1.2. *The Neo-Utilitarians*

In strong contrast to the classical utilitarians, the new advocates of happiness as a measure of progress are intending not to justify the use of income but to provide a replacement or supplement to it. The new advocates started with Richard Easterlin at the beginning of the 1970s—at around the same time that development economists were struggling to find an alternative to GNP (Seers 1972, Easterlin 1974). The approach was taken up by others, mainly in relation to developed countries (e.g. Clark and Oswald 1994, Frey and Stutzer 2002, Kahneman 2003), most enthusiastically by Layard (2011) and Dolan (2014), who argue, unlike most others, that happiness should be the only

of satisfaction. The old "law of diminishing utility" thus leads securely to the proposition: Any cause which increases the absolute share of real income in the hands of the poor, provided that it does not lead to a contraction in the size of the national dividend from any point of view, will, in general, increase economic welfare.'

objective and all other aspects of life are only valuable if instrumental to the promotion of happiness. According to Dolan: 'Happiness is all that matters in the end' (Dolan 2014, 189). Initially, less attention was paid to developing countries, but Carol Graham and others have undertaken a large amount of empirical work on the extent and correlates of happiness in developing countries (Graham and Pettinato 2002, Graham 2009, Graham 2011). Moreover, Bhutan has instituted a measure of Gross National Happiness as a replacement for GNP. No other country has done so, but some governments are introducing subjective well-being measures alongside measure of income (e.g. the UK government).

Mill and Layard provide very similar justifications for adopting happiness as the goal and metric. Both argue that every person seeks happiness and this gives it supremacy as a measure of progress. Mill (Mill et al. 1998, 81) states:

> No reason can be given why the general happiness is desirable, except that each person, so far as he believes it to be attainable, desires his own happiness . . . we have not only all the proof which the case admits of, but all which it is possible to require, that happiness is a good: that each person's happiness is a good to that person, and the general happiness, therefore, a good to the aggregate of all persons.

And Layard states:

> It is thus self-evident that the best society is the happiest. (Layard 2011, 224)

> [I]t [happiness] is... supremely important because it is our overall motivational device. (Layard 2011, 24)

> [W]e are programmed to seek happiness. (Layard 2011, 224)

This justification is not convincing for several reasons—which we will develop further later in the chapter. It assumes that what we want (our overall motivational device) is what ought to happen, yet we also have motives (such as jealousy, hatred of others, love of others) which can override the happiness motive, the fulfilment of which would clearly not provide a satisfactory measure of societal progress. Moreover, to state that something is 'self-evident' is not a reason at all, but simply an assertion of belief by the author.

2.2. Definitions and Measurement

There are many interpretations of what is meant by the 'happiness' objective. According to Layard it is a 'subjective feeling'; it is 'feeling good, enjoying life'. For Graham, it is 'subjective wellbeing'. Aristotle's *eudaimonia* is far from simply a feeling: it is associated with human flourishing, living well, having a virtuous life, and fulfilment of human potential. Indeed, it comes closer to the capabilities approach—discussed in Section 2.3—than that of neo-utilitarians, which is also how happiness is interpreted by Franklin (2010).

There are also differences among those who stick to a subjective measure of happiness: for example, J.S. Mill differentiated different types of pleasure, famously saying that poetry was more desirable than pushpin. But this would make it very difficult (and arbitrary) to measure. Psychologists have differentiated between an affective or emotional component and a cognitive or judgemental component of well-being. Stone and Mackie (2014) differentiate between evaluative well-being and experienced well-being. In addition, there is the issue of *time*: subjective measures of well-being (particularly affective measures or experienced well-being) have been shown to vary according to age (Blanchflower and Oswald 2004, Graham 2009) and according to the time of day (Kahneman et al. 2004). Hence any reported measure will vary according to the time of day of the survey and the age of the respondent (and for some the season of the year), especially for affective measures. Layard (2011) proposes that the objective should be to maximize lifetime happiness for any individual, which deals with the problem of time in some ways, but obviously raises major (and almost certainly insuperable) problems of measurement.

Empirical work on happiness uses surveys of people's perceptions of their lives, but the questions vary—some relate closely to feelings and others to a considered evaluation of more objective conditions. Questions include: 'Did you smile or laugh a lot yesterday?' and 'Generally speaking how happy are you with your life?' These two are both primarily directed at the affective component. Other questions are more cognitive, for example: 'Generally speaking how satisfied are you with your life?' and 'Imagine a ladder from 0–10 with 10 the best possible life: on which step do you stand?' These last two questions may not be answered with reference to feelings at all, but may represent a considered judgement of a person's objective condition in relation (especially for the last question) to what a person knows about other possible lives. The interpretation of any measure of societal (or personal) happiness then depends on the precise question which forms the basis for the measure.[5] Generally speaking, empirical studies find much higher correlations between objective conditions—such as incomes—and answers to 'ladder of life' questions than with answers to the more affective questions on how happy a person is. Moreover, interpretations of the questions may differ across cultures and according to the precise translation adopted. These ambiguities, in themselves, make happiness an unsatisfactory measure of societal progress.

[5] Research shows correlations of approximately 0.5 between answers to the second and third questions (Blanchflower and Oswald 2004).

2.2.1. *Adding Up and Distributional Issues*

Measures of happiness used in cross-country comparisons are based on an average of answers by a representative sample of the population in just the same way as for GNP, despite the fact that in general the questions are answered ordinally so it is not appropriate to add up and compare answers. Distributional issues are then dealt with, in principle, by identifying how inequality of *incomes* affects happiness. Most evidence suggests that people compare their position to a reference group (often the average situation), which means that the rich get additional happiness from inequality while the happiness levels of the poor, for a given income level, are likely to be worse the greater the inequality (Kingdon and Knight 2007, Graham and Felton 2006, Knight and Gunatilaka 2011). There is virtually no correlation between measures of life satisfaction and inequality across countries, and in econometric exercises across countries levels of income per capita and HDI show a significant positive relationship with life satisfaction, but distribution of income, as measured by the Gini coefficient, adds nothing. Alesina et al. (2004) find that inequality does not affect happiness in the US but has a strong negative impact on the poor in Europe. Graham (2009), comparing Honduras and Chile, finds that inequality in Latin America makes the poor three percentage points less happy, but the rich five percentage points happier. It is difficult to come to firm conclusions on redistribution on this basis since the scoring is ordinal.[6] If one did interpret them cardinally, these findings would only justify redistribution if a decision was taken to weight the feelings of the poor more heavily than those of the rich. Doing so requires one to move outside the happiness metric and call on other values.

To summarize the discussion on measurement, using happiness as a way of evaluating progress involves many problems arising from disagreements about definitions; differences in how people answer questions according to the nature of the question, age, and even time of day, as well as culture; problems of adding up answers across people to arrive at a national figure; and the weak basis for distributional judgements. Yet it might still be better than the alternatives. According to Layard (2011), one must have a single metric, and happiness is the best one on offer—indeed who can be against happiness? It is then necessary to consider alternatives before coming to conclusions. Section 2.3 will briefly discuss some alternatives for defining and measuring progress offered by the HD and capability approaches, an HR approach, and, for distributional issues, theories of justice.

[6] But see Cowell and Flachaire 2017 for suggestions on how to derive inequality measures from an ordinal distribution.

2.3. Alternative Approaches

A number of ways of defining development objectives have been suggested by those seeking alternatives to the use of income (particularly GNP) as a measure of societal progress. Some involve using income as the metric, but modifying it to allow for distributional concerns (Chenery et al. 1979). But others have rejected incomes altogether as an objective, though typically it remains an important means for achieving other objectives (Seers 1969, Morris 1977, Hicks and Streeten 1979, Sen 1980, Streeten et al. 1981, UNDP 1990, Sen 1999a). We will not discuss these many views, reviewed in Chapter 1, but focus on the HD approach, Sen's capabilities approach from which it is largely derived, and HR approaches to development.

We reviewed the origins and basic characteristics of the two approaches—HD and Sen's capabilities approach—in Chapter 1. As stated in the first *Human Development Report*: 'Human development is a process of enlarging people's choices. The most critical ones are to lead a long and healthy life, to be educated and to enjoy a decent standard of living. Additional choices include political freedom, guaranteed human rights and self-respect' (UNDP 1990, 1). The development of the HD approach owed much to Sen's view that the expansion of individuals' capabilities or freedoms should be the objective of development, and to the basic needs approach that gave priority to advancing people's basic needs. All these approaches reject income as a measure of progress in development, although they accept that it is an important instrument to advance these objectives. HD, capabilities, and basic needs all involve *plural* objectives. And none of them refers to people's subjective evaluations of their condition (or to happiness measures). A critical feature of the capabilities framework is the emphasis placed on the importance of *agency*, so that it is not only levels of achievement in capabilities, but how they are achieved which matters, in particular whether goals are achieved by processes freely chosen by the person, or ones with which they concur. Thus what Sen calls 'wellbeing achievements' may be overridden by agency goals.

Human rights refer to certain inalienable rights to which everyone is entitled as a human being. An HR approach to development sees the objective of development as being one of promoting the universal realization of these rights. As Jefferson stated (repeated in the US Constitution): 'We hold these truths to be self-evident: that all men are created equal; that they are endowed by their Creator with certain unalienable rights'. HR approaches have their origin in theories of natural rights, developed by various philosophers from the seventeenth century. They were recognized constitutionally in Britain in the 1689 Bill of Rights, in the US Declaration of Independence and the US Constitution of 1776, and in France with the Revolution and the Declaration of the Rights of Man and the Citizen in 1789.

At an international level, it was the UDHR following the Second World War which provided the foundation for the HR approach to development. The UDHR's preamble stated that 'recognition of the inherent dignity and of the equal and inalienable rights of all members of the human family is the foundation of freedom, justice and peace in the world'. This was followed by agreement to a succession of covenants, including the two 1966 International Covenants on Civil and Political Rights and on Economic, Social and Cultural Rights, and a number of more specific covenants. Internationally agreed human rights include rights to adequate food, education, housing, water and sanitation, employment, and more generally, the right to 'development', as well as a variety of political rights. Adopting an HR approach means that progress in development is to be assessed by progress in achieving these universal rights. In practice, this is not easy since the rights are rather general. Nonetheless, the general direction needed for progress is clear. Again the approach is pluralist, does not specifically include income, and does not include any subjective evaluations.[7]

Neither the capabilities/HD nor the HR approach specifically includes a judgement about distribution, although there are some distributional implications from giving priority to universal access to some critical capabilities, and equally to the fulfilment of HR at a basic level. Moreover, the HR conventions include the elimination of discrimination. Nonetheless, the approaches recognize the importance of considering and promoting a just distribution, even though for a more comprehensive view of justice in relation to the distribution of outcomes or resources one has to turn to philosophers such as Rousseau (1968 [1762]), Rawls (1971), Locke (1773), or Nozick (1974), or to more recent philosophers such as Anderson (1999).[8] The question of what constitutes an equitable distribution is a critical issue for anyone concerned with societal progress.

It is clear that the HD, capability, or HR approaches differ substantially from the happiness approach. In the first place, the objectives are pluralistic (including a number of incommensurable elements); second, they all concern 'objective' observable conditions and none makes reference to subjective evaluations; third, for the capability approach, agency and well-being are important; and finally, justice across individuals and groups is an important consideration for each, and not only the summation of individual achievements.

These differences pose a challenge for the happiness approach, if subjective evaluations differ from objective ones. For example, if people with poor

[7] The US Constitution, of course, famously includes the rights to 'life, liberty and the pursuit of happiness', but it is notable that the right is to the *pursuit* of happiness, not to happiness as such, and its achievement would be measured by people's freedoms rather than their levels of happiness.

[8] See Stewart (2013a) for a summary of some views on distributional justice.

nutrition and health display high subjective happiness indicators; or, if high values of subjective indicators are achieved, despite a lack of agency (e.g. through ill-treated labour); or if societies show high average achievements on life satisfaction (and even low dispersion), with a highly unequal distribution across genders or races. These differences get to the heart of the question of whether happiness is a good indicator of progress. Given these dilemmas, would one choose to accept the happiness indicator or the more objective and agency-sensitive ones? Should justice be viewed purely instrumentally, in terms of whether it raises happiness? Similarly, for agency? Layard has stated that happiness is the ultimate goal and 'goods like health, autonomy and freedom are "instrumental goods"' (Layard 2011, 113). Our view is that given such dilemmas, we would regard the objective and agency-sensitive indicators as decisive, not the subjective ones. This does not rule out *any* role for subjective indicators, as will be discussed further in Section 2.6. But it rules out their exclusive use.

The dilemma would, of course, not exist if there were a perfect correlation between subjective and objective indicators. But there is not, as Tables 2.1 and 2.2 and Figure 2.1 show. Table 2.1 shows the relationship between the three components of the HDI and a cross-country survey of life satisfaction. The correlation is lowest for income per capita and highest for life expectancy.

Table 2.1. Correlations between happiness score and HDI and components, around 2015

HDI components	Correlation coefficient with country happiness score, around 2015
Life expectancy	0.787
Mean years of schooling	0.727
Gross national income per head, adjusted[a]	0.695

Source: World Happiness Report 2017; UNDP, Human Development Report Office Data.
a. Purchasing power parity (PPP) 2011 (US$); income per head is capped at US$75,000.

Table 2.2. Correlation between happiness score and HDI, by level of HDI, around 2015

Country grouping	Correlation coefficient with country happiness score, around 2015
Very high HDI	0.613
High HDI	0.126
Medium HDI	0.497
Low HDI	0.454
All countries	0.842

Source: World Happiness Report 2017; UNDP, Human Development Report Office Data.

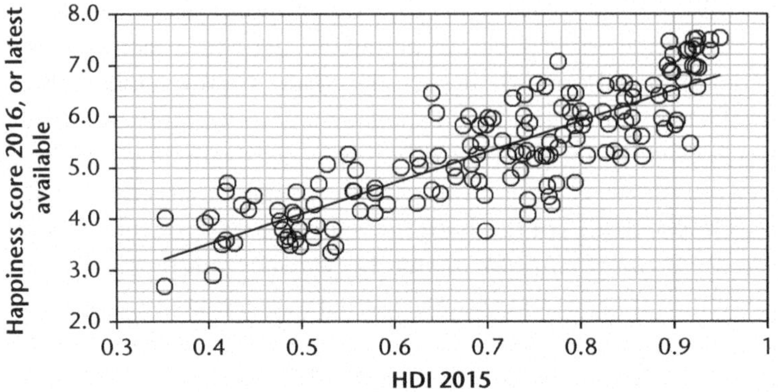

Figure 2.1. Scatter of happiness score and HDI, latest year available

While a correlation of 0.84 might be thought to be quite high (even sufficiently high to make one question the reality of any such dilemma, as mentioned above), when one does the same correlation for subsets of countries according to their level of HD, one finds much lower correlations (see Table 2.2 and Figure 2.1).

One reason for the weak correlations is that people adapt to poor circumstances. Section 2.4 summarizes some evidence of such adaptations.

2.4. Some Problems With the Happiness Approach As a Guide to Development Policy

2.4.1. *Adapting to Conditions*

As Graham notes, 'there is evidence of a great deal of upward and downward adaptation as well as a clear role for innate character traits in mediating the relationship between happiness and a range of environmental variables' (Graham 2009, 214). Expectations about life conditions, and hence satisfaction with them, has been shown to be partially dependent on people's local reference group, as shown by research in China and South Africa (Kingdon and Knight 2004, Knight and Gunatilaka 2011). Hence poor people living in low-income neighbourhoods or countries tend to be more satisfied with their lives, relative to a particular income level, than poor people living in high-income environments. Similarly, it has been frequently shown that reporting of ill health rises with incomes and education—as expectations of normal health rise (Sen 2002). Likewise, country regressions suggest that employed people are happier if the aggregate unemployment level is higher, and that unhappiness from unemployment diminishes as the unemployment persists (Graham 2009). Similarly, where the crime 'norm' is higher, suffering from crime has a less negative impact on happiness than where crime is rare (Graham and Hoover 2007).

None of this is unexpected. But it shows that people do adapt to their circumstances, making a happiness measure an unsatisfactory way of assessing development progress—unless one believes that all that matters is perceptions, i.e. that if a poor woman is chronically unwell and malnourished and yet declares her life satisfactory, we should not be concerned with her conditions.

2.4.2. *Happiness Has Little to Do with Development*

A further problem for the use of happiness measures as the way of assessing development, and of guiding development policy, is that such a large proportion of the determinants of individual happiness lies outside the realm of development policy, or is only indirectly affected by such policy.

Completely unaffected by development policy are factors such as genetics and temperament (which appear to account for about half a person's level of happiness), upbringing, age, marriage, and religion, all of which have been shown to affect levels of happiness. Then there are factors indirectly influenced by development policy: behavioural factors—such as friendships, exercise, and narcotics and alcohol consumption; the social context—the extent of social networks and social institutions; the political context—the degree of personal freedom and absence of repression; and the extent of personal security. These are areas in which development policy does play an important, albeit indirect, role. Policies affecting them can and should be influenced by people's perceptions and preferences, in addition to other factors, including the relationship with HR and their implications for other aspects of development.

Finally, the factors directly affected by development policy which have been shown to influence (or at least be correlated with) life satisfaction include economic circumstances (incomes positively for the most part, and unemployment negatively); the state of health, which consistently has a strong positive impact; and educational levels (no consistent pattern has been observed, however). Some correlations between a range of factors and levels of happiness across individuals for particular countries (or regions) are shown in Table 2.3.[9]

Quite apart from the central question of this chapter—how far we should assess progress by measures of perceived well-being as against capabilities or

[9] Helliwell and Wang (2013) find that income per capita and life expectancy at birth are significantly positively related to levels of happiness, and they also find a positive relationship with country levels of social support, freedom to make life choices, and generosity, and (negatively) with perceptions of corruption with a cross-country regression of 149 countries for 2012.

Table 2.3. Some correlates with happiness measures across individuals, various years

Period covered	US	Latin America	Russia	Central Asia	Afghanistan
	1972–98	2001	2000	2004	2009
Age	Neg	Neg	Neg	Neg	Neg
Age squared	Pos	0	Pos	Pos	0
Male	Neg*	Neg	Pos*	NS	NS
Married	Pos***	Pos	Pos	Pos***	NS
Log income	Pos	Pos**	Pos**	Pos***[b]	Pos***[c]
Education	Pos	Neg	Pos	Pos	NA
Black[a]	Neg**	Neg	Pos	Neg*	NA
Student	Pos	Pos	Pos	NA	NA
Retired	Pos*	Neg	Neg**	NA	NA
Unemployment	Neg***	Neg***	Neg***	Neg***	Neg
Self-employed	Pos	Neg	Pos***	NA	
Health	Pos***	Pos***	Pos***	NA	NA
Farmer	NA	NA	NA	Neg*	NA
Living in Taliban district	NA	NA	NA	NA	Pos**
Psuedo R2	0.075	0.062	0.033	0.096	0.197

Notes: *** = significant at 1 per cent; ** = significant at 5 per cent; * = significant at 10 per cent.

Source: Graham (2009); (a) except for US this variable is a 'minority'; (b) self-assessed socio-economic status; and (c) household assets.

HR fulfilment—the fact that only a fraction of variation in measures of happiness is associated with development policy would make this a rather clumsy way of assessing progress, as so much 'noise' is picked up in these measures (Lykken and Tellegen 1996).

2.5. Possible Adverse Policy Implications

There are several ways in which policy implications arising from the use of a happiness approach could have adverse implications for development viewed as the expansion of capabilities or the fulfilment of HR: first, some policies which worsen objective conditions for some might increase measures of happiness; second, policies which improve objective conditions might reduce happiness; third, policies may be introduced to encourage the adaptation to poor conditions, rather than being directed at improving the conditions; and fourth, some serious problems may be neglected.

2.5.1. *Policies which Worsen Objective Conditions for Some May Raise Happiness*

Going by the evidence on the importance of reference groups and/or prevailing norms and conditions for satisfaction, it follows that worsening the conditions of a reference group, without changing/improving the conditions of the individuals outside this reference group, would improve the conditions of the latter. In a similar way, an increase in general unemployment would improve the happiness of the unemployed, and a rise in the crime rate would improve the happiness (or lessen the unhappiness) of those subject to crime, according to empirical studies. Of course, this need not mean that the best policy, from a happiness perspective, is to worsen general conditions, because one needs to take into account the population as a whole: the reference group whose conditions are worsened, those suffering additional unemployment, and the people subject to additional crime are likely to find their satisfaction worsening. However, if the reference group is small in number relative to the people of direct concern, the net effect (assuming heroically that one can add this up) may indeed be positive if the situation of the reference group deteriorates. In this context, there could be no improvement in the situation of the group of concern, and deterioration in the reference group situation, yet overall an improvement in happiness. (Of course, the opposite may obtain if the reference group is large relative to the people of concern—then the overall situation would be likely to worsen if the situation of the reference group worsens.)

Essentially this means that we may not need to improve the objective position of the poor (their health/incomes, etc.) so long as there is a reduction in reference group circumstances which improves the happiness of the poor more than it worsens that of the reference group. In contrast, those concerned with capabilities or HR would argue that development policy should aim for improved realization of these for poor people, irrespective of what happens to the reference group.

2.5.2. *Policies which Improve Objective Conditions May Reduce Happiness*

An improvement in objective conditions may reduce happiness in a variety of ways. One is if economic growth raises expectations faster than incomes. Or, going back to the previous discussion and focusing on the poor, if it raises the conditions of the reference group faster than that of the poor. Similarly, a spread of health entitlements may lead people to assess ill health more adversely as their standard of what is normal rises. A reduction in unemployment, while positive for those who get jobs, may be outweighed by increased unhappiness arising from unemployment among those remaining unemployed—though this could be offset by rising expectations of getting a job.

2.5.3. *Policies May be Introduced to Encourage Adaptation to Bad Conditions, Rather than Tackling the Conditions*

This is probably the most serious consequence of adopting happiness as the exclusive measure of development—since there is some evidence that it is occurring in places—while the earlier issues were theoretical possibilities, perhaps unlikely to have effect in practice. For example, psychologists have developed interventions to counter what they describe as poverty-related stress (e.g. Rienks and Wadsworth 2012).[10] Indeed, a joint venture between Stanford and the Harvard Kennedy School created a Stress Reduction Lab aimed at reducing the negative effects of poverty on those experiencing it. In India, evidence of rising mental health problems among the poor has led the UN to recommend that: 'Mental health issues should be integrated into all broader development and poverty eradication policies and programmes as a key indicator of human development' (UNDESA-WHO 2010). This is not to argue that mental health programmes do not have a role: mental ill health is an important source of unhappiness and is especially prevalent among the poor (Patel 2001, Layard et al. 2013). But the main effort needs to be devoted to eliminating the conditions giving rise to poverty, not to making it acceptable—i.e. to eradicate poverty, rather than to alleviate some symptoms.

2.5.4. *Neglect of Serious Issues*

Assessments of happiness can only relate to the present generation; there could be speculation about developments for future generations, but these lack empirical foundation. At worst, this means that the present generation's happiness is maximized at the expense of future generations—the environment, for example, is likely to be neglected. To the extent that the present generation's happiness is affected by prospects for future generations, this extreme conclusion would be modified, but it is unlikely to be sufficient to ensure the well-being of future generations. Moreover, to the extent that the present generation has a commitment to protecting the well-being of future generations, this is more likely to be an agency goal—derived from principles that a person has—rather than a well-being one, yet the happiness surveys do not incorporate agency goals if they do not affect current perceived well-being. As well as neglect of future generations, people alive today who are unable or less able to articulate their perceived well-being—such as infants, children, the very old, and those with particular problems—may also be left out except to the extent that their well-being affects those who are able to articulate their state of well-being. Doubtless, those who advocate happiness as a measure of progress would agree that some modifications are needed to deal with these issues, but this gets one away from the pure happiness approach and into more complex ways of assessing progress.

In sum, the happiness approach provides a weak and sometimes misguided approach to development policy. Many of the determinants of individual

[10] We are grateful to Nandini Gooptu for ideas for this section.

happiness are independent of development policy. Some elements which form a central part of HR or capabilities do not appear to affect happiness in a systematic way—such as education. And some ways of enhancing happiness can be consistent with no improvement or even worsening of objective conditions. Consequently, measures of happiness should not displace HD or other ways of assessing development progress and of guiding policy, including the HR approach, the expansion of capabilities or freedoms, and the search for justice. These are not instrumental approaches, justified only to the extent that they advance the happiness objective, but fundamental constituents of progress.

2.6. Is There Any Role for Subjective Evaluations in Our Measuring of Progress in Development?

Do the severe problems with using happiness as the sole way of assessing development mean that we should abandon all such subjective assessments of progress? This seems extreme. It would seem difficult to count a country as progressing, even with marked improvements in the objective indicators of capabilities, if *all* assessments of subjective evaluations showed *strong deterioration*. Several approaches have been suggested for incorporating both objective and subjective evaluations in assessments of progress.

For example, the Sarkozy Commission concludes that '[m]easures of both objective and subjective well-being provide key information about people's quality of life' (Stiglitz et al. 2010, 18). This, indeed, is the approach adopted by Bhutan in its famous Gross National Happiness indicator, which includes nine domains and thirty-three indicators, with psychological well-being forming one of the nine domains, and four indicators associated with it (see Table 2.4). In like vein, Sen has argued that happiness 'can be seen as a very important human functioning, among others', and hence be included as one of the elements in assessing progress, and also that it may be of 'great circumstantial relevance in checking whether people are succeeding or failing to get what they value', i.e. a way of assessing how effectively other goals are being met (Sen 2009, 276). Kroll (2013) has amalgamated the HDI with a happiness indicator to assess country progress, and also suggested that correlations with happiness should determine the priority to be given to the objective elements of the HDI.

Four different approaches to the role to be given to indicators of happiness can be distinguished in these views. First, the view that psychological well-being should be added to the dashboard of elements to be included in a multidimensional evaluation of progress. This is broadly Sen's view and that of the Sarkozy Commission. But the problems of measurement and

Table 2.4. Elements of Bhutan's Gross National Happiness Index

	Domain	Number of Indicators
1	Psychological wellbeing	4
2	Health	4
3	Time use	2
4	Education	4
5	Cultural diversity & resilience	4
6	Good Governance	4
7	Community vitality	4
8	Ecological diversity and resilience	4
9	Living standards	3
	Total	33

Source: Ura et al. (2010).

mismeasurement remain, as well as that of adaptation to poor circumstances. Hence one would need to be cautious before taking this element of the dashboard too seriously.

The second view is that a combined index should be developed to assess country progress, including basic capabilities *and* a happiness indicator. This is what the Bhutan Index does and is also advocated by Kroll. Apart from the usual problems of choosing a system of weighting, this could distort assessments—from an HR or HD perspective—by allowing subjective measures to compensate for poor performance on basic indicators of capabilities. Given the severe theoretical and empirical problems raised by a happiness measure, as already discussed, we conclude this is an undesirable approach.

The third view adopted by Kroll (and advocated by Layard in arguing that everything other than happiness only has instrumental value) is that correlates with measures of happiness should be used to evaluate the priorities to be given to other objectives. This, however, puts happiness back in the driving seat, and could result in serious distortions of priorities from a capabilities perspective.

A fourth view that Sen appears to advocate is that measures of happiness could be useful in evaluating the effectiveness of implementation of policies directed towards enhancing capabilities. Here one needs to revert to a dashboard approach. As the sole means of evaluating implementation, the impact on subjective well-being would be unsatisfactory. The impact on the actual capability—e.g. whether children are indeed being educated and at what standard—is critical in evaluating implementation of, for example, an education project. However, the impact on subjective well-being could be a supplementary criterion, with some significance in itself, and more so for indicating defects in implementation that might otherwise have been missed—e.g. that the location of the school involved high transport costs. This involves going beyond the measured indicator of well-being to an investigation into why the project had not improved subjective well-being.[11] As so many factors affect people's overall well-being, this does not appear to be a good indicator to use for project evaluation. More straightforward is simply to ask participants whether they feel they have benefited from the project or not, if there are any serious problems with it, and why.

Thus, of the four ways of incorporating a happiness indicator into evaluation of development progress, the only one with some value, in our view, is to include it in the dashboard of multiple indicators. But here we need to differentiate small and big changes, and positive and negative ones. Small changes in any happiness indicator can be ignored given measurement problems. Attention is warranted for *large negative changes*. If there is progress in the objective indicators but *significant deterioration* in subjective ones—not due to measurement issues—this could be a signal that the development path has problems which need to be explored. As Adrian Wood put it,[12] we should be concerned with avoiding and reducing misery, and indicators of this are relevant to assessments of development progress.

In contrast, large positive changes, if unaccompanied by improvements in objective indicators such as nutrition, health, education, or security, on their own would not, in our view, be an indication of major progress in development in poor countries. The situation is perhaps different in rich countries where for most people achievements with respect to basic indicators might be regarded as satisfactory, and a large improvement in general satisfaction might therefore be accepted as constituting real progress. And we should note that it is only the happiness of those surveyed that is included, so that progress may be at the cost of those left out, including, but not only, future generations.

2.7. Conclusion

The utilitarians of the eighteenth and nineteenth centuries made a major contribution: they put human happiness at the centre of the evaluation of progress, rather than religion or hierarchy and privilege which then broadly prevailed. Others, such as Tom Paine, similarly challenged privilege and hierarchy, from an HR perspective. Both schools undoubtedly contributed to

[11] There is also the question of whose subjective wellbeing should be included: the wellbeing of the participants (children in this case), their families, others indirectly affected—e.g. those living near a new school—and the broader community?

[12] In a contribution to a seminar at the Oxford Department of International Development, October 2013. This is close to the view of Popper who thought that rather than maximize pleasure, the principle should be to 'minimize pain' (Smart 1958, Popper 2002), although what is advocated in this chapter is not precisely this—i.e. not invariably minimizing pain as the overriding principle, but bringing it into consideration as one element.

improvements in public policy and the abysmal conditions facing many who lived then.

Over time, however, the way that the utilitarian approach was interpreted had defects. It provided the basis for measurement of national income and its use as the main criterion of progress. Yet national income misses out many important elements in human progress—and became particularly unsatisfactory once economists adopted an ordinal approach to utility, rejecting the strong redistributive message of Pigou and others. The major achievement of the neo-utilitarians has been to challenge GNP and measures of income more generally as measures of progress, by reaffirming the initial utilitarian approach with its focus on human happiness, and showing that changes in income are not necessarily correlated with changes in happiness. Instead of using income as a measure of utility, the neo-utilitarians advocated a direct measure of happiness to be ascertained by surveys. They thus challenged the use of GNP, and dealt with some of its problems as a measure of progress. But the approach had its own problems, especially as the sole measure of progress, and particularly in poor countries.

This chapter has reviewed some major problems of the neo-utilitarian approach, including those of measurement and adaptation. Above all, the objection to the neo-utilitarian approach is that human progress involves promoting HD and HR, advancing human fulfilment or flourishing, realizing agency objectives, and promoting a just distribution, sustained over generations. Cross-country surveys of human well-being can come nowhere near to measuring this extensive array of objectives.

3

The Relationship between Human Development and Economic Growth

3.1. Introduction

HD is taken here as the ultimate objective of human activity, displacing economic growth as argued in Chapter 1.[1] Nonetheless, economic growth is likely to be an important instrument for advancing HD. Indeed, the relationship is two-way. On the one hand, economic growth provides the resources to permit sustained improvements in HD. On the other, improvements in HD and consequently in the quality of the labour force are an important contributor to economic growth. The aim of this chapter is to explore the two-way links between the two both at the conceptual and empirical levels, and to consider priorities in the phasing of policy: in particular, we examine the common assumption that countries should first establish strong economic fundamentals (i.e. promote economic growth), and that only then can they afford to promote HD.[2]

HD is often defined as a process of enlarging people's choices in a way that enables them to lead longer, healthier, and fuller lives (UNDP 1990). This definition is very broad. For the purpose of exploring the links between HD and economic growth theoretically, and especially empirically, we need to narrow it down. In this chapter we shall consider the HD of a country to consist of the health and education of its people, recognizing that this is a very reductionist interpretation. We are here following the HDI, except that we do not include the income component because our aim is to explore the relationship between economic growth and HD, and it would confuse matters to have incomes on both sides of the relationship.

[1] Vidya Diwakar is co-author of this chapter, with particular responsibility for Section 3.3. The chapter draws on earlier papers to which Alejandro Ramirez, Tavneet Suri, and Michael Boozer contributed. We are grateful for their permission to use the material here.

[2] Adelman and Morris (1973) provide an early exception to this rule, arguing that investment in education should be given priority.

The chapter is organized as follows: Section 3.2 identifies the major links between economic growth and HD. Section 3.3 presents some empirical cross-country evidence on these links. Section 3.4 develops a typology of country cases, some representing the mutual enhancement of HD and economic growth and some demonstrating asymmetric performance. The final section, Section 3.5, concludes.

3.2. The Two Chains

We view HD as the central objective of human activity and economic growth as potentially a very important instrument for advancing it. At the same time, achievements in HD themselves can make a critical contribution to economic growth. There are thus two distinct causal chains to be examined: one runs from economic growth to HD, as the resources from national income are allocated to activities contributing to HD; the other runs from HD to economic growth, indicating how, in addition to being an end in itself, HD helps increase national income. The two chains are pictured in Figure 3.1.

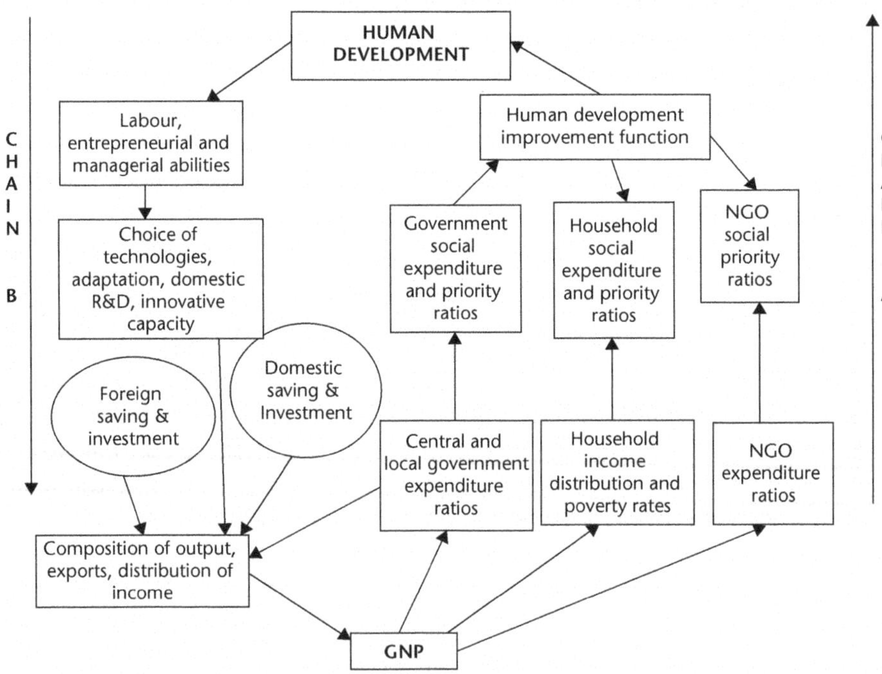

Figure 3.1. The relationship between HD and GNP

3.2.1. *Chain A: From Economic Growth to HD*

GNP contributes to HD mainly through household and government activity; civil society—e.g. through community organizations and other non-governmental organizations (NGOs)—also plays a role. The same level of GNP can lead to very different performance on HD according to the allocation of GNP among and within these institutions and variations in their behaviour.

Households' propensity to spend their after-tax income on items which contribute directly to HD (e.g. food, potable water, education, and health) varies, depending on such factors as the level and distribution of income across households as well as on who controls the allocation of expenditure within households. In general, poor households spend a higher proportion of their incomes on these basic HD items than those with higher incomes, and similar results flow from greater female control over household income.

When levels of poverty are high, either because national income per head is low or because it is badly distributed, the expenditure of many households on HD is bound to be low. Large differences in poverty levels arise from the variation across societies in the level and distribution of GNP per capita. While evidence indicates that, in general, poverty is reduced with economic growth,[3] the extent of the reduction varies greatly with the distribution of income and its change over time (Bourguignon 2003, Chakrangi and Ram 2010). A comparative analysis of Brazil, China, and India, for 1981–2005, for example, showed that the elasticity of poverty with respect to growth varied hugely, from 3.2 per cent in Brazil to less than 1 per cent in India and China, but poverty fell most in China because of its very high growth rate (Ravallion 2009). The nature of the growth process is relevant here: in particular, the extent to which growth is based on the generation of employment and on increasing rural incomes. Where the output mix is labour-intensive and rural incomes rise rapidly, incomes are likely to become more equal and poverty reduction to be greater than if growth is urban-biased and capital-intensive (Lipton 1977, Stewart 1977, Lipton and Ravallion 1995).

Expenditure on HD-related items is strongly affected by the rate of poverty reduction. For example, if poor households receive extra income, they increase their food expenditure and calorie consumption significantly. Of thirty-eight studies in different countries, one-third indicate that at least one-half of additional income is spent in this way (Strauss and Thomas 1995). Evidence—for example, for Bolivia, Brazil, Chile, China, Côte d'Ivoire, Ghana, India, Indonesia, Pakistan, the Philippines, Malaysia, Nicaragua, and

[3] For example Bruno et al. (1999), in a study of twenty countries, show that a 10 per cent increase in average income per capita, 1984–93, was associated with a 20 per cent fall in the proportion of people living on less than US$1 a day.

Peru—also indicates the positive effects of a change in family income on child schooling (Birdsall 1985, Behrman and Wolfe 1987, King and Lilliard 1987, Deolalikar 1993, Alderman et al. 1997).

Similarly, studies in a number of countries, including Brazil, Chile, China, Côte d'Ivoire, Mexico, and Nicaragua, have shown that an increase in household income has a positive effect on health, with some studies showing a higher response among low-income households in response to an increase in income than among high-income households (Birdsall et al. 1995, Yang and Kanavos 2012, Fillenbaum et al. 2013, Aguila et al. 2015). In Thailand, for example, health improved fastest among the poorest sections of society between 1990 and 2000 at a time when poverty fell from 18 per cent to 2 per cent, while there were also pro-poor health interventions (Vapattanawong et al. 2007). Long-term panel studies in India, Peru, and Vietnam show that children's height for their age depends both on total food expenditure and on the pattern of food expenditure (Humphries et al. 2017). An overview of thirty-four studies conducted in developed countries found a strong positive impact of additional household financial resources on a variety of child outcomes, including schooling and health (Cooper and Stewart 2013).

The distribution of income affects both education and health, in part because it affects the poverty rate for a given national per capita income.[4] An estimate for the 1990s suggested that if the distribution of income in Brazil had been as equal as Malaysia's, school enrolment among poor children from poor households would have been 40 per cent higher (Birdsall et al. 1995). A sample of 108 countries (Checchi 2003) found that inequality negatively affected female primary education and secondary education overall. Moreover, socio-economic inequality appears to affect health over and above the effect of poverty, with relative as well as absolute income mattering.[5] But the effects of poverty as such are not always clearly differentiated from the effects of inequality.[6] More equal societies have been found to have better health overall (Wilkinson and Pickett 2006, Wilkinson and Pickett 2008, Kondo 2012).

Where women control cash income, it appears that expenditure patterns are geared relatively more towards HD inputs, such as food and education (Quisumbing and Maluccio 2000, Guzmán et al. 2008). For example, among Gambian households, the larger the proportion of food under women's control the larger household calorie consumption (von Braun 1988). Similarly, in

[4] For evidence regarding China, Mexico, and India see Ming et al. (2005), Lopez-Acevedo (2006) and Majumdar and Mooij (2011).

[5] One of the pathways relating socio-economic status to health is through social capital, since social networks transmit information about health and education. Asymmetric social capital—with poor groups having poorer networks from the perspective of health information—can enhance health inequalities. For empirical evidence supporting this, see Uphoff et al. (2013).

[6] One study of low- and middle-income countries showed that both individual and relative wealth affected health (van Deurzen et al. 2014).

the Philippines it has been shown that consumption of calories and proteins increases with the share of income accruing to wives (Garcia 1990). In Côte d'Ivoire, an increase in women's share of cash income was associated with significantly higher spending on food and reduced spending on alcohol and cigarettes (Hoddinott and Haddad 1995).

Turning to the government, the allocation of resources to improving HD is a function of total public sector expenditure, of how much of this flows to the HD sectors, and of the way in which it is allocated within these sectors. This can be expressed in the form of three ratios: the public expenditure ratio, defined as the proportion of GNP spent by the various levels of government; the HD allocation ratio, defined as the proportion of total government expenditure going to the HD sectors; and, finally, the HD priority ratio, defined as the proportion of total HD sector expenditure going to 'priority areas'. Within the HD sectors, some expenditures are clearly much more productive in terms of achieving advances in HD than others; for example, basic education, especially at an early stage of development, is generally recognized to have a larger impact on HD than tertiary education. But the precise definition of what constitutes a 'priority area' will inevitably vary according to a country's stage of development, rendering this third ratio more arbitrary and difficult to measure than the other two. There exist very large variations across countries in each of these ratios, which means that the same level of GNP may be associated with very different levels of government spending on HD priorities (UNDP 1991, Stewart 1995).

The underlying determinants of these three ratios are complex, but include the following: (a) the tax capacity of the system; (b) the strength of the demand for military expenditure and for other non-HD priorities of the government; and (c) the varying interplay between bureaucratic forces, vested interests, and popular pressures. It should be noted that all three ratios are affected by the extent of decentralization of government: real decentralization, i.e. devolution, tends to increase the total revenue available; it often raises the HD allocation ratio; and it almost always improves the HD priority ratios (UNDP 1991, ch. 3, Ranis and Stewart 1994). However, a survey of nineteen countries found that decentralization was not invariably 'pro-poor'; it can be co-opted by local elites (Jütting et al. 2004; see also Bardhan and Mookherjee 2006).

The significance of public expenditure choices for improving HD is illustrated by a comparison between Kenya and Malawi. In the 1980s, a similar proportion of national income went to public expenditure (27 per cent in Kenya, 30 per cent in Malawi), but Kenya had a significantly higher social allocation ratio (47 per cent compared to 35 per cent in Malawi) and social priority ratio (34 per cent compared to 14 per cent in Malawi) so that the proportion of GDP going directly to HD-improving priorities in Kenya was over three times that of Malawi (5.1 per cent compared to 1.5 per cent) (UNDP 1996, 71).[7] Similarly, in 2012, Ethiopia and Uganda had the same proportion of GDP going to government expenditure (about a fifth), but Ethiopia devoted almost half of this to the social sectors, while Uganda spent a quarter on education and health, with the result that the proportion of GDP going to the social sectors in Ethiopia was double that in Uganda. Statistical analysis of the relationship between social spending and education and health outcomes is shown in a study of 118 developing countries between 1971 and 2000 (Baldacci et al. 2008). The authors estimate that an increase in spending on education of 1 per cent of GDP is associated with three additional years of schooling per child, and a one percentage point GDP rise in expenditure on health services raises the under-five survival rate by 0.6 per cent.

The importance of economic growth for raising resources to support HD is illustrated by country comparisons. In 2000, health expenditure per head was about the same in Nicaragua and Guyana; but over the decade 2000–10, GDP per head (constant prices) increased by 16 per cent in Nicaragua but only by 6 per cent in Guyana. With a similar increase in the proportion of GDP going to health in the two countries, health expenditure per capita (PPP 2005 prices) doubled in Nicaragua compared with an increase of 50 per cent in Guyana. This meant that by the end of the decade Nicaragua's health expenditure per head was over 40 per cent greater than that of Guyana. Similarly, in Ghana health expenditure per head was just 43 per cent of that of Côte d'Ivoire in 2000. But by 2010, due to faster growth, health expenditure per head rose by 90 per cent in Ghana compared with 26 per cent in Côte d'Ivoire, so that Ghana's health expenditure per head had then reached 65 per cent of the level in Côte d'Ivoire.

Finally, NGO or other civil society activity, on which information is more scattered, is typically heavily oriented towards HD objectives (e.g. generating incomes for the poor and on schools, nutrition, and health projects). Resources are derived from private donations and governments, in each case including both foreign and domestic sources. There are considerable variations in the extent, vitality, and effectiveness of NGO activities across countries, depending on their history, culture, tax laws, and actual or perceived government deficiencies in providing services. In most contexts, NGOs play a supplemental or even marginal role, but in a few areas—e.g. Building Resources Across Communities (BRAC), and the Grameen Bank in Bangladesh, the Harambee Schools in Kenya, and the Self Employed Women's Association in India—they can constitute a major source of HD enhancement. In Bangladesh, for example, non-government-financed schools account for over 40 per cent of

[7] These calculations adopt a narrow definition of social priority expenditure, including only pre-primary and primary education and primary healthcare.

primary school enrolment and over 90 per cent of secondary, compared with 4 per cent and 11 per cent respectively in Ethiopia. Further discussion of their role, alongside that of other social institutions, is contained in Chapter 7.

Expenditures on HD inputs are clearly not objectives in themselves, but rather constitute instruments for achieving advances in various dimensions of basic well-being. A further important link in Chain A, therefore, is the effectiveness of these expenditures in raising HD levels, i.e. what type of provision is most productive at what level of development, and how different combinations effect a change in HD. We shall call this link in the chain the 'human development improvement function' (HDIF); it resembles a production function in that it relates the inputs into HD, such as public expenditure on health services or water, to the HD objective of achieving better health. An illustration of the type of relationship represented in the HDIF is whether and how far the provision of safe water is complementary to, or a substitute for, education in contributing to improvements in health. Another example is the combination of preventive health spending and nutrition levels which most effectively yields improvements in infant mortality. The relationships embodied in the HDIF are complex, depending on individual and community behaviour and the existence of local knowledge about relevant technologies. Moreover, the relevant arguments of the HDIF are bound to differ at different stages of development and among different cultures. Societal norms can be important in determining the relationships in HDIF, as further argued in Chapter 7.

Some aspects of the HDIF have been considerably illuminated by a great deal of detailed empirical work. We give just a few examples here. One is the abundant evidence that education, especially of females, tends to improve infant survival and nutrition (Behrman and Wolfe 1987, Thomas and Henriques 1991). An investigation into low- and middle-income countries for 1990–2011 found that '39.6% of the child mortality decline from 1990–2000 and 17.5% of the child mortality decline from 2000–2011 can be attributed to increases in female schooling' (Schäferhoff et al. 2015). Moreover, it is not only a parent's education but the general education level in the community that can affect child health (Moestue and Huttly 2008). There is also growing evidence that cash transfers (conditional and unconditional) can improve the nutrition, health, and education of both young and old (Parker et al. 2008, Behrman and Parker 2013), and research in Ghana and Nepal has shown that in rural areas the provision of basic health services, including adequate drugs, significantly increases child health and survival (Lavy et al. 1996, Hotchkiss et al. 2002).

Conditions liable to bring about an improvement in the efficiency of the HDIF include better information about available technologies and the appropriate combinations of inputs; the generation of new and more effective technologies; changing social norms; and enhanced motivation to make use of available options, e.g. sending children to schools and clinics. Such motivation appears to be influenced by social norms, education levels, the power structure within the family, as well as incentives and the magnitude of opportunity costs.

It should be clear from this discussion of the various links in the economic growth–HD chain that, in general, we would expect important causal connections to exist between the economy and HD achievements, but these connections are *not automatic*: the strength of the links in Chain A varies according to a large range of factors, including the structure of the economy, the distribution of assets, and the policy choices made. The richness of the social capital of a society affects these choices and the strength of links at each stage; when people act together to promote their well-being, when public morality is high, when the community monitors malfeasance, and when it participates extensively in public life, *ceteris paribus*, we can expect all the links in Chain A to be stronger.

In summary, we would hypothesize from this review of the links in Chain A that the connection between GNP and HD is likely to be stronger:

- the lower the poverty level: for a given level of GNP per capita, this means the more equally income is distributed;
- the more income households allocate to HD at a given income level: this may be related both to the level of female education and to female control over income within the household;
- the higher the proportion of GNP devoted to priority social expenditure by the government;
- the greater the effective contribution of social institutions, including community organizations and other NGOs; and/or
- the more efficient the HDIF.

3.2.2. *Chain B: From HD to Economic Growth*

Turning our attention to the second chain, from HD to economic growth, there is an obvious presumption, supported by ample evidence, that as people become more healthy, well nourished, and educated they contribute more to economic growth. Higher levels of HD, in addition to being an end in themselves, affect the economy through enhancing people's capabilities and consequently their creativity and productivity.

Clearly, the health and education of a population represent one of the main determinants of the composition and growth of output and exports and constitute an important ingredient in a system's capacity to borrow foreign technology effectively.

This instrumental effect of HD—which is incorporated in Chain B—must not, however, let us forget the intrinsic importance of HD. The fundamental premise, which underlies the whole HD approach, is that HD is intrinsically valuable, irrespective of any impact on productivity; for example, improving the lives of those who may never (or never again) be producers, such as the severely disabled and the old. Improving their (and other) human lives is, of course, an important part of advancing HD, irrespective of any impact on productivity, and enters the end point of Chain A (i.e. societal HD).

Specific links from HD to economic growth, summarized in Chain B, include the ways that: (a) the health and basic education of workers raise their productivity; (b) secondary education, including vocational education, facilitates the acquisition of skills and managerial capacity; (c) tertiary education supports the development of basic knowledge, the appropriate selection of imported technologies, and the development and adaptation of domestic technology; and (d) secondary and tertiary education contributes to key institutions of government, law, and the financial system, among others, which are all essential for economic growth as well as other important societal objectives.

Empirical evidence at both micro and macro levels further illuminates these relationships. At a *micro* level, numerous studies indicate that increases in earnings are associated with additional years of education, with the rate of return varying with the level of education. While social rates of return (which defined narrowly deduct the publicly financed costs of education but make no other adjustments to the private returns) are below the private, they are still typically greater than returns to most physical investment. The returns to primary schooling tend to be greater than the returns to secondary and tertiary education (Psacharopoulos and Patrinos 2004). However, the method for estimating these returns assumes that additional incomes earned as a result of additional education represent the returns. There are several problems with this assumption (Bennell 1996). One is that they may represent private returns but not necessarily social, defined broadly to include externalities such as contributions to health and innovation. Moreover, the view is sometimes challenged by the argument that education performs a signalling function, differentiating between people of different innate ability, rather than itself raising productivity. However, investigations in rural Pakistan and in urban Kenya and Tanzania, differentiating between additional earnings due to cognitive achievement and those due simply to schooling, showed that cognitive achievement accounted for a high proportion of the extra earnings (Knight and Sabot 1990). Chevalier et al. (2004) also find little support for the screening or signalling explanation of the relation between education and wages using UK data, while Card (2001) estimates that the contribution of innate ability, as against that of education, does not account for more than 10 per cent of the total return. A second reason for concern with the rate of return estimates is that they may be good indicators of marginal change, but the returns would vary if there were a substantial, non-marginal change as might happen with a major policy adjustment leading to changes in the structure of earnings.

More direct evidence on the effect of education on productivity comes from investigations of farm and firm productivity. In agriculture, evidence suggests positive effects of education on productivity among farmers using modern technologies, but less impact, as might be expected, among those using traditional methods (Rosenzweig 1995, Foster and Rosenzweig 1996, Reimers and Klasen 2013). A study in Thailand showed that farmers with four or more years of schooling were three times more likely to adopt fertilizer and other modern inputs than less-educated farmers, while in Nepal the completion of seven or more years of schooling led to substantial increases in productivity in wheat and rice (Jamison and Moock 1984, Birdsall 1993).[8]

Education is also an important contributor to technological capability and technical change in industry. Statistical analysis of the clothing and engineering industries in Sri Lanka, for example, showed that the skill and education levels of workers and entrepreneurs were positively related to the rate of technical change of the firm (Deraniyagala 1995). There is also evidence of a positive impact on firm productivity from studies of industrial firms in a number of countries, including Kenya, Tanzania, Uganda, Belgium, Ghana, Iran, and South Africa (Frazer n.d., Jones 2001, Aggrey et al. 2010, Lebedinski and Vandenberghe 2013, Burger and Teal 2014). But not all studies find a significant positive effect of education on firm productivity (e.g. Söderbom and Teal 2004, Kleynhans and Labuschagne 2012).

Education alone, of course, cannot transform an economy. The quantity and quality of investment, domestic and foreign, together with the overall policy environment and the quality of institutions, form other important determinants of economic performance. Yet the level of HD has a bearing on these factors, too. The quality of policymaking and of investment decisions is bound to be influenced by the education of both policymakers and managers; moreover, the volume of both domestic and foreign investment is likely to be larger when a system's human capital supply is more plentiful.

From a *macro* perspective, the so-called 'new growth theories' aimed to endogenize technical progress by incorporating some of these same effects, emphasizing education as well as learning and research and development (R&D). According to Lucas (1988), for example, the higher the level of education of the workforce the higher the overall productivity of capital because the more educated

[8] Examination of the early stages of India's Green Revolution indicates that the benefits from schooling arose more from developing farmers' capacity for learning from their own or others' experiences, rather than from providing them with an initial information advantage (Foster and Rosenzweig 1996).

are more likely to innovate, and thus affect everyone's productivity. In other models, a similar externality is generated as the increased education of individuals raises not only their own productivity but also that of others with whom they interact, so that total productivity increases as the average level of education rises (Perotti 1993). A complementary view is that technical progress depends on the level of R&D in an economy (Romer 1990). By investing labour and capital in R&D, a firm is able to improve not only its own profitability but also the productivity of the firms which consume its output. Again, education plays a key role, both in contributing to R&D and via interactive learning.

The impact of education on the nature and growth of exports, which, in turn, affect the aggregate growth rate, is another way in which HD influences macro performance. The education and skills of a developing country's labour force influence the nature of its factor endowment and consequently the composition of its trade. It has been argued that even 'unskilled' workers in a modern factory normally need the literacy, numeracy, and discipline which are acquired in primary and lower secondary school (Wood 1994). Theoretical models incorporating skills and learning as important determinants of comparative advantage have led to modifications of the simple two-factor Heckscher–Ohlin model, helping to explain the Leontief paradox and the dramatic success in the manufactured export growth of some developing countries, notably those of East Asia (Pack and Westphal 1986, Leamer 1993). Investigations have shown a significant positive correlation between the growth of manufactured exports and the growth of GDP, although serious identification problems remain (Ram 1985, Edwards 1993, Hsiao and Hsiao 2006), while a number of empirical studies have shown the positive effect of education on economic growth at a macro level, with its size varying according to the measure of education and the particular macro growth model adopted (Barro 2001, Johnes 2006, Barro 2013).

Improved health and nutrition have also been shown to have positive effects on productivity, especially among poorer individuals (Behrman and Deolalikar 1987, Behrman 1993, Savedoff and Schultz 2000, Sohn 2000, Schultz 2002, Bloom et al. 2004). Numerous studies have shown a negative effect of malaria on workers' productivity and earnings, leading to sizeable effects on national income in countries in sub-Saharan Africa where incidence is high (Picard and Mills 1992, Nur 1993, Najera and Hempel 1996, Dillon et al. 2014). According to Jobin (2014, 1 of online paper): 'Following annual expenditures of about $0.2 billion for suppressing malaria, the mean per capita Gross Domestic Product of fourteen African countries increased 98% after 7 years of intervention, while it improved only 66% in 9 comparable but untreated countries.' Taking a more holistic view of health, Bloom and Canning (2005) found that a 1 per cent improvement in adult survival rates improves labour productivity by 2.8 per cent, on the basis of cross-country panel data for 1960–95. Although Acemoglu and Johnson (2007) argue that the major improvement in life expectancy from the 1940s did not increase per capita incomes, this has been questioned by Bloom et al. (2014), who show that the improvement in health did affect growth and incomes positively, allowing for conditional convergence.

A range of labour productivity gains has been observed associated with calorie increases, including in studies of farmers in Sierra Leone, sugar cane workers in Guatemala, and road construction workers in Kenya (Immink and Viterri 1981, Wolgemuth et al. 1982, Strauss 1986). In these cases productivity enhancement appears to follow fairly immediately as current intakes of calories or micro-nutrients are increased. In other cases the effects are medium run (as reflected in weight) or long run (as reflected in height), based on evidence from Bangladesh, Brazil, India, Sri Lanka, and the Philippines (Behrman and Deolalikar 1988, Pitt et al. 1990, Haddad and Bouis 1991, Strauss and Thomas 1997). A study in Cali, Colombia, found that a health and nutrition programme, alongside preschool education, increased the lifetime earnings of individuals from 2.5 to 8.9 times those of an illiterate worker's (Selowsky 1981). And for South Korea, Sohn (2000) finds that improved nutrition raised labour inputs by 1 per cent per annum during 1962–95. Estimates by Hoddinott et al. (2013) for benefit–cost ratios of interventions to prevent stunting range from 4 (in the Democratic Republic of the Congo) to 48 (in Indonesia).

There is also a positive feedback from improved education to greater income equality which, in turn, is likely to favour higher rates of growth. As education becomes more broadly based, low-income earners are better able to seek out economic opportunities. For example, a study of the relation between schooling, income inequality, and poverty in eighteen countries of Latin America in the 1980s found that one-quarter of the variation in workers' incomes was accounted for by variations in schooling attainment; it concluded that 'clearly education is the variable with the strongest impact on income equality' (Psacharopolous et al. 1992, 48). Mughal and Diawara (2011) found that the level of secondary and tertiary education was significantly negatively associated with inequality, on the basis of panel data for sixty-five developing countries during 1980–2005. Similarly, Cornia (2014) found that the ratio of secondary and tertiary education to primary or no education was significantly associated with a decline in inequality in Latin American countries during 1999–2009.

Finally, education may affect per capita income growth via its impact on the denominator, i.e. population growth. There is consistent evidence from every region of the world that greater female education reduces fertility (Schultz 2007). High fertility rates in Africa led some to question whether Africa was an exception (Bledsoe et al. 1998, Bongaarts and Casterline 2013), but the evidence suggests it is not. For example, a study of fourteen African countries for the mid-1980s showed a negative correlation between female schooling and fertility in almost all countries, with primary education having a negative impact in about half the countries and no significant effects in the other half, while secondary education invariably reduced fertility (Ainsworth et al. 1996). A study for 1994–2010 confirms the role of education in Africa's demographic transition (Mveyange 2015).

As in Chain A, the strength of the various links in Chain B can vary considerably and there is no *automatic* connection between an improved level of HD and increases in per capita GNP. Thus, it is not enough to create a larger pool of educated people; there must also exist opportunities for them to be productively employed. Relevant here are the savings and investment rates, the policy setting, and the quality of the system's social institutions.

Although high rates of savings and investment by themselves, as shown by past East European experience, do not guarantee high levels of sustained growth, normally a positive relationship between investment and growth prevails, with its strength depending on such factors as the policy environment, the quantity and quality of human resources, the availability of technology choices, and the flexibility of the institutional framework. As pointed out earlier, both domestic investment and foreign direct investment are influenced by a country's HD level—particularly the education and skill levels of the workforce. But differences in economic growth across societies are again not only due to the level of inputs but also by how effectively they are used and for what purpose. One important influence is the incentives set by economic policy. Another derives from people's motives and behaviour patterns which depend on prevalent norms and networks as well as on public and private systems devised to manage resources.

Income distribution also appears to be important in Chain B, as it is in Chain A. Considerable evidence suggests that more equality tends to be associated with higher growth (Alesina and Rodrik 1994, Birdsall and Sabot 1994, Persson and Tabellini 1994, Deininger and Olinto 2000), although this view has been challenged (Li and Zou 1998). However, evidence suggests that high levels of inequality make it more difficult to sustain growth (Berg et al. 2008).

Among the explanations put forward for this is one derived from the relationships in Chain A, i.e. that a more equal distribution of income implies better nutrition and a stronger demand for education, and hence raises labour productivity. Other explanations derive from political economy considerations, for example, that an unequal distribution of income may be associated with greater political instability, which is more likely to interrupt economic progress (Alesina and Rodrik 1994).

In summary, the connection between HD and GNP, represented by Chain B, is likely to be stronger:

- the more attuned to the needs of the economy is the educational system—this depends on the stage of development, e.g. primary education at an earlier stage, secondary and vocational at a later stage, the quality of education at all stages, etc.;
- the higher the investment rate;
- the more appropriate the economic policy setting;
- the more supportive the quality of the social capital in place; and
- the more equal the distribution of income.

Once again the nature of the policies or institutions which determine the strength or weakness of particular links in Chain B will vary with the stage of development a country has reached. For example, the adoption of labour-intensive methods is critical at an early stage when there is still much unemployment and underemployment, but later on more capital and skill-intensive methods are needed; institutions facilitating the productive use of small rural savings are especially important early on; and a more differentiated financial intermediation network is required at a later stage.

3.3. Cross-Country Empirical Analysis, 1970–2014

The preceding discussion led us to a set of hypotheses about the links between HD and economic growth for both causal chains: from economic growth to HD (Chain A) and from HD to economic growth (Chain B). In this section, we present cross-sectional ordinary least squares (OLS) regression results on the two-way correlations between HD and economic growth. This stems from a recognition that HD is both an input into development as well as an outcome, as the two chains postulate. The distinction between correlation and causality must be stressed here; our analysis examines relationships highlighting the former, while avoiding any robust claims of causality. This is because HD and economic growth are mutually reinforcing, insofar as an improvement in either one should theoretically improve the other. In this setting, claims of causality become problematic. Consequently, we avoid such claims, instead attempting to investigate the existence and extent of the co-dependency between HD and economic growth through a correlations framework. To reduce the inevitable problems of endogeneity, we use time-lags for the data in the regressions.

In our investigation, all HD variables are highly correlated so we do not measure their separate associated effects in a single regression. For example, life expectancy and the poverty headcount display a correlation coefficient of –0.76 during 1970–2014, while for the poverty headcount and gross female primary enrolment, the corresponding coefficient is –0.75. The two gendered education variables—gross female secondary enrolment rate and the ratio of male to female secondary enrolment—are also correlated at –0.57 over the same period. A full list of variables and countries included in the data are presented in Box A.3.1 and Table A.3.4 of the Appendix, while summary graphs are presented in Figure A.3.1 (also in the Appendix).

In this model, we characterize the key independent variables—in the first chain (A), infant mortality, gross secondary enrolment (for the total population and among females), and life expectancy; and in the second chain (B), economic growth—in two ways. We control for initial levels of each variable in 1970 and the rate of change between 1970 and 2014. The logic is that country starting points often explain a large amount of the subsequent change in that variable (i.e. the rate of change),[9] and that different variables have different lag times in affecting the dependent variable. For some variables, initial levels display stronger associations with progress in the dependent variables than changes, while for others the reverse holds true (which could also reflect reverse causation)—but controlling for both in the same specifications enables a more balanced assessment of progress.

3.3.1. *Chain A: From Economic Growth to HD*

In Tables A.3.1 and A.3.2, we examine associations of lagged economic growth with improvements in HD. Specifically:

$$HD_i = \alpha + \tau y_{i0} + \varphi g_i' + HD_i'\delta + w_i'\theta + n_j + \epsilon_i \tag{1}$$

where y_{i0} is the initial GDP per capita in 1970,[10] g is the growth rate of GDP per capita from 1970 to 1990, *HD*'s are vectors of initial and lagged change HD variables, the *w*'s are other controls (Gini coefficient, and public education and health expenditures), and the *n*'s are the regional dummies.

3.3.1.1. ECONOMIC GROWTH IS CORRELATED WITH IMPROVEMENTS IN HD . . .

Results presented in Tables A.3.1 and A.3.2 (in Appendix A) indicate that economic growth is significantly positively correlated with improvements in the rate of change of both life expectancy and infant mortality in almost

[9] Rodríguez Takeuchi and Samman (2015) found that the initial levels for six of seven MDG variables accounted for between 49 per cent (primary education) and 90 per cent (sanitation) of subsequent progress.

[10] GDP is preferred over per capita GNP (or GNI) as the data are available for a larger number of countries.

all specifications, including all the baseline specifications (see column 1 in Table A.3.1, and column 7 in Table A.3.2) and when introducing controls (see columns 2, 3, and 5–9 in Table A.3.1, and columns 8 and 9 in Table A.3.2). The level of GDP per capita in the initial year (1970) is also associated with subsequent improvement in life expectancy and infant mortality, significantly in most cases.

As a caveat, it is worth noting that a low initial level of GDP per capita does not mean that countries cannot make significant improvements in HD. For example, we observe that Mali, Nepal, Cambodia, Guinea, Malawi, Bangladesh, and Burkina Faso all fall within the bottom quartile in terms of countries' GDP per capita in 1970, yet they made some of the largest improvements in life expectancy over the forty-five-year period. Indeed, the regression-based associations are by no means deterministic but rather emphasize the additional gains to be made in multidimensional well-being through early advances in output as measured by GDP per capita.

The impact of income is less clear-cut in the case of education (see Table A.3.2), with GDP per capita growth showing a significant association with change in gross secondary enrolment in only one of the three specifications (see column 3 in Table A.3.2). Both the levels of per capita income and of growth have a positive association with aggregate secondary enrolment change, but are not significant. However, GDP per capita is significantly associated with the increase in the female enrolment rate in two cases (see columns 5 and 6 in Table A.3.2), and growth in per capita income is positively and significantly associated with change in female enrolment in one specification (see column 6 in Table A.3.2).

For every one of the HD variables, there is evidence for some catch-up or convergence across countries, with lower improvements the higher the initial levels.

We also observe that public spending on social sectors is effective in promoting HD outcomes. For example, the average ratio of public health expenditures to GDP is associated with an improvement in life expectancy in every case where the variable is included (see columns 5, 6, 8, and 9 in Table A.3.1) and with the reduction in infant mortality (see columns 8 and 9 in Table A.3.2), and the change in the ratio of education expenditure to GDP is consistently positively and significantly related to increases in the secondary school enrolment rates (both total and female) (see columns 2, 3, 5, and 6 in Table A.3.2). In contrast, against expectation, the distribution of income (measured here by the average Gini coefficient, 1970–2014) does not show a significant association with improvements in the life expectancy (see columns 3 and 4 in Table A.3.1) or the other HD variables (not shown here).

Finally, Tables A.3.1 and A.3.2 indicate that there is a lower improvement in life expectancy and infant mortality for a given growth rate visible in African countries, which may be due to the impact of HIV/AIDS over the period. In contrast, the change in education, for a given growth of GDP, was greater in Africa than elsewhere.

3.3.1.2. ...AND IMPROVEMENTS IN ONE ELEMENT OF HD ARE ALSO CORRELATED WITH IMPROVEMENTS IN OTHER ELEMENTS OF HD

Equation (1) also allows us to examine relationships between different types of HD variables, and whether controlling for improvements in these may affect the direction or extent of association between economic growth and HD. We only present the whole set of regression results for equations with life expectancy as the dependent variable (see Table A.3.1), even though, as shown in Table A.3.2, similar correlations exist across other HD outcomes as well. Our justification for focusing on life expectancy as opposed to another HD outcome is first, practically, for clarity of analysis, and second, because changes in growth, education, and infant mortality over time are also likely, in theory, to manifest in changes in life expectancy.

Accordingly, we present our results around life expectancy in columns 1–9 of Table A.3.1. This analysis shows that HD variables can sometimes have synergistic effects. We observe that the initial level of education, though not the lagged change, has a positive association with improvements in life expectancy. Overall, secondary enrolment has a larger association than female secondary enrolment, though ultimately both are important conduits to improved life expectancy over the long term. Finally, we observe that improving gender parity in secondary education in favour of girls is associated with improvements in life expectancy (see column 9 in Table A.3.1).

Against expectations the Gini coefficient does not show any significant association.

3.3.2. *Chain B: From HD to Economic Growth*

To examine the reverse relationship—from HD to economic growth—we first employ the following OLS model:

$$g_i = \alpha + HD_i'\tau + z_i'\theta + n_j + \epsilon_i \tag{2}$$

where g is the average growth rate of GDP per capita for country between 1970 and 2014, HD's are the gross secondary enrolment rate overall and of the female subset, infant mortality rate, and life expectancy (both the initial value to control for starting conditions, and the rate of change for all HD measures), the z's are other explanatory variables (the gross capital formation rate and the Gini coefficient), and the n's are regional dummies (with Asia as the reference group). Results are presented in Table A.3.3 (in the Appendix).

3.3.2.1. ECONOMIC GROWTH BEGETS MORE HD, BUT HD IS ALSO SIGNIFICANT FOR ECONOMIC GROWTH

Table A.3.3 exhibits two familiar correlations also found in earlier work covering the 1960–2001 period (Suri et al. 2011). These are: (a) a positive effect of gross capital formation that is statistically significant across a majority of specifications; and (b) a conditional convergence effect which we derive from the negative coefficient on the initial GDP per capita. In other words, investment is associated with economic growth,[11] and those countries in our dataset with a lower GDP in 1970 tended to catch up somewhat with richer countries over the period.

We also observe in the table the strong correlation of economic growth with initial HD *levels* in all specifications that only include the HD variable and regional controls (i.e. columns 1, 3, and 5 in Table A.3.3). This holds in every case but one, when other controls (gross capital formation rate, and the Gini coefficient) are introduced. While the Gini coefficient is not statistically significant, it almost always shows a negative relationship with economic growth across specifications (i.e. more inequality is associated with lower growth). In most cases, *changes* in the HD variables (infant mortality, and both measures of enrolment rate change) also are correlated significantly with economic growth. In fact, changes in IMR (infant mortality rate per 1,000 live births) have a much stronger association with economic growth than the initial level of IMR.

In contrast, initial *levels* of gross enrolment in secondary education both overall and among females have a stronger association with economic growth than their respective *change* variables. Comparing initial levels, we observe that female secondary enrolment has a stronger association with economic growth than the overall gross secondary enrolment rate (see columns 5–8 in Table A.3.3), echoing the literature which emphasizes the multiple spillover effects of female education, given women's role as primary care givers within households (UNICEF 2004). However, we should note that Barro (2013) found that it was only secondary schooling of males, not females, that had a significant association with economic growth, during 1960–95 for one hundred countries, using average years of school attainment of adults at secondary school and above as the education variable. Moreover, we explored whether the male/female enrolment ratio had a significant association with growth in addition to secondary enrolment rates and did not find significant results in

[11] We also substituted the domestic savings rate for gross capital formation (not shown here), which gave similar results.

terms of either levels or change in the male/female enrolment ratio (see columns 9 and 10 in Table A.3.3).

3.3.2.2. REGIONAL VARIATIONS IN HD'S INFLUENCE OVER ECONOMIC GROWTH

Finally, across most specifications the dummy variables for both Africa and Latin America are negative, indicating that Asian countries are more efficient in converting HD into economic growth than the two other regions.

3.3.3. *Summarizing the Relationship Between HD and Economic Growth*

In summary, the findings broadly endorse our hypotheses, where we have data to test them:

(a) *HD and economic growth improvements generally move together over the long run*, with evidence of mutual interaction. This was also found in Suri et al. (2011) using an earlier timeframe.

(b) *Increases in a country's economic growth appear to be sustained either if HD levels are high initially and/or if an improvement takes place.* This indicates that it is not only the early levels of secondary education or infant mortality which matter for economic growth; investments in improving HD can also raise economic growth. Similarly, HD improvements can result from improvements in economic growth, reaffirming the presence of two-way correlations.

(c) *HD variables have synergistic effects*, with improvement in one leading to improvements in others, reflecting the strong correlations among these variables. The importance of improving HD levels early on is again stressed in order for these synergistic effects to manifest over the long run. In turn, one could expect these synergisms to translate into improved economic growth through Chain B, contributing ultimately to a virtuous cycle between HD and economic growth.

The two chains, Chains A and B, taken as a whole, showed a significantly positive effect of economic growth on HD and a significantly positive effect of HD on economic growth. With respect to specific links in each of the chains, our findings broadly confirmed our hypotheses, apart from that for income distribution. As measured by the Gini coefficient, income distribution had virtually no effect in Chain A (from economic growth to HD); it had an inverse association in Chain B (more equality associated with higher growth), but was insignificant. For improvements in life expectancy as the dependent variable in Chain A, the higher the health expenditure, and the higher the initial secondary enrolment, for a given level and growth of GNP per capita, the larger the improvement. For Chain B, the relationship between HD and economic growth was stronger the higher the investment rate. The regional dummies were mostly negative for both Africa and Latin America in both chains, showing worse conversion from growth to HD than Asia.

3.4. Virtuous and Vicious Cycles and Lopsided Development

The existence of two chains linking HD and economic growth is thus strongly supported by both the conceptual framework and the empirical evidence presented. This means that an economy may be on a mutually reinforcing upward spiral, with high levels of HD leading to high growth and high growth in turn further promoting HD. Conversely, weak HD may result in low growth and consequently poor progress towards HD improvement. The strength of the links in the two chains determines the extent of mutual reinforcement between HD and economic growth, in either direction.

Country performance can therefore be usefully classified into four categories: *virtuous*, *vicious*, and two types of *lop-sidedness*, i.e. lopsided with strong HD/weak growth (called 'HD-lopsided'), and lopsided with weak HD/strong economic growth ('EG-lopsided'). In the virtuous cycle case, good HD enhances growth, which in turn promotes HD, and so on. In the vicious cycle case, poor performance on HD tends to lead to poor growth performance which in turn depresses HD achievements, and so on. The stronger the linkages in the two chains described in Sections 3.2.1 and 3.2.2, the more pronounced the cycle of economic growth and HD, either in a positive or dampening direction. Where linkages are weak, cases of lopsided development may occur. On the one hand, good economic growth may not bring about good HD, if, for example, there are weak linkages such as a particularly low social expenditure ratio; on the other hand, good HD performance may not generate good economic growth if there is a dearth of complementary resources because of low investment rates. Such cases of lopsided development are unlikely to persist. Either the weak partner in the cycle eventually acts as a brake on the other partner, leading to a vicious cycle case, or if the linkages are strengthened, possibly by policy change, a virtuous cycle case results.

One way of classifying countries into the four categories is to compare their performance on HD and economic growth with the average performance of all developing countries. Figure 3.2 presents this classification for 1970–2014 for all developing countries for which data were available, excluding the countries of the former Soviet Union because of the special circumstances affecting their development over these decades. The vertical and horizontal grid lines represent average performance for the period, with countries given equal weight.

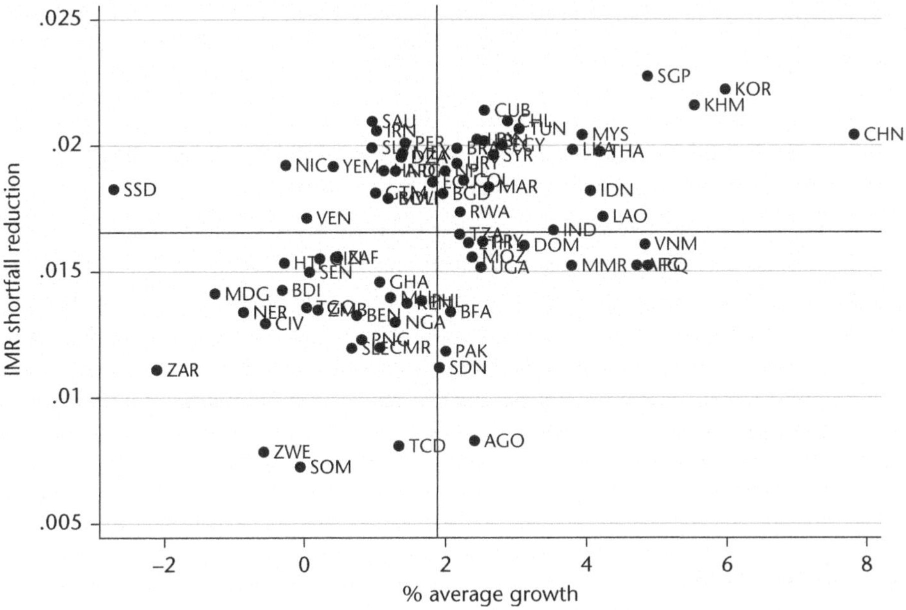

Figure 3.2. Classification of country performance, 1970–2014

Most developing countries appear as either virtuous (top-right quadrant), or vicious (bottom-left quadrant); a significant number showed an HD-lopsided pattern, and fewer an EG-lopsided one. A strong regional pattern emerges, with East Asia heavily represented in the virtuous cycle case (eight out of the eleven East or South East Asian countries) and sub-Saharan Africa in the vicious category (twenty altogether, or two-thirds of sub-Saharan African countries). Over half the countries in Latin America are in the HD-lopsided quadrant. In the EG-lopsided category, half are from sub-Saharan Africa, and the remaining half are scattered among the other regions.

The important issue for policy purposes is how a country may move towards inclusion in the virtuous cycle category. Much can be learned about this by looking at the ways in which countries changed across categories over time. Taking the movements of countries over the four decades 1970–80, 1980–90, 1990–2000, and 2000–14 (see Table A.3.4 in the Appendix) we find the following:

- Of the twenty-two countries initially classified as 'vicious', four remained there throughout the decades (Benin, the Democratic Republic of the Congo, Senegal, and Togo), and four moved in and out of the category.[12]

[12] Sierra Leone was in the vicious category for three decades and in the EG-lopsided category just for the 2000s. Zambia was also in the vicious category for three decades and moved into the virtuous category in the 2000s.

- Of the countries that succeeded in escaping from the vicious category for more than a single decade, and not falling back, four moved into the EG-lopsided category—Burma, Burkina Faso, Ghana, and the Sudan—and six moved into some combination of HD-lopsided and virtuous (namely, Bolivia, Peru, Nepal, Madagascar, Malawi, and Niger), among those countries for which we have data over the whole period.
- Turning to the twenty-one countries that started as 'virtuous', three remained virtuous throughout (Singapore, Thailand, and Sri Lanka), while China, Indonesia, South Korea, Malaysia, Cuba, Uruguay, Egypt, and Tunisia were in the virtuous category for three of the four decades. The performance of a few countries deteriorated such that they ended up in the vicious category by the 2000s: these were Ecuador, Algeria, Iraq, and Saudi Arabia.

3.5. Conclusion

The analysis in this chapter has suggested that economic growth and HD form a mutually reinforcing cycle of causation with success in one tending to promote success in the other. The two are connected in what we have described as two chains, with the links being the main elements that enhance or reduce the connections between the two.

Our analysis, drawn from many studies, and largely confirmed by our own empirical cross-country analysis, suggests that Chain A—which links economic growth to HD—is stronger the higher the allocation of GNP to the social sectors, and within them social priorities; the more equally income is allocated; and the more efficient the HD improvement function (i.e. the function relating household consumption to HD outcomes), which is likely to be affected by complementarities among different inputs, and the female share of household income and of household decision-making. Chain B, which links HD to economic growth, is likely to be stronger the greater the investment ratio, the more efficient the economic policies, and the stronger the prevailing institutions. While a voluminous literature provides evidence of the importance of all these elements, in our own investigations we found that besides the impact of HD on economic growth, social sector expenditure was significant in Chain A and female secondary enrolment (which may proxy for female control over income and decision-making), and the investment share was significant in Chain B. Against expectations, the Gini coefficient was not significant in either chain, although the signs were mostly in the expected direction (i.e. showing a negative association). We were unable to test for some of the other factors mentioned (social priority ratios, the quality of institutions or policies) for lack of data. In addition, we found the substantive presence of correlations between the HD variables themselves. This reflects synergisms whereby, for example, a rise in education may improve nutrition, which in turn would enable individuals to exploit the fruits of education more successfully. In this way, improving HD initially and over time can lead to a higher level of equilibrium in both HD and economic growth over the long term.

The results of this chapter confirm the presence of an interactive cycle between HD and economic growth. This reaffirms the importance of HD, including education and health, not only with respect to its intrinsic value for human dignity and the development of human capabilities, but also in terms of its instrumental value as a propeller of economic growth.

Chapters 4 and 5 will now investigate in more depth the conditions for success and failure in HD, using country cases. Chapter 4 explores some of the relevant characteristics of the most and least successful countries in promoting HD. Chapter 5 will return to the issue of transitions, providing case studies of countries that were able to move from the vicious category to the virtuous one, and a review of the developments behind the opposite movement, from the virtuous to the vicious category. In terms of sequencing, this implies that HD must be promoted at an early stage for sustained growth as well as advancing HD itself.

Appendix A

Some notes on our procedures:

1. Countries in Europe and Central Asia are excluded from the analysis, as are those with populations less than two million at any point in the 1970–2014 period, and those that are considered 'developed' at the start of the period—proxied by whether the country is in both the top quartile in IMR and in GDP per capita (see Table A.3.4 for a complete list of countries included).
2. HD variables were interpolated to increase country inclusion in the regressions.
3. Initial values are for 1970, unless data are missing, in which case the value of the nearest year from 1971–4 was adopted.
4. Change variables indicate annual relative change in the variable.
5. Where change is not denoted for a time period in the variable name of regression tables, the variable is averaged over the period indicated.
6. GDP per capita is divided by 100 in regressions for ease of unit analysis.
7. The definition of the variables used is given in Box A.3.1. The countries covered are shown in Table A.3.4.

8. The source for variables used in the analysis is the World Bank's World Development Indicators (World Bank n.d.). Exceptions are the GDP per capita (UNSD 2016) and the GDP per capita growth rates, which have been constructed by the authors from UNSD values.
9. Table A.3.1 and A.3.2 give the results of the tests for Chain A, from GDP to HD; and Table A.3.3 gives the result for the tests of Chain B, from HD to economic growth. Box A.3.1 explains the variables used. Table A.3.4 shows the country classification.

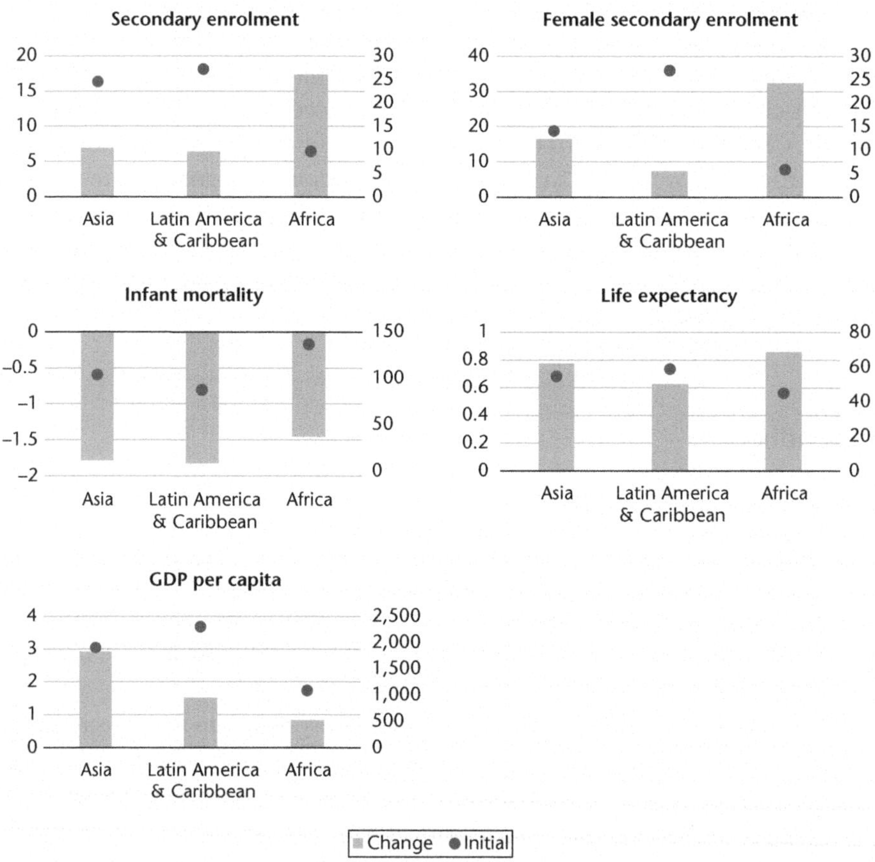

Figure A.3.1. HD and economic growth by region, initial values and change, 1970–2014

Table A.3.1. From economic growth to the change in life expectancy, 1970–2014

Variables	(1)	(2)	(3)	(4)	(5)	(6)	(7)	(8)	(9)
GDP per capita, 1970	0.00253**	0.00475***	0.00513	0.00197	0.00413***	0.00325*	0.00510***	0.00474***	0.00392**
	(0.000994)	(0.00121)	(0.00336)	(0.00283)	(0.00116)	(0.00167)	(0.00161)	(0.00167)	(0.00153)
GDP per capita growth, 1970–90	0.0403***	0.0452***	0.0381*	0.0307	0.0408***	0.0383**	0.0465***	0.0423**	0.0349**
	(0.0143)	(0.0145)	(0.0225)	(0.0185)	(0.0143)	(0.0158)	(0.0152)	(0.0158)	(0.0150)
LE, 1970	–0.0455***	–0.0553***	–0.0453***	–0.0548***	–0.0572***	–0.0468***	–0.0533***	–0.0551***	–0.0598***
	(0.00414)	(0.00548)	(0.00735)	(0.00636)	(0.00558)	(0.00575)	(0.00554)	(0.00562)	(0.00635)
GSER, 1970		0.00628**	0.00700*	0.00534*	0.00674**	0.00740**			0.00758**
		(0.00246)	(0.00395)	(0.00311)	(0.00269)	(0.00353)			(0.00317)
GSER change, 1970–90		0.00467	–0.000823	0.000262	0.00478	0.000651			0.00546
		(0.00566)	(0.00635)	(0.00582)	(0.00533)	(0.00540)			(0.00581)
GSERF, 1970							0.00429*	0.00428	
							(0.00248)	(0.00266)	
GSERF change, 1970–90							–0.000749	–0.000114	
							(0.00388)	(0.00388)	
GSERMF, 1970									–0.0366**
									(0.0152)
GSERMF change, 1970–90									–0.0366
									(0.0358)
Gini coefficient, 1970–2014			2.34e-05	–0.00553					
			(0.00582)	(0.00655)					
Public health expenditure (per cent of GDP) average, 1970–2014					0.0512**	0.0542***		0.0481**	0.0511**
					(0.0211)	(0.0188)		(0.0238)	(0.0242)
LAC	0.0829	0.120**		0.194*	0.0641		0.0844	0.0335	0.0617
	(0.0552)	(0.0506)		(0.101)	(0.0604)		(0.0554)	(0.0662)	(0.0792)
Africa	–0.267***	–0.267***		–0.287***	–0.290***		–0.264***	–0.289***	–0.287***
	(0.0762)	(0.0771)		(0.0998)	(0.0811)		(0.0764)	(0.0823)	(0.0865)
Constant	3.113***	3.431***	2.856***	3.723***	3.429***	2.807***	3.433***	3.428***	3.577***
	(0.216)	(0.250)	(0.382)	(0.343)	(0.247)	(0.249)	(0.266)	(0.261)	(0.296)
Observations	74	68	56	56	66	66	63	61	61
R-squared	0.667	0.710	0.581	0.710	0.730	0.630	0.684	0.699	0.726

Robust standard errors in parentheses; omitted region is Asia.
*** Significance at 1 per cent level, ** significance at 5 per cent level, * significance at 10 per cent level

Table A.3.2. From economic growth to the change in HD (measured by education and IMR change, 1970–2014)

	GSER change, 1970–2014			GSERF change, 1970–2014			IMR change, 1970–2014		
Variables	(1)	(2)	(3)	(4)	(5)	(6)	(7)	(8)	(9)
GDP per capita, 1970	0.0301	0.0314	0.102	0.0249	0.365**	0.364**	−0.00490***	−0.00583***	−0.00720***
	(0.0412)	(0.0903)	(0.0781)	(0.129)	(0.142)	(0.150)	(0.00131)	(0.00178)	(0.00235)
GDP per capita growth, 1970–90	0.442	0.478	1.332*	0.0645	1.923	2.781*	−0.0556***	−0.0487***	−0.0491**
	(0.406)	(0.569)	(0.670)	(0.986)	(1.204)	(1.477)	(0.0170)	(0.0171)	(0.0194)
LE, 1970			−0.327			−0.974			
			(0.314)			(0.647)			
LE change, 1970–90			−2.570			−1.940			
			(2.747)			(6.131)			
IMR, 1970		−0.0361			0.0458		−0.00134	−0.00305***	−0.00284**
		(0.0321)			(0.0771)		(0.000884)	(0.00108)	(0.00112)
IMR change, 1970–90		−2.295			−1.449				
		(1.797)			(3.403)				
GSER, 1970	−0.499***	−0.451***	−0.328***					−0.00725**	
	(0.0979)	(0.0963)	(0.0918)					(0.00332)	
GSER change, 1970–90								−0.00436	
								(0.00612)	
GSERF, 1970				−0.878***	−0.763**	−0.569**			−0.00397
				(0.290)	(0.286)	(0.256)			(0.00345)
GSERF change, 1970–90									0.00138
									(0.00465)
Public education expenditure (% of GDP), 1970		−1.064	−0.203		−1.751	−0.492			
		(0.982)	(0.941)		(2.160)	(1.914)			
Public education expenditure (% of GDP) change, 1970–2014		1.707***	1.689***		3.189***	2.957***			
		(0.401)	(0.380)		(0.780)	(0.770)			
Public health expenditure (% of GDP) average, 1970–2014								−0.0661***	−0.0610**
								(0.0239)	(0.0270)
LAC	0.791	−1.265	1.389	1.563	1.203	5.553	−0.108	−0.00315	−0.00661
	(1.606)	(2.356)	(2.690)	(3.825)	(4.896)	(5.319)	(0.0768)	(0.0889)	(0.0972)
Africa	3.632	10.93**	7.489*	8.467	22.25**	16.52**	0.221**	0.248**	0.236**
	(2.563)	(4.072)	(3.813)	(6.331)	(9.835)	(7.744)	(0.100)	(0.110)	(0.106)
Constant	18.06***	13.92**	28.01*	28.73***	4.818	59.23*	−1.432***	−0.943***	−1.079***
	(2.812)	(5.270)	(16.34)	(5.524)	(12.13)	(34.63)	(0.128)	(0.196)	(0.197)
Observations	63	44	45	57	39	40	70	64	59
R–squared	0.475	0.644	0.641	0.317	0.530	0.548	0.467	0.538	0.524

Robust standard errors in parentheses; omitted region is Asia.
*** Significance at 1 per cent level, ** significance at 5 per cent level, * significance at 10 per cent level

Table A.3.3. From HD to change in economic growth (dependent variable is GDP per capita growth, 1970–2014)

Variables	(1)	(2)	(3)	(4)	(5)	(6)	(7)	(8)	(9)	(10)
GDP per capita, 1970	−0.0301***	−0.0583***	−0.0252***	−0.0450***	−0.0255***	−0.0641***	−0.0274***	−0.0569***	−0.0235**	−0.0535***
	(0.00523)	(0.0175)	(0.00508)	(0.0161)	(0.00942)	(0.0227)	(0.00866)	(0.0200)	(0.00938)	(0.0184)
IMR, 1970	−0.0114***	−0.00933*								
	(0.00401)	(0.00530)								
IMR change, 1970–90	−0.706***	−0.679***								
	(0.181)	(0.193)								
LE, 1970			0.110***	0.0767**						
			(0.0231)	(0.0339)						
LE change, 1970–90			0.391	0.200						
			(0.349)	(0.393)						
GSER, 1970					0.0502***	0.0334**			0.0532***	0.0336*
					(0.0184)	(0.0157)			(0.0197)	(0.0180)
GSER change, 1970–90					0.0471*	0.0358			0.0517**	0.0376
					(0.0246)	(0.0287)			(0.0251)	(0.0281)
GSERF, 1970							0.0640***	0.0444***		
							(0.0198)	(0.0152)		
GSERF change, 1970–90							0.0289**	0.0288*		
							(0.0133)	(0.0147)		
GSERMF, 1970									−0.0916	0.0456
									(0.179)	(0.0913)
GSERMF change, 1970–90									0.0263	0.137
									(0.206)	(0.251)
Gross fixed capital formation (% of GDP), 1970–2014		0.0919		0.0825		0.155**		0.0935*		0.103*
		(0.0604)		(0.0655)		(0.0583)		(0.0487)		(0.0556)
Gini coefficient, 1970–2014		−0.0236		−0.0106		−0.00712		0.00183		−0.00999
		(0.0294)		(0.0299)		(0.0382)		(0.0399)		(0.0453)
LAC	−1.559***	−0.209	−1.823***	−0.730	−1.361***	0.303	−1.731***	−0.349	−1.550***	0.0233
	(0.390)	(0.679)	(0.370)	(0.739)	(0.445)	(0.926)	(0.476)	(1.005)	(0.494)	(1.012)
Africa	−1.145***	−0.471	−1.265***	−0.877*	−1.798***	−0.907**	−1.698***	−1.101**	−1.634***	−1.018*
	(0.418)	(0.422)	(0.400)	(0.452)	(0.455)	(0.442)	(0.438)	(0.506)	(0.449)	(0.512)
Constant	2.913***	1.537	−2.842**	−2.433	1.938***	−0.892	1.982***	−0.0492	1.985**	0.232
	(0.754)	(1.914)	(1.379)	(1.857)	(0.587)	(1.608)	(0.449)	(1.468)	(0.744)	(1.765)
Observations	70	58	74	60	68	56	63	51	63	51
R-squared	0.489	0.507	0.495	0.481	0.398	0.520	0.389	0.412	0.405	0.398

Robust standard errors in parentheses; omitted region is Asia.
*** Significance at 1 per cent level, ** significance at 5 per cent level, * significance at 10 per cent level

Table A.3.4. Country classification by decade, 1970s to 2000s

	Country classification			
	1970s	1980s	1990s	2000s
East Asia and Pacific				
Cambodia			EG-lopsided	Virtuous
China	Virtuous	EG-lopsided	Virtuous	Virtuous
Indonesia	EG-lopsided	Virtuous	Virtuous	Virtuous
Korea, Rep.	Virtuous	Virtuous	EG-lopsided	Virtuous
Lao PDR		EG-lopsided	Virtuous	EG-lopsided
Malaysia	Virtuous	Virtuous	Virtuous	EG-lopsided
Burma	EG-lopsided	Vicious	EG-lopsided	EG-lopsided
Papua New Guinea	Vicious	Vicious	EG-lopsided	Vicious
Philippines	EG-lopsided	Vicious	HD-lopsided	EG-lopsided
Singapore	Virtuous	Virtuous	Virtuous	Virtuous
Thailand	Virtuous	Virtuous	Virtuous	Virtuous
Vietnam		EG-lopsided	Virtuous	EG-lopsided
Latin America and Caribbean				
Argentina	HD-lopsided	HD-lopsided	Virtuous	Vicious
Bolivia	Vicious	Vicious	Virtuous	HD-lopsided
Brazil	Virtuous	HD-lopsided	HD-lopsided	HD-lopsided
Chile	HD-lopsided	Virtuous	Virtuous	Vicious
Colombia	Virtuous	Virtuous	HD-lopsided	EG-lopsided
Cuba	Virtuous	Virtuous	HD-lopsided	Virtuous
Dominican Republic	Virtuous	HD-lopsided	Virtuous	EG-lopsided
Ecuador	Virtuous	HD-lopsided	HD-lopsided	Vicious
El Salvador	HD-lopsided	HD-lopsided	Virtuous	HD-lopsided
Guatemala	EG-lopsided	HD-lopsided	Virtuous	Vicious
Haiti			HD-lopsided	Vicious
Honduras	Virtuous	HD-lopsided	HD-lopsided	HD-lopsided
Mexico	Virtuous	HD-lopsided	Virtuous	HD-lopsided
Nicaragua	HD-lopsided	HD-lopsided	HD-lopsided	Vicious
Paraguay	EG-lopsided	Virtuous	HD-lopsided	Vicious
Peru	Vicious	HD-lopsided	Virtuous	Virtuous
Uruguay	Virtuous	HD-lopsided	Virtuous	Virtuous
Venezuela, RB	HD-lopsided	HD-lopsided	HD-lopsided	Vicious
Middle East and North Africa				
Algeria	Virtuous	HD-lopsided	Vicious	Vicious
Egypt, Arab Rep.	Virtuous	Virtuous	Virtuous	HD-lopsided
Iran, Islamic Rep.	HD-lopsided	HD-lopsided	Virtuous	HD-lopsided
Iraq	Virtuous	EG-lopsided	EG-lopsided	Vicious
Lebanon		HD-lopsided	Virtuous	HD-lopsided
Libya			Virtuous	HD-lopsided
Morocco	EG-lopsided	Virtuous	HD-lopsided	Virtuous
Saudi Arabia	Virtuous	HD-lopsided	HD-lopsided	Vicious
Syrian Arab Republic	Virtuous	HD-lopsided	Virtuous	HD-lopsided
Tunisia	Virtuous	Virtuous	Virtuous	HD-lopsided
Yemen, Rep.			Vicious	HD-lopsided
South Asia				
Afghanistan				EG-lopsided
Bangladesh	Vicious	EG-lopsided	Virtuous	Virtuous
India	Vicious	EG-lopsided	Virtuous	EG-lopsided
Nepal	Vicious	Virtuous	Virtuous	HD-lopsided
Pakistan	Vicious	EG-lopsided	Vicious	Vicious
Sri Lanka	Virtuous	Virtuous	Virtuous	Virtuous

Sub-Saharan Africa				
Angola		EG-lopsided	Vicious	EG-lopsided
Benin	Vicious	Vicious	Vicious	Vicious
Burkina Faso	Vicious	EG-lopsided	EG-lopsided	EG-lopsided
Burundi	Vicious	EG-lopsided	Vicious	Vicious
Cameroon	EG-lopsided	EG-lopsided	Vicious	Vicious
Chad	Vicious	EG-lopsided	Vicious	EG-lopsided
Congo, Dem. Rep.	Vicious	Vicious	Vicious	Vicious
Côte d'Ivoire	HD-lopsided	Vicious	Vicious	Vicious
Ethiopia		Vicious	HD-lopsided	Virtuous
Ghana	Vicious	Vicious	EG-lopsided	EG-lopsided
Guinea		EG-lopsided	HD-lopsided	Vicious
Kenya	EG-lopsided	EG-lopsided	Vicious	HD-lopsided
Madagascar	Vicious	Vicious	HD-lopsided	HD-lopsided
Malawi	Virtuous	Vicious	Virtuous	HD-lopsided
Mali	EG-lopsided	Vicious	Vicious	Vicious
Mozambique		Vicious	Virtuous	Virtuous
Niger	Vicious	Vicious	HD-lopsided	HD-lopsided
Nigeria	Vicious	Vicious	Vicious	EG-lopsided
Rwanda	EG-lopsided	Vicious	EG-lopsided	Virtuous
Senegal	Vicious	Vicious	Vicious	Vicious
Sierra Leone	Vicious	Vicious	Vicious	EG-lopsided
Somalia		EG-lopsided		
South Africa	HD-lopsided	HD-lopsided	Vicious	Vicious
South Sudan				HD-lopsided
Sudan	Vicious	Vicious	EG-lopsided	EG-lopsided
Tanzania		EG-lopsided	Vicious	Virtuous
Togo	Vicious	Vicious	Vicious	Vicious
Uganda		Vicious	EG-lopsided	Virtuous
Zambia	Vicious	Vicious	Vicious	Virtuous
Zimbabwe	Vicious	EG-lopsided	Vicious	Vicious

Virtuous = above average on HD change and economic growth; HD-lopsided = above average on HD, below on economic growth; EG-lopsided = above average on EG, below on HD; vicious = below average on both HD change and economic growth. Averages are means of country performance.

Box A.3.1. LIST OF VARIABLES AND DESCRIPTIONS

EG variables

GDP per capita: Gross domestic product per capita in constant 2010 US$

GDP per capita growth (annual %)

HD variables

IMR: Infant mortality rate (per 1,000 live births)

LE: Life expectancy at birth, total (years)

GSER: Gross enrolment ratio, secondary, both sexes (%)

GSERF: Gross secondary educational enrolment of females (% gross)

GSERMF: Gross secondary educational enrolment, male to female ratio

Controls

Public education expenditure (% of GDP)

Public health expenditure (% of GDP)

Gross domestic savings (% of GDP)

GINI index (World Bank estimate)

Poverty headcount ratio at $1.90 a day (2011 PPP) (% of population)

Regions: LAC (Latin America and Caribbean), Africa, and Asia (reference group removed from regression outputs)

4

Success and Failure in Human Development, 1980–2014

4.1. Introduction

The aim of this chapter is to review countries' experience in advancing HD since 1980.[1] We briefly explore general progress across all countries, and then identify countries that were most and least successful in advancing in HD. The aim is to investigate whether (and which) particular characteristics of the economy and of policy are associated with these outcomes. In this chapter we look at the variables often associated with success and failure in HD across the selected countries. While we define success and failure for this purpose according to progress on basic HD, as measured by reductions in the IMR and economic growth, we also look beyond these basic features and explore other aspects such as political freedoms, inequality, and environmental sustainability, to see how far achievements on these indicators (both in levels and changes) are associated with success and failure with respect to basic HD.

4.2. Aggregate Achievements

There has been major progress in realizing HD among developing countries since the early 1960s when the majority of developing countries became independent.[2] The three components of the HDI each saw significant progress almost everywhere. Life expectancy in Africa increased from just thirty-six in

[1] This chapter draws on some material from Ranis and Stewart (2012). We are grateful for permission to reuse it here (copyright © United Nations Development Programme, reprinted by permission of Taylor & Francis Ltd, <http://www.tandfonline.com>, on behalf of the United Nations Development Programme).

[2] While India gained independence in 1947, most developing countries in Asia, Africa, and the Middle East became independent in the 1950s and 1960s. However, Latin American countries, of course, had become independent long before then, in the nineteenth century.

1950 to sixty by 2015 after dipping a bit in the 1990s due to HIV/AIDS, while in Asia it increased from forty-two in 1950 to seventy-five by 2015 (data from Roser 2017). Life expectancy in Latin America went from fifty-six in 1960 to seventy-five by 2015. Among low-income countries, less than half of the population of primary school age was enrolled in primary school in 1970 and only 13 per cent in secondary school. By 2014, virtually all children of primary age were enrolled (with a gross enrolment ratio of 104) and 41 per cent of secondary school-age children were at school. Among middle-income countries most children were in primary school in 1970 (gross enrolment ratio at 91 per cent) but only one-third of the age group were in secondary school. By 2014, the gross primary school enrolment ratio among middle-income countries was 105 per cent and the secondary school ratio was 76 per cent. Incomes also rose over this period, with some fluctuations: GDP per capita in high-income countries more than doubled between 1970 and 2015; middle-income countries grew fastest, tripling their per capita incomes; while per capita incomes among low-income countries grew most slowly, with an increase of only 23 per cent between 1982 and 2015.[3]

The HDI, which is a composite, albeit crude, measure of HD, with the three components being life expectancy, a measure of educational achievements, and adjusted income, consequently also showed significant progress. This is shown by region for 1980–2013 in Figure 4.1. The base year used is 1980 as it is

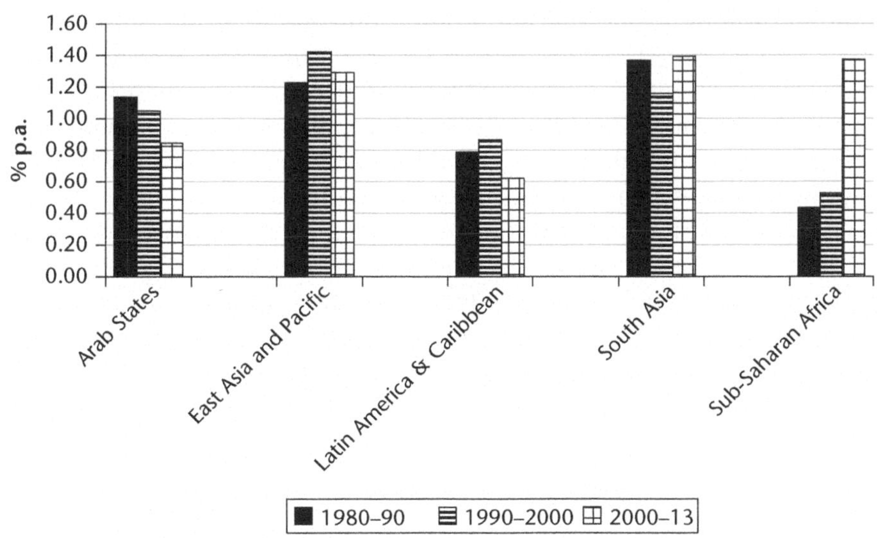

Figure 4.1. Change in HDI by region, 1980–2013, % p.a.
Source: World Bank (n.d.)

[3] Data are all from World Bank (n.d.) unless otherwise stated.

the first year for which the UNDP provides data on HDI. Asia showed the greatest advances. Sub-Saharan Africa made poor progress in the 1980s and 1990s, reflecting weak economic performance associated with the debt crisis and adjustment programmes, as well as the devastating effects of HIV/AIDS on health. But Africa did extremely well over the 2000s as economic growth accelerated and the spread of AIDS/HIV was contained and the disease extensively treated with retroviral drugs.

Although these data suggest a fair amount of success overall, country performance differed quite substantially. In this chapter we aim to identify factors associated with success and failure, by investigating the experience of selected countries that did particularly well or particularly poorly.

A major issue, of course, is how to identify success and failure. In this chapter we follow the classification of countries put forward in Chapter 3, into 'virtuous', 'HD-lopsided', 'EG-lopsided', and 'vicious' categories. These categories show performance on economic growth and the non-income dimensions of basic HD, as measured by reductions in the infant mortality rate.[4] In Chapter 3 we categorized developing countries according to whether they performed above or below the mean for all developing countries on these two fundamental aspects of basic HD over the four decades—the 1970s, 1980s, 1990s, and 2000s (see Table A.3.4 in the Appendix to Chapter 3).

Using these categories, success in promoting basic HD might be defined as being persistently above average on each dimension (in the virtuous category), and poor performance as being persistently below average on each (in the vicious category). Or we might define success as moving from poor to good performance (from vicious to virtuous), and failure as moving from above average to below average. Here we combine these two approaches, adopting examples from each (see Tables 4.1 and 4.2).

Persistent success (i.e. being consistently in the virtuous category) is rare: the only examples are Singapore, Thailand and Sri Lanka. Eight countries managed to be in the virtuous category for three of the four decades, as shown in Table 4.1. There are many more cases of movement from poor performance to good as shown in Table A.3.4 in the Appendix to Chapter 3.

In what follows, we explore the performance of three successful and (up to) three weak performing countries from each region, hereafter described as good and weak HDI performers respectively. The good performers selected are: for East and South East Asia, China, South Korea, and Thailand; for South Asia, Bangladesh, Nepal, and Sri Lanka; for sub-Saharan Africa, Ethiopia, Mozambique, and Rwanda; for Latin America, Bolivia, Cuba, and Peru; and

[4] The availability of data makes this a good shorthand measure.

Table 4.1. Countries with successful basic HD experiences, 1970s to 2000s

(i)	East and South East Asia	South Asia	Sub-Saharan Africa	Latin America and the Caribbean	Middle East and North Africa
Virtuous for four decades	• Singapore • Thailand	• Sri Lanka			
Virtuous for three decades	• China • Indonesia • South Korea • Malaysia			• Cuba • Uruguay	• Egypt[a] • Tunisia
Successful transition from vicious to virtuous		• Bangladesh • India[b] • Nepal[a]	• Ethiopia • Mozambique • Rwanda[c] • Tanzania • Uganda • [Zambia][d]	• Bolivia[a] • Peru	

Notes: [a] Lapsed to HD-lopsided in the 2000s; [b] Went from vicious in the 1970s to EG-lopsided then virtuous then EG-lopsided again. [c] went from EG-lopsided in 1970s to vicious, then EG-lopsided and then virtuous; [d] also appears as weak case, as was in the vicious category for three decades.

Table 4.2. Countries with particularly weak basic HD performance, 1970s to 2000s

(ii)	East and South East Asia	South Asia	Sub-Saharan Africa	Latin America and the Caribbean	Middle East and North Africa
Persistent poor performance, vicious over four decades			• Benin • Democratic Republic of the Congo • Senegal • Togo		
Poor performance in three of the four decades	• Papua New Guinea	• Pakistan	• Burundi • Côte d'Ivoire • Mali • Nigeria • Sierra Leone • [Zambia][a] • Zimbabwe		
Moved from virtuous (1970s) to vicious (2000s)				• Ecuador • Guatemala[b]	• Algeria • Iraq • Saudi Arabia

Notes: [a] Zambia appears as both a weak case having been in the vicious category for three decades, as well as a successful case for moving into the virtuous category in the 2000s; [b] Guatemala moved from virtuous in the 1990s (rather than the 1970s) to vicious in the 2000s.

for the Middle East and North Africa, Tunisia and Egypt.[5] We select Papua New Guinea as the only weak performer in East and South East Asia and Pakistan in South Asia, according to our criteria, and to help comparisons we also add Burma, although it was only in the vicious category for one period

[5] Only these two countries in the Middle East and North Africa qualify according to our criteria.

and EG-lopsided for the remainder. For sub-Saharan Africa, as weak performers, we select the Democratic Republic of the Congo, Côte d'Ivoire, and Zimbabwe; in Latin America, Ecuador and Guatemala; and in the Middle East and North Africa, Algeria, Iraq, and Saudi Arabia.

We should emphasize that here we are defining 'good' and 'poor' performance by *improvement or decline over time,* not absolute ranking which is due to historic circumstances and is not so informative about what countries need do to achieve higher levels of basic HD.

In the rest of this chapter we explore whether the more successful countries, as selected above, differ in any systematic way from the unsuccessful ones.

4.3. Identifying Proximate Causes of Success and Failure on Basic HD 1980–2014

First we identify a range of indicators that previous work suggests is associated with success or failure as suggested in Chapter 3, as well as by other cross-country investigations and case studies (Ranis et al. 2000, Ranis and Stewart 2000, Molina and Purser 2010, McGuire 2010, Suri et al. 2011). Among the variables associated with success/failure on HDI according to these studies are:

- the social expenditure ratio (i.e. health plus education expenditure as a proportion of GDP);
- the level of education of the population;
- the ratio of female to male secondary enrolment rates;
- the level and growth in per capita incomes;
- income distribution; and
- poverty rates.

We recognize that two of these indicators—income per capita and educational enrolment rates—are components of the HDI, but research suggests that each is also an input into the other two components so they are therefore included (Behrman 1990, 1996, Ranis et al. 2000).

In principle, both levels of variables and changes in these variables might be relevant to explaining success and failure in change in basic HD over time. The levels are potentially relevant because the size, for example, of social expenditure ratios is likely to affect the expansion of services over time. Income distribution levels, as well as the change in income distribution, will affect how different groups behave towards education. And the enrolment rate in education is likely to affect the take-up of new health interventions. Below we explore both levels and changes in the variables, data permitting.

Our aim is to determine whether there are systematic patterns or combinations of patterns associated with particular success or failure. The econometric studies, exemplified in Chapter 3, indicate broad associations in general, but they do not indicate whether the association is shown for all particularly successful or unsuccessful countries. For each of the indicators listed we assembled data for the average of the period 1980–2014 (or latest available date), though in many cases data were only available for the more recent years, and for some countries no data were available at all.

4.3.1. *Social Indicators*

The good performers in East and South East Asia devoted more government expenditure to education as a percentage of GDP in both periods, but in South Asia, both Bangladesh and Sri Lanka had quite low expenditure, below that of Pakistan. And in Africa the good performers had greater expenditure than the poor performers in the 2000s but not in the 1980s—among the good performers the ratio increased substantially between the two periods, while it fell in two of the three poor performers. Among Latin American countries too, education expenditure was higher in good than poor performers in the 2000s but not in the 1980s (see Figure 4.2). The Middle Eastern countries all showed high education expenditure ratios without any systematic differences between good and poor performers. Health expenditure data are only available from 1995. Here the good performers tended to outspend the poor performers, especially by 2014, apart from the Middle East (see Figure 4.3).

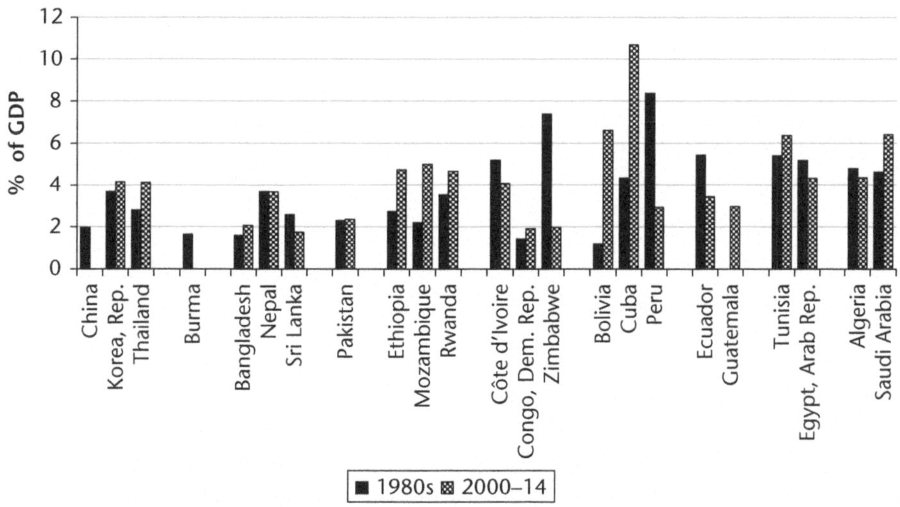

Figure 4.2. Education expenditure as % of GDP, 1980s and 2000s
Source: World Bank (n.d.)

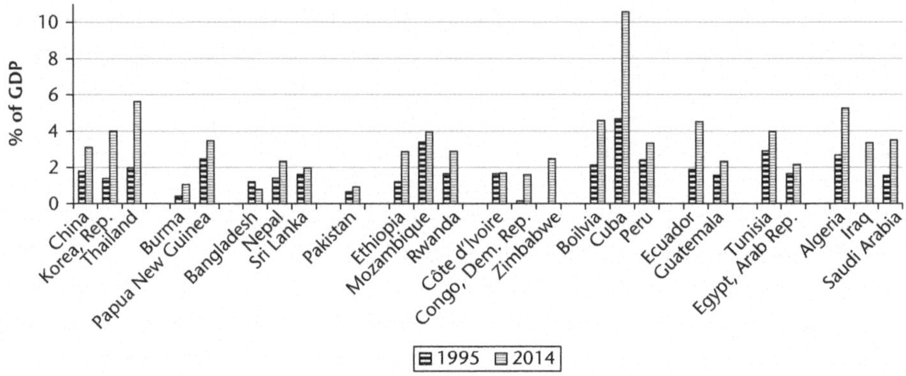

Figure 4.3. Public expenditure on health as % of GDP, 1995 and 2014
Source: World Bank (n.d.)

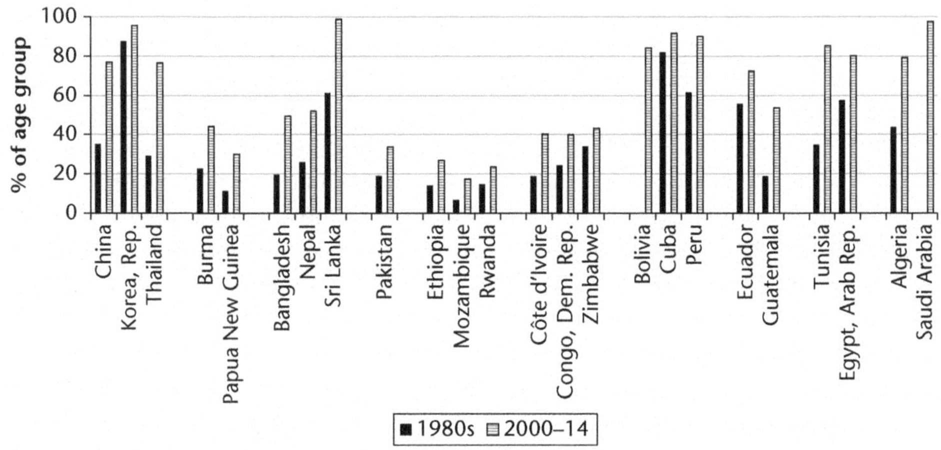

Figure 4.4. Gross secondary enrolment ratio, % of age group, 1980s and 2000s
Source: World Bank (n.d.)

Pakistan is a notably low spender on health (a weak performer), but Bangladesh—a good performer—also spends relatively little. In contrast, Cuba's expenditure is exceptionally high at over 10 per cent of GDP.

When it comes to secondary school enrolment (see Figure 4.4) in Latin America and Asia the good performers outperformed the poor performers in both the 1980s and 2000s, but this is not the case in Africa, where the poor performers have higher enrolment rates. However, the average proportionate increase in secondary enrolment was greater in every region among good HDI performers apart from Latin America, where the enrolment rates were already high and therefore there was less room for improvement.

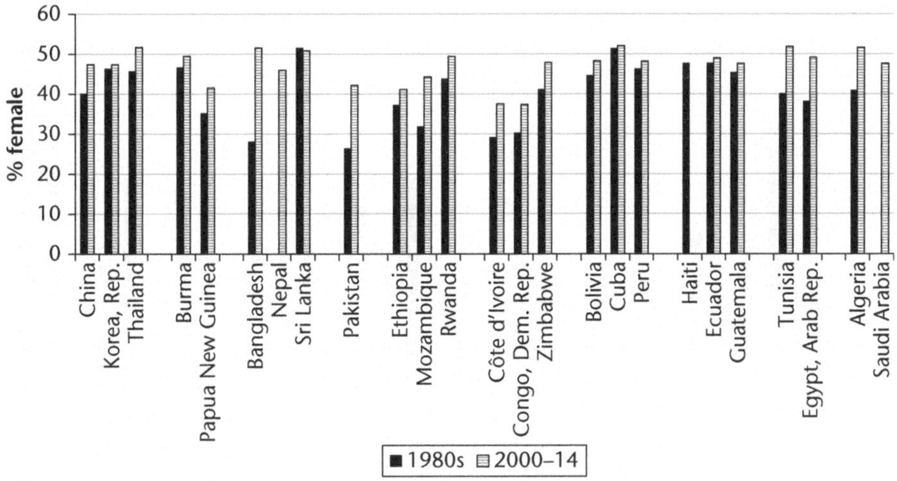

Figure 4.5. Female % in total secondary enrolment 1980s and 2000s
Source: World Bank (n.d.)

Generally the good performers had higher female enrolment as a proportion of the total in both periods.

4.3.2. *Economic Performance*

The good HDI performers did not invariably have higher per capita incomes in 1980 than the poor performers—in fact, in sub-Saharan Africa good HDI performers had lower incomes than the poor performers (see Figure 4.6). Some good performers had very low incomes, such as Nepal and Bangladesh and the three sub-Saharan African countries, showing that a low initial level of income does not prevent success in improving basic HD.

However, growth rates in per capita income among good performers were generally higher than among poor performers (see Figure 4.7). Exceptions were Mozambique and Cuba, both of which had negative growth, as did all the sub-Saharan African poor performers and Iraq.

There were no systematic differences in income distribution across the categories, according to the limited data. In the 1980s, the good performers mostly had a more equal income distribution than the poor performers, with the exception of Tunisia and Thailand which had notably high inequality. The most unequal country was Guatemala. In many cases, where data are available, income distribution worsened between the 1980s and 2000s, among both sets of countries. Rwanda and Cuba (good HDI performers) both saw substantial rises in inequality. However, in South Korea, Thailand,

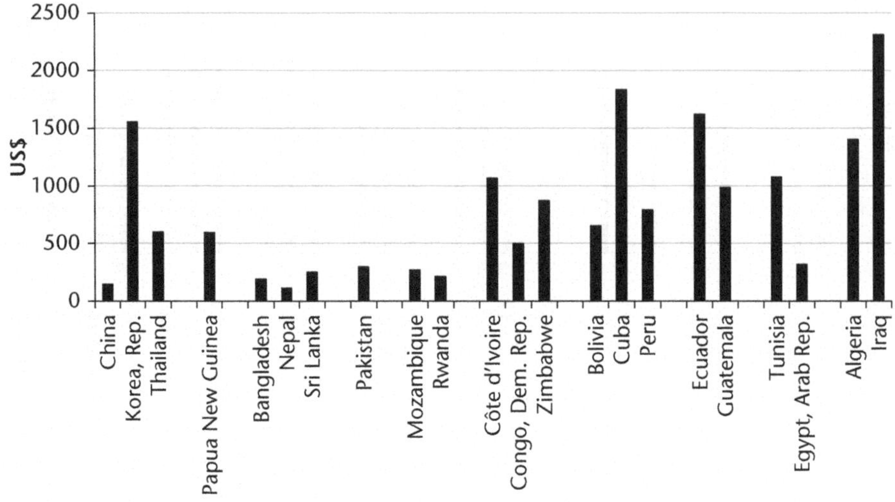

Figure 4.6. Income per capita, 1980, in US$
Source: World Bank (n.d.)

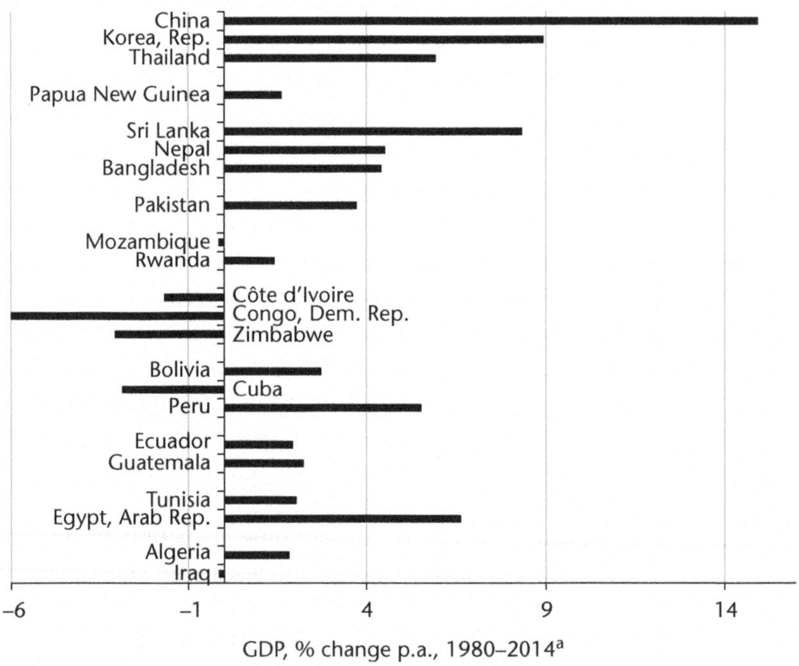

Figure 4.7. Annual growth in GDP, 1980–2014
a. Dollar income growth is deflated by US rate of inflation
Source: World Bank (n.d.)

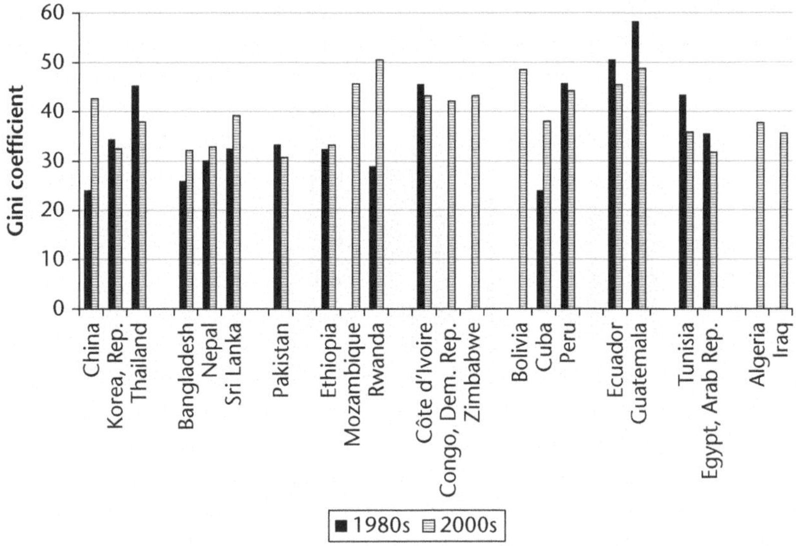

Figure 4.8. Inequality in the 1980s and 2000s
Source: World Bank (n.d.); WIDER WIID; Prieto (2008) for Cuba

Egypt, and Tunisia (among the good performers) and in Ecuador and Guatemala (among the poor), inequality fell (see Figure 4.8).

Poverty estimates for around 2012 (Figure 4.9) do not show major differences between successful and unsuccessful countries. Very low poverty rates are observed in Ecuador, a poor performer, while some of the good performers had high poverty rates, notably the three sub-Saharan African countries. Although systematic data are not available for the period as a whole, for countries for which we have data it seems poverty fell more among the good performers, with very large reductions in the headcount ratio in China (eighty-one percentage points reduction between 1981 and 2012), Nepal (fifty-nine percentage points between 1984 and 2010), and Ethiopia (thirty-one percentage points between 1995 and 2010). Poverty worsened significantly in some of the poor performers, including Côte d'Ivoire, Zimbabwe, and Iraq.

In sum, in relation to levels of educational and health expenditure and secondary enrolment in 1980, there are few systematic differences between good and poor performers in basic HD. However, good performers tended to increase their expenditure ratio more than poor performers so that by the 2000s most had higher expenditure on education as a proportion of GDP and higher secondary enrolment rates. Female secondary enrolment as a proportion of the total was mostly better among good performers (Figure 4.5). In a number of respects the good performers outperformed the poor ones in

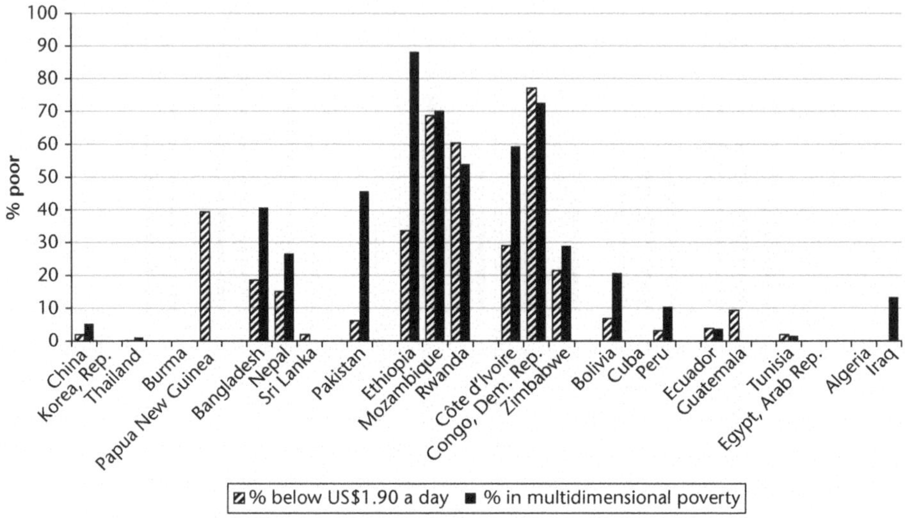

Figure 4.9. % of population in poverty, most recent date
Source: World Bank (n.d.), UNDP, HDRO data

changes over time: increases in education and health expenditure, rises in secondary school enrolment and female to male enrolment ratios, growth in per capita income, and reductions in poverty. All these changes would be expected to contribute to better basic HD achievements. But it is important to note that there were exceptions: countries with low social expenditure ratios that did well, such as China and Bangladesh; and countries with low or even negative growth that did well, such as Cuba and Mozambique. There were also countries that performed poorly in basic HD improvements, while having high levels of social expenditure and school enrolment (such as Saudi Arabia) and quite large reductions in poverty (such as Ecuador).

While we find some common tendencies, the differences among the good performers are notable. Basically, countries achieve success in a variety of ways:

- First, some countries had good and fairly equitable growth combined with only moderate social expenditure—South Korea and Sri Lanka followed this path.
- Second, the success of some countries derived mainly from high social expenditure. These countries succeeded despite low or even negative growth and high inequality—Cuba is a clear example, as is Mozambique.
- Third, some countries forged a path somewhere between these two extremes, combining good, but not spectacular growth and a quite equitable distribution, supported by moderate levels of social expenditure.

This is the path followed by Nepal and Bangladesh. This is probably the path that is easiest for many countries to replicate.

The poor performers can also be divided into three categories:

- First, countries that combined weak social expenditure, negative or very low growth, and poor distribution—the path of the Democratic Republic of the Congo and Burma (though data are lacking for income growth).
- Second, countries that had relatively good social expenditure, combined with negative growth and a highly inequitable distribution—Côte d'Ivoire and Zimbabwe. Zimbabwe's social expenditure also fell dramatically over the period.
- Third, there are countries that combined fairly low (and falling, in the case of Ecuador) social expenditure with positive growth but high inequality—Ecuador and Guatemala are examples.

In principle, the last category of country among the poor performers is in the strongest position—and indeed both Ecuador and Guatemala were only in the vicious category for one period; countries should be able to get out of the poor category by improving their social expenditure and distribution.

Close examination of both the more and the less successful cases confirms the view that there is no single path to good or poor performance, but rather alternative routes.

4.4. Beyond Basic HD

It is now well accepted that the HDI represents a reductionist measure of HD. In Chapter 6, drawing on philosophical investigations of what constitute the features of a 'full' life, we identify eleven dimensions in addition to those represented by the HDI. Here we take a subset of these because of a lack of consistent and reliable data for the others. We include:

- political rights and civil liberties as measured by the polity2 score;
- gender empowerment as measured by the Gender Inequality Index (GII);
- environmental quality and sustainability; and
- human security as measured by two variables: the homicide rate and the incidence of violent political conflict.

We look at the levels of achievement and changes between 1980 and the latest year available in the 2000s, or for a shorter period when data are restricted. We then compare our 'good' and 'poor' HDI performers with the performance on these indicators of 'HD beyond the HDI' to explore whether countries that do well or badly on basic HD also do well on other indicators.

4.4.1. *Political Rights Index*

Both among the countries that did exceptionally well and those that did poorly on the basic HD, there was mostly improvement in the index of political freedom between the 1980s and the 2000s (Figure 4.10); the majority of countries were in negative territory in the 1980s; and those countries that got positive scores in the 1980s included both good and weak HDI performers. By the 2000s just four countries had scores of minus 5 or less: two good HD performers (Cuba and China) and two weak ones (Burma and Saudi Arabia). Hence the evidence suggests that lack of democratic rights does not necessarily impede progress on basic HD. This evidence challenges the view that better political rights are either necessary or sufficient to generate improvements in HD (McGuire 2010, Przeworski et al. 2000). It supports the more ambiguous findings about the relationship between democracy and HD of Tsai (2006). Democracy provides the space for political action to promote basic HD, but active participation, organization, and struggle may be necessary to translate this into improved HD (Tsai 2006, Stewart 2010).

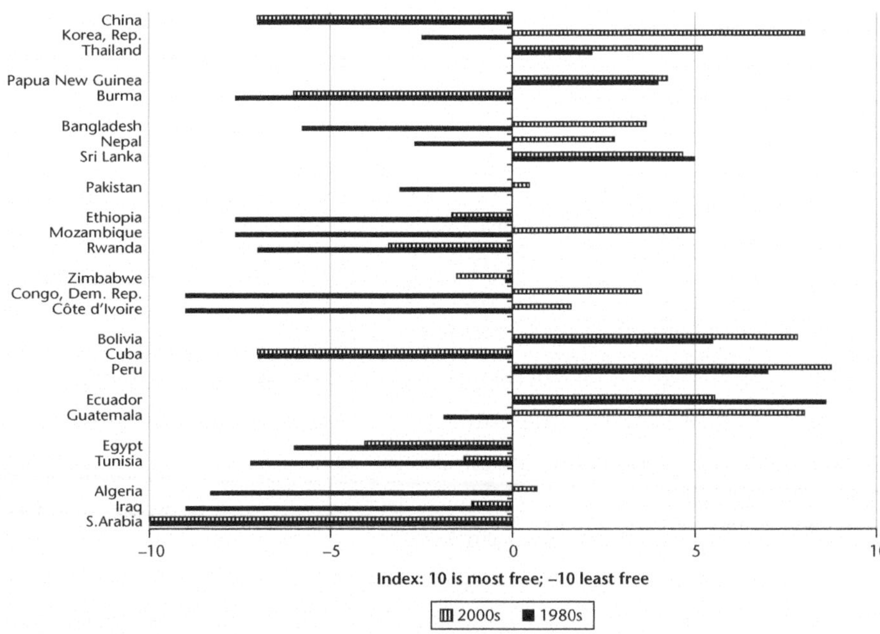

Figure 4.10. Political freedom index (polity2), 1980s and 2000s

Source: Center for Systemic Peace Polity Project, www.systemicpeace.org/polityproject.html (accessed 15 January 2017)

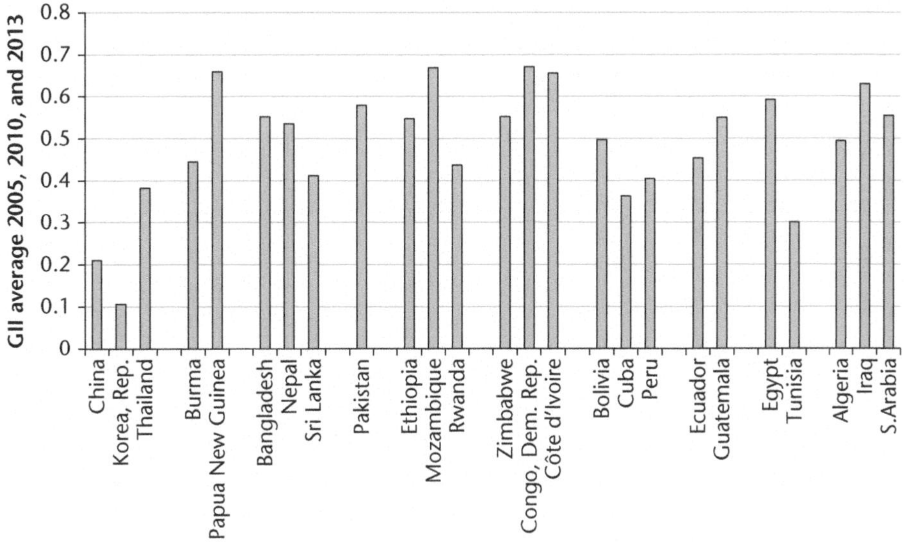

Figure 4.11. Gender Inequality Index (GII), average 2005, 2010, and 2013
Source: UNDP, HDRO data

4.4.2. *Gender Empowerment*

Gender empowerment here is measured by the UNDP's GII. This is a composite measure which includes gender inequality in reproductive health, political empowerment, and labour market participation. Higher values imply more inequality. The better HDI performers tend to show lower gender inequality than the weak performers in each region (Figure 4.11). In each region the most unequal country is a weak HDI performer: Papua New Guinea, Pakistan, Guatemala, Democratic Republic of the Congo, and Iraq are all weak HDI countries, although Mozambique, a good performer, has high gender inequality.

4.4.3. *Homicides and the Incidence of Violent Conflict*

We use the numbers of prosecuted homicides per 100,000 people and the incidence of violent conflict as measures of human security.[6] The data for homicides are particularly suspect as they depend on reported homicides and their prosecution, and understate actual homicides to an unknown extent.[7] Figure 4.12

[6] This is a narrow definition of human security, which is broader than this and includes security against all kinds of risks—economic, health, and physical threats (UNDP 1994, CHS 2003).

[7] According to the UN Office on Drugs and Crime (UNODC n.d., 2): 'The comparison of intentional homicide figures between countries and regions is, to some extent, a comparison not only of the level of intended killing of persons, but also of the extent to which countries and regions deem that a killing should be classified as such. In essence, societies define those killings that it perceives as acceptable and those that it does not.'

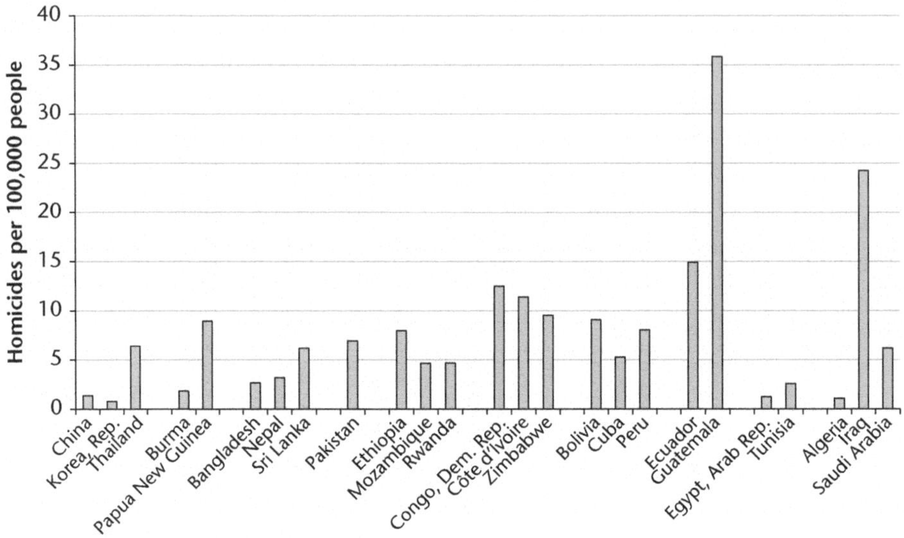

Figure 4.12. Intentional homicides per 100,000 people, average 2000–14
Source: World Bank (n.d.)

shows how the good and poor performers fared during 2000–14. Mostly the good performers in each group show lower rates than the poor performers. Security against crime, especially against homicide, is an important dimension of HD. The exceptionally low rates in South Korea, China, Bangladesh, Egypt, and Nepal enhance their claim to be good performers, while the very high rates in Guatemala and Iraq accentuate their poor basic HD performance. However, among the poor HDI performers, Algeria and Burma had notably low rates of homicide.

Political violence is another important aspect of insecurity. Figure 4.13 shows the years of intense conflict in the countries that did especially well or poorly on basic HD encompassing both internal and interstate conflict. Violent conflicts affected both good and weak HDI performers. Thus Sri Lanka, Ethiopia, and Mozambique had substantial high-intensity conflict incidence. Yet for Zimbabwe, a poor performer, no conflict was recorded. In a few of the 'good' cases, conflict incidence was great in the first half of the period, and recovery from conflict permitted good transitions, as we shall see in detail in Chapter 5, for example, in Ethiopia and Mozambique. Some of the conflicts were located in peripheral parts of the country and consequently had a relatively small impact on national income and average achievements on HD, as in Sri Lanka, but nonetheless had strong negative effects on the local populations both in relation to the security dimension of HD and in terms of the economic and service underpinning of other central dimensions of HD. Low-intensity conflict (deaths of more than twenty-five persons a year)

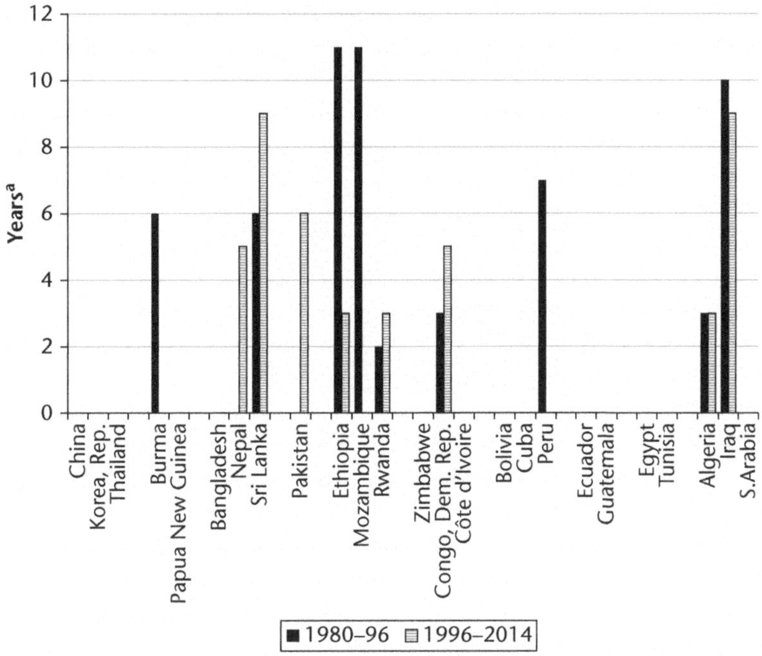

Figure 4.13. No. of years in intense conflict, 1980–2014

Note: Intense conflict = deaths of >1,000 p.a.

a. No entry indicates zero years in conflict

Source: UCDP/PRIO Armed Conflict Dataset Codebook, Version 4-2016 (Gleditsch et al. 2002, Petterson and Wallensteen 2015)

show a similar pattern: the conflicts experienced in Guatemala and Côte d'Ivoire were of this type (so do not show up in Figure 4.13).

4.4.4. *Environment*

We use two measures for the environmental dimension: first the Environmental Progress Index (EPI), which is a composite measure of the vitality of the ecosystem (twelve indicators) and environmental health (seven indicators). This is a useful indicator of environmental issues as a valued dimension of HD, and as an input into other valued dimensions of HD, particularly health. The EPI includes carbon emissions as one component, accounting for 12.5 per cent of the index, but it is useful to look at this separately because of its importance for climate change. There is no marked difference between good and poor HDI performers on EPI in any region, although on average the good HDI performers show better EPI (see Figure 4.14).

Carbon emissions tend to be related to per capita income. In East and South East Asia, the good HDI performers, which have higher incomes, also show

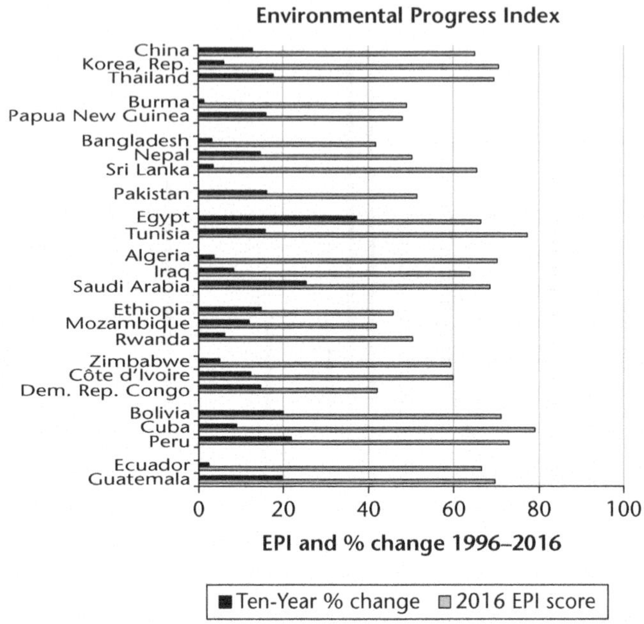

Figure 4.14. Environmental Progress Index (EPI) and ten-year change, 1996–2016
Source: Yale Center for Environmental Law & Policy (YCELP) and the Center for International Earth Science Information Network (CIESIN) at Columbia University

significantly higher emissions than the poor performers (see Figure 4.15). In the Middle Eastern region, the three poor HDI performers also show exceptionally high emissions, which may be because they are oil producers. No particular relationship can be found in other regions, though Saudi Arabia, a poor HDI performer, shows the highest emissions in this set of countries.

Taking these additional dimensions of HD into account indicates that good performance on basic HD does not necessarily mean that countries also perform well on other dimensions of HD. We explore this issue further in Chapter 6. In general, there is a lack of consistency across different dimensions, and a weak relationship between the non-HDI dimensions and improvement in basic HD. For example, Sri Lanka and Ethiopia, good HDI performers, experienced high levels of violent conflict, while Zimbabwe, a low-HDI performer, recorded none. Mozambique, another good performer, had a relatively low EPI and Burma, a weak performer, did well on EPI. Political rights were poor over the whole period in some good HDI performers, including China and Cuba, while others had weak rights initially but improved over time, including South Korea and Nepal. A number of the poor HDI performers showed progress in political rights, such as the Democratic Republic of the Congo and Côte d'Ivoire. And, as just noted, some of the good HDI performers

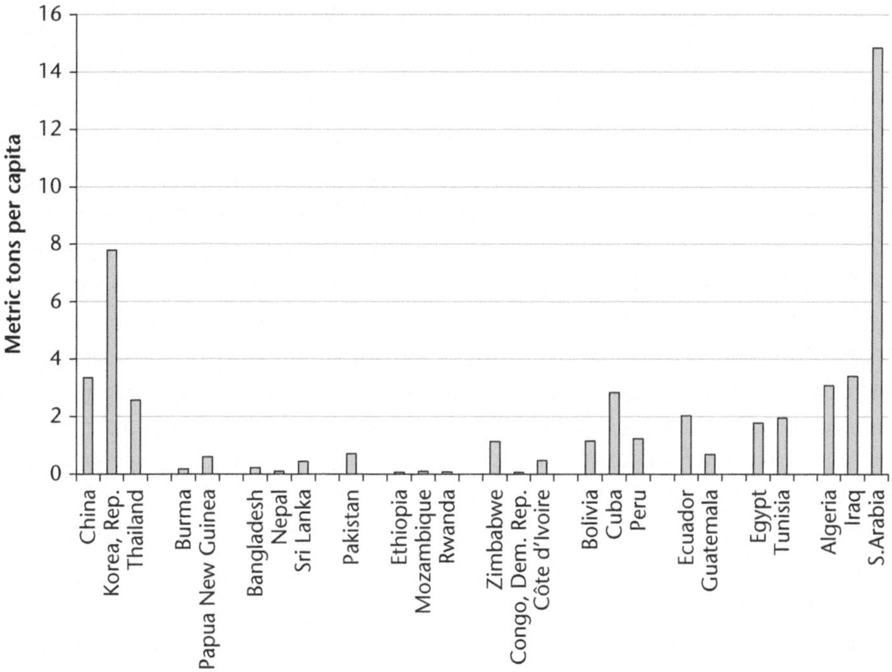

Figure 4.15. CO_2 emissions per capita, 1980–2013, average
Source: United Nations MDG indicators (mdgs.un.org)

did particularly badly on carbon emissions, notably the three East Asian countries. Among the dimensions reviewed here, those most closely related to progress on basic HD were the homicide rate and gender inequality, both mostly worse among the poor HDI performers.

Looking across the dimensions for each country, South Korea stands out as doing well on average in every dimension apart from carbon emissions. In contrast, good HDI performer Ethiopia did poorly on almost every non-HDI dimension, apart from carbon emissions. Among the weak HDI performers there was more consistency: Pakistan, Iraq, Côte d'Ivoire, and Saudi Arabia did poorly on almost every dimension.

4.5. Conclusion

The aim of this chapter was to ascertain whether we could observe systematic patterns of policy related to success and failure on basic HD, and how far success or failure on basic HD was related to other, wider dimensions of HD.

We identified three countries which had performed exceptionally well over time and up to three weak performers, during 1980–2014, from five regions—East and South East Asia, South Asia, sub-Saharan Africa, Latin America, and the Middle East. A regional approach allows, to some extent at least, for differing initial conditions. The countries were selected in this way to illustrate conditions for exceptional progress or fall-back.

Having identified the countries, we explored whether there was an association of success and failure on basic HD with a number of variables associated in the literature, and by regression analysis in Chapter 3, with HD outcomes. Our main conclusion is that there are no unique patterns leading to success or failure; rather, there are alternative paths to either positive or negative outcomes.

Certain characteristics were common to almost all success cases compared with the weak cases: these were a high ratio of female to male enrolment in secondary school and a low GII. The successful countries mostly spent more on health as a proportion of GDP, and in three regions—the Asian regions and Latin America—the secondary enrolment rate was higher by the 2000s, but not in sub-Saharan Africa or the Middle East. The success cases experienced faster economic growth, apart from Cuba. The exceptions indicate that there are alternative paths to success.

Success was associated with varying combinations of good performance on growth, equitable distribution, and high social expenditure. Some countries had exceptional performance on one or another of these elements. But some followed an intermediate road, experiencing good but not spectacular growth, a fairly equitable distribution, and moderate levels of social expenditure. Nepal and Bangladesh are examples. We suggest that this route is likely to be the easiest to replicate.

We also found varying patterns of poor performance, this time with exceptionally weak performance on the three elements just identified: growth, equity, and social expenditure. Some had poor performance on all three elements—such as the Democratic Republic of the Congo and Côte d'Ivoire. But some did well on one but were dragged down by poor performance on the others. For example, Zimbabwe had relatively high social expenditure but poor growth and an inequitable distribution. Worsening inequality combined with fairly low social expenditure led to poor basic HD performance despite positive economic growth—as was the case in Ecuador and Guatemala.

For the most part, country performance with respect to important dimensions of HD not encompassed in the HDI shows little correlation between the non-HDI dimensions and performance on basic HD. In summary, this suggests that it cannot be assumed that promoting basic HD, as measured by IMR reductions and economic growth, will necessarily also lead to improvements in other aspects of HD. It is necessary to promote each of the important dimensions of HD individually.

Analysing success and failure in HD over more than three decades is evidently a difficult task. Much depends on the metrics chosen, and the move from correlation to proving causation has not been attempted here. But by exploring differences between the successful and weak performers on a number of characteristics, while paying attention to differing initial conditions, some patterns of success and failure emerge. In the end, however, there are invariably important country-specific political and historical dimensions which defy quantification and yet help determine outcomes. We examine country-specific political and economic factors for selected countries in Chapter 5.

5

Successful Transition Towards a Virtuous Cycle of Human Development and Economic Growth

Country Studies

Chapter 4 explored performance on some of the major economic and social characteristics associated with exceptionally good or poor performance, which we defined in two ways: as exceptional performance both in improving HD and economic growth over three or four decades (the virtuous cycle category); or as exceptional transitions from poor performance on both HD and growth to good performance on both between the 1970s and 2000s. We found that countries that were particularly successful in these terms did not follow a single path: while all tended to have exceptional improvements in secondary school attendance and a higher female to male ratio of school attendance, they showed different combinations of growth, income distribution, and social expenditure. Poor performers were defined in a similar way to good performers: either they had persistently weak improvements in HD and low growth over three or four decades, or they fell back from good performance to the vicious category over the decades. The negative transition cases (Ecuador, Guatemala, and Algeria) experienced moderate growth rates, while the persistently poor performers showed weak or negative growth, as indeed followed from the selection criteria. For both types of weak performance, again, there were different combinations of inequality in distribution and social expenditures across these poorly performing countries.

The aim of this chapter is to go beyond the statistical overview presented in Chapter 4, particularly with respect to positive transitions, and to explore in more depth the economic conditions experienced, the policies followed, and the political economy underlying the adoption of these policies in countries which transitioned successfully from a weak HD position to strong one.

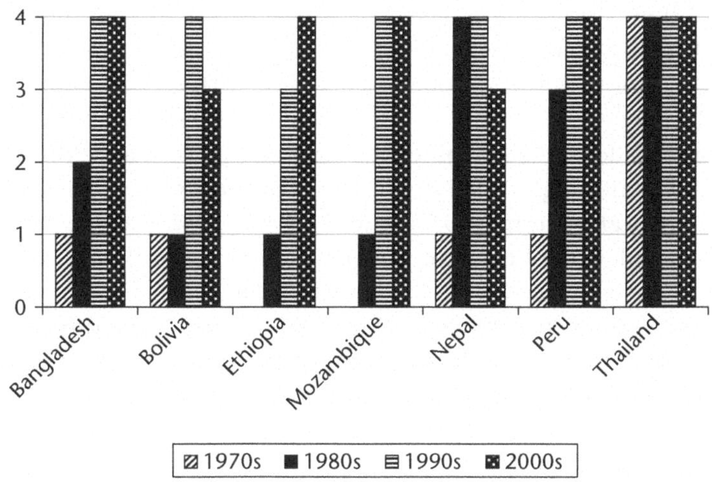

Figure 5.1. Positive transitions to be explored, 1970s–2000s
Note: HDI categories: 1 = vicious; 2 = EG-lopsided; 3 = HD-lopsided; 4 = virtuous
Source: Table A.3.4

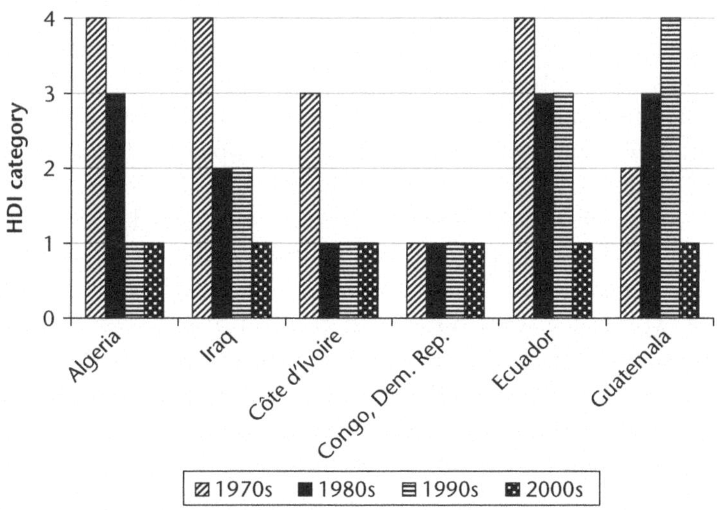

Figure 5.2. Negative transitions to be explored, 1970s–2000s
Note: HDI categories: 1 = vicious; 2 = EG-lopsided; 3 = HD-lopsided; 4 = virtuous
Source: Table A.3.4

We aim to put some flesh on the findings in Chapter 4, but with a special focus on *transitions* from poor to good policies, as well as very briefly reflecting on reversals. Of the countries listed as especially successful in Chapter 4 (see Table 4.1), we select Bangladesh and Nepal from South Asia, Ethiopia and Mozambique from sub-Saharan Africa, and Bolivia and Peru from Latin

America—all of which are successful transition countries—for more in-depth analysis. We also look at the experience of Thailand as one of only three countries in the world to sustain itself in the virtuous category over four decades. The experience of these seven countries is illustrated in Figure 5.1.

We also consider some examples of worsening performance for lessons on what to avoid, although only briefly. The countries selected with worsening experience are taken from Table 4.2 in Chapter 4. We include the negative transition experiences of Ecuador, Guatemala, Algeria, and Iraq, each moving from the virtuous category in the 1970s (the 1990s in the case of Guatemala) to the vicious one in the 2000s; and we also consider Côte d'Ivoire and the Democratic Republic of the Congo, which stayed in the vicious category for three and four decades, respectively (see Figure 5.2).

5.1. Positive Transitions

5.1.1. *Bangladesh*

Bangladesh progressed from the vicious category in the 1970s, first to an EG-lopsided category during the 1980s, and then into the virtuous category in the 1990s and 2000s. In 1970, life expectancy was only forty-four years. This was just before Bangladesh achieved independence, having suffered as the exploited eastern wing of Pakistan from 1947. The war that led to the split in 1971 involved a very sharp (but temporary) fall in incomes. In 1980, male adult literacy was 40 per cent and female 18 per cent, malnutrition was over 60 per cent, and under-five mortality at 240 per 1,000 live births. By 2013, male literacy was 63 per cent and female 56 per cent, malnutrition had fallen to 17 per cent, and under-five mortality to forty-one per 1,000 live births. Life expectancy at birth had risen to seventy-one years. Clearly HD in Bangladesh had greatly advanced over the forty-year period: Bangladesh had moved from the UNDP's low-HDI category to the medium-HDI category.

Underlying these improvements were accelerating economic growth, a rise in social expenditures, a relatively equal income distribution, and a greatly improved position of women. Growth in incomes per capita was very low in the 1970s (in many years negative); it recovered somewhat in the 1990s, ranging between 2 per cent and 3 per cent per annum; and it then accelerated to between 4 per cent and 5 per cent per annum in the 2000s. This improvement was supported by rising investment. Gross capital formation as a percentage of GDP was only 8.7 per cent in 1973; by 2013 it had risen to 28.3 per cent. Education expenditure as a percentage of GDP was only 1.1 per cent in 1979, rising to a maximum of 2.4 per cent in 2000, but falling to 1.9 per cent in 2009. Health expenditure was higher at around 3.5 per cent of GDP from

1995 (earlier data are not available). These are low rates (especially for education). Income distribution, however, was relatively equal: the Gini coefficient was just 0.283 in 1983; it rose a little to 0.331 in 2000 but then fell slightly to 0.32 in 2010. The poverty rate fell from 70 per cent in 1983 to 44 per cent in 2010. It would thus appear that a combination of accelerating and well-distributed growth was the major impetus behind the HD improvements, not social expenditure. We need to get beneath these statistics to understand the causes of this achievement.

It is difficult to argue that Bangladesh has been well governed since its independence: the first prime minister was murdered, and there has been a succession of coups; the Bangladesh government is also notoriously corrupt. It was the worst performer on Transparency International's corruption index in 2005, and in 2014 it was 145th out of a total of 174 countries. On political rights, Bangladesh has fluctuated between 3 and 5, according to the Freedom House index (where 1 is most free and 7 least).

This is not a case of an effective and egalitarian state promoting HD. Indeed, one observer (Sobhan 2002, 6) noted:

> The patronization by successive governments of a criminal class, who have become instrumental to the functioning of our principal political parties has brought the machinery of law enforcement into contempt.... The days when bureaucrats were driven by a sense of public mission, built on expectations of professional recognition and advancement, remain in distant memory. In such circumstances the administrative system is rarely capable of implementing any policy and is largely seen as an agency for rent seeking from the helpless citizens.... The health care and education services have degenerated to a point where it is a misnomer to term them as a public service.

Others have criticized social protection programmes for 'administrative complexity, high cost, high leakages, mistargeting, weak governance, less transparency and accountability, political capture, and corruption in program implementation' (Masud-All-Kamal and Saha 2014, abstract).

Since Bangladesh gained independence from Pakistan in 1971, the government has oscillated between authoritarian military domination and democracy, and in the democratic phases between two political parties, each of which aims to prevent the other from advancing governance effectively (Rahim 1997, Kabir 1999). However, despite an apparently dysfunctional state, progress occurred largely due to two types of non-state actors: first, an enormously enterprising and extensive set of NGOs; and second, a dynamic private sector, especially in garments and textiles. They contributed to the provision of services and to incomes for the poor, and probably of most significance, both have helped empower women.

Two major NGOs (BRAC[1] and the Grameen Bank), supplemented by many others, have extended credit to millions of the poor, especially women, and provided education and other services (Lovell 1992, Holcomb 1995, Nath 1997, Bornstein 2005, Rohde 2005, Hulme 2008). The Grameen Bank lends to around nine million people, of whom over 90 per cent are poor women. It has also moved into other activities, including telecommunications and garments production. BRAC claims to cover more than one hundred million people, with services that include health and educational programmes and social enterprises as well as micro-credit. While there is some doubt about how far the micro-credit expansion has raised incomes, it seems generally agreed that it has been empowering for women (Mahmud 2002, Pitt et al. 2006, Banerjee et al. 2014, Chowdhury 2009, Rashid 2014).

The second important set of non-state actors were those responsible for the garment industry in Bangladesh, mainly small- and medium-size enterprises, many of whom had little previous entrepreneurial experience. These firms seized the opportunities to expand low-cost textile and garments production offered by the Multi Fibre Agreement initially and, despite pessimistic prognoses, sustained efficient production for the low-quality end of Western markets even after this agreement ended in 2005 (Quddus and Rashid 2000, Islam 2001, Erfan 2004). Very low wages (less than half those of China and well below other countries in the region) and some domestic tax incentives helped the expansion (Ahmed 2009). From 1978, exports of garments grew from US$1 million to US$26 billion in 2014 and accounted for 84 per cent of merchandise exports (data from WTO), while exports rose from 3 per cent of GDP in 1975 to 20 per cent in 2014. About half the firms are small-scale (Malhotra 2006). The industry employs approximately four million workers, of whom 90 per cent are women (Ghosh 2014). The majority of these women come from rural areas and remit part of their pay back, spreading the benefits. Moreover, experience working in the city empowers women, despite the poor conditions. Upon interviewing female workers, Hyder found a sense of empowerment as well as social mobility among these workers: 'The garments industry has created the rise of financially independent and successful women in Bangladesh and is responsible for a dramatic shift in paradigm for Bangladeshi society' (Hyder 2009, 2). Some of the earnings from the garment work went to the education of children in the family. In one case, earnings allowed for the college education of a daughter: 'in three generations, Khadijah's family had gone from rural housewife to blue-collar working woman to college graduate' (Hyder 2009, 1).

[1] BRAC first stood for the 'Bangladesh Rehabilitation Assistance Committee'; but over time this changed to the 'Bangladesh Rural Advancement Committee' and then 'Building Resources across Communities'.

Female empowerment was also increased by a dramatic improvement in the gender parity of primary and secondary education in Bangladesh over these decades: the ratio was 0.3 in 1973 and 1.1 (i.e. more girls than boys were enrolled) by 2013. As noted, the expansion of micro-credit, largely directed towards women, also made a contribution here.

Enhanced female empowerment affects HD in several ways: most directly, it increases female participation in and control over household decisions. Much evidence shows this improves the nutrition, education, and health of children (see Chapter 3). It also has a direct effect on the freedom of those in work. As one worker said: 'I like it here. I make my own decisions'; and another: 'I can do whatever I like. I can enjoy myself. I have freedom' (interviews quoted in Weiss 2014).

These two sets of actors—locally initiated and managed NGOs and local entrepreneurs—supported by the state, at least intermittently, played a major role in bringing about the virtuous and mutually supportive cycle of relatively egalitarian economic growth and impressive progress in HD in Bangladesh.

5.1.2. *Nepal*

Nepal is another low-HDI country in South Asia that progressed from the vicious category in the 1970s to the virtuous one in the 1980s and 1990s. However, this was interrupted by the civil war from 1996 to 2006, leading to about 10,000 deaths and a lapse in growth in the early 2000s. Nonetheless, for the 2000s as a whole progress in HD was sustained, so Nepal moved into the HD-lopsided category in the 2000s. Yet, as in many countries, the average achievements conceal substantial horizontal inequalities along caste, ethnic, gender, and spatial lines. Indeed, Nepal is said to have seven axes of exclusion (UNDP 2009).

Nepal's indicators in the 1970s were very poor: the under-five mortality rate in 1971 was over 240, even higher than that of Bangladesh, and the adult literacy rate was also worse (9.2 per cent for females and 32 per cent for males in 1981). Gross primary enrolment was only 27 per cent and secondary 12 per cent. But there was substantial progress over subsequent decades. Life expectancy at birth was forty-two years in 1970 and had reached 68.4 years by 2013. The adult literacy rate rose from 32 per cent in 1981 to 72 per cent in 2012. Universal primary education had been achieved and gross secondary enrolment was 67 per cent by 2014. Over these decades, Nepal rose up the ranks of the HDI to be top of the low-HDI category in 2014.

In the 1970s and 1980s Nepal was ruled by a monarch, but democratic institutions and political parties were reintroduced in 1990 following popular pressure. The 1990 Constitution 'acknowledged that the country was multi-ethnic and multi-lingual', and put forward principles for eliminating discrimination along the lines of caste and gender. Yet it contained some exclusionary provisions, including establishing Hinduism as the official religion and Nepali as the only official language, and outlawing sectarian and ethnic political parties (UNDP 2009, 84). Political and socio-economic horizontal inequalities persisted, on geographic, class, and caste lines. These inequalities and deprivations resulted in the outbreak of a 'People's War' in 1996, led by Maoists (Murshed and Gates 2005). The bitter conflict ended with a peace agreement in 2006; the Maoists gained power and established a republic. Constitutional discussions continued throughout the 2000s. Politically, Nepal thus seems unpromising territory for successful HD transition for much of the period.

Economic growth was low in the 1970s (just 0.4 per cent per capita per annum), reflecting a very low rate of investment, contributing to the vicious category in the 1970s. The growth rate increased in each successive decade—even during the People's War there was only one major dip—and it reached an average of 2.8 per cent per capita per annum in the 2000s, still below neighbouring countries and developing countries as a whole. This was paralleled by a large increase in investment, which went from 8 per cent in 1971 to 20.5 per cent in 2000, reaching 37 per cent in 2014. Productivity and export growth lagged behind that of the South Asian region in the 2000s, which accounted for Nepal's lapse into the HD-lopsided category in this decade.

Income distribution was remarkably equal in the early 1980s (the first years for which data are available) with a Gini coefficient of 0.21, but it appears to have risen significantly since then to 0.4 in 2000 and 0.465 in 2010. The rising inequality was associated with growth in non-agricultural activities from the 1980s and stagnation in agriculture. Despite the worsening distribution, growth, social programmes, and remittances resulted in a sharply declining poverty rate which was almost 75 per cent in 1984, falling to 47 per cent in 2003 and just 15 per cent in 2010 using the US$1.90-a-day standard. The MPI headcount was 44.2 per cent in 2011, having fallen from 64.7 per cent in 2006.

The improvements in HD were due to a combination of state and donor action, community and NGO initiatives, and remittances. The 1990 Constitution included a guarantee of universal access to education. Education expenditure as a percentage of gross national income (GNI) was just 0.9 per cent in the 1970s, rising from 2.3 per cent in the 1980s to 2.6 per cent in the 1990s, and to 2.9 per cent during 2000–9. The 1990s also saw a substantial expansion in healthcare, including primary healthcare centres. Health expenditure accounted for over 5.5 per cent of GNP from 1995 onwards. Social security schemes are patchy, although they have been extended over the years, especially since 2006 (Khanal 2012). A universal pension scheme was introduced in the 1990s for those over seventy-five, widows, and disabled people. But its estimated coverage was 30 per cent for the elderly and less for the other categories (Asian Development Bank 2009). Formal sector social security protections exist for a minority of the workforce (estimated at around 10 per cent).

After the war ended, donors and government programmes of support were targeted at deprived areas and groups: these programmes were on a large scale, covering around three to four million people out of a total population of twenty-eight million (Brown 2012, Stewart 2012a). The Nepalese government introduced an employment scheme guaranteeing one hundred days of employment per household in districts 'severely impacted by the conflict and which currently suffer from a serious problem of isolation, unemployment and poverty' (World Bank 2007, 1), the coverage of which was greatly extended by the World Bank. Other donors, such as the United States Agency for International Development and the UK's Department for International Development, also introduced large programmes to create employment and support small enterprise in those districts worst affected by the conflict, targeted towards low castes and minorities. But while the government is committed to providing social protection for all, in practice 'programmes are fragmented and are driven by populist or political concerns and do not constitute a comprehensive strategy' (Khanal 2012, 2).

Nepal has long had a tradition of community networks and partnerships—*Guthis*, *Dhikurs*, and *Parma* (informal collective institutions). A formal initiative, the Small Farmer Development Programme, began to mobilize poor farmers in 1975. Social mobilization increased after democratization in 1990. A range of interest groups developed to represent the deprived, including organizations of Dalits, of nationalities (peoples of different ethnicities and national origins), and of women. A coalition of NGOs lobbied for the abolition of bonded labour. There were active efforts to instigate social mobilization in the 1990s throughout the country, resulting in SMCs (socially mobilized communities) estimated to cover nearly 40 per cent of households in 2002, with about half the membership being female (Sah 2003). An evaluation of SMCs found that people perceived they had a positive impact on livelihoods, health, and education (UNDP 2004a). However, the ultra-poor were often excluded.

Remittances also played a major role. Migration and remittances rose sharply in the 2000s. As many as four million people are estimated to have migrated, or one-third of the male working population, mainly to the Middle East. By 2012 remittances accounted for around a quarter of GNP, far more than exports (8 per cent) or aid (4 per cent). Remittances reached about 56 per cent of households. However, it has been argued that they have had a negative impact on the economy, via a 'Dutch disease' effect, and have depressed agricultural productivity because of the effects on incentives of recipient households (Tuladhar et al. 2014). While remittances increased in the 2000s, the export share of GNP declined. Nonetheless, remittances helped to reduce poverty, amounting to as much as two-thirds of the income of recipient households. They are estimated to have accounted for one-third to one-half of the poverty reduction between 1996 and 2004 according to one study (World Bank 2006a).

A substantial fall in gender inequality also contributed to the HD improvements in Nepal. There was a sharp improvement in the Gender Development Index (GDI) from 1996 to 2011 (UNDP 2009, Government of Nepal and UNDP 2014), largely due to rising life expectancy among women and increases in school enrolment.[2] Female parliamentary representation improved significantly in 2008 as a result of a law requiring one-third of seats to be held by women. The Gender Empowerment Measure (GEM) increased by 45 per cent between 2001 and 2011. Nepal's rank in the GDI was 102 in 2013 and its GII[3] rank was 98, both considerably above the HDI rank at 145. Its ranking on both is better than that of Bangladesh.

In summary, the poor performance in the 1970s was due to abysmal initial conditions, with very low investment and social expenditures. Rising investment accounted for the improvements in growth in the following decades, interrupted by the war in the late 1990s and early 2000s. Very low inequality in the 1980s, combined with growing per capita income, contributed to poverty reduction in that decade. Following democratization in the 1990s, government commitment to social programmes grew, promoted by active social mobilization and non-governmental initiatives, including the spread of SMCs. In the 2000s, remittances played a major role in poverty reduction and post-conflict social programmes were expanded, especially to conflict-affected areas and groups, sustaining progress on HD.

5.1.3. *Thailand*

Thailand is a particularly interesting case, achieving sustained success in growth and HD over all four decades, despite experiencing rather high inequality by Asian standards and a turbulent political situation, particularly

[2] The GDI 'measures gender inequalities in three basic dimensions of human development: health, measured by female and male life expectancy at birth; education, measured by female and male expected years of schooling for children and female and male mean years of schooling for adults ages 25 years and older; and command over economic resources, measured by female and male estimated earned income'. It represents the ratio of women's to men's HDI for gender inequalities in life expectancy, education, and earned incomes (UNDP 2016, technical notes, 5).

[3] The GII, introduced in Chapter 4, includes inequalities in seats in parliament, education, and labour force participation, as well as the maternal mortality and adolescent birth rates.

since 2004. Moreover, it is also of interest as one of the few developing countries never to have been colonized.

Thailand's growth in GDP was almost 6 per cent on average for the period 1970–2014, being highest in the 1970s and 1980s at over 7 per cent per annum and falling to around 4 per cent per annum from 2000. The growth was led by an increase in labour-intensive exports and industrial output: exports increased by almost 10 per cent annually over the whole period and industrial value increased by 7.2 per cent per annum. Agriculture also experienced sustained growth, though the population working in agriculture declined from 1990. Growth was supported by high investment, especially in the 1990s when the ratio of gross capital formation to GDP reached over 40 per cent, but it declined sharply with the financial crisis suffered by East Asian countries in the late 1990s. The crisis also reduced growth—indeed it became negative for a short period. Multiple sources for income distribution show considerable differences in the estimated Gini coefficient at any one time. For example, in 1962 one estimate is for a Gini of 0.41 and another of 0.58 according to WIDER's comprehensive dataset (WIDER n.d.). Taking the lower estimate for each year, it seems that there has not been much change over the decades, with the Gini hovering around 0.41.[4] The poor benefited from trickle-down from growth, and poverty fell sharply: while over 40 per cent of the population were below the World Bank's US$3.20 a day in 1981, this had fallen to 1.5 per cent by 2012. Other measures of poverty show similar trends.

Government expenditure in Thailand on health and education rose over the decades, though it was not exceptionally high: educational expenditure accounted for 3 per cent of GDP in 1971 and had risen to over 5 per cent in 2011, while health expenditure was 1.7 per cent in 1995 (data not available earlier) and more than doubled to 3.7 per cent by 2013. This, of course, implied a fast increase in absolute expenditure given the rapid rise in GDP. There were big increases in school enrolments: the gross secondary education enrolment rate rose from 18 per cent in 1971 to 86 per cent in 2012, and the gender balance of primary and secondary education improved—the parity rate was 0.87 in 1971 (fewer girls than boys in school) and was just over 1 by 2014. The GDI, a ratio of women's to men's HDI values, was also 1 in 2014.[5] Water and sanitation improved dramatically: by 2014, 98 per cent of the population had an improved source of water. By 2013 virtually every birth was attended by a skilled health worker. These improvements in the conditions for health and education were reflected in dramatic

[4] The World Development Indicators show some equalizing tendency since 1980 with a Gini coefficient of 0.45 in 1980 falling to 0.39 in 2012.

[5] Thailand's ranking for the GDI in 2014 was 76, which is significantly above its ranking for the HDI (at 93).

improvements in health: the under-five mortality rate came down from seventy-two per 1,000 live births (about half the middle-income average) in 1971 to 12.3 in 2015—the average under-five mortality for middle-income countries in 2015 was forty-one; and maternal mortality fell from one hundred per 100,000 births to 10.5, a third of the average rate for middle-income countries. Evidence for 1990–2000 shows a sharp reduction in inequality in infant mortality rates across social groups: the excess mortality between the poorest and richest quintile declined by 55 per cent (Vapattanawong et al. 2007). These are remarkable achievements, as reflected in the fact that Thailand is one of just three countries to be in the virtuous category for all decades. We now turn to some policies underlying this achievement.

5.1.3.1. SOCIAL PROTECTION

While those in the formal sector (civil servants and private employees) were covered by health insurance and pensions, the almost two-thirds of the labour force in the informal sector had only informal and ad hoc coverage before 2001. Since then a series of protections have been introduced, including an allowance for older people and for those with disabilities, and universal rights to healthcare and to twelve years of education, free in public schools and subsidized in private ones (ILO 2013).

5.1.3.2. RURAL POVERTY

Sustained agricultural progress led to a fall in rural poverty. This was supported by government investments in rural infrastructure and programmes for agricultural credit, as well as pricing policies that supported agriculture. Initially, agriculture grew by absorbing more labour, but once the labour supply began to fall, there was emphasis on new technologies, supported by government extension and research (Leturque and Wiggins 2010).

5.1.3.3. URBAN CONDITIONS

A commitment to reducing urban poverty was driven in part by protests and organization among the poor themselves, and by the TRT (Thai Rak Thai Party), a progressive political party led by Thaksin Shinawatra which gained a large electoral majority in 2001. In the early 1990s, after protests and demonstrations by the urban poor, the 'Four Regional Slum Network' was initiated, a nationwide organization of poor communities, which actively advocated for the rights of the poor. As a result, in the 1990s representatives of the poor contributed to the drafting of successive national plans. When Thaksin gained power in 2001 he was committed to universal healthcare, a debt moratorium for small farmers, soft loans for community development, and housing for the poor. As one Thai person stated: 'the government declared its battle against poverty' (quoted in Bhatkal and Lucci 2015, 26). One of the programmes introduced was Baan Mankong, a national programme for urban development based on community participation, which aimed for security of tenure for the poor, housing improvements, and improved housing quality (Bhatkal and Lucci 2015). The programme was well financed and has had considerable success. It continued despite the political upheavals of the mid and late 2000s.

5.1.3.4. HEALTH SECTOR POLICIES

There appears to have been a long-term commitment to improving health. By 1950, there was a hospital in every province (Thailand Government 2007). From 1975 it was a constitutional requirement that the government should provide health services to those with low incomes. Pro-poor health insurance schemes were initiated in the 1970s, user charges were waived for the poor in 1975, and a subsidized voluntary health insurance scheme was introduced in 1983 targeted at the near-poor. However, there remained highly unequal access to health services, and a large fraction of the population was not covered by the system. In 1978, rural doctors formed an association (the Rural Doctors' Society[6]) which acted as a pressure group for improved rural health facilities. Rural health facilities improved so that by 1989 there was a health clinic in every village, with a resource switch from urban hospitals (Wibulpolprasert and Pengpaibon 2003). In 2002, universal healthcare was introduced: 'A person shall enjoy an equal right to receive standard public health service, and the indigent shall have the right to receive free medical treatment from State's infirmary' (2002 National Health Security Act).[7] According to Harris (2015), this was made possible by a network of progressive bureaucrats, many of whom had been part of the Rural Doctors' Society, who set the agenda and fought for its implementation against the opposition of much of the medical profession and the World Bank, but with the support of active civil society organizations, the World Health Organization (WHO), and the ILO. Their activities in the 1990s—including the organization of a mass petition for universal healthcare—led Thaksin to make the issue a flagship of

[6] The Rural Doctors' Society was formed by a small group of exceptional young doctors committed to public service, working in the poorest rural areas. Later on, many obtained senior jobs in the Ministry of Health and elsewhere and formed a formal network, Sampran Forum, to share experience and ideas. One member explained his support for universal health: 'When I was a rural doctor, I saw many people taken ill and becoming almost penniless. They had to sell their farmland or even their daughter to pay for their medical treatment. It was such a painful experience that we dreamt of providing medical care to the sick' (quoted in Harris 2015, 172).

[7] There is some opposition to the government-supported universal health service provision from private hospitals (Fernquest 2013). The World Bank has also drawn attention to its costs and questioned its affordability (World Bank 2012). However, World Bank research papers show that the service has reduced the amount of sick leave and increased employment (Wagstaff and Manachotphong 2012a, 2012b).

his campaign. Harris shows the 'strategic role played by a network of bureaucrats within the Thai state' who drew on 'strategic resources in the political, bureaucratic, civil, and international realms to advance their agenda' (Harris 2015, 166).

In short, it seems that sustained economic success—largely led by the private sector, and based on labour-intensive industrial exports and diversification and export expansion in agriculture—supported poverty reduction in Thailand. Government policies and expenditure played an important role in the economic success, especially through rural infrastructure. The reduction in monetary poverty contributed greatly to HD success, but improvements in education, health care, and water and sanitation were also essential components. A set of welfare state type provisions for supporting the old, those with disabilities, and the poor were introduced in the 2000s, in addition to universal health care, which was largely free at delivery.

These impressive HD achievements occurred despite considerable political turbulence. Pro-democracy uprisings against military rule took place in the early 1970s and the early 1990s. In addition, there was a Communist-inspired insurgency in the 1970s. Rebellion by the three south-east provinces, where Malay Muslims live, in contrast to the vast majority of the Thai population who are Buddhist, had been ongoing for much of the period, becoming especially fierce from 2004. The mass protests led to the adoption of democratic institutions in 1993, followed by peaceful elections. As already noted, Thaksin's TRT gained power in 2001 with a progressive agenda, promising health services, support for villages, and employment—which he largely delivered on. Re-elected in 2005, there was a military coup against him in 2006, which the military justified as a response to the 'yellow shirt' (middle- and upper-class) protests. The movement demanded that power be returned to the king. A 'red shirt' movement then developed with street protests against the military government. Elections were called in 2011, won by the Pua Thai Party led by Yingluk Shinawatra, Thaksin's sister, who continued with his policies. This led to renewed yellow shirt protests, in particular provoked by an amnesty for those indicted for political offences, including Thaksin himself, and her government was overthrown by a military coup in 2014 (Kurlantzick 2011, Ungpakorn 2013, Ungpakorn 2015).

Thus progress in HD in Thailand occurred against a turbulent political background. Social movements played both positive and negative roles. Positively, organizations like the Rural Doctors' Society and the network for the urban poor formed a pressure group for reforms, as did the urban network of the poor. Negatively, the yellow shirt movement brought down progressive democratic governments. Yet the pro-HD policies, it appears, were not reversed. Bureaucrats committed to HD policies, especially in health, also played an important role in policy change and implementation.

5.1.4. *Ethiopia*

The 1970s and 1980s were years of economic stagnation, high levels of poverty, and very poor education and health services in Ethiopia. Primary enrolment was just 15 per cent in 1970 and secondary enrolment 3.8 per cent. In 1993 primary enrolment was still as low as 22 per cent, and in 1996 secondary enrolment was 11 per cent. Education expenditure was just 1.6 per cent of GDP in 1981. The immunization rate for infants was 4 per cent (measles) in 1980. In 2000, only 5.6 per cent of births were attended by a skilled health worker. Per capita incomes fell during the 1980s and 1990s. Hence Ethiopia was in the vicious category for the 1970s (presumably, although growth data are lacking) and 1980s.

Political turbulence is undoubtedly a major factor in explaining Ethiopia's poor economic performance in the 1980s and 1990s. Haile Selassie, the long-term dictator, was deposed in 1974, but this was followed by coups and uprisings until the socialist People's Revolutionary Democratic Front gained power in 1991 and established a Federal Constitution in 1994. However, a war about the border with Eritrea continued until a peace treaty in 2000. Since then there has been broad political stability. The government is authoritarian and suppresses opposition forcefully. Devastating droughts occurred periodically (1972–3, 1984–5, 1998–2000, and 2008–9, and the end of 2015). When combined with political instability and conflict, the droughts led to mass famine as these factors meant that relief efforts were late and poorly directed, the worst case being in the 1980s when perhaps as many as one million people died (Clay and Holcomb 1986, de Waal 1991). Per capita economic growth was negative in the 1980s and 1990s, when socialist planning gave way to a market-oriented strategy, and it reached 6 per cent per annum in the 2000s (Figure 5.3). Although democratic freedoms remain limited,[8] since 1995 the stable government has been able to devote resources and energy towards development, with a focus on improving education and health and raising agricultural output. There was a complementary industrial strategy, aiming to develop and promote labour-intensive exports (Gebreeyesus 2016). Aid also increased massively (see Figure 5.4): it amounted to 6.7 per cent of national income in 1981 and had risen to almost 38 per cent by 2003, but then fell back to 16 per cent by 2013. In 2006 aid accounted for almost 60 per cent of government expenditure.

Education expenditure as a share of GDP had risen to 3.9 per cent by 2013, and health expenditure, which was 3 per cent in 1995, had risen to 5.1 per cent. Educational enrolments rose sharply from 1993, with primary education reaching 83.6 per cent by 2006, and secondary 29 per cent.

[8] Freedom House classified Ethiopia as 'not free' in 2015.

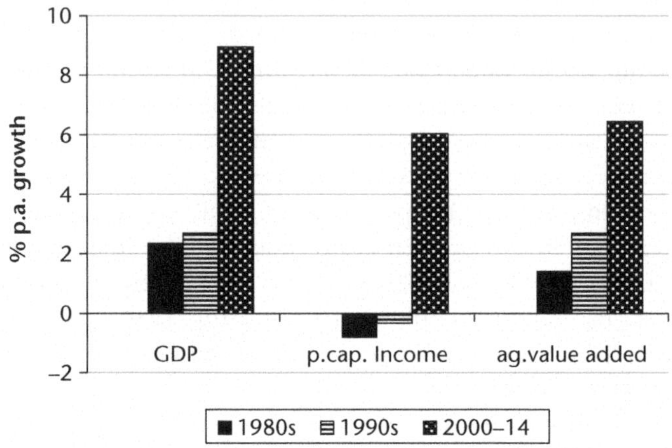

Figure 5.3. Annual growth in Ethiopia, 2000–14
Source: World Bank (n.d.)

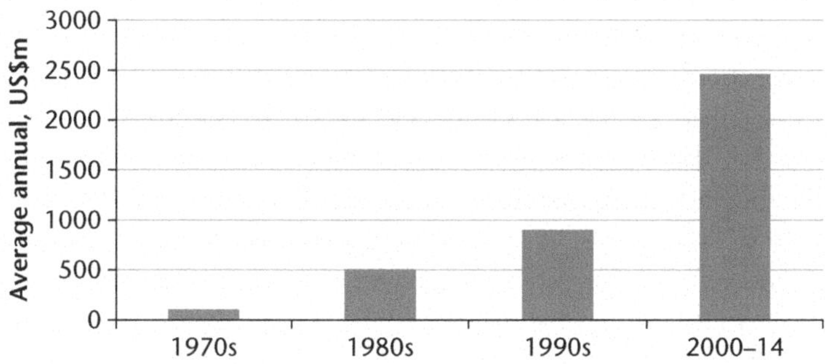

Figure 5.4. Net annual aid to Ethiopia, 1970s–2014
Source: World Bank (n.d.)

These rates represent a considerable improvement, although they are still lower than those for low-income countries as a whole. The gender parity rate for primary and secondary enrolment also improved greatly, from 0.4 in 1971 to 0.9 by 2012. Immunization rates rose from 13 per cent in 1992 to over 70 per cent in 2014. Skilled birth attendance had risen to 27.7 per cent by 2016 and under-five mortality fell sharply (see Figure 5.5). Maternal mortality also improved, though it remained very high at 676 per 100,000 births in 2011. The government also devoted considerable investment to rural infrastructure, including roads, agricultural extension services, and improved seeds and fertilizer. Road density increased by more than half, 9,000 new farmer training centres were established, and 60,000 agricultural support workers were employed (ODI 2015). The growth rate of agriculture value added was far higher in the 2000s than in previous decades (see Figure 5.3).

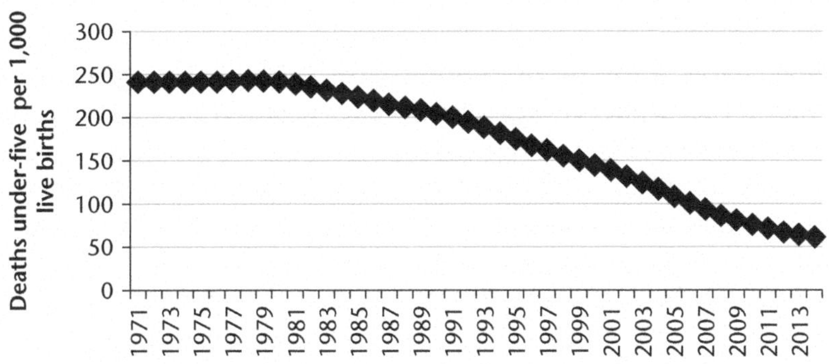

Figure 5.5. Under-five mortality in Ethiopia, 1970–2014
Source: World Bank (n.d.)

Cereal production rose nearly fourfold between 1994–5 and 2009–10, and by a further 50 per cent by 2014–15, due to improved seeds, fertilizer, agricultural extension, and the road network (Dorosh and Rashid 2015, ODI 2015). Manufacturing value added kept pace with the growth of GDP, and textile exports increased fourfold in the 2000s (Gebreeyesus 2016).

It is notable that the droughts of the 2000s did not lead to mass deaths because relief systems were much more effective. The government improved food security, with better early warning systems and communication, as well as a Productive Safety Net Programme (PSNP) to assist the poorest and most vulnerable. The PSNP combines cash and food transfers and is estimated to have reached almost eight million people in 2013. The combination of agricultural-based growth and the PSNP led to a large reduction in poverty: the headcount was estimated at almost 70 per cent of the population in 1981 and had fallen to 33.5 per cent by 2010 (US$1.90 a day, 2011, PPP). Income distribution appears to have been relatively equal. While estimates of income distribution vary according to source (see WIDER n.d.), the Gini estimates hover around 0.32, but with some estimates much higher and some lower.

It is thus easy to understand why Ethiopia was in the vicious category in the 1980s (and presumably the 1970s), with extremely low incomes, negative growth in per capita incomes, and exceptionally poor education. Political stability, together with a government committed to advancing development, is responsible for the improvements from the mid-1990s. The two main thrusts of the strategy adopted from around 1990—a focus on agricultural growth and progress in health and education—account for the transition to HD-lopsided and then the virtuous category. This was supported by large aid flows, especially to the health sector.

5.1.5. *Mozambique*

Mozambique was at war for most of the years from 1964 to the early 1990s, first a war of independence against the Portuguese colonists, which culminated in independence in 1975, and then a civil war in which each party was supported by outside powers—the left-wing FRELIMO (*Frente de Libertação de Moçambique*) by Cuba and Russia, and the conservative RENAMO (*Resistência Nacional Moçambicana*) by South Africa. Around a million people were believed to have been killed in this civil war, and several million displaced. The civil war came to an end with a 1992 peace agreement after the external support dissolved with the end of the Cold War and of apartheid in South Africa. These two wars left Mozambique in a state of severe underdevelopment: 'The independence war and the decolonization process entailed the total disruption of formal economic activity' (Chingono 2001, 91). Social and economic infrastructure was destroyed, and new investment virtually came to a halt. Gross investment fell to as low as 3.5 per cent of GDP in the mid-1980s. It is estimated that almost 60 per cent of primary schools were closed or destroyed (Bruck 2001, 67). There was a 30 per cent reduction in establishments involved in agricultural marketing between 1982 and 1988 (Bruck 2001, 69). Agricultural production fell by around 35 per cent between 1974 and 1992 when the civil war ended, with an even greater fall in food production per head (Stewart and Samman 2001). Tax revenue was less than 3 per cent of GDP in 1983–6. The secondary enrolment rate was just 8 per cent in 1983 and the primary rate around 60 per cent. The infant mortality rate was 174 in 1980. The wars saw massive forced migration, much of it internal. About a quarter of the population was displaced internally and another 10 per cent left the country (Bruck 2001). In 1993, the World Bank categorized Mozambique as having the lowest per capita income in the world. The prolonged and pervasive conflict accounts for Mozambique's position in the vicious category in the 1980s.

The rapid transformation to the virtuous category was due to an impressive post-war recovery, supported by large aid inflows. Aid per head in the 1970s was around US$10 (2012 prices), and rose almost sevenfold by the 1980s. From 1990 to 1994 it accounted for almost 60 per cent of GNI. Subsequently, it continued to rise in absolute terms but fell as a proportion of GNI, accounting for about a fifth of GNI by the late 2000s (Jones and Tarp 2015). Investment also recovered and reached 36 per cent of GNP by 1999, rising even further subsequently. From 1993, food production and exports (almost entirely primary products) grew, as did per capita income (see Figures 5.6 and 5.7). Mining investment rose, largely through foreign direct investment (Jones and Tarp 2015). The net barter terms of trade deteriorated sharply during the 1980s, compounding the other problems, and they continued to deteriorate in the 1990s. As in most of Africa, terms of trade improved in the 2000s but remained

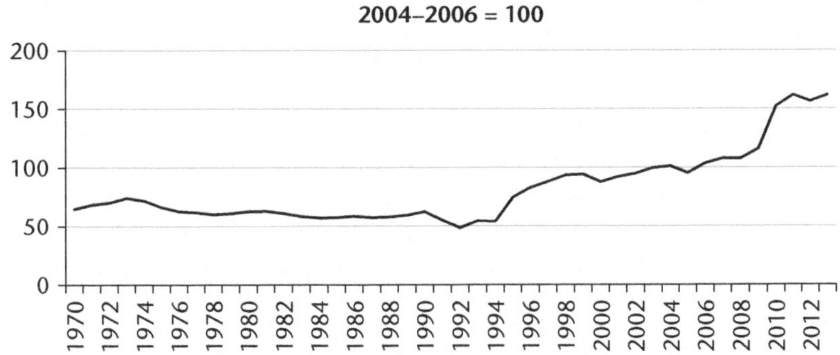

Figure 5.6. Mozambique: food production index, 1970–2012
Source: World Bank (n.d.)

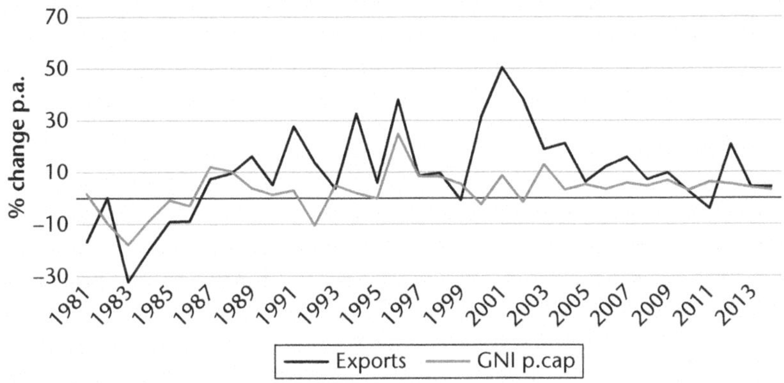

Figure 5.7. Mozambique: % change per annum in exports and GNI per capita, 1981–2014
Source: World Bank (n.d.)

much below the 1980 value, and the terms worsened again after 2010. There was little change in the Gini coefficient, which remained at around 0.45 between 1996 and 2008. The poverty headcount fell from 85 per cent in 1996 (below US$1.90 a day), but was still 68.7 per cent in 2008, while the MPI headcount was 82.3 per cent in 2003, falling to 70.3 per cent in 2011.

The proportion of GDP devoted to health and education expenditure also increased. By 2013, Mozambique was spending almost 7 per cent of GDP on the health sector and the same on education, both above the average for low-income countries. These expenditures led to an expansion in school enrolment. Primary enrolment was estimated at just 39 per cent in 1971; the rate was 63 per cent by 1990 and universal primary education was achieved by 2013. Secondary enrolment rates were much lower: just 5.4 per cent in

1980 and only 6 per cent in 2000, but the rate had risen to 26 per cent by 2013. The infant mortality rate improved somewhat in the 1980s, and much more rapidly in the 1990s and 2000s, falling from 160 per 1,000 live births in 1990 to 57 in 2015. However, as in Ethiopia, maternal mortality remained high at 680 per 100,000 births in 2011. A possible contributory factor in the later success of Mozambique was the decentralization policy adopted in the 1990s. Municipalities, with elected mayors and councils, got most power, while rural districts continued to be controlled from the centre. However, most local governments remained relatively weak (Ames et al. 2010). In 2009, elected provincial assemblies were introduced, but provincial governors continued to be appointed by the centre.

These achievements occurred in a context of democratic institutions, though the legitimacy of the elections was constantly challenged, and in the 2004 elections the Electoral Commission found that 5 per cent of the vote had gone missing and reallocated one parliamentary seat. FRELIMO, the winners of the civil war, have consistently gained a majority and dominated government, partly because they represent the majority southern population. Initially, the FRELIMO government adopted a socialist strategy including nationalization, land reform, and planning. There was a switch to market reforms in the 1990s. However, the emphasis on improving health and education remained. Both the first two post-war presidents, Joaquim Chissano and Armando Guebeza, retired as required by the Constitution after two terms. Both followed a pro-growth and pro-poverty reduction strategy. RENAMO, the opposition party, initially formed a peaceful opposition, although they instigated some violent kidnappings and ambushes from 2012. They have had increasing success at elections but remain in a minority. The elected provincial assemblies permit some power-sharing in regions dominated by RENAMO. Freedom House rates Mozambique as 'partly free', with a score of 3 for civil liberties and a score of 4 for political rights in 2015, which is considerably better than Ethiopia which scored 6 in each category.

In summary, Mozambique's transitional success is partly a consequence of the economy rebounding from a devastating civil war, supported by large aid flows. More favourable terms of trade, political stability, and economic reforms contributed to continued progress on both economic growth and HD. The government ideology consistently favoured HD.

5.1.6. *Bolivia*

Bolivia obtained political independence in 1825, and this was followed by a number of wars with neighbouring countries, in which Bolivia lost a good deal of territory. From that point onwards, the country was ruled by a Ladino elite which neglected the indigenous peoples who formed the great majority of the population.[9] A revolution in 1952 was followed by nationalization of major assets, including the mines, and a modernizing import-substituting strategy. However, with a succession of military coups from 1964, the situation of the indigenous population remained very poor. Civilian rule was re-established in 1982, followed in 1985 by a drastic stabilization plan, supervised and initiated by Jeffrey Sachs and supported by the IMF and the World Bank, to deal with the debt situation, arising in part because of a sharp fall in the price of tin, together with a very high inflation rate. This plan involved huge cutbacks in public expenditure, and led to declining income and rising poverty. An Emergency Social Fund was introduced in 1987 to provide employment for those affected, but it was by no means sufficient (Stewart et al. 1995). A new government in 1993 continued with the liberalization agenda, privatizing assets and deregulating the economy. This was accompanied by extensive decentralization and renewed emphasis on the social sectors. The government also introduced a pension for the elderly (*Bonosol*), partly to compensate for pension reform. Peasant and workers' movements had developed from the 1950s. They gained strength from the 1980s onwards, partly as a reaction to the impoverishment of the 1980s, and united in the *Movimiento al Socialismo-Unzaguista*, which won elections in 2005, with Eva Morales, the leader of the movement, becoming president. Morales initiated changes in the Constitution, to give more power to indigenous people, and in economic policy, including renationalizing hydrocarbons, some land reform, increasing social investments, and introducing cash transfer schemes.

This political history partly explains Bolivia's trajectory. Per capita income stagnated in the 1970s (falling by 3 per cent over the decade); it then fell by 18 per cent between 1980 and 1990, due to the stabilization policies and a major deterioration in the terms of trade. The terms of trade continued to worsen in the 1990s but improved substantially in the 2000s. Growth began to recover, rising by 19 per cent in the 1990s and another 22 per cent during 2000–10. Gross investment was stagnant in the 1970s and fell in the 1980s; it was just 11.6 per cent in 1989, rising to 18 per cent by 2000 and remaining at around that rate. Social expenditures fell during the 1980s: public expenditure on health and education together accounted for 4 per cent of GDP in 1981 and 3.8 per cent of a (lower) GDP in 1990. However, expenditures subsequently rose. By 1994 the total—including public and private—health and education expenditure together accounted for 9.3 per cent of GDP, rising to 13.1 per cent in 2010. The decentralization policies were partly responsible for the improvement. In 2004, 20 per cent of national tax revenue was devolved to local districts, while

[9] According to Klein (1993, 237), at that stage it was 'a typical racist state in which the non-Spanish speaking indigenous peasantry was controlled by a small Spanish-speaking white elite' (translated by and quoted in Faguet 2012, 13).

democratically elected mayors and councils were instituted. The ownership of social, economic, and cultural infrastructure was passed to local authorities. The change in responsibilities led to a big switch in expenditure towards education, water and sanitation, and urban development. It also redirected resources away from the three major cities to the rest of the country, benefitting poorer districts and leading to broad equality of expenditure per capita across districts. The responsiveness of priorities to local needs increased (Faguet 2003). Further decentralization occurred in 2005, when two-thirds of hydrocarbon revenues were devolved to departments, and direct elections were introduced for departmental heads (*prefectos*). Departments and municipalities became responsible for over a third of public expenditure and as much as 60 per cent of investment (World Bank 2006b). Between 1998 and 2010, the proportion of public expenditure devoted to education rose by six percentage points, but the proportion going to health fell somewhat. Morales introduced two cash transfer schemes, the *Bono Juancito Pinto* in 2006, conditional on school attendance, which had reached 96 per cent of low-income children by 2008; and the *Bono Juana Azurduy* for pregnant women and children under two years, which was conditional on attending health clinics and getting the children immunized. This was intended to reduce maternal mortality and improve infant nutrition and health.

Poverty, extreme poverty, and inequality all rose in the 1990s, peaking around 2000. The poverty rate (US$3.10 poverty line) fell from 41 per cent in 2000 to 19 per cent in 2010; extreme poverty (US$1.90) fell from 30 per cent to 12 per cent in 2009 and 7.7 per cent in 2013. The Gini coefficient was 0.581 in 2000 and rose to 0.585 in 2005, but subsequently fell to 0.497 in 2009. The MPI headcount also fell from 36.3 per cent in 2003 to 20.5 per cent in 2008. Primary enrolment was 90 per cent or more throughout the period, and secondary enrolment, which was just 42 per cent in 1990, had risen to 80 per cent by 2013. Access to improved sanitation facilities showed a similar trend. The national coverage fell between 1975 and 1990 (when it was 28 per cent), but subsequently rose steadily such that half the population was covered by 2013.

Bolivia's poor performance on HD and economic growth in the 1980s was due to the drastic stabilization programme, combined with very limited priority given to social investments. Its success from 1990 was due to the recovery of the economy, massive democratic decentralization, and Morales' land reforms and cash transfer programmes. The workers' and peasant movements undoubtedly played an important role in securing the election of Morales and bringing about these changes.

5.1.7. *Peru*

Peru was in the vicious category for the 1970s. This was a decade of massive change in asset ownership and management, initiated by General Velasco who had taken power in a coup in 1968. He adopted a radical agrarian reform replacing the large, privately owned haciendas with cooperatives; he also undertook extensive nationalization of major industries, and promoted ISI. He made efforts to give the indigenous population greater recognition, introducing a law to make Quechua a second official language, although this was never implemented. The reforming agenda slowed down after he was deposed by others from the military in 1975. In the short run, the reforms had a negative impact on production. Agricultural production was disrupted, and the state-owned industries made losses. The indices of crop production and food production fell over the decade. The public sector (and the trade balance) went into massive deficit (as much as 10 per cent of GDP), while inflation accelerated. Over the 1970s, growth in per capita incomes was slow and inequality continued to be very high, with a Gini coefficient of around 0.6 (see WIDER n.d.). Moreover, social sector expenditure was relatively low, with health and education together accounting for just over 3 per cent of GDP.

The 1970s also saw the politicization of the rural population. The agrarian reform conferred few benefits on the indigenous population (Thorp and Paredes 2010). Elected positions in the cooperatives were confined to those who could read and write Spanish, and many of the indigenous population felt that control over them had passed from the landlords to the state. Young militants initiated a Revolutionary Vanguard party, and the Peasants Confederation (*Confederación Campesina del Perú*) became more radical and membership greatly expanded (Thorp and Paredes 2010). *Sendero Luminoso*, the Shining Path movement, began its recruitment among poor peasants during that decade.

Democracy was restored in 1980. Fernando Belaúnde, who had been president in the 1960s, was returned to power, followed by Alan Garcia in 1985. Yet '[i]ronically, the return to democracy coincided with the eruption of political violence' (Thorp and Paredes 2010, 148). Violence, instigated by the Shining Path and provoking strong government reactions, intensified throughout the 1980s and accounted for around 70,000 deaths, the majority indigenous. The economy continued to decline, with high debt, worsening terms of trade, escalating inflation, and the effects of the 1982–3 El Niño. Neither the orthodox, IMF-supported policies of Belaúnde, nor the more unorthodox policies of Garcia, were effective, and growth declined and poverty rose sharply throughout the decade (Stewart 1995, 180). However, there was some improvement in income distribution over the 1980s. The political and economic context explains the below average economic performance of Peru in the 1980s, but it is difficult to understand how the country moved into an HD-lopsided category in this decade. While education and health expenditure rose as a proportion of government expenditure, the share of government expenditure in GDP fell sharply, so that per capita expenditures on health and education also appear to have fallen significantly (Stewart 1995, 184). Nonetheless, there was a steady improvement in secondary enrolment from the 1970s (primary enrolment was already virtually comprehensive), agricultural production recovered, and immunization rates rose impressively from 16 per cent in 1980 to 72 per cent in 1990.

The 1990s were years of post-conflict recovery. Alberto Fujimori changed policies radically after he came into power in 1990: he brought the Shining Path rebellion to an end following the capture of the leaders in 1992, and he introduced neoliberal policies with 'shock therapy', cutting the budget deficit and reversing the previous interventionist policies by abolishing price controls, liberalizing trade, and privatizing assets. '[T]he Fujimori government also carried out a "pacification" strategy that combined intelligence-based counter-insurgency with the expansion of the reach of state services in rural areas.... Roads, schools, clinics, sewerage systems, electrification schemes and small-scale irrigation works were built across the country' (Orihuela 2012, 196). A social fund, the Social Development and Compensation Fund (FONCODES) Project, was introduced to provide a safety net for the poor, with over 40,000 rural development projects. There were major improvements in the provision of clean water, sanitation facilities, and electricity (Orihuela 2012). Economic growth recovered (see Figure 5.8), and poverty and malnutrition declined.

In 2001, Fujimori—accused of being dictatorial and repressive—was replaced by Alejandro Toledo, the first indigenous president. He continued with the liberalization policies, under the auspices of the IMF, privatizing assets, encouraging foreign investment, and introducing a number of bilateral

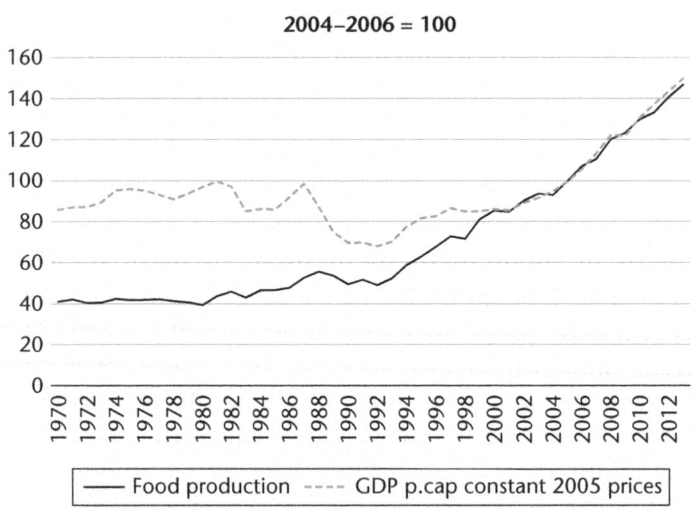

Figure 5.8. Peru: GDP per capita and food production indices, 1970–2012
Source: World Bank (n.d.)

trade agreements. He also improved the position of indigenous Peruvians, supporting bilingual education, promoting indigenous organizations, and adopting a decentralization initiative covering health, education, food, and social development programmes. Decision-making (but less so resources) was transferred to democratically elected regional and municipal governments, with a requirement that 15 per cent of candidates should have an indigenous background. A set of social programmes aimed to improve the position of the poor, including extending the existing safety nets so that over a third of the population were covered by 2004, and access to healthcare in remote regions was improved (St John 2010). Garcia succeeded Toledo and broadly continued the Toledo policies of combining market liberalization with the expansion of social programmes.

The 2000s were years of rapid economic growth in Peru: for the decade average annual growth in per capita incomes was 3.7 per cent, more than double that of the preceding decade. This was partly due to the policy changes, but also to a sustained improvement in the terms of trade which rose by more than 50 per cent over the decade. Investment, which had fallen sharply in the 1980s, recovered in the two subsequent decades, reaching 25 per cent of GDP in 2010 (much the same as it was in 1980). There was also a fall in inequality: while the Gini coefficient was over 0.5 in the 1990s, by 2010 it was 0.45. Consequently, poverty fell substantially. The headcount ratio, which had risen in the 1980s and been broadly constant in the 1990s, fell from 30 per cent in 2000 (US$3.90 a day) to 13 per cent in 2010. The MPI headcount almost halved, falling from 19.5 per cent in 2005 to 10.5 per cent in 2012. The increase in per capita incomes was reflected in expanded education and health budgets, with the proportion of GDP devoted to these sectors remaining broadly constant for education and rising in the case of health. There was an expansion in secondary enrolment which reached over 90 per cent by 2010, and expenditure per primary and secondary student increased; health expenditure per head rose rapidly.

In sum, the virtuous category for Peru in the 1990s was due to two types of recovery: recovery from conflict and from economic mismanagement, combined with policies designed to improve the conditions of the rural poor. The virtuous category in the 2000s was due to success in sustaining and accelerating economic growth, while income distribution improved, and there was continued expansion of social expenditures.

5.2. Common Features of Transitional Success

The countries reviewed here all started in the 'vicious' category (apart from Thailand) and this, in some ways, made it easier for them to achieve large improvements as the starting point was so poor. All apart from Bolivia and Thailand had experienced civil war, which had undermined growth and HD. A further contributory factor to the 'vicious' categorization was economic mismanagement and drastic stabilization programmes. Ending civil wars and reversing the worst aspects of the adverse economic policies provided a platform for progress on both economic growth and HD. In a number of cases, generous aid flows supported the recovery—notably in the two African cases as well as in Bangladesh and Nepal. Moreover, there was an explicit attempt to reach the marginalized population with social programmes as part of reconciliation and to prevent conflict recurrence. This was especially apparent in the cases of Peru and Nepal.

The examples of these countries show, like the findings in Chapter 4, that differing combinations of growth, income distribution, and social expenditures can advance basic HD. Bangladesh is an interesting case of egalitarian distribution with quite low social expenditures. In contrast, Bolivia started with low social expenditures, but these rose to quite high levels; it also initially had high inequality which fell somewhat in the 2000s. Thailand too had relatively low social expenditures and quite high inequality (though improving), but it sustained an exceptionally high rate of growth over four decades. These findings do no more than repeat what we found in Chapter 4. What is much more interesting is the differing agents and institutions behind the improvements.

As before, there is no automatic connection between political freedoms and performance. Ethiopia, for example, does very well, despite being classified as 'unfree', while Thailand did not sustain democracy, experiencing periodic interventions by the military. Mozambique is democratic, although the fairness of its elections has been questioned; Peru made huge progress under Fujimori, who was democratically elected yet also autocratic. From a political freedom perspective, this is a mixed bag. Democratic or not, in every case the leaders of the countries do seem committed to advancing the well-being of the population. In both Bolivia and Peru, the first presidents to be of indigenous origin aimed (not always successfully) to reverse centuries of discrimination. In Bangladesh, the early post-war governments were determined to reverse the discrimination against the population as a whole exercised by West Pakistan. In Thailand, Thaksin's TRT was committed to reaching the poor rural population.

Different institutions and actors made contributions to promoting HD in the various countries. Decentralization helped advance HD in Bolivia, Mozambique, and Ethiopia by orienting expenditures towards popular priorities. In Bangladesh, large local NGOs were important in providing services (especially education and micro-finance). Extensive community organizations (SMCs) played a role in Nepal, while the Four Regional Slum Network was important in advocating for social policies to benefit the poor in Thailand.

Also in Thailand, progressive bureaucrats played a critical role in advancing universal healthcare. For Thailand, it was the combination of these strong advocates with a progressive government looking for innovative social policies which was responsible for success in HD.

The nature of the private sector was also relevant to advancing HD. In Bangladesh, small and medium-sized enterprises in the textile industry provide employment for young women, which both empowered them and enabled them to send remittances to their families which helped to reduce poverty. In both Mozambique and Ethiopia increased growth of agriculture was based on small farm producers, and thus spread the benefits of growth. In contrast, in Peru growth was concentrated in the south of the country and hardly touched the remote rural areas where many of the poor indigenous population were located (Thorp and Paredes 2010, Orihuela 2012).

In summary, the stories of successful transitions point to pluralistic conclusions: there is no single magic recipe for success in either economic conditions and decisions, or in political structures. Politically, a determination to advance the well-being of the population does seem to be a necessary condition, but this can be motivated in a variety of ways: through left-wing ideology, identification with particular deprived groups, a desire to advance conflict-prevention, or the need to secure popular support for re-election. Economically, avoiding catastrophic mismanagement, leading to massive budget deficit and accelerating inflation, or (conversely) excessive cutbacks such as those of the 1980s, seems to be a necessary condition. Improving terms of trade also helped each of these countries in the 2000s, while the adverse terms of trade of previous decades was definitely a severe handicap. These findings are broadly confirmed when we explore the experience of the negative transitions.

5.3. Negative Transitions

In the case of the positive transitions, the aim is to find out what might be replicated elsewhere to promote HD, while the lessons from negative transitions are, in contrast, what not to do. In all the negative transition countries, there was very poor economic performance in the 1980s (see Figure 5.9). This was partly accounted for by the world recession at the beginning of the decade, worsening terms of trade, the accumulation of debt, and the stabilization policies followed during that decade. For Algeria, Iraq, and Ecuador, the 1970s was a decade of expansion, based on import-substitution policies and financed by accumulating debt. This supported expansion of the social sectors and good HD performance. Poor growth continued in the 1990s for many of the countries but for different reasons. In Algeria, there was an insurgency by the Islamic Salvation Front, a temporary military takeover of the government,

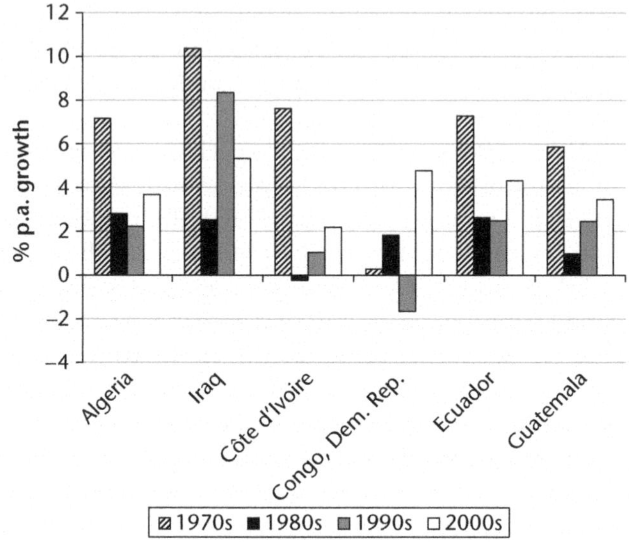

Figure 5.9. Average annual % growth in GDP, weak performers, 1970s–2000s
Source: World Bank (n.d.)

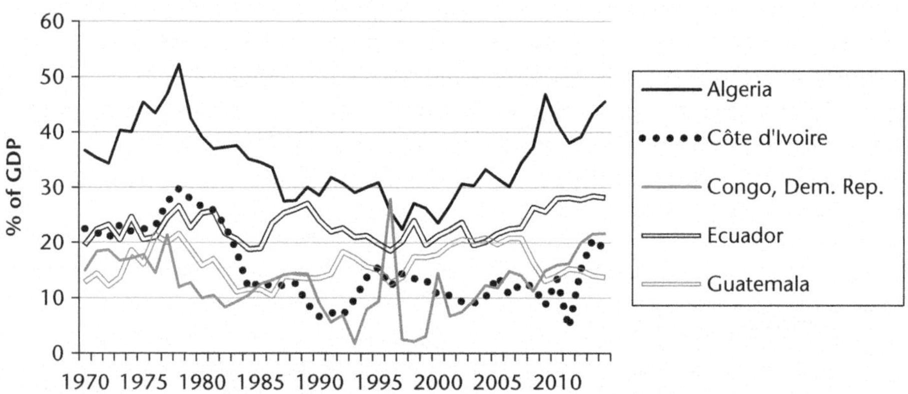

Figure 5.10. Gross capital formation as % of GDP, weak performers, 1970–2013
Source: World Bank (n.d.)

and a state of emergency that lasted through the 2000s—years that were punctuated by suicide bombings. In the 1980s, continuing into the 1990s, Ecuador, Guatemala, and Côte d'Ivoire were suffering from debt burdens and deflationary adjustments. Growth did recover in the Latin American cases in 2000s, but not as much as elsewhere, possibly due to the falling rate of investment experienced in the previous decades (see Figure 5.10)—hence their relatively poor economic performance. Iraq's growth fell dramatically in the 2000s, due to the invasion by the US and coalition forces, while Côte d'Ivoire's growth became negative as a result of the civil war in the early 2000s but recovered after. The Democratic Republic of the Congo was subject to endemic conflict over the decades, accounting for its persistently weak performance. Political turbulence was also evident, for example, in Ecuador where there were four presidents in five years at the end of the 1990s.

Both Ecuador and Guatemala had notably high inequality (Gini 0.5 or more), but with some improvement in the 2000s. Inequality was not remarkably high in the other negative transition countries. As shown in Chapter 4, Ecuador and Guatemala, along with the Democratic Republic of the Congo, spent relatively little on education. Poverty was exceptionally high in the Democratic Republic of the Congo (over 80 per cent in the 2000s), but not so elsewhere. Indeed, there was a big decline in poverty in Guatemala from the 1990s and a modest decline in Ecuador, while the poverty rate rose in Côte d'Ivoire.

In sum, the negative transition countries were blown off course by a combination of economic adversities associated with the debt crisis and worsening terms of trade, and/or by conflict in their territories. Another factor was mismanagement—illustrated notably by Democratic Republic of the Congo and also in the case of Zimbabwe (not explored here). Unlike the positive transition countries, these countries lacked the ideology and agency to overcome these adversities by using developmental policies as exemplified in the positive cases.

5.4. Conclusion

This chapter has explored the processes underlying positive transitions. Countries adopted different approaches, some relying primarily on state programmes (sometimes associated with decentralization of governmental activities), others on NGOs and communities. In some countries, the private sector spread the benefits of growth across the population; in some countries and phases, aid was hugely important, while in others foreign direct investment played more of a role. Nor was there uniformity of political conditions, with some autocratic and some more democratic states; but for all the positive transition cases, the improvement in the condition of the mass of the population remained a major objective of governmental policies, albeit for different reasons.

The negative transition cases suffered from economic setbacks due to external or political developments, and were unable to overcome these effectively. Furthermore, in these cases the extensive presence of dynamic agents—among NGOs, bureaucrats, communities, or the private sector—that we find in the positive cases appears to have been lacking. Moreover, during the decades when performance deteriorated, the countries' leadership changed quite frequently, so that short-run objectives tended to prevail over longer-term developmental ones.

The role of social institutions (including NGOs) and political factors (including social movements) was clearly important in accounting for both success and failure. These are explored further in Chapters 7 and 8.

6

Human Development

Beyond the HDI

6.1. Introduction

HD goes well beyond the HDI, with which it is often equated, as we argued in Chapter 1.[1] As noted there, the first *Human Development Report* defined HD as 'a process of enlarging people's choices. The most critical ones are to lead a long and healthy life, to be educated, and to enjoy a decent standard of living. Additional choices include political freedom, guaranteed human rights and self-respect' (UNDP 1990, 10). The HDI itself is thus a reductionist measure, incorporating just a subset of possible human choices. In fact, the measure, which includes life expectancy, literacy, years of education, and a modified measure of income, is directed at the choices referred to as 'most critical' in the first report.

It has long been recognized that the HDI is, therefore, a very incomplete measure of HD, leaving out many aspects of life which are of fundamental importance. The aim of this chapter is to identify a wider set of measures regarding the choices which might qualify as part of HD, and to analyse how well or how poorly the more extensive list of choices is in practice represented by the HDI, using international cross-country data.

Our first task is to identify which aspects of life might reasonably qualify as part of HD. To do this we survey a few of the many attempts that have been made to define the full life; although these generally have different philosophical underpinnings, they are in broad agreement about the main

[1] This chapter draws on material from Ranis et al. (2006). We are grateful to the UNDP for permission to use the material here.

dimensions to be included. In light of this, we have drawn up a list of the categories of life we feel are good candidates to be included as part of HD. Having identified the main categories we wish to include as dimensions of HD, we then try to identify indicators of performance in each of the categories, bearing in mind both measurability and data availability. For each category we then explore the relationships among the indicators, aiming to identify a limited number of indicators to represent each category. We then show how far these measures correlate across countries with the widely accepted measures of progress, including the HDI, income per capita (PPP), and under-five mortality. This enables us to see whether extending our measures of HD beyond the HDI so as to incorporate a broader concept of HD requires a wider set of indicators to represent country performance than the HDI, or indeed per capita income. Insofar as it does, this should permit improved measurement of progress, analysis, and policy choices.

We should note that, as with most attempts to assess HD (or indeed Sen's capabilities approach, with which it is closely connected, see Sen 1999a), we can only observe actual achievements rather than the range of *ex ante* choices available. The actual set of achievements on any variable, of course, indicates that it is a member of the set of possible choices, but the range of choices presumably goes far beyond actual performance, as options *not* chosen are not included.

6.2. Defining the 'Full Life', or a Broad Definition of HD

Defining what makes for a fulfilled life has been a central theme of philosophers and politicians throughout history. Aristotle's *Ethics*, for example, was devoted to identifying the conditions needed to achieve *eudaimonia*, commonly interpreted as 'the best life' (Bostock 2000, 15).

Alkire (2002) lists thirty-nine attempts to identify what makes for a flourishing life, produced over the years 1938–2000. Here we will consider seven (see Table 6.1),[2] each of which adopts a different philosophical approach and justification:

1. Rawls identifies primary goods through 'deliberative rationality'. According to *A Theory of Justice*, primary goods 'are in general necessary for the framing and execution of a rational plan of life ... following full deliberative rationality, that is, with careful consideration of the relevant facts and

[2] Five of these are contained in Alkire (2002); the sixth and seventh were produced subsequently.

Table 6.1. Requirements for human flourishing

Authors	Rawls (1999 [1972])	Finnis et al. (1987)	Doyal and Gough (1991)	Nussbaum (2000)	Narayan-Parker et al. (2000)	Camfield (2006)	Burchardt and Vizard (2011)
Defining concepts	Primary goods	Basic human values	**Basic needs** and intermediate needs[a]	Central human functional capabilities	Dimensions of well-being	Quality of life	'Internationally agreed HR'
Bodily well-being		Bodily life: health, vigour, and safety	**Physical health** Nutrition: food and water Healthcare Safe birth control and child bearing Safe physical environment	Life Bodily health Bodily integrity	Bodily well-being Access to health services Good physical environment		Life Health
Material well-being	Income and wealth		Protective housing Economic security		Material well-being Food Assets	Food Shelter	Standard of living
Mental development		Knowledge Practical reasonableness	Basic education	Senses Imagination Thought Emotions Practical reason Play		Education (Bangladesh and Ethiopia, not Thailand or Peru)	Education and learning
Work	Freedom of occupation	Skilful performance in work and play	Work		Work		Productive and valued activities
Security			Physical security		Civil peace Physically safe environment Lawfulness (access to justice) Personal physical security Security in old age		Physical security Legal security

(*continued*)

Table 6.1. Continued

Authors	Rawls (1999 [1972])	Finnis et al. (1987)	Doyal and Gough (1991)	Nussbaum (2000)	Narayan-Parker et al. (2000)	Camfield (2006)	Burchardt and Vizard (2011)
Social relations	Social bases of self-respect	Friendship	Significant primary relationships	Affiliation Social bases for self-respect	Social well-being Family Self-respect and dignity Community relations	Family	Individual, family, and social life Identity, expression self-respect
Spiritual well-being		Self-integration Harmony with ultimate source of reality				Religion (important in Bangladesh and Thailand)	
Empowerment and political freedom	Rights, liberties, opportunities Powers and prerogatives of office and positions of responsibility Freedom of movement		Autonomy of agency Civil and political rights Political participation	Control over one's environment	Freedom of choice and action		Participation, influence, voice
Respect for other species				Other species			

Notes: [a] Intermediate needs are instrumental for the achievement of basic needs; basic needs are in bold and intermediate are in normal type.

Source: Derived from Alkire (2002), Doyal and Gough (1991), Narayan-Parker et al. (2000), Camfield (2005).

after a careful consideration of the consequences' (Rawls 1999 [1972], 359 and 380). They are derived from 'some general facts about human wants and abilities' and the necessities of social interdependence.[3]

2. Finnis' approach is derived from practical reasoning (Finnis 1980, Finnis et al. 1987), which has a lot in common with 'deliberative rationality', as it is derived from imagination and experiences (Nussbaum 2000, 39; also see Finnis et al. 1987, table 3.2, 110–11).
3. Doyal and Gough's definition of basic needs is based on the principle of the avoidance of serious harm, where harm is defined as preventing people realizing activities which are essential to their plan of life (Miller 1976, Doyal and Gough 1991).
4. Nussbaum's list is developed on the basis of what is termed 'overlapping consensus' (a concept developed by Rawls (1993) as a basis for justice in a plural society) plus intuition as to what is needed to be 'truly human' (Nussbaum 2000).[4] An overlapping consensus is an informed view of what people agree about, even if they have different overall philosophies or religions.
5. The analyses by Narayan-Parker and others (Narayan-Parker et al. 2000) in the *Crying Out for Change: Voices of the Poor*, derived from thousands of interviews and focus groups with poor people throughout the developing world, purport to represent what the poor themselves identify as their needs.
6. A similar exercise was conducted by the ESRC Research Group Wellbeing in Developing Countries (Camfield 2006), in which people in four countries were consulted as to what makes for a good quality of life.
7. Burchardt and Vizard (2011) developed ten domains to encapsulate the major dimensions of a capability approach, derived partly from International HR agreements and partly from consultative exercises.

Broadly, the approaches can be classified into two types: some aim to identify the *constitutive elements* of a good or flourishing life (Aristotle and Finnis), while others are concerned primarily with the *necessary requirements* of such a

[3] Rawls adds 'the Aristotelian principle' which, roughly interpreted, is that more complex and sophisticated activities are generally preferred, and hence more desirable, than simpler ones. For example, according to Rawls (1971) algebra would be preferred to arithmetic and chess to checkers (draughts) because they are more complex activities.

[4] By 'overlapping consensus', we take John Rawls' meaning as interpreted by Nussbaum, that 'people may sign on to this conception, without accepting any particular metaphysical view of the world, and particular comprehensive ethical or religious view, or even any particular view of the person or human nature'. However, Nussbaum argues that the 'primary weight of justification remains with the intuitive conception of truly human functioning and what that entails' (Nussbaum 2000, 76).

life (e.g. Doyal and Gough and Rawls on primary goods).[5] This is one reason why the seven sets of requirements for human flourishing are not in total agreement—those looking at the constitutive requirements of a good life place less emphasis on material aspects, while those exploring the necessary requirements for such a life tend to emphasize the material aspects. For example, Finnis et al. and Nussbaum are quite thin on material aspects, but emphasize non-material aspects such as friendship and emotions, which are omitted by Doyal and Gough, and get short shrift from Narayan-Parker et al. (2000). Environmental issues appear explicitly in Nussbaum, and are only discussed briefly by others. Nussbaum is the only author to record 'respect for other species' as a significant dimension.

It is not our aim here to select among these lists (or characteristics) but rather to identify a comprehensive view of the dimensions of HD. People and societies may or may not choose to promote all the aspects identified, and we do not wish to make the choices for them. Hence, as a starting point, the relevant set of dimensions is the set which includes all the elements that have been identified as possible aspects of human flourishing. The aim, then, is to try to measure country achievements on these manifold dimensions. There are obvious problems with such measurement, including identifying what a good indicator of each dimension would ideally be, and then finding what (normally imperfect) measures are available in practice. Such measures are likely to vary across societies. To make the measurement issue easier, we first draw up a comprehensive set of broad dimensions to use as a starting point to search for indicators of achievement. For example, we identify 'community well-being' as an important dimension of HD; then, as indicators of this elusive concept, we include measures of 'crime rate', 'alcohol use', 'corruption', 'orphan rate', 'AIDS deaths', '% in civic associations', 'trust in others', 'rule of law', 'confidence in public institutions', 'tolerance of neighbours', and 'natural disaster rates' .

It is useful to start with the broad dimensions (shown in Table 6.1), first, because objectives of HD are generally thought of in this way. Second, while there may be agreement on these broad categories, there is not necessarily the same agreement on selection of elements and indicators of the broad dimensions. For example, we may agree that political freedom and political participation are important dimensions of HD, but this does not imply a precise form of government and constitution. Third, the best ways of achieving progress in broad dimensions may vary across countries according, for example, to the level of development or geography, and consequently appropriate indicators of achievements may vary. Fourth, partly because of this, data availability varies across countries, i.e. each country may have data on some indicators relevant to any single broad category, but not consistent data across others.

[5] We are grateful to M. Qizilbach for making this point.

In the light of the efforts to identify dimensions of human flourishing just cited, we propose the following broad dimensions of HD:

1. The HDI itself. This, of course, is itself a multidimensional indicator which includes health, education, and a measure of income (i.e. it broadly covers bodily health, literacy, and basic aspects of material well-being). We include it as a single measure because it is the generally accepted measure of achievement on HD. This is what we define in this book as 'basic HD'.
2. Mental well-being (i.e. an individual's psychological state).
3. Empowerment.
4. Political freedom.
5. Social relations.
6. Community well-being.
7. Inequalities.
8. Work conditions.
9. Leisure conditions.
10. Political security (i.e. freedom from political violence or instability).
11. Economic security (i.e. freedom from economic fluctuations).
12. Environmental conditions.

In contrast to the lists in Table 6.1, we have not included spiritual well-being here, given problems of definition and measurement, nor have we included respect for other species, though we do consider environmental sustainability. On the other hand, we have separated social relations from community well-being. The former is a matter of people individually having satisfactory relations with others, including such indicators as divorce rates, the importance of family and friends, and tolerance for different types of neighbours. The latter, in contrast, is a function of the well-being of a community as a whole and includes such elements as low crime rates and a thriving civil society. We have also separated empowerment from political freedom, as the former relates to the power (or lack of it) of the relatively disempowered, such as poor people, women, and other groups with little power, while the latter relates to liberal political conditions more generally. We have added inequalities as a general category, which in principle should measure inequalities in the other categories. We do this because the existence of various inequalities independently affects people's well-being, especially that of the poor. An alternative approach would be to weight each dimension according to how it is distributed, but this would be highly complex and would also conceal the independent contributions of levels of achievement and distribution. We have two conditions to represent security, or the absence of risks: one encompasses political security (or freedom from risk of political violence), and the other encompasses economic security (or freedom from risk of loss of livelihood through various vicissitudes).

Any list of dimensions is inevitably both subjective and ethnocentric. This is illustrated by the differences across countries and generations which the ESRC Research Group Wellbeing in Developing Countries found in how people define the quality of life (Camfield 2005). Hence, anyone finding this type of approach helpful should be able to amend the categorization to reflect different views. This applies especially across different cultures.

6.3. Selection of Indicators and Procedures for Their Use

Ideally, there would appear to be many potential elements and indicators for each of the broad dimensions identified in Section 6.2. In practice, however, there are difficulties. In the first place, some of the categories of HD are in principle difficult to measure (for example, mental well-being). Second, some of the available data are based on surveys of performance and some on perceptions of observers, with the latter involving an obvious element of subjectivity. Third, data are often lacking, or seriously incomplete, covering only a small sample of countries. Fourth, some indices are themselves constructed out of a variety of elements and sources in ways that might be subject to challenge. Thus we are aware of the many limitations and pitfalls of data in this field. What we have done is to collect whatever we could find; hence our choice of indicators is to a certain extent dictated by data availability. Additional efforts to improve data are clearly warranted.

Table 6.2 presents our initial set of dimensions and proposed elements/indicators of these dimensions. We should note that some of the indicators represent achievements on the chosen category, while others represent failure (e.g. with respect to mental well-being, life satisfaction is a measure of achievement and suicide a measure of failure)—and the data of course need to be interpreted accordingly.

Our basic purpose is to identify a set of indicators which broadly represent the more all-encompassing version of HD, covering the categories identified in Section 6.2. For this, we need to know how far existing core indicators already achieve this. We shall, therefore, correlate representative indicators of each category with what we call the three core indicators. These core indicators are those commonly used to assess country performance: HDI, per capita income, and under-five mortality rates. The HDI, as noted, represents a reductionist approach to measuring HD, incorporating basic aspects of health, education, and material well-being. Income per capita is, of course, the most common way of assessing overall country performance, used in particular by the World Bank. We have also chosen under-five mortality because it is often used as a

Table 6.2. Dimensions and indicators

Mental well-being	Empowerment	Political freedom	Social relations	Community well-being	Inequality	Work conditions	Leisure conditions	Economic stability	Political security	Environmental conditions
Male suicide rate	Poverty rates: • international income poverty[a] • national income poverty • HPI	Political and civil liberties	Friends very important	Crime rate	Income Gini	Unemployment	Telephone availability	GDP cycle	Political stability	Environmental sustainability index
Female suicide rate	GEM	Freedom of worship	Family very important	Alcohol use	HI	Employment conditions	Internet use	CPI fluctuations	Refugee flows	
Life satisfaction	Female/male secondary education enrolment	Political terror index	Tolerance of neighbours	Corruption	Rural–urban inequality	Informal employment	Radio use	Manufactured/ total exports	Collective violence	
Prisoners per population	Unmet need for contraceptives	Political freedom	Crude divorce rate	Orphan rate	GDI	Child labour	Cinema attendance	Foreign portfolio investment/ GDP	Political violence	
	Married girls, aged 15–19	Freedom of the press		AIDS deaths	Happiness inequality	Minimum wage policy	Newspaper circulation	Terms of trade fluctuations		
	Ratio of females in parliament	Juridical independence		% in civic associations	Health inequality		TV ownership	Social security coverage		
	Union density			Trust in others						
				Rule of law						
				Public institutions						
				Population affected by natural disasters						
				Tolerance of neighbours						

Notes: [a] For the years we did this exercise, the international poverty rate was US$1 a day (PPP).

Source: See Table B.6.1 (Appendix B) for full details of the sources of data.

proxy for the non-income part of basic HD. We use all three indicators in spite of the fact that they are highly correlated with each other, because we wish to investigate whether different core indicators are better or worse at representing the other categories of HD.

In exploring each dimension we have two objectives. First, to explore the relationships among the variables within each set, which we will do by calculating rank order correlations among them across developing country performance for the same time period. Second, we aim to identify variables that would be appropriate to represent each dimension as a whole so that we can explore how the dimensions relate to HDI and the two other core measures of country performance. However, where variables in a particular category are not highly correlated with each other, we choose more than one variable to represent the category.

We decided on a number of rules of procedure. When the sample size for an indicator is twenty-five or less, we do not select that variable as one of the indicators representing the category. We define the rank order correlation as being 'very high' when the correlation coefficient is above 0.8; 'high' when the correlation coefficient is 0.6 and over, and below 0.8; 'moderate' when it is 0.3 and over, and below 0.6; and low when it is below 0.3. In determining which variables represent others because of high intercorrelation, we take 0.6 and above as our requirement. Only significant correlations (at the 5 per cent level) are counted and all statements about correlations refer only to significant ones.

To select which of two or more variables that are correlated at the required level is chosen to represent the category, we first consider which variable 'carries' (i.e. is correlated with, at the required rate) most other variables. When they are equal, we consider which shows the greater level of correlation with the other variables.

An alternative procedure would have been to adopt principal components analysis. A disadvantage of this method is that one is left with mechanically generated composite indicators, which can obscure the variable of interest while the weights that are used are not immediately transparent.

6.4. Correlations Within the Dimensions

Adopting the procedures outlined in Section 6.3, we get the following results.

6.4.1. *Mental Well-Being*

Our mental well-being indicators (see Table 6.3) cover measures of unhappiness, as shown by suicide, lack of adjustment to society as shown by the prison

Table 6.3. Mental well-being indicators

	Male suicide	Female suicide	Life satisfaction	Prisoners
Male suicide	1			
	44			
Female suicide	0.8632*			
	0			
	44	46		
Life satisfaction	−0.0403	−0.0228	1	
	0.874	0.926		
	18	19	30	
Prisoners	0.2588	0.0536	0.2881	1
	0.0898	0.7235	0.1226	
	44	46	30	124

Notes: The first row is the correlation measure, the second shows the significance level (* = all observations that are significant at the 95 per cent level), and the third row shows the number of observations available for each calculation. Indicators retained to represent the category are shaded.

Source: See Table B.6.1 in the Appendix.

population, and life satisfaction. Of the indicators available, male and female suicide are highly correlated, and neither is correlated with the other variables—i.e. a measure of life satisfaction, unhappiness, and prisoners per population. It is therefore not particularly important which we select, but we choose the male suicide rate because, in most countries, it is larger than the female rate. The other variables—life satisfaction and prisoners—are not significantly related to each other.

We therefore select life satisfaction, prisoner population, and male suicide as independent indicators of mental well-being.

6.4.2. *Empowerment*

Empowerment and political freedom are clearly related. However, our interpretation of 'empowerment' concerns the power of weak groups in society to have some autonomy and control over their lives, while political freedom relates primarily to formal political liberties and is treated separately. Our empowerment indicators include various measures of poverty and of the status of women, as well as a measure of unionization (see Table 6.4).

The international poverty rate is highly correlated with national poverty rates, the Human Poverty Index (HPI), and the share of girls aged 15–19 years who are married, while the other poverty indices are highly correlated with fewer variables within the category. Therefore, following our procedures, we adopt the international poverty rate as an indicator for this dimension.

The UNDP's GEM is highly correlated with the proportion of female parliamentarians. We choose GEM because it represents a wider range of female

Table 6.4. Empowerment indicators

	Poverty1day	PovNational	HPI	GEM	FemSecMale	ContraceptiveLack	MarriedGirls	FemParliamnt	UnionDensity
International poverty rate	1								
	70								
National poverty rate	0.7271*	1							
	0								
HPI	0.7350*	0.5392*	1						
	0	0							
	66	66	94						
GEM	−0.0537	−0.1712	−0.5318*	1					
	0.7742	0.4133	0.0014						
	31	5	33	40					
Female/Male secondary enrolment	−0.4073*	−0.3535*	−0.5831*	0.2623	1				
	0.003	0.0101	0	0.1403					
	51	52	68	33	92				
ContraceptiveLack	−0.5883*	−0.3245*	−0.7539*	−0.0647	0.5799*	1			
	0	0.0156	0	0.7864	0				
	52	55	64	20	53	79			
MarriedGirls 15–19 years	0.6264*	0.5937*	0.5498*	−0.3393*	−0.5017*	−0.5033*	1		
	0	0	0	0.0322	0	0			
	70	68	86	40	83	68	112		
FemParliamnt as prop. of total	−0.0073	−0.0436	−0.1283	0.8685*	0.1957	0.0815	−0.1051	1	
	0.9519	0.7202	0.228	0	0.0692	0.4838	0.2882		
	70	70	90	40	87	76	104	127	
UnionDensity	−0.0453	−0.145	0.0015	0	0.2097	0.076	−0.2508	0.1016	1
	0.8023	0.4616	0.9936	1	0.3253	0.7368	0.1462	0.5615	
	33	28	32	19	24	22	35	35	36

Notes: The first row is the correlation measure, the second shows the significance level (* = all observations that are significant at the 95 per cent level), and the third row shows the number of observations available for each calculation. Indicators retained to represent the category are shaded.

Source: See Table B.6.1 in the Appendix.

empowerment. The ratio of female to male secondary education is not highly correlated with any other variable, though it is moderately (negatively) correlated with the poverty measures and the rate of teenage marriage, and (positively) with the unmet need for contraceptives. The rate of union density is not correlated with any of the other variables, while unmet need for contraceptives is not highly correlated with other variables in the category.

Consequently, we choose the international poverty rate, GEM, the ratio of female/male secondary education, the unmet need for contraceptives, and union density as representing the empowerment category.

6.4.3. *Political Freedom*

As indicators for political freedom (see Table 6.5) we have chosen two composite indicators, 'political rights and civil liberties', produced by Freedom House, and 'political freedom', prepared by the World Bank, as well as distinct indicators of political terror (Amnesty International), freedom of worship (Freedom House), and free press and juridical independence (World Economic Forum). Both 'political and civil liberties' and 'political freedom' are highly correlated with each other, and with free worship and freedom of the press, and can

Table 6.5. Political freedom indicators

	PolrtCivlib	FreeWorship	PolTerror	PolFreedom	FreePress	JuridIndp
PolrtCivlib	1					
	137					
Freeworship	0.7951*	1				
	0					
	39	39				
PolTerror	0.3420*	0.1728	1			
	0.0002	0.2996				
	111	38	111			
PolFreedom	−0.9351*	−0.7942*	−0.4492*	1		
	0	0	0			
	136	39	111	136		
FreePress	0.7526*	0.5551*	0.251	−0.6894*	1	
	0	0.0027	0.0621	0		
	61	27	56	61	61	
JuridIndp	0.2096	0.3264	0.3106*	−0.4378*	0.1856	1
	0.1049	0.0966	0.0198	0.0004	0.1522	
	61	27	56	61	61	61

Notes: The first row is the correlation measure, the second shows the significance level (* = all observations that are significant at the 95 per cent level), and the third row shows the number of observations available for each calculation. Indicators retained to represent the category are shaded.

Source: See Table B.6.1 in the Appendix.

therefore be used to represent them. There is not much to choose between these measures, but we select 'political and civil liberties' as its correlation with free press is a little higher. Political terror and juridical independence are not highly correlated with any other variables and we select them as well.

6.4.4. *Social Relations*

This is an area where information is particularly scarce and available samples are small. We have indicators for values placed on friends and family, tolerance for different types of neighbours,[6] as well as the divorce rate (see Table 6.6). The crude divorce rate is moderately (negatively) correlated with the importance of families, but there are no high correlations among the variables. We therefore retain all four variables—the value placed on families, value placed on friends, tolerance of neighbours, and the divorce rate—to represent this category.

6.4.5. *Community Well-Being*

We have a wide variety of potential indicators here (see Table 6.7). However, there are only small samples for trust in others, the crime rate, and the share of the population involved in civic work, and, therefore, we drop them.

Table 6.6. Social relations indicators

	FriendsVeryImpt	FamilyVImpt	NgbTol	CrudeDivorce
FriendsVeryImpt	1			
	75			
FamilyVimpt	0.3563*	1		
	0.0017			
	75	75		
NgbTol	−0.0388	0.1856	1	
	0.7464	0.1185		
	72	72	73	
CrudeDivorce	−0.1367	−0.3792*	−0.2633	1
	0.3489	0.0072	0.0771	
	49	49	46	68

Notes: The first row is the correlation measure, the second shows the significance level (* = all observations that are significant at the 95 per cent level), and the third row shows the number of observations available for each calculation. Indicators retained to represent the category are shaded.

Source: See Table B.6.1 in the Appendix.

[6] Tolerance for different kinds of neighbours seemed to us to be a feature both of social relations and of community well-being, so we included the indicator in both categories.

Table 6.7. Community well-being indicators

	Crime	Alcohol	Corruption	Orphans	AIDS	CivicWork	Trust	RuleofLaw	PublicInst	NatDisaster	NgbTol
Crime	1										
	17										
Alcohol	0.4893*	1									
	0.0462										
	17	128									
Corruption	0.0847	0.2089*	1								
	0.7466	0.0469									
	17	91	93								
Orphans	−0.1121	−0.04	−0.4405*	1							
	0.6907	0.7047	0.0001								
	15	92	70	93							
AIDS	0.1149	0.0974	−0.4777*	0.7162*	1						
	0.6718	0.3532	0	0							
	16	93	77	84	94						
CivicWork	0.2857	0.5242	0.1956	0.1242	−0.1736	1					
	0.5345	0.0543	0.5028	0.7006	0.5707						
	7	14	14	12	13	14					
Trust	−0.4	−0.4856*	−0.2464	0.2721	−0.0904	−0.2187	1				
	0.2861	0.0139	0.2351	0.2458	0.6967	0.5183					
	9	25	25	20	21	11	25				
RuleofLaw	−0.1495	0.1223	0.8879*	−0.4519*	−0.4707*	0.0396	−0.0131	1			
	0.5668	0.1691	0	0	0	0.893	0.9505				
	17	128	93	93	94	14	25	134			
PublicInst	0.05	0.1585	0.8866*	−0.1665	−0.3060*	0.1963	−0.0805	0.8229*	1		
	0.8541	0.2265	0	0.2528	0.0244	0.5013	0.7086	0			
	16	60	61	49	54	14	24	61	61		

(*continued*)

Table 6.7. Continued

	Crime	Alcohol	Corruption	Orphans	AIDS	CivicWork	Trust	RuleofLaw	PublicInst	NatDisaster	NgbTol
NatDisaster	−0.1054	0.0117	−0.2887*	0.1217	0.1899	−0.0485	0.2936	−0.1526	−0.4470*	1	
	0.6873	0.8958	0.0052	0.2453	0.0683	0.8693	0.1544	0.0806	0.0003		
	17	128	92	93	93	14	25	132	60	134	
NgbTol	−0.5394	0.0981	0.0764	0.215	−0.0185	−0.2421	−0.0574	0.1006	0.2162	−0.2679	1
	0.1076	0.6059	0.6935	0.3245	0.9301	0.4255	0.79	0.597	0.2691	0.1523	
	10	30	29	23	25	13	24	30	28	30	30

Notes: The first row is the correlation measure, the second shows the significance level (* = all observations that are significant at the 95 per cent level), and the third row shows the number of observations available for each calculation. Indicators retained to represent the category are shaded.

Source: See Table B.6.1 in the Appendix.

AIDS deaths[7] and the incidence of orphans are highly correlated with each other. At the time of writing, AIDS deaths represented a more comprehensive negative condition, being a cause of the high orphan rates and of other problems in society, so we have chosen it. The three variables, rule of law, public institutions, and corruption, are all highly intercorrelated, with little to choose among them. We have chosen the rule of law (a World Bank measure of the extent to which agents have confidence in the rules of society and abide by them) as a more comprehensive indicator than the other two. The share of the population involved in natural disasters was not highly correlated with any of the other indicators, nor was tolerance of neighbours. Consequently, we select AIDS deaths, the rule of law, tolerance of neighbours, and the rate of natural disasters as representative of community well-being.

6.4.6. *Inequalities*

Of the various measures of inequality (see Table 6.8), the GDI, the UNDP's composite measure of gender inequality, is very highly correlated with happiness inequality. We select GDI because it encompasses a broader set of variables. While health inequality is moderately correlated with the income Gini coefficient, the correlation is not high enough to allow us to eliminate either indicator, as is also the case with rural–urban inequality and horizontal inequality (HI). Consequently, we select the income Gini, HI, rural–urban inequality, GDI, and health inequality to represent this category.

6.4.7. *Work Conditions*

We have five indicators of work conditions (see Table 6.9)—the unemployment rate at a recent date, child labour (5–14 years), an index of employment conditions reflecting the regulatory situation, informal employment as a proportion of the total, and an index indicating the existence of a minimum wage policy. Child labour is inversely correlated with the unemployment rate, although there are only twelve cases of countries with both sets of data. We retain unemployment because the indicator is available for a much larger number of countries. However, it is well known that data for this (as well as for child labour) are unreliable and variable, since definitions differ markedly across countries. Since none of the other indicators is highly correlated with each other, although there is a moderate correlation between minimum wage policy

[7] The use of AIDS deaths as an important element of community well-being is emblematic of the way appropriate indicators are time and place specific. This exercise was done when the AIDS epidemic was at its height and lethal. As AIDS incidence declines and the illness becomes chronic rather than lethal, it may no longer be an appropriate indicator.

Table 6.8. Inequality indicators

	IncomeGini	HI	RurUrbIneq	GDI	HappyIneq	HealthIneq
IncomeGini	1					
	78					
HI	0.1803	1				
	0.1719					
	59	78				
RurUrbIneq	−0.2788	−0.4065*	1			
	0.0577	0.0125				
	47	37	48			
GDI	−0.1016	−0.0646	0.0136	1		
	0.3824	0.5795	0.9268			
	76	76	48	122		
HappyIneq	−0.1307	−0.151	0.0572	0.9982*	1	
	0.2844	0.212	0.7189	0		
	69	70	42	111	111	
HealthIneq	0.2950*	0.2248	−0.0305	−0.0186	−0.0775	1
	0.0288	0.1127	0.8579	0.8881	0.574	
	55	51	37	60	55	61

Notes: The first row is the correlation measure, the second shows the significance level (* = all observations that are significant at the 95 per cent level), and the third row shows the number of observations available for each calculation. Indicators retained to represent the category are shaded.

Source: See Table B.6.1 in the Appendix.

Table 6.9. Work conditions indicators

	Unemployment	EmplConditions	InformalEmpl	ChildLabour	MinWagePol
Unemployment	1				
	67				
EmplConditions	−0.0391	1			
	0.7964				
	46	76			
InformalEmpl	0.192	0.14	1		
	0.4452	0.4862			
	18	27	28		
Childlabour	−0.7881*	0.1617	−0.0387	1	
	0.0023	0.4401	0.9002		
	12	25	13	41	
MinWagePol	0.0279	0.3922*	0.2263		1
	0.8755	0.0085	0.2468	1	
	34	44	28	16	47

Notes: The first row is the correlation measure, the second shows the significance level (* = all observations that are significant at the 95 per cent level), and the third row shows the number of observations available for each calculation. Indicators retained to represent the category are shaded.

Source: See Table B.6.1 in the Appendix.

and employment conditions, we retain the remaining three variables—informal employment, minimum wage policy, and employment conditions—as well as the unemployment rate, to represent the work conditions category.

6.4.8. *Leisure Conditions*

We have six variables in this category (see Table 6.10)—phone availability, internet use, radio use, television ownership, newspaper use per person, and cinema attendance. The first five are all highly correlated with each other. We choose phone availability because the correlations are highest, and cinema attendance (which is moderately related to the other variables) as our indicators for this category.

6.4.9. *Economic Security*

Variables chosen for economic security because they are likely to cause fluctuations in incomes include the share of manufacturing exports (inversely), portfolio investment as a share of GDP, and fluctuations in the terms of trade (see Table 6.11). We also include the actual GDP business cycle. Individual

Table 6.10. Leisure conditions indicators

	PhoneAvail	InternetUse	RadioUsage	CinemaAtt	Newspaper	Television
PhoneAvail	1					
	135					
InternetUse	0.9064*	1				
	0					
	134	134				
RadioUsage	0.7235*	0.6928*	1			
	0	0				
	130	129	130			
CinemaAtt	0.5078*	0.4712*	0.3717*	1		
	0.0022	0.0049	0.0304			
	34	34	34	34		
Newspaper	0.8204*	0.8067*	0.6766*	0.4299*	1	
	0	0	0	0.0284		
	67	66	67	26	67	
Television	0.8249*	0.7728*	0.6775*	0.4348*	0.8068*	1
	0	0	0	0.0102	0	
	130	129	128	34	66	130

Notes: The first row is the correlation measure, the second shows the significance level (* = all observations that are significant at the 95 per cent level), and the third row shows the number of observations available for each calculation. Indicators retained to represent the category are shaded.

Source: See Table B.6.1 in the Appendix.

Table 6.11. Economic insecurity

	GDPcycle	CPIcycle	ManufExpts	Portfolio	TermsofTrade	SocSecPol
GDPcycle	1					
	108					
CPIcycle	0.1137	1				
	0.2944					
	87	92				
ManufExpts	−0.4426*	−0.2529*	1			
	0.0001	0.0389				
	72	67	76			
Portfolio	0.0312	0.1669	0.229	1		
	0.7891	0.1838	0.0866			
	76	65	57	79		
TermsofTrade	0.2117	0.4209*	−0.5989*	0.0224	1	
	0.0577	0.0003	0	0.866		
	81	69	56	59	89	
SocSecPol	0.0201	−0.0815	0.0965	0.5786*	−0.0537	1
	0.8983	0.6266	0.57	0.0002	0.7423	
	43	38	37	36	40	46

Notes: The first row is the correlation measure, the second shows the significance level (* = all observations that are significant at the 95 per cent level), and the third row shows the number of observations available for each calculation. Indicators retained to represent the category are shaded.

Source: See Table B.6.1 in the Appendix.

economic vulnerability is likely to result from these macro-fluctuations and also from fluctuations in the inflation rate, although individual economic insecurity may be reduced by social security coverage. Our data for all these variables are for 1980–2000, apart from social security which relates to 2000. A high correlation was observed between the terms of trade fluctuations and the share of manufacturing exports in output. Since terms of trade fluctuations are likely to have an immediate effect on many people's incomes, we retain it instead of manufacturing exports as a share of total exports. None of the other variables were highly correlated, although portfolio share of investment and social security polices were moderately positively correlated, presumably because each is higher at higher levels of per capita income. We therefore retain all the other indicators noted above.

6.4.10. *Political Security*

The four indicators in this area (see Table 6.12) are as follows: 'political stability', a composite index reflecting the likelihood of the overthrow of government compiled by the World Bank; net refugee outflows as a proportion of the population during 1998–2002 (from the Office of the United Nations High Commissioner for Refugees, UNHCR); an index of collective violence,

Table 6.12. Political stability indicators

	PolStability	Refugees	CollViolence	PolViolence
PolStability	1			
	125			
Refugees	−0.4202*	1		
	0.001			
	58	58		
CollViolence	−0.6072*	0.4692*	1	
	0	0.0003		
	109	56	109	
PolViolence	−0.6153*	−0.0407	0.6217*	1
	0	0.7617	0	
	125	58	109	137

Notes: The first row is the correlation measure, the second shows the significance level (* = all observations that are significant at the 95 per cent level), and the third row shows the number of observations available for each calculation. Indicators retained to represent the category are shaded.

Source: See Table B.6.1 in the Appendix.

including excessive civilian targeting (from Marshall 2002) and political violence, defined as any type of armed conflict from 1990 (derived from Marshall 2005). Political stability, collective violence, and political violence are all highly intercorrelated. We choose political violence since the correlation coefficients are higher than in the other two cases. The refugee flow indicator is only moderately correlated with the other indicators and is therefore retained as an indicator representing this dimension.

6.4.11. *Environmental Conditions*

We have just one composite indicator for this category, environmental sustainability, produced by the World Economic Forum, Yale Center for Environmental Law and Policy, and the Center for International Earth Science Information Network (CIESIN), which will therefore represent this category.

6.5. Relating the Selected Indicators to the Core Indicators

Using the selected indicators to represent each dimension, we now explore how these relate to the three core measures used to assess country performance for the same period of time—the HDI, income per capita (PPP), and under-five mortality. We start with the HDI, currently the most prominent measure of HD performance. Table 6.13 shows the correlations between HDI and the thirty retained indicators representing our eleven categories. We then follow similar procedures as before, i.e. we eliminate any variable which has a

Table 6.13. Correlations between retained indicators and HDI

Indicator	HDI ranking	Indicator	HDI ranking	Indicator	HDI ranking
HDI ranking	1	NgbTolerance	−0.1017	InformalEmpl	−0.295
			0.5929		0.1275
	126		30		28
MaleSuicide	0.3041*	CrudeDivorce	0.6764*	MinWagePol	−0.2115
	0.0448		0.0008		0.1535
	44		21		47
LifeSatisfaction	0.6877*	AIDSdeaths	−0.6585*	PhoneAvail	0.8585*
	0		0		0
	30		93		125
Prisoners	0.5817*	RuleofLaw	0.6528*	CinemaAtt	0.5074*
	0		0		0.0019
	117		126		35
International poverty rate	−0.7843*	AlcoholUse	0.2483*	GDPcycle	−0.1127
	0		0.0058		0.2502
	70		122		106
Contraceptive	0.7610*	NatDisaster	−0.3223*	CPIcycle	−0.3413*
	0		0.0003		0.0009
	75		124		92
GEM	0.4555*	IncomeGini	0.0621	Portfolio	0.2466*
	0.0031		0.5891		0.0295
	40		78		78
FemSecmale	0.5666*	HorizIneq (HI)	0.3370*	TermsofTrade	−0.171
	0		0.0033		0.1176
	90		74		85
UnionDensity	0.0606	RurUrbIneq	−0.5379*	SocSecPol	0.6072*
	0.7257		0.0001		0
	36		48		46
PolrtCivlib	−0.2991*	GDI	0.013	Refugees	0.0276
	0.0007		0.8916		0.8428
	126		113		54
PolTerror	−0.2719*	HealthIneq	−0.3866*	PolViolence	−0.4276*
	0.0048		0.0021		0
	106		61		126
JuridIndp	−0.3344*	Unemployment	−0.0266	EnvSustain	0.2553*
	0.0084		0.8309		0.0152
	61		67		90
FriendsVeryImpt	0.1404	ChildLabor	−0.7339*		
	0.4594		0		
	30		39		
FamilyVimpt	−0.1849	EmplConditions	−0.1506		
	0.3281		0.1941		
	30		76		

Notes: Variables retained are shaded.

Source: See Table B.6.1 in the Appendix.

Table 6.14. The relationship of indicators to the core measures

Category of human development	Indicators eliminated	Indicators retained
Mental well-being	Life satisfaction	Male suicide rate Prisoners
Empowerment	US$1 a day poverty Contraceptive access	GEM Female/male secondary education Union density
Political freedom	None	Political/civil liberties Political terror Juridical independence
Social relations	None	Value of friends Value of family Tolerance of neighbours Divorce rate
Community well-being	AIDS deaths Rule of law	Alcohol consumption Natural disasters Tolerance of neighbours
Inequalities	None	Income Gini Horizontal inequality Rural–urban inequality GDI Health inequality
Work conditions	Child labour	Unemployment Employment conditions Informal sector proportion Minimum wage policy
Leisure conditions	Phone availability	Cinema attendance
Economic stability	Social security	GDP cycle CPI cycle Portfolio investment Terms of trade
Political stability	None	Political violence Refugee flows
Environment	None	Environmental sustainability

Notes: Shaded areas indicate retained indicators.

Source: See Table B.6.1 in the Appendix.

high correlation (i.e. above 0.6) with the core indicator. Life satisfaction, the rate of contraceptive use, the divorce rate, the rule of law, phone availability, and social security policies are all highly positively correlated with the HDI, while international poverty rate, AIDS deaths, and the rate of child labour are highly correlated negatively. The HDI may therefore represent all these indicators. Table 6.14 summarizes our results, showing which indicators are retained for each category.

This exercise shows that HDI alone does not encompass many other important dimensions of HD, even on our rather modest requirements of a 0.6 correlation. For each of the eleven categories, at least one other variable needs to be included in order to assess the overall state of HD, and altogether

Table 6.15. Correlation among basic indicators of HD

	HDI ranking	Income PPP	Under 5 mortality	Adult iliteracy	Maternal mortality	Life expectancy	Infant mortality
HDIranking	1 126						
IncomePPP	0.8789* 0 113	1 113					
Under5mort	−0.8789* 0 125	−0.8258* 0 112	1				
Adultillit	−0.8091* 0 106	−0.7082* 0 99	0.7393* 0 107	1 108			
MatMortality	−0.8760* 0 115	−0.8227* 0 105	0.9177* 0 120	0.6895* 0 105	1 120		
Lifeexpectancy	0.8784* 0 120	0.7462* 0 109	−0.9184* 0 125	−0.6216* 0 107	−0.8745* 0 120	1 126	
Infantmort	−0.8762* 0 125	−0.8142* 0 112	0.9947* 0 136	0.7393* 0 107	0.9050* 0 120	−0.9135* 0 125	1 136

Notes: The first row is the correlation measure, the second shows the significance level (* = all observations that are significant at the 95 per cent level), and the third row shows the number of observations available for each calculation. Indicators retained to represent the category are shaded.

Source: See Table B.6.1 in the Appendix.

we add thirty-one indicators. The correlations with under-five mortality yield exactly the same results as HDI. Under-five mortality also shows similar correlations with the basic elements of HD as with HDI (see Table 6.15). HDI is, of course, a much more widely accepted measure. But the under-five mortality rate has advantages for some purposes, since it is more precise in terms of changes over time and less complicated to calculate.

In relation to per capita income (PPP), for the most part the results were the same as for HDI (see Table B.6.2 in the Appendix). The differences were as follows:

- In the mental well-being category, life satisfaction was moderately rather than highly correlated with income, so that the three variables—life satisfaction, prisoners, and male suicide—would need to be retained.
- In community well-being, in contrast to HDI, AIDS deaths are only moderately correlated with income, and thus should be retained.
- In all the other categories, the same indicators are retained as in the case of the HDI.

Thus HDI is a somewhat more encompassing general indicator of HD than PPP per capita income. Income per capita is, of course, also a less good measure of basic HD than HDI, which is designed for this very purpose. This is confirmed by the stronger correlations of HDI with life expectancy, infant mortality, maternal mortality, and adult illiteracy than shown by per capita income (see Table 6.15).

Given the fact that, for most categories, more than one variable (and in most cases several) emerges as a result of following these procedures, the question arises whether one should seek a composite indicator for each category similar to the HDI. We should note the very fact that since more than one variable emerges we are left with variables that are *not* highly correlated with one another. The weighting of the variables in any composite is bound to be arbitrary, yet there could be advantages from the point of view of comparing country performance in different categories and also changes over time.

6.5.1. *High-Income Countries*

Performing the same exercise for high-income (OECD) countries, we found a good deal of similarity with the developing country story (see Table B.6.3 in the Appendix). Here we used the same indicators for comparability, though, not surprisingly, data were not available for some indicators (e.g. child labour), while different indicators might be more appropriate for some of the categories for richer countries (e.g. the share of manufacturing exports is probably not relevant to economic stability in the OECD countries). For the most part the results were very similar. One interesting difference was that the various indicators of inequality showed much higher correlation with each other among the rich countries than in the developing countries. The HDI was a poorer indicator of our various categories of well-being than in the case of developing countries—with seven out of the eleven categories having no indicator correlated with HDI at above the cut-off rate, whereas for developing countries this applied only in four out of the eleven categories. Two interesting examples are that in developing countries both life satisfaction and poverty proved to be correlated with HDI whereas neither was in the case of the OECD countries. Income per capita and under-five mortality each performed even worse than HDI in the case of the OECD countries.

6.6. Conclusions

This chapter has considered how well the HDI represents HD when broadly defined. Following other contributions in this area, we identified eleven categories of HD which seem to encompass all the major dimensions of HD. For each category, we then identified a potential set of indicators which seem to us plausible measures and for which data are available. We investigated correlations among these measures and, in order to reduce the number of variables representing each category, we included only one indicator for any set of indicators that are highly correlated with each other, also retaining any indicator that does not show a high correlation with the other indicators in its category. The aim was to include only variables which are broadly independent of each other.

Our next step was to see how well the selected variables for each category are correlated with the HDI. Any variable in any category that was highly correlated with HDI was then eliminated on the grounds that these variables were already encompassed by the HDI measure. We were left with thirty-one variables, each representing an independent dimension of HD showing that the HDI is not adequate as a measure of a broad definition of HD.

We subsequently performed the same exercise with two other commonly used aggregate measures of country progress—income per capita (PPP) and under-five mortality—in order to determine whether they 'carried' a larger set of our HD indicators. We found that under-five mortality performed exactly as the HDI, while income per capita did less well, i.e. using income alone misses even more dimensions of a broader conception of HD than using HDI alone. And, of course, income per capita is also a less good indicator of the basic elements of HD. Carrying out the same exercise for OECD countries gave similar results, although the HDI represented a smaller proportion of indicators. Both PPP income and under-five mortality did worse than HDI in this respect.

This chapter has explored empirical correlations but did not attempt to investigate causality. We recognize that our procedures are somewhat arbitrary and a change in the data used, thresholds, etc. would yield somewhat different results. Our basic purpose, however, is not to be definitive but to show that extending the concept and measurement of HD to a broader set of dimensions seriously affects the way one should measure and assess country performance. We are open to the deployment of alternative categories, indicators, data sources, and rules of procedure.

An alternative approach to the procedures adopted here would be the application of principal components analysis to each category to reduce the number of retained (or independent) indicators. However, unless the original indicators are sufficiently correlated to be effectively summarized in a new single measure without significant loss of information, the problem of multidimensionality will persist; and even when successful, the new indicator is likely to pose problems of interpretation, as it ultimately remains a hybrid measure with reduced intuitive appeal since principal component measures are constructed as a linear combination of the original dimensions.

Appendix B

Table B.6.1. Summary of indicators and sources

Indicator	Code	Notes	Date	Source
Core indicators				
HDI rank	HDI	Composite of life expectancy, adult literacy and mean schooling, and per capita GDP	2002	UNDP 2004
GDP per capita (PPP)	IncomePPP	PPP US$	2002	World Bank WDI
Child mortality rate	Under5Mort	Mortality under five years old, per 1,000 live births	2002	UNDP 2004
Physical well-being				
Adult illiteracy	AdultIllit	Adult illiteracy rate (% age 15 and above)	2002	UNDP 2004
Maternal mortality	MatMortality	Maternal mortality rate (per 100,000 live births)	2000	MDG website <http://www.un.org/millenniumgoals/>
Life expectancy	LifeExp		2000–5 estimate	WHO <http://www.who.org>
Infant mortality	InfantMort	Mortality under a year per 1,000 live births	2002	UNDP 2004
Individual mental well-being				
Suicide rates	MaleSuicide, FemSuicide	Per 100,000 people	2003	WHO <http://www.who.org>
Life satisfaction	LifeSatis	0–10 ladder, with 10 most satisfied	1990s	World Database of Happiness <http://worlddatabaseofhappiness.eur.nl/>
Population incarcerated (%)	Prisoners	Per 100,000 of population	2004	King's College World Prison Brief <http://www.prisonstudies.org>
Empowerment				
Population living below US$1/day (%)	Poverty1day		1990–2002	World Bank WDI
Population living below the national poverty line (%)	PovNational		1990–2001	World Bank WDI

(continued)

Table B.6.1. Continued

Indicator	Code	Notes	Date	Source
Human Poverty Index (HPI)	HPI	Composite of deprivation in life expectancy, illiteracy, lack of access to safe water and health services, and malnutrition	2002	UNDP 2004
Gender Empowerment Measure (GEM)	GEM	Composite of gender inequality in parliament, occupational status, and income	2002	UNDP 2004
Ratio of female to male secondary school enrolment	FemSecMale		2000–1	UNDP 2004
Unmet need for family planning	Contraceptive Lack	% of sexually active men/women not using modern contraception who do not want children for at least two years	Date between 1990–2002	Population Reference Bureau <http://www.prb.org/>
Currently married females aged 15–19 (%)	MarriedGirls		Date between 1985–2002	*World Fertility Report* <http://www.un.org/en/development/desa/population/publications/fertility/world-fertility>
Women in parliamentary seats (%)	FemParliamnt		2004	Inter-Parliamentary Union (IPU)
Union density	UnionDensity	% of labour force affiliated with labour unions	1997	ILO Laborstat <http://laborsta.ilo.org>
Political and cultural freedom				
Combined political rights and civil liberties indicator	PolRtCivLib	Scale of 1–7 with 1 most free; average of 'political rights' and 'civil liberties' scales	2003	Freedom House <https://freedomhouse.org/>
Freedom of worship	FreeWorship	Scale of 1–7, with 1 most free, Religious Freedom in the World	2000	Freedom House <https://freedomhouse.org/>
Amnesty International political terror index	PolTerror	Scale of 1–5, with 5 most repressive	Avg. 2000–3	Amnesty International <https://www.amnesty.org.uk/>

Voice and accountability index	PolFreedom	Measures political rights and ability of citizens to participate, higher numbers better	2002	World Bank Governance Indicators <http://info.worldbank.org/governance/wgi/>
Freedom of the press	FreePress	Business leaders perceptions, 104 countries (rank order)	2004	Freedom House <https://freedomhouse.org/>
Juridical independence	JuridIndp	Business leaders perceptions, 104 countries (rank order)	2004	Porter et al. (2004)
Social relationships				
Friends very important	FriendsValue	Lower numbers indicate more importance	1999–2001	World Values Survey Data Base <http://www.worldvaluessurvey.org/>
Family very important	FamilyValue	Lower numbers indicate more importance	1999–2001	World Values Survey Data Base <http://www.worldvaluessurvey.org/>
Neighbour tolerance	NgbTol	Average response to whether would want to live next to various types of people; lower numbers indicate more tolerance	1999–2001	World Values Survey Data Base <http://www.worldvaluessurvey.org/>
Crude divorce rate	CrudeDivorce	Ratio of number of divorces to population	2001 or most recent	
Community well-being				
People victimized by crime	CrimeRate	% of population	Year between 1990–2001	UNDP 2004
Alcohol consumption, recorded	AlcoholUse	Per capita litres pure alcohol, ages 15+	2003 data	WHO (2004) <http://www.who.int/>
Corruption index	Corruption	Scale of 0–10, with 10 least corrupt	2004	Transparency International <http://www.transparency.org.uk/>
Orphaned children	OrphanCount	% of children without one or both parents	2003	UNICEF (2004)
Estimated AIDS deaths	AIDS	% of population	2003	MDG website <http://www.un.org/millenniumgoals/>
Participation in civic associations	CivicWork	% of economically active population (includes paid and volunteer work)	2003	Johns Hopkins Comparative Nonprofit Sector Project <http://ccss.jhu.edu/research-projects/comparative-nonprofit-sector-project/>

(continued)

Table B.6.1. Continued

Indicator	Code	Notes	Date	Source
Trust in others	Trust	Extent to which people feel 'most people can be trusted', lower numbers show more trust	1999–2001	World Values Survey Data Base <http://www.worldvaluessurvey.org/>
Rule of law	RuleofLaw	Extent to which agents have confidence in and abide by rules of society; the higher the better	2002	World Bank Governance Indicators <http://info.worldbank.org/governance/wgi/>
Public institutions index	PublicInst	Business leader perceptions of quality of public institutions	2004	Porter et al. (2004)
Share of population affected by natural disasters	NatDisaster	Average for period of number affected each year divided by total population	Average of data 1980–2000	Calculated from the US Office of Disaster Assistance and the Center for Research on the Epidemiology of Disasters (OFDA/CRED) International Disaster Database <http://www.emdat.be/> and World Bank WDI
Neighbour tolerance	NgbTol	Average response to whether would want to live next to various types of people; lower numbers indicate more tolerance	1999–2001	World Values Survey Data Base <http://www.worldvaluessurvey.org/>
Inequalities				
Gini of income	IncomeGini		Year between 1990–2000	UNDP (2004b)
Horizontal inequalities	HI	Range from −2 to +4, higher number represents more disadvantage	2000	Minorities at Risk database <http://www.mar.umd.edu/mar_data.asp>
Rural–urban inequalities	RuralUrbIneq	Ratio rural–urban poverty	Year between 1990–2002	World Bank WDI
Gender Development Index	GDI	HDI adjusted to account for gender inequality	2001	UNDP 2004
Life satisfaction inequality	HappyIneq	Dispersion of responses on 0–10 ladder of life satisfaction (std dev.)	1990s	World Database of Happiness <http://worlddatabaseofhappiness.eur.nl/>

Inequality in healthcare	HealthIneq	Perceived inequality in access to healthcare, rich and poor, business leaders survey; lower number indicates less inequality	2004	Porter et al. (2004)
Work conditions				
Unemployment rate	Unemployment		Year between 1992–2003	ILO Laborstat <http://laborsta.ilo.org>
Extent to which employment conditions are regulated	EmpConditions	Index 1–100, with higher number reflecting more regulation	1999	Djankov et al. (2002); <http://www.nationmaster.com>
Share employed in informal sector	InformalEmp	% of labour force employed in unofficial economy in capital city of each country as % of official labour force	2000	ILO Laborstat <http://laborsta.ilo.org>
Child labour	Childlabour	% aged 5–14 involved in labour	Year between 1999–2001	UNICEF <https://data.unicef.org>
Existence of minimum wage policy	MinWage	Dummy equals 1 if minimum wage policy exists in country	2000	ILO Laborstat <http://laborsta.ilo.org>
Leisure conditions				
Telephone/cell phone subscribers	PhoneUse	Per 100 population	2002	MDG website <http://www.un.org/millenniumgoals/>
Internet users	InternetUse	Per 100 population	2002	MDG website <http://www.un.org/millenniumgoals/>
Radios	RadioUsage	Per 1,000 people	1997	UNESCO <http://data.uis.unesco.org/>
Cinema attendance	CinemaAtt	Per 1,000 people	Average 1995–9	UNESCO <http://data.uis.unesco.org/>
Newspaper circulation	Newspapers	Per 1,000 people	Average 1997–2000	UNESCO <http://data.uis.unesco.org/>
TV ownership	TV	Per 1,000 people	Average 1997–2000	UNESCO (data.uis.unesco.org/)
Economic stability				
GDP cycle	GDPcycle	Average annual deviation from mean	1981–2002	World Bank, WDI
CPI cycle	CPIcycle	Average annual deviation from mean	1981–2002	World Bank, WDI

(*continued*)

Table B.6.1. Continued

Indicator	Code	Notes	Date	Source
Share of manufactured exports in total	ManufExpts	Average of 1980, 1990, and 2000 (or closest year)	1980–2000	World Bank, WDI
Portfolio cycle	Portfolio	Average for period of share of portfolio investment (current US$ excluding liabilities constituting foreign authorities' reserves) as share of GDP	1980–2000	World Bank, WDI
Terms of trade cycle	TermsTrade	Average annual deviation from mean	1980–2000	World Bank, WDI
Social security policy	SocSecPolicy	Measures social security benefits as average of old age, disability, death benefits; sickness/health benefits; unemployment benefits	2000	International Social Security Association data <https://www.issa.int/en/country-profiles>
Political stability				
Political stability measure	PolStability	Composite reflecting perceptions of likelihood of destabilizing or overthrow of government	2002	World Bank Governance Indicators <http://info.worldbank.org/governance/wgi/>
Net refugee outflow	Refugees		1998–2002	UNHCR (2002) <http://www.unhcr.org/uk/statistics/unhcrstats/4a07e87d6/unhcr-statistical-yearbook-2002.html>
Collective political violence in 1990s	CollViolence	Reflects levels of violence within country and whether excessive civilian targeting, scale of 0–8, with 8 worst	1990s	Integrated Network for Social Conflict Research <http://www.systemicpeace.org/inscrdata.html>
Countries with major episode of political violence since 1990	PolViolence	Dummy equals 1 if any type of armed conflict	1990	Derived from data given in Marshall (2005)

Environmental well-being				
Environmental sustainability index	EnvSustain	Multicomponent measure of progress towards environmental sustainability; higher measure indicates greater progress	2002	Yale Center for Environmental Law and Policy, and CIESIN <http://www.ciesin.org>

Note: WDI = World Development Indicators <http://databank.worldbank.org/data/reports.aspx?source=world-development-indicators>.

Table B.6.2. Correlations between retained indicators and per capita income

Indicator	IncomePPP	Indicator	IncomePPP	Indicator	IncomePPP
IncomePPP	1 113	NgbTol	–0.129 0.4967 30	InformalEmpl	–0.1158 0.5574 28
Malesuicide	0.1575 0.3318 40	CrudeDivorce	0.6663* 0.0025 18	MinWagePol	–0.3431* 0.0182 47
LifeSatisfaction	0.5540* 0.0015 30	AIDSdeaths	–0.5447* 0 89	PhoneAvail	0.8708* 0 113
Prisoners	0.6229* 0 107	RuleofLaw	0.6748* 0 113	CinemaAtt	0.4968* 0.0045 31
Poverty1day	–0.7592* 0 70	AlcoholUse	0.2718* 0.0039 111	GDPcycle	–0.1729 0.0822 102
Contraceptive Lack	0.6497* 0 71	NatDisaster	–0.3084* 0.0009 112	CPIcycle	–0.4379* 0 86
GEM	0.4735* 0.002 40	IncomeGini	0.1911 0.0937 78	Portfolio	0.2430* 0.0383 73
FemSecmale	0.5404* 0 82	HorizIneq (HI)	0.3487* 0.0027 72	TermsofTrade	–0.2962* 0.008 79
UnionDensity	0.0802 0.642 36	RurUrbIneq	–0.5347* 0.0001 48	SocSecPol	0.6419* 0 46
PolrtCivlib	–0.3471* 0.0002 113	GDI	–0.0671 0.4966 105	Refugees	–0.0677 0.6442 49
PolTerror	–0.2806* 0.0059 95	HealthIneq	–0.4017* 0.0015 60	PolViolence	–0.4530* 0 113
JuridIndp	–0.4524* 0.0003 60	Unemployment	0.1517 0.2354 63	EnvSustain	0.2990* 0.0054 85
FriendsVeryImpt	0.0937 0.6225 30	ChildLabour	–0.7154* 0 38		
FamilyVimpt	–0.1909 0.3123 30	EmplConditions	–0.2259 0.0513 75		

* Moderate correlation with PPP income per head.

Source: See Table B.6.1.

Table B.6.3. Selected indicators for OECD countries, and relationship to HDI

Category of HD	OECD countries		
	Indicators retained within each category	Indicators eliminated, because high correlation with HDI	Indicators not correlated with HDI and therefore retained
Mental well-being	Male suicide Life satisfaction Prisoners	None	Male suicide Life sat**, Prisoners*
Empowerment	GEM HPI2 F/M secondary Unions Married teenage girls	GEM	HPI2* F/M secondary Unions Married teenage girls
Political freedom	Political/civil liberties Political terror Political freedom	None	Political/civil liberties Political terror Political freedom
Social relations	Value of friends Value of family Tolerance of neighbours Divorce rate	Value of friends	Value of family Tolerance of neighbours Divorce rate
Community well-being	Civic association Rule of law Alcohol use Trust in others Tolerance of neighbours AIDS deaths Natural disasters	Civic association	Rule of law Alcohol use Trust in others Tolerance of neighbours AIDS deaths* Natural disasters
Inequalities	Health inequality Horizontal inequality	None	Health inequality Horizontal inequality
Work conditions	Long-run unemployment Minimum wage	None	Long-run unemployment** Minimum wage
Leisure conditions	Library books Internet use Phone availability	Library books	Internet use Phone availability
Economic stability	GDP cycle Social security policies	None	GDP cycle Social security policies
Political stability	Regime durability Political stability Political violence	Regime durability	Political stability Political violence
Environment	Environmental sustainability	None	Environmental sustainability

* High correlation with under-five mortality; ** High correlation with PPP income per head.

7

Capabilities and Human Development

Beyond the Individual—The Critical Role of Social Institutions and Social Capabilities

7.1. Introduction

Individuals cannot flourish alone: indeed they cannot *function* alone.[1] When they are born the family provides their life support. In turn families cannot function independently of the societies in which they are located. Being a member of a family, of a locality, and of the larger society is an essential component of a flourishing existence. Moreover, these groupings can provide good conditions for the individual, or bad ones, so it is not only their existence but their nature which is relevant to HD. Thus a major task of the HD approach—which aims to assess human progress and to identify the conditions for human flourishing—is to explore the nature of social institutions which are favourable for human flourishing, as against those that impede it.

The capability approach, developed by Sen (1999a) and Nussbaum (2000), which provides the theoretical underpinning of much discussion of HD, is essentially individualistic. Development consists of the expansion of *individuals'* capabilities or freedoms. These are defined as what a person can be ('beings') or do ('doings'). The objective of development is then to expand the set of capabilities of each individual. From this capability set, an individual makes choices and thus translates the potential to be or do a variety of things into actual beings or doings, or what are called 'functionings'. It is these

[1] We are grateful to Maurice Kigler, Seeta Prabhu, Bina Agarwal, the HDRO, and discussions in seminars in UNDP, HDRO, and UNDP New Delhi for very useful comments on an earlier draft. This chapter uses material from Stewart (2013b). This was originally commissioned as a background paper by the Human Development Report Office of UNDP and some of it was used in the *Human Development Report 2013*. We are grateful to the UNDP for permission to reuse it here.

functionings that we observe. The HD approach tends to focus on functionings rather than capabilities because of its major concern with assessing progress—functionings can be observed and measured, while it is much more difficult to measure capabilities, although there have been a number of attempts both theoretical and empirical (e.g. Schokkaert and van Ootegem 1990, Burchardt and Le Grand 2002, Anand et al. 2005, Anand et al. n.d.). Nonetheless, like the capabilities approach, the HD approach maintains that freedom of individual choice is a central aspect of satisfactory development. As stated in the *Human Development Report*, 'Human Development is a process of enlarging people's choices' (UNDP 1990, 10). This implies that if we could show that a set of functionings was not chosen freely, this would constitute a serious defect even if the actual set of achieved functionings was deemed to be good.

Whether we are discussing capabilities or functionings, progress is assessed by how *individuals* are affected. In this respect the two approaches share the views of the utilitarian approach which they aim to replace. How does this individualism relate to the essentially social quality of human existence? In principle, the individualism of the capabilities approach and the social features of human life appear quite compatible. Expanding individual capabilities forms the end, or the objective, while identifying and promoting good social institutions is a means to this objective. Yet in two ways, the primacy of individualism in the capabilities approach is at odds with the flourishing of social beings. First, individuals are so bound up with others that it can be difficult to disentangle them and treat them as separate; as Etzioni stated: 'a basic observation of sociology and psychology *is that the individual and the community "penetrate" one another* and require one another, and that individuals are not able to function without deep links to others' (Etzioni 1993, 65, italics added). We shall explore whether this means that the strict means–end nexus partially breaks down. Second, as a consequence of the emphasis on individual choice and individual flourishing, there has been a tendency in analysis of HD to neglect the study of social institutions and capabilities. This is not to claim that the capabilities approach or HD approach ignores the importance of the instrumental role of social institutions (e.g. Sen 1999a, Drèze and Sen 1989, UNDP 1993, Drèze and Sen 2013), but that it has given it insufficient emphasis. Indeed, Sen has gone somewhat beyond recognition of the instrumental aspect of social arrangements[2] to a hint, at least, of a more fundamental role that society plays in determining individual capabilities: 'in valuing a person's ability to take part in the life of the society itself,

[2] Sen (1999a, 116) refers to 'the advantage of group activities in bringing about substantial social changes'.

there is an implicit valuation of the society itself, and that is an important aspect of the capability perspective' (Sen 2009, 246).

This chapter explores these issues in order to consider how the social can be better integrated into the HD approach—in analysis, research, and policy. The discussion is organized into the following four sections: Section 7.2 considers some definitional issues. Section 7.3 explores ways in which *social capabilities* contribute to individual flourishing, in order both to show how important social capabilities are and to lay down the broad boundaries of what we are discussing. Section 7.4 considers factors relevant to assessing social well-being at an aggregate level, going beyond particular social institutions to societal relationships, including a discussion of the concepts of social cohesion and social inclusion. Section 7.5 considers implications of the analysis of social institutions for the HD approach, including for research, data collection, and policy recommendations.

7.2. Some Definitions

We need to start with definitions. *Social institutions* are understood here as all institutions in which people act collectively (i.e. involving more than one person), *excluding profit-making market institutions and the state.* They include formal NGOs, informal associations such as neighbourhood associations or social clubs, cooperatives and producer associations, sports clubs and savings associations, and much more. They influence, and are influenced by, both state and market. While both state and market have been subject to much investigation in relation to HD and the capabilities approach, the role of collective activities outside the state and the market has been given a much less central place.

Following North's (1991, 97) well-known broad definition of institutions as 'humanly devised constraints that structure political, economic and social interactions', social institutions include norms and rules of behaviour. Social institutions thus encompass both organizations, such as those listed above, and norms—in each case they may be formal or informal. Social norms influence behaviour and are consequently important in determining the HD impact of goods and services intended to promote HD, whether provided by the state, the market, or social organizations. We define *social capabilities* as what such institutions can be and do, like the definition of individual capabilities as what individuals can be or do.[3]

[3] Roy (2012) has suggested these should be termed *relational capabilities*. Ibrahim (2006) uses the term 'collective capabilities' to incorporate the collective dimension of human action—which is very similar to the way the term 'social capabilities' is used.

Social capabilities are needed firstly, for all those activities which, by their essence, can only be done in a group, and not individually; and secondly, for many activities which could in principle be carried out alone, but which would be carried out much more effectively if done collectively. Examples of the first type are playing football, participating in a book club or an orchestra, a neighbourhood group, or a policing group, an army, a library, a social club or dating agency, a group to protect the environment, or communal worship. Examples of the second include a mass of activities where there are economies of scale so that carrying out such activities individually is highly uneconomic; the provision of health services is an example. There are some organizations to which both arguments apply—for example, in education there are clear economies of scale, so providing education collectively is more economic, but there are also intrinsic virtues of collective provision since social interaction among children is important in itself as part of the educational experience.

Some of these activities could be provided by the market—e.g. private sports clubs, or education for profit. However, where there are large externalities, market provision will not occur and any collective action needs to be provided, or supported, either by the state or by non-state social institutions (or some combination). The division of responsibility between state and non-state institutions varies across countries (and time). For example, there is more of a tradition of state provision of social capabilities in Europe (and especially northern Europe) than in the US, where non-state groups play a bigger role. There is also often a blurring of the distinction between state and non-state because the state frequently subsidizes non-state activities (e.g. subsidies to the arts and sports).

But some activities *cannot* be carried out by the state. Political economy-type collective action is non-state by its nature, and indeed arises largely in order to gain control over the state or to pressure it to take some action. Non-state social institutions therefore supplement state activities in areas where there are large externalities, or where the market would fail because people are too poor to buy what is considered (by the state or by particular groups) as being essential or of high priority—like universal education or health services; they also provide services which the state may regard as of lesser priority (e.g. libraries or theatres). They also act where the state cannot, as in political and social movements.

Turning to rules, regulations, and social norms: while the state is responsible for manifold laws and regulations, informal norms (which we call here social norms) are by definition outside the control of the state. They are the outcome of innumerable social interactions over time—among individuals and social institutions and also through market influences. They can, however, be influenced by deliberate actions by both state and non-state actors.

7.3. Why Analysis of Social Institutions and Social Capabilities is Essential for HD

Social institutions and social capabilities are critically important in determining individual capabilities because: (a) they have a direct impact on them—most individual capabilities cannot exist without social capabilities; (b) societal norms affect the choices people make within any capability set and individuals' behaviour towards others, thus affecting other people's capabilities; (c) they affect the functioning of all other societal institutions, i.e. both state and market institutions; and (d) social institutions and social capabilities are critical determinants of the power and influence of particular groups (and individuals in these groups), at macro, meso, and micro levels. At macro levels, they influence the policy choices governments make and thereby the aggregate level and distribution of capabilities. Similar effects can be observed at meso and micro levels. Moreover, they also influence the terms individuals receive in market activities—including their terms of exchange, wages, and conditions of work. Chapter 8 is devoted to analysing the politics behind HD improvements, and consequently the issue of collective action and power at a macro level will be covered there rather than in this chapter.

Societies vary hugely in the number, functions, effectiveness, and distributional consequences of social institutions, and consequently in the range of social capabilities that may contribute to advancing HD. While considerable work has been devoted to cataloguing variations in the state and the market across countries, and reasons for and consequences of these variations, the same sort of cataloguing has rarely been carried out for non-state social institutions.[4] The more amorphous social norms have been even more neglected. Yet 'good' social norms from the perspective of HD can make a large difference to behaviour and consequently to capabilities and HD outcomes.

7.3.1. *The Impact of Social Institutions and Capabilities on Individual Capabilities*

To illustrate this, it is helpful to consider a list of some central capabilities. Though Sen has resisted drawing up a list of specific capabilities, arguing that it is for individuals and their collective deliberations to determine the capabilities they have reason to value, there have been a large number of attempts to delineate the main conditions needed for human flourishing, as discussed in Chapter 6. Table 6.1 summarized seven such efforts.

[4] Notable exceptions are Edwards (2004) and Oxhorn et al. (2004).

Table 7.1. Role of social institutions in affecting major capabilities

Capability	Social organization	Social norms
1. Bodily well-being	NGOs, communities, and families provide goods and services	Norms of health behaviour, attitudes to violence
2. Material well-being	Cooperatives, NGOs, family (including remittances), producer organizations, workers' organizations	Attitudes to employment, discrimination
3. Mental development/ well-being	Family and community effects	Societal norms (positive or negative)
4. Work	Workers' associations	Norms towards female and child work
5. Security	Warring groups and criminal gangs (negative), community associations (positive)	Societal norms
6. Social relations	Family and community Clubs and associations	
7. Spiritual well-being	Religious organizations	Societal norms
8. Empowerment and political freedom	Political parties, social movements and peoples' associations basis of empowerment	Norms of hierarchy and discrimination
9. Respect for other species and for natural environment	Community action, NGOs	Norms of behaviour

Drawing on the nine different dimensions of capabilities in Table 6.1, Table 7.1 points to the role of social institutions in underpinning each of these critical capabilities. As can be seen from Table 7.1, besides the state and the market, social institutions—including the family, community, and neighbourhood associations, trade unions, social movements, political parties, and NGOs—are all important in influencing the production of different capabilities, while social norms also play a critical part in determining behaviour which in turn affects capability sets. Not all social institutions have a *positive* impact: for example, norms of discrimination can be adverse for employment, education, health, and the material and mental well-being of some groups (including women), while criminal gangs and warring groups undermine security.

Moreover, there are possible conflicts in the conditions needed to achieve different capabilities: for example, between material well-being and environmental conditions, at least in the short term; and possible trade-offs between the growth of market influences, which may improve material well-being, and conditions supportive of those capabilities which depend on having a cohesive society. This is supported by the evidence showing that there is not a high positive correlation among many of the main dimensions of HD as shown in Chapter 6, which suggests that conditions which give rise to some capabilities may not be conducive for others. When grouping the dimensions of HD into four broad categories—basic HD (as measured by the HDI), and social, economic, and political aspects of development and classifying country performance accordingly, few countries do well or badly on *all* categories and most tend to show mixed performance, some doing better in one aspect (e.g. social) and worse on others (e.g. economic or political) and conversely (see Appendix C and more extended discussion in Ranis et al. 2009). These inconsistencies in performance across dimensions of HD suggest that it may not be possible to categorize institutions into those which are good (or bad) for HD as a whole, but only into those which are good or bad for some aspects of HD.

7.3.2. *Social Institutions, Norms, Choices, and Individual Autonomy*

Norms are a form of social institution that have a powerful impact on human behaviour. Social norms include both moral commandments (often sanctioned by religion) and numerous behavioural norms without a clear ethical basis which affect behaviour in general or in particular situations. An example of the latter is a norm, prevalent in many Latin countries, that people take a siesta in the afternoon. Almost every action we take is influenced by some norms—for example, in relation to noise-making (or not), ways of dealing with people (levels of politeness and of social distance), eating habits, cleanliness, punctuality, technology use, and so on. Some norms are related to health behaviour and directly affect health capabilities, and others affect the effectiveness of particular institutions—e.g. the norm of doing homework is helpful for improving the learning impact of school. Some affect distribution of capabilities, for example, across genders. Section 7.3.1 sketched out how norms contribute to capability-affecting behaviour. Here we want to consider how social norms affect *choices* among capabilities.

A critical building block of much of the capabilities approach and HD analysis is the assumption that individuals are autonomous and make their own decisions in light of their own preferences, personality, etc. While the aim of development is to expand people's capabilities, it is the individual who has the responsibility of choosing which capabilities to make use of, which to develop, etc. Underlying this view is the assumption that the individual is in the best position to know what she wants and is ethically the right person to make these decisions. Yet giving moral primacy to individual choice only makes sense if the individual is truly autonomous. If people are programmed to take decisions in a particular way—as in some science fiction stories—we would not regard their individual choices as necessarily the best choices. Yet without assuming a science fiction scenario, social institutions have a major influence on individual choices, limiting individual autonomy. On the one hand, social norms—outside the control of any one individual but formed by interactions among individuals, and with social, state, and market institutions over time—greatly influence those choices. On the other hand, individuals' freedom of choice is often constrained by various social institutions to which they belong which may heavily influence, or even determine, particular choices. Consider child labour: individual decisions on this are affected by social norms—whether it is considered fine for children to work, as in many developing countries, or outrageous, as in some Western countries; in addition, it is not the child, usually, but the family (parents or grandparents) who make the decision for the child. In other cases, it is the community that constrains free choice, ostracizing, stoning, or even killing people who make choices (e.g. of marriage) which contravene social rules.[5]

It follows that the autonomous individual is something of a myth—doubtless it represents the aspiration and belief (and perhaps is closer to a reality) among those philosophers who make it an essential component of their analysis. But most people are far from having complete freedom of choice: they have degrees of freedom, but their choices are heavily influenced by norms and institutions (market as well as social), with the extent of freedom varying across societies. Hence we cannot ignore the social institutions nor the influence exerted by the market, but must assess these norms and institutions to see whether they are promoting choices that enhance HD. And indeed, we may go further and try to encourage social institutions which are considered to promote HD, and to deter or prevent those which are deleterious to HD, assuming that there is some acceptable way of determining HD priorities.

However, once we agree that the individual is not autonomous, and hence not necessarily the best judge of HD-promoting capabilities, we enter very difficult territory because we can no longer rely on individual decisions to constitute the correct decisions from a capabilities approach or HD perspective, given the strong influences of norms and institutions. It is here that Etzioni's statement becomes particularly meaningful: *'the individual and the community "penetrate" one another'*. There are several routes that might follow from this conclusion: one is to take the decisions out of the hands of individuals and give them to the state. Yet this is clearly unsatisfactory on many grounds. First, how can the state be trusted to know, and if it knows, to take the best decisions? Even if democratic, the state will not be able to take into account the aspirations and capacities of each individual, and is likely to be swayed by particular interests. Moreover, there is clear value for individuals in being in control over their own lives, in being active agents. Although not a

[5] We should note that what we now regard as social norms which have negative impacts on human capabilities are by no means confined to low-income societies. 'Negative' social norms in relation to homosexuality or to race, for example, were pervasive in Western societies until recently and still apply in parts of society. Moreover, what Western societies approve of in relation to restrictions on privacy generally, and especially on the freedom of people labelled as 'terrorists', as well as the treatment of animals, may well be regarded as abhorrent in the future.

perfect solution, given the real constraints on individual autonomy, a second route in relation to decisions about what functionings to choose among private goods in a capability set (i.e. those which affect the consuming person but not others) is to leave such decisions to the individual. However, given that the individual may not recognize (or know about) the full implications of their choices, this route has to be accompanied by efforts to improve information about the consequences of certain behaviours. There remain many decisions which affect people other than the individual—in many cases the family and often people outside the family. Here policies are needed towards social (and market) institutions so as to increase their positive and reduce their negative impacts on individual choices in relation to HD; in some situations, this may justify regulation, reducing the freedom of choice of some individuals. These are complex areas where judgement is required. Because of the influence of social norms on behaviour and the impact of individual behaviour on others, there is no theoretical justification for leaving all decisions to 'autonomous' individuals. Yet, as should be clear by now, there are no simple rules about how much it is justified to influence individual behaviour, nor about who should do the influencing.

Here are a few examples to illustrate the point:

- Health-promoting behaviour involves hand-washing and the use of bed nets in malaria affected areas. To achieve this a family needs certain material resources (water, soap, bed nets). They also need to change their behaviour and this requires a change in norms of behaviour, which can be affected by information via the education sector, the media, and leaders. Evidence suggests that simply providing bed nets, without changing norms, results in only a minority of people using the nets (Banerjee and Duflo 2012). Moreover, to secure such a change may require overriding the preferences of children (to sleep without bed nets).
- Another type of health-promoting behaviour is to stop substance abuse, including consumption of tobacco, alcohol, and drugs. Here, as well as information, restrictions on the sale of these items (or their taxation) are likely to be desirable.
- The long-run well-being of children (health, earnings, etc.) is generally affected by whether they go to school. Here the family has to be persuaded, induced, or compelled to send the child to school, possibly at the expense of loss of earnings from child labour.
- In many societies, equality of opportunities for women requires a major change in social norms as well as restrictions on discriminatory behaviour.
- Families can be trapped in poverty by informal norms that support early marriages and dowry requirements.

In each of these examples, it is assumed that there are some priority objectives—of promoting health, promoting child education, promoting gender equality—which justify policies to change social institutions and to restrict individual choice. Yet individuals, and indeed societies, may reject these objectives—for example, some reject the objective of gender equality. Should those who wish to advance HD override local views where they are inconsistent with the assumed dominant objectives? Nussbaum (2000) has suggested that this is a false dilemma, and indeed that there is a broad and shared 'overlapping' consensus on many values, while Sen (1997) has argued that although there is a large diversity of views many Asian thinkers value freedoms as much as, and in a similar way to, many Western thinkers. Yet in practice there do appear to be conflicts between the values espoused within and across societies. One possible justification for giving primacy to certain objectives is with reference to universal HR as the 'final court' (Vizard 2006). But we must recognize that some argue that these agreed rights are basically Western-imposed conceptions (Mutua 2001).

Ultimately, giving primacy to certain objectives as advancing HD is a matter of values—derived, as shown in Chapter 6, from many philosophical approaches. The various approaches briefly summarized there—which span many centuries—are in considerable agreement about the main categories, but not about how one should define the objectives precisely, or meet them, nor about priorities within them. Sen has argued that these issues should be decided by 'deliberative democracy' (Sen 1999b, Crocker 2006), and others by participatory processes (Chambers 1997, Narayan-Parker et al. 2000). Both have a role to play, but for both, social institutions influence choices, as a result of the influence of social norms on choices and of social institutions on power. These issues will be discussed further in this chapter and in Chapters 8 and 9.

This section has shown that social institutions do indeed penetrate the individual, in the sense of contributing to the way they see the world and the choices they make. Consequently, the autonomous individual is a bit of a myth. It follows that social institutions, and particularly social norms, must themselves be an object of policy so as to promote institutions which not only contribute to the effective production of capability-creating conditions, but also that influence individual choices among capabilities in a positive way from the perspective of agreed HD priorities, such as promoting health and education and limiting violence and substance abuse. If we believe that one set of outcomes (and choices) is superior to another from an HD perspective, then we need to try and change social institutions so that they favour such outcomes. This assumes that a broad agreement can be reached on HD-promoting activities and outcomes, whether by discussion and consensus or by appeal to HR conventions.

7.3.3. *Social Institutions and Power*

Policy change is the outcome of a political struggle in which different groups (and individuals) provide support for particular changes. In this struggle, uncoordinated individuals are generally powerless. They are also powerless to improve the conditions they face in the market. Yet by getting together to support particular changes, individuals can acquire power collectively. As the *Human Development Report of the Dominican Republic* (UNDP 2008, 47), states: 'El empoderamiento individual y el colectivo, para ser sostenibles, tienen que ser simultáneos' (individual and collective empowerment can only be sustained together).[6]

Collective social institutions that have been shown to be effective in supporting change include producer groups, workers' associations, social movements, and political parties. Organizations uniting people are especially crucial for poorer people, since rich individuals can exercise influence through their wealth. Yet groupings of poor people also face the biggest obstacles from lack of finance, low levels of education, poor social networks, and powerful opposition from richer agents (Thorp et al. 2005). Nonetheless, there are many cases of poor individuals improving their conditions by acting collectively at macro, meso, and micro levels (Heyer et al. 2002, Thorp et al. 2005). Examples of the ways that collective action has changed national politics and policy are discussed in Chapter 8, which is focused on the politics of policy change towards HD. Here we discuss the micro and meso levels, and examples of social institutions which have improved the conditions of poor participants through collective action.

Ultimately, as we have already shown, country progress on HD depends on a combination of the macroeconomic structure, economic growth, and government policies. However, within the limits set by these conditions, poor people can improve their own position, and their own set of capabilities, by their own actions. When the deprived come together as a group their position may advance both as a result of cooperation in production leading to greater output, improved marketing, and consequently higher incomes; and because they develop a stronger bargaining position. In many cases, groups perform both production and bargaining functions. Here are some examples of how social institutions among the most extreme deprived groups can improve their position by collective action, primarily by enabling them to bargain effectively with employers or the state:

[6] This report investigates many of the relationships between collective action, empowerment, and HD outcomes (see UNDP 2008, diagram 1.4). It also develops individual and collective empowerment indices.

- An analysis of sex workers in Calcutta shows how one of the most diverse, fragmented, internally competitive, and conflictual sets of individuals improved their conditions and their self-respect as a result of collective organization in a group which bargained for improved conditions (Gooptu 2002).
- Similarly, women in a squatter community in Cape Town (Crossroads) came together to form a highly successful action group which challenged state-sponsored eviction attempts and was even instrumental in the overthrow of apartheid. The group gained the assistance of middle-class rights groups, and obtained media publicity for their cause (Kaplan 1997).
- One of the most marginal set of workers are scavengers, who collect and sell waste products on to middlemen—they are mostly associated with disease and squalor, perceived as a nuisance and probably criminal, and highly exploited. Studies in Asia and Latin America have found that scavengers obtained only about 6 per cent of the price paid to the middlemen. Yet organization of scavengers into groups has resulted in successful cooperatives which significantly improved the conditions of members. In Colombia, for instance, the cooperative *Recuperar* in Medellín by the mid-1990s had almost 1,000 members, 60 per cent of whom were women, with individuals earning 1.5 times the minimum wage and being eligible for loans and scholarships from the cooperative (Medina 1998).
- Women's groups (often organized for productive purposes, such as in cooperatives, or for micro-finance) have also been shown to empower women (Chen 1983, Mahmud 2002, Kumar and Quisumbing 2010, Argawal 2010).
- In Mumbai, an alliance of associations of slum and pavement dwellers improved the position of these most invisible and deprived groups by bargaining with the state, strengthening their position by careful self-enumeration, and permitting people to assert their welfare rights (Menon 2010).
- In Bolivia, a water rights movement culminated in a 'Water War, a popular uprising that kicked out Bechtel, a multinational company that had privatized the water in everything from communally built wells to rain cisterns. Many citizens from across the economic spectrum couldn't afford the exorbitant rates set by the company, so they joined together in protests and road blockades, sending Bechtel packing and putting the water back into public hands.' (Dangl-Znet 2009).
- Some groups start small, but eventually cover very large numbers: for example, The National Dairy Cooperative Federation brings together cooperative federations from across eighteen Indian states; the Self-Employment

> Women's Association in India had 1.5 million members in 2015; and Sri Lanka's Movement of Thrift and Credit Cooperative Societies (SANASA) is an umbrella organization covering over 8,000 individual cooperatives.

However, if the change advocated requires state action, state capacity is needed as well as political support. Muñoz et al. (2006) compare rural indigenous areas in Peru with stronger and weaker local collective institutions, and show that in the areas with a relatively well-organized state (Bambamarca and Espinar), jointly organized activities promote security and improve conditions generally, while in the area with weaker state institutions (Ayacucho) there was little social or economic collective action and the Shining Path was able to exploit the situation to mobilize for violence. Even in the better-organized areas, the indigenous peoples were unable to improve their conditions greatly because of weak state capacity. Muñoz et al. attribute this to weak institutions at the intermediate level: 'if the intermediate level is controlled by political parties that are fragmented, corrupt and prone to personalism and favouritism, then the connections go sour' (Muñoz et al. 2006, 23).

The benefits from these collective efforts often extend beyond material returns. They can also contribute to enhancing the dignity of members and other aspects of well-being—all part of HD. As one member of a small farmer's group in Nepal stated: 'Because we are a group now and we stick to each other, we have suddenly become more powerful. The moneylenders are afraid to exploit us now. The government officials speak to us, they even speak nicely. We are also no longer afraid to enter the bank or the office of the cooperative society' (Bhasin 1979). Similarly, a women's organization in Pakistan helped to initiate a rose production cooperative among the poorest women in the village in 1995: apart from economic benefits, participants noted that 'People in the village now respect me' (Alkire 2002, 1). Further, 'In the early morning I pick flowers. When I do this I feel I have done swab [holy work]. Inner peace comes' (Alkire 2002, 278).

While it is clear that collective action groups among the poor can be effective in improving the conditions of the group concerned, this is unlikely to provide a general solution to improving HD for two reasons. First, the improvements in living conditions are limited so long as those involved continue to work in low-productivity activities—the scavengers, for example, can improve the terms they get, but they will continue to work long hours, with almost no technology, in extremely poor conditions, for low returns. Second, there are many obstacles to the formation of such groups, which limit their coverage. Organization, communication, and leadership are all needed, yet very poor people lack the education and resources to facilitate these (Thorp et al. 2005) Moreover, the groups often face fierce opposition from those they are confronting. An extreme example of this was a Farmers'

Federation in Thailand formed to enforce land rights among the landless. Twenty-one leading members were assassinated and the Federation eventually collapsed (Ghai and Rahman 1981). For these reasons, there are limits to what we can expect from micro-group formation. Despite the many problems, where micro-initiatives succeed, not only do they bring distinct benefits for members, but they can also be stepping stones to mobilization on a greater scale. This was the case with the National Cooperative Dairy Federation in India which began as a few cooperatives and now coordinates activities throughout India, and has become a major actor in milk distribution and the determination of prices.

Hence, while these social institutions can improve the lives of participants in a variety of ways, national policy change is often required to sustain the expansion of HD. Chapter 8 therefore considers the politics underlying such change and collective action on a larger scale.

7.3.4. *The Relationship between Social Institutions and Capabilities and Individual Capabilities*

As stated at the outset of this chapter, the capabilities approach has always defined capabilities as pertaining to individuals, and furthermore that the objective of development is to expand individual capabilities/freedoms. We have shown here the critical importance of social capabilities for providing the conditions for individuals to flourish. Good social conditions affect not only individuals' capabilities and outcomes (functionings) in a particular society at the present time, but also those who will be living in future generations (including the lives of children already born). Clearly, social capabilities are of huge *instrumental* importance for advancing HD today and across generations. Moreover, as argued earlier, social norms affect the very choices that individuals make—not only among the capabilities they may have reason to value, but those which would not be classified as being valuable—such as drug taking, abuse of others, and violence. In this way social institutions and norms 'penetrate the individual', making it difficult to separate them completely. Promoting HD then requires the support and encouragement of institutions and norms that influence individuals in ways that promote valuable capabilities.

Thus while the quality of development—valued or non-valued outcomes—ultimately depends on what happens to individuals, both those alive today and across generations, the nature of social institutions is also of critical importance. When assessing societies from an HD perspective, it is therefore necessary to include not only today's individuals' outcomes (life expectancy, nutrition, education, political participation), but also the social institutions which affect their choices and outcomes, and affect those of future generations. Moreover, prevalent social institutions together with individual capabilities and interactions influence the development of social institutions themselves and consequently future possibilities. In addition, there are aspects of society that affect individuals but *cannot* be assessed by focusing on individuals alone—those that involve, by definition, relationships among the individuals in society. Social cohesion and social inclusivity are among the terms which summarize such relationships, and represent critical conditions for individual flourishing. They are discussed further in Section 7.4. This focus on the social does not imply that one can have a valued outcome at a societal level while individual capabilities flounder, but rather that one needs to investigate the quality of social institutions and social capabilities as providing an essential foundation for the flourishing of individual capabilities.

In Figure 7.1 we present a diagrammatic representation of some of the relationships sketched above between social institutions and individual capabilities. Note the two-way arrows indicating that social institutions affect individuals, but that they in turn are formed by individuals.

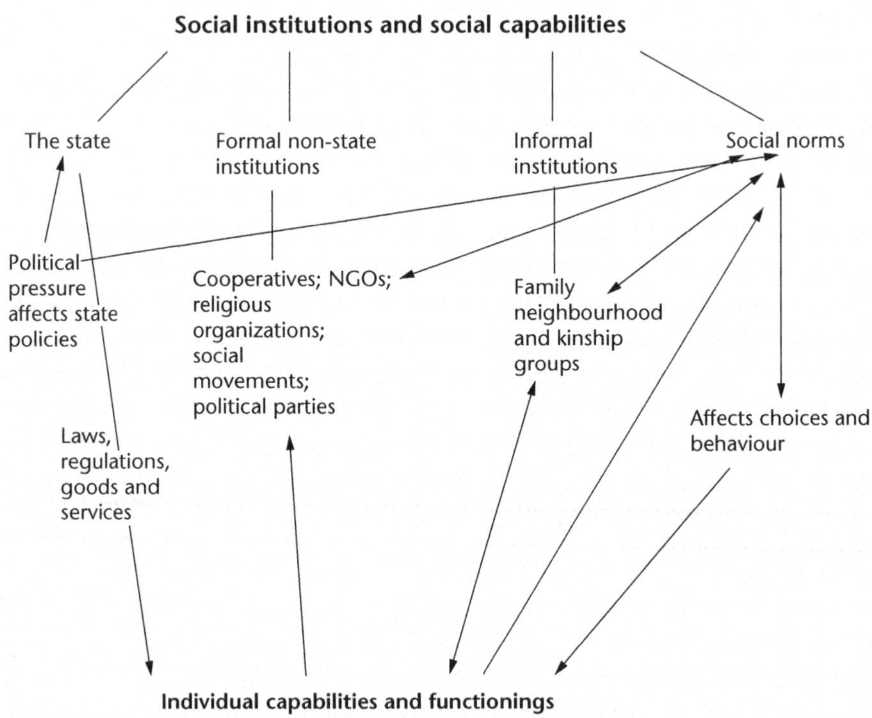

Figure 7.1. The relationship between social institutions and individual capabilities

This section has laid out three different ways in which social institutions (including norms) affect individual capabilities and functionings: first, as essential inputs or means to achieve virtually every significant capability, or important dimension of HD; second, as affecting the choices people make; and third, as affecting individuals' relative power and consequently their market conditions, their access to politically granted benefits, and the political economy of policy choice (see Chapter 8). Section 7.4 will discuss ways of approaching a macro-level assessment of social institutions, both in relation to the types of social institutions discussed, and also in relation to aggregate concepts of social cohesion and social inclusion, which go beyond the individual institutions considered in this section to the relationships across society.

7.4. Analysing a Society's Social Institutions and Social Capabilities

This section presents some considerations which should inform analysis and assessment of social institutions and social capabilities at a country level. It considers the relationship between these and concepts that are often used in aggregative assessments of society, notably including social cohesion and social inclusion, which go beyond particular institutions to consider societal relationships as a whole. It provides a diagrammatic representation of the various relationships, and it makes suggestions for how one might go about empirically assessing social institutions in particular societies from an HD perspective.

7.4.1. *Classifying and Cataloguing Social Institutions and Capabilities*

Clearly not all social institutions and capabilities are desirable from an HD-promoting perspective. For example, non-state institutions and social norms can encourage antisocial behaviour, such as drug trading and consumption, criminality, and violent conflict. So, to put it crudely, we have 'good' and 'bad' social institutions from an HD perspective. In the tradition of capabilities analysis, 'bad' capabilities (those that people do not have reason to value) are not defined as capabilities, and we could do the same here, so that social capabilities and the institutions that produce them are by definition desirable. However, we argue that it would be better to classify all social institutions and social capabilities (good and bad) as such and subsequently sort them into those that promote HD and those that do not, and may even undermine it. This classification would be more transparent, but as already pointed out, some institutions may be good in some respects but not in others, so it may not be possible to make a clear categorization.

A critically important part of any cataloguing of social institutions is to classify them into the HD-promoting, the HD-neutral, and the HD-undermining categories, in order first to assess the richness of particular societies in terms of the HD-promoting institutions (which could be called 'social capital', although this has so many different definitions that it causes confusion to use the term[7]); and second to identify the conditions which give rise to good or bad social institutions (including norms).

7.4.2. *Macro and Micro Aspects of Social Institutions*

While Table 7.1 explored the relationships for each of the selected dimensions independently, it is also useful to aggregate across dimensions and social institutions and consider whether we can identify the *general* features of major social institutions—such as the family, the community, and society as a whole—as well as general features of social norms, which together provide a positive environment for a range of dimensions of HD, so as to identify social institutions which are broadly good for HD. While there can be some ambiguity—for example, a family may support the flourishing of some individuals but not others (perhaps due to gender), or at some times and not others—it still may be possible to identify general tendencies.

A cataloguing and classification of social institutions in each society would provide details of the range of institutions in existence in any society. Nonetheless, it could miss the big picture. In assessing social aspects of a society, it is necessary also to look at society as a whole, and assess the overall quality of social aspects of life in the society. The overall quality does in part depend on the number and quality of social institutions, including the quality of social norms. Yet the overall quality of society goes beyond both organizations and norms. It is possible to have a society with broadly good social institutions, yet there could be dysfunctional family relationships ('living alone', or the converse 'living in an oppressive family'); one where relations across cultures are highly limited (a 'silo' society, as Malaysia is sometimes described); a highly hierarchical society where there are strong social institutions at different levels of society but little contact across levels (a 'class' or caste-ridden society); and/or a stratified society, where economic and social mobility is limited, which would almost certainly be present in hierarchical or silo societies but is also often present in others (Sampson and Morenoff 2006, Stewart and Langer 2008, Clark 2014).

[7] There is no clear and unique definition of social capital (Dolfsma and Danreuther 2003, Foley and Edwards 1999). For this reason, the particular definition adopted by a study will depend on the discipline and level of investigation (Robison et al. 2002). Not surprisingly, considering the different frameworks for looking at social capital, there is considerable disagreement and even contradiction in the definitions of social capital (Adler and Kwon 2002, Claridge 2012). 'Social capital' was used by Putnam to mean membership of non-state social organizations (excluding the Church) (Putnam et al. 1993). But many others have used it to refer to the quantity of interactions between people.

These aspects are all relevant for an assessment of how satisfactory the social conditions are for HD. It is here that concepts of *social cohesion* and *social inclusion* become relevant—these are macro concepts aimed at assessing the quality of the social aspects of life for society as a whole.

Social cohesion is a complex concept which is impossible to define precisely.[8] The concept has its origins in Durkheim's notions of social solidarity and social integration. As Ranci (2011, 2795) states: 'This is a fuzzy concept, including heterogeneous dimensions such as social integration, solidarity, inequality, place attachment or identity. Many different definitions have been proposed in order to reduce its vagueness.' The rather ill-defined nature of the concept is illustrated by some definitions that have been suggested. For example, Bécares et al. (2011, 2773) state that:

> Social cohesion is a multicomponent concept, formed of various dimensions which together contribute to society's collective project and well-being... common values and a civic culture, social order and social control, social solidarity and reductions in wealth disparities, social networks and social capital, and territorial belonging and identity.

The OECD (2011) approach is similar:

> A cohesive society works towards the well-being of all its members, minimising disparities and avoiding marginalisation. It entails three major dimensions: fostering cohesion by building networks of relationships, trust and identity between different groups; fighting discrimination, exclusion and excessive inequalities; and enabling upward social mobility.

Kearns and Forrest (2000, 996) define a cohesive society as 'one where conflict between societal goals and groups, and disruptive behaviours, are largely absent or minimal', and Table 7.2 shows their specification of the multiple domains that contribute to a socially cohesive society (Forrest and Kearns 2001).

It has been suggested that there are two distinct approaches to defining social cohesion: one broadly emanating from Europe, and the other from North America (Hooghe 2012). On the one hand, Europeans emphasize the role of social exclusion, or inequalities and marginalization, as weakening social cohesion. A fundamental aspect of a socially cohesive society is then the shared perception that the distribution of power and material resources is fair. The European approach focuses on the role of government in ensuring that this objective is achieved (Council of Europe 2007, Bécares et al. 2011). On the other hand, the North American approach places much more emphasis on the behaviour and beliefs of individuals in relation to one

[8] The discussion on social cohesion here draws on Langer et al. (2017).

Table 7.2. The domains of social cohesion

Domain	Description
Common values and a civic culture	Common aims, objectives, moral principles, and codes of behaviour; support for political institutions and participation in politics
Social order and social control	Absence of pervasive conflict or threats to existing order; absence of incivility; effective informal social control; tolerance; respect for difference; intergroup cooperation
Social solidarity and reductions in wealth disparities	Harmonious economic and social development and common standards; redistribution of public finances and opportunities; equal access to services and welfare benefits; ready acknowledgement of social obligations and willingness to assist others
Social networks and social capital	High degree of social interactions within communities and families; civic engagement and associational activities; easy resolution of collective action problems
Place attachment and identity	Strong attachment to place; intertwining of personal and place identity

Source: Forrest and Kearns (2001, 2129).

another: their links with one another (in what is often defined as 'social capital'); shared norms of behaviour; agreed intersubjective meaning (or shared understandings); and high levels of trust in others—to describe the bonds that bring people together and the result of this ('solidarity') (Cole 1988, Putnam 2000). This distinction is mainly one of emphasis, as the quotations above illustrate.

Both approaches to the concept were developed to describe social cohesion in developed societies. Here we draw on them to define social cohesion for multi-ethnic developing countries. In this context, we believe that three aspects are critical components of social cohesion:

- The extent of *inequalities*, both horizontal and vertical (stemming from the European approach). Horizontal (or group) inequalities (HIs) are particularly critical for social cohesion in multi-ethnic societies because it is sharp inequalities between ethnic (or religious or regional) groups that fuel political conflict, often leading to violence (Stewart 2008, Cederman et al. 2011). HIs are especially relevant to social cohesion in multi-ethnic societies because competition and conflict tends to run along group (often ethnic) lines. Political and cultural recognition and social HIs are all relevant to social cohesion, as well as economic inequalities. But vertical inequalities are also relevant, since high and rising vertical inequality can undermine bonds among people (Uslaner 2008).
- The level of *trust* among people generally, and particularly across groups, is a powerful indicator of how cohesive a society is—of the strength of the 'glue' that binds people together. Where trust across groups is low,

conflict is more likely (Gambetta 1988),[9] and economic progress can be impeded (Knack and Keefer 1997, Zak and Knack 2001, Beugelsdijk et al. 2004). This element broadly reflects the North American perspective on social cohesion.

- The third critical element, in multi-ethnic societies, is the strength of people's adherence to national *identity* in relation to their group (or ethnic) identity. This component is important for multi-ethnic societies, especially those, such as in Africa, where national boundaries have not developed organically but were created relatively recently by colonial powers. The strength of identities is related to the perceived importance of HIs, since if group identities are relatively weak HIs may not be perceived at all, or if perceived, not regarded as important. It is also relevant because group conflict is more likely if group identities are perceived as strong relative to national ones. Conversely, if people put major emphasis on national identities it indicates that they regard themselves as involved in a shared national project. We need to emphasize that this does *not* imply that giving importance to group identity is inconsistent with social cohesion. In flourishing multi-ethnic societies, people value both their group and their national identities. The term 'multiculturalism' (Kymlika 1995) is sometimes used to describe such a society—one which allows for 'the rich tapestry of human life and the desire among people to express their own identity in the manner they see fit' (Bloor 2010, 272). However, some have interpreted multiculturalism as involving the separate living of each group with limited interactions among them, and this may clearly undermine national social cohesion. Multiculturalism has consequently been displaced by monoculturalism in some European countries, with assimilation to the dominant culture being actively advocated. Yet this too is likely to undermine social cohesion because it causes resentment among the groups whose cultures are suppressed. A socially cohesive society requires both diversity and unity, with both group and national identities being valued. Only where group identities take strong precedence over national ones is national cohesion likely to be be threatened.

Drawing on these three components, we believe that social cohesion can best be represented as a triangle composed of each of the three (see Figure 7.2).

Each of the three elements are indicators of social cohesion; they also reinforce each other. For example, a society with high HIs is more likely to emphasize ethnic as against national identities, and trust across groups is likely to be lower where ethnic identity is given particular prominence.

[9] There is, of course, a two-way relationship between conflict and trust where conflict also destroys trust (Nee 1996, Spence 1999, Warren 1999).

Assessing the extent of social cohesion in a society then requires some attempt to measure these three elements, and composite indicators can be devised (Langer et al. 2017). An alternative (or complementary) approach is to assess social cohesion by looking at outcomes—the absence of violent conflict, low levels of criminality, and so on. There is obviously no single correct way of approaching this complex issue: the important point being made is that the overall state of society is an important element in determining how far HD has progressed.

When it comes to social cohesion and social inclusion we are not talking about the relationship between individuals and social institutions (as depicted in Figure 7.1), but how individuals relate to others in society (the extent and nature of social interactions, trust among individuals and groups, inequality between individuals and groups, and exclusion). Figure 7.3 illustrates the features of social cohesion diagrammatically.

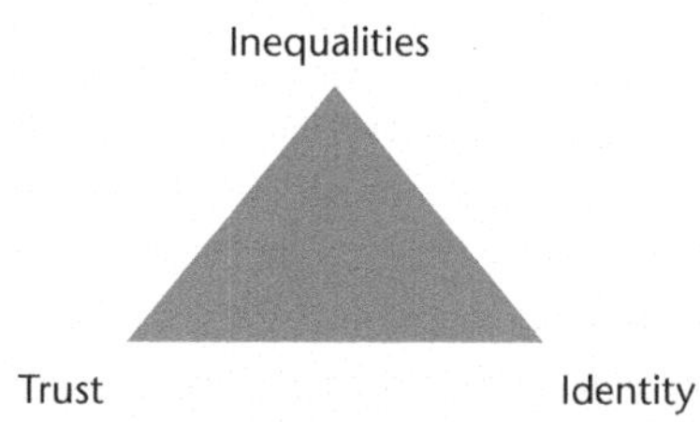

Figure 7.2. Social cohesion triangle

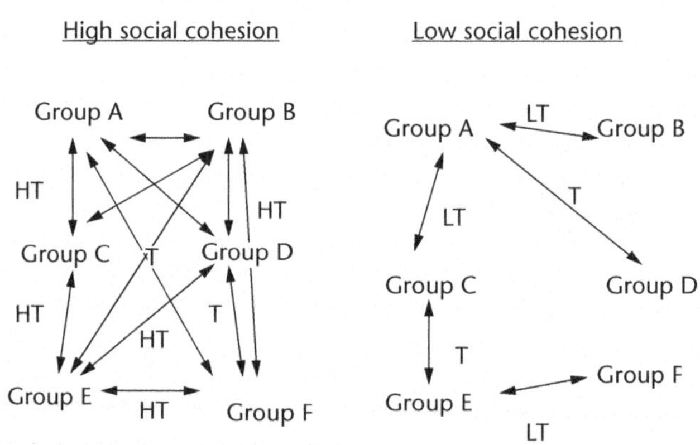

Groups may be divided by religion, ethnicity, gender, region, class, caste, race, etc.

Lines represent significant quantity of social interactions. HT = high trust between members of the groups; T = medium trust; LT = low trust.

Figure 7.3. High and low social cohesion

The concept of *social inclusion* is another way of viewing the overall societal situation, which cannot be assessed by looking only at individual well-being or capabilities. Social inclusion is present where no group or groups suffer multiple disadvantages (economic, political, social, and cultural). A society with high degrees of social exclusion would not qualify as socially cohesive, since by definition it would be hierarchical and stratified, and social inclusion is a contributory element of social cohesion, as already noted. Large HIs are associated with social exclusion and a lack of social cohesion. Measurement of social exclusion/inclusion and HI involves examining both objective indicators by group (of income, assets, social service access, political access and participation, and cultural recognition) and, where possible, perceptions of inequality by group (Mancini et al. 2008, Langer and Mikami 2011). High vertical inequality (across individuals) may also be an indicator of hierarchy.

In addition to measures of social cohesion and social inclusion, other indicators may be argued to reflect the overall well-being of a society: for example, homicide rates and other indicators of criminality and abuse; mental breakdown and suicide rates; and the number of abandoned children.

A full assessment of social aspects of a society then involves four types of measurement and description:

1. a cataloguing of social institutions and social norms;
2. measurement of social interactions;
3. measurement of social exclusion/HIs/vertical inequality; and
4. assessments of societal outcomes, including social cohesion.

7.5. How Does a Focus on Social Institutions and Capabilities affect the Capabilities Approach or HD Approach?

It is helpful to treat this question on four levels: analytic, empirical, policy, and assessment.

7.5.1. *Analytic Level*

At the level of analysis, it suggests that those concerned with the capabilities approach/HD should go beyond the individual where so much of the work to date has been focused and investigate the questions covered briefly in this chapter, including:

- the interactions between groups and individuals;
- incentives and constraints on collective action;
- the formation of groups;
- the relationship between groups and politics and policy outcomes;

- the role of norms in influencing behaviour; and
- how norms are formed.

7.5.2. *Empirical Level*

Empirical work is needed as follows:

- To identify the nature of social institutions and norms that are associated with improvements in the capabilities approach/HD, recognizing that different institutions emerge historically and a range of institutions may (in differing combinations) be consistent with good outcomes.
- To catalogue social institutions in a number of countries and identify the conditions which give rise to 'good' social institutions from an HD perspective.
- To explore the relationship between indicators of social cohesion (interactions, trust, inequalities), as well as other factors,[10] and HD outcomes, especially social outcomes such as homicide, criminality, and suicide.

7.5.3. *Policy Level*

Potentially, this approach opens up a large arena for policy, though before arriving at policy conclusions the analytic and empirical work just noted is needed. Policy areas include:

- Policies to promote social institutions (including norms) which would support the capabilities approach. For example, in relation to regulations and norms, policies need to support health-promoting behaviour and to discourage or even outlaw health-destroying behaviour; similarly, policies with respect to discriminatory behaviour (whether by gender or by ethnic or other group).
- Policies that facilitate empowering social institutions, notably forming groups among the poor for production and bargaining, such as cooperatives, borrowing groups, and workers unions, with a particular focus on promoting women's groups because of the generally relative lack of power among women.
- Policies that promote socially cohesive outcomes, including encouraging interactions across groups (e.g. via the education system, the media, spatial planning, transport).
- Policies to reduce horizontal and vertical inequalities.

[10] Political and economic conditions may, of course, also influence these outcomes.

7.5.4. *Assessment Level*

This is an area where systematic data (within and across countries) are particularly rare. Data are required in order to obtain a picture of the 'social health' of each country, which would include the nature and quantity of social institutions, social interactions, trust, and social mobility; inequalities; and social outcomes. These are not data that are included in national accounts. Nonetheless, the World Values Surveys and the Global Barometer Surveys provide some evidence on trust in others (but often not by group); in some countries there are data for cross-group marriages, but generally not other cross-group interactions; global crime statistics are available for some outcomes (e.g. homicide, suicide, criminality); a number of sources provide data for domestic violence; social surveys sometimes provide data on marriage breakdowns; data on vertical inequality are widely available (if not necessarily accurate); data for HIs by ethnicity can be calculated from many of the DHS surveys, and for HIs by region from most of the surveys, as well as from the Ethnic Power Relations dataset, and geocoded datasets developed by Cederman et al. (2011), while inequality across demographic groups (gender/age) often forms part of surveys and national accounts. Making an aggregate assessment of the strength of social institutions country by country is difficult because of deficient data and because different indicators may move in different directions (this is discussed in Chapter 8).

Nonetheless it is important to complement information on socio-economic and political conditions promoting (or inhibiting) HD with some indicator(s) on the strength of social institutions and aggregate societal conditions.

7.6. Conclusion

This chapter has sketched the main ways that social institutions affect capabilities and HD in an instrumental way: how they affect the very choices people make and the things they value, thereby limiting the autonomy of the individual and posing a major theoretical challenge as to how to identify 'good' influences and 'good' choices. It has also argued (to be developed further in Chapter 8) that collective action—a critically important social institution—can affect the design and implementation of policy relevant to HD. Finally, the chapter considered a holistic approach to society, with relations among people and institutions determining the degree of social cohesion and social inclusion, both of which, in addition to particular social institutions, are important for developing a peaceful and sustainable society in which HD can flourish.

Social interactions are a quintessential part of human life, and their quantity and quality determine what we might call a person's social capabilities (i.e. those capabilities an individual may enjoy that involve relations with others). Moreover, we all live embedded in social institutions—in the family, the neighbourhood, the nation—and these and the nature of social norms that we face deeply affect the nature and quality of our daily life. In other words, we cannot get away from society and retreat into a monadic existence of autonomous individuals, and if we did we would be immeasurably impoverished. That being so, the study of and policy towards social institutions must form an essential component of our approach to HD.

Appendix C

In Ranis et al. 2009, we classified dimensions of country performance into four categories: basic HD, as measured by the HDI, economic performance, social and community relations, and political freedoms and stability dimensions. Most of the data were for selected years between 1990 and 2004, apart from the measure of economic stability which used data for 1981–2002. For each of the four dimensions we classified country performance as to whether it was in the top quartile of low- and middle-income country performance (high), in the bottom quartile (low), or in the

Table C.7.1. Classification of countries according to HD, economic, political, and social performance

	Sub-Saharan Africa	Latin America	Middle East	East and South East Asia	South and Central Asia
Overall classification					
High	2	6	2	2	3
Medium	15	14	11	8	7
Low	25	1	2	1	0
Proportion imbalanced (%)	57	43	29	18	30
Nature of imbalances in performance across dimensions					
Social superior*	6	0	1	0	1
Social deficient**	−1	−2	0	−1	0
Political superior*	10	0	2	0	0
Political deficient**	0	−1	0	−1	0
HD superior*	2	2	0	0	0
HD deficient**	−5	0	0	0	−1
Economically superior*	0	1	1	0	1
Economically deficient**	0	−3	0	0	0

Notes: * A country was identified as superior in one dimension if it was high in one dimension and medium or low in the others; ** it was classified as deficient in a particular dimension if it was classified as low in one or medium or medium and high in the others.

Source: Ranis et al. (2009).

middle two quartiles (medium).[11] Table C.7.1 provides some results of the exercise, showing that a substantial proportion of countries (57 per cent in sub-Saharan Africa and 43 per cent in Latin America and the Caribbean, for example) show imbalances, doing well in some respects but not in others. In sub-Saharan Africa, there was a clear tendency to do better on social and political aspects than the economic dimensions and basic HD.

[11] Given that each dimension was constituted by several indicators, it was possible for country performance on any single indicator to include elements that were in the top quartile and some in the middle two quartiles or the bottom quartile. The classification in these cases is explained in Ranis et al. (2009, 127).

8

The Politics of Progress in Human Development

> Governments do not change magically through some 'historical radical transformation' but only through actual struggles of the time.
>
> Wolfe 1974, 154

> Rise like lions after slumber,
> In unvanquishable number
> Shake your chains to earth like dew
> Which in sleep had fallen on you—
> Ye are many—they are few
>
> Shelley, *The Masque of Anarchy*, 1832

8.1. Introduction

Previous chapters in this book have analysed the origins of the HD approach and its main characteristics, and explored the experience of countries that have been more, and those that have been less, successful in promoting HD. We have identified a set of policies that are likely to promote HD. But we have not investigated why some governments adopt HD-promoting policies to a greater extent than others. To do so we need to understand the underlying political economy of policy choice towards HD, which is the aim of this chapter.

In general, analysis of both HD and capabilities approaches has been stronger on normative issues—what should happen, and what policies are needed to make this occur—than on political economy. In analysing the capabilities approach, Sen touches on politics, from a philosophical perspective, by pointing to the need for democratic deliberation and a 'reasoned consensus' as the way to take the approach forward. Later in this chapter we consider whether this is sufficient for the analysis of the politics of HD, in light of the observed political struggles aimed at advancing HD. As seen earlier in the book, the HD approach has generally been rather pragmatic, identifying and characterizing those societies that, in practice, have been successful, but has done little analysis of the underlying politics. This chapter aims to build on and go beyond these efforts. To do so, we explore a set of theoretical and empirical perspectives.

We start by drawing on Karl Polanyi's 'double movement', which helps to explain progress (and regress) in HD at a high level of generality (Sections 8.2 and 8.3). While Polanyi's sweep of forces provides an overarching framework, more analysis is needed regarding what we might call the meso- and micro-foundations of the Polanyi changes. Historical evidence (including from Polanyi) shows that forms of collective action of protest and advocacy provide such building blocks. Consequently, the second theoretical perspective considered is that of collective action, and here we draw on theories of social movements, such as those by Tilly and Tarrow (Section 8.4). While these theories were developed to describe events in developed countries, we shall consider their relevance to contemporary developing countries. The determinants of group action at the micro level, discussed in Chapter 7, is also relevant here. Drawing these analyses together, we come to some conclusions about the underlying political economy of determinants of progress in HD, and consider how these approaches relate to the ideas of dominant capabilities theorists (Section 8.6).

8.2. Polanyi and Swings in Policy

In his classic work, *The Great Transformation*, Polanyi (1944) analysed factors underlying broad swings in policymaking over the long term, drawing heavily on the experience of Britain in the eighteenth, nineteenth, and early twentieth centuries. The swings he points to consist of movements between strong government (and other) regulation of the economy and the unregulated market. This periodicity is powerfully illustrated for Europe, focusing on the period from the eighteenth to the mid-twentieth century. Polanyi shows how the regulatory and interventionist stance that had governed economies from medieval times gave way to market forces in the nineteenth century, and then, as a reaction to the harsh human consequences of this change, the role of the market was curtailed and that of the state increased in a series of steps—whose timing and nature differed among countries—culminating in the mid-twentieth century, in the introduction of the welfare state and Keynesian macroeconomic management in Western Europe, and the Communist state which advanced HD in a different way in the USSR and Eastern Europe.

Polanyi's main thesis is that each system, whether dominated by the market or by the state, has consequences which provoke intellectual, political, and policy reactions, which in turn lead to a reaction against the ruling model and a return to its opposite. For example, interventionist strategies lead to inefficiencies and severe constraints on entrepreneurial activities, which eventually result in an abandonment of the model, deregulation, and the establishment of a market-driven model; but this in turn has harsh consequences for human conditions and for economic stability, which leads to political pressures for renewed state interventions and eventually a policy change in this direction. The major contribution of Polanyi was not only to identify these cycles, but to show how change required a combination of new ideas and political action, emanating from political pressures:

> Our thesis is that the idea of a self-adjusting market implied a stark utopia. Such an institution could not exist for any length of time without annihilating the human and natural substance of society.... Inevitably, society took measures to protect itself, but whatever measures it took impaired the self-regulation of the market, disorganised industrial life, and thus endangered society in yet another way.
>
> (Polanyi 1944, 3)

Polanyi draws on the experience of Europe, and especially England, in the years between about 1700 and the time of his writing (1944) to illustrate this.

Although, according to Polanyi, market transactions of some kind are pervasive throughout human history, in economic systems prior to nineteenth-century Europe the market played a subordinate role. 'Though the institution of the market was fairly common since the later Stone Age, its role was no more than incidental to economic life' (Polanyi 1944, 45). In contrast, 'the control of the economic system by the market ... means no less than the running of society as an adjunct to the market. Instead of economy being embedded in social relations, social relations are embedded in the market' (Polanyi 1944, 60).

Until reforms in the nineteenth century, England had a highly regulated economy. From medieval times, trade within and between countries was subject to strict regulations, much of it administered by guilds. Tolls and prohibitions restricted trade between towns. Though many of these were abolished in the sixteenth and seventeenth centuries, they were replaced by extensive government regulation. Equally, land was embedded in social relations and controlled politically and socially, rather than through the market. Labour was subject to numerous regulations and controls, including those governing the relations of master, journeyman, and apprentice, by guild, custom, and statute, while there were severe restrictions on labour mobility, since each parish had the duty to provide for their own destitutes. In general, '[t]he economic system was submerged in general social relations; markets were merely an accessory feature of an institutional setting controlled and regulated more than ever by social authority' (Polanyi 1944, 70).

Adam Smith (among others) provided the intellectual justification for removing market restrictions, arguing that a laissez-faire market would promote efficiency and growth, while others (including Bentham) advocated a free market in land. The political impetus for reform came from an emerging entrepreneurial class, first making money by using the 'enclosed' (or appropriated) lands to keep sheep and sell wool, and then moving into manufacturing and exporting.[1] Their activities were constrained by the heavy regulations in existence and they used their growing power to oppose them. Political reforms reflected the growth of this class, as the 1832 Reform Act enlarged the franchise so that representatives of the emerging industrial entrepreneurial class gained representation in the reformed House of Commons (Thompson 1963, Foot 2005, Fraser 2013).

Land was the first factor of production to be 'freed', with the enclosure movement of the late eighteenth century, and formal restrictions on land transfers in England were abolished in 1801.[2] A competitive labour market resulted from legislation relaxing the restrictions on labour mobility, the Combination Laws of 1799 and 1800 which banned workers' unions, and the Poor Law reform of 1834 which provided only minimal and demeaning support for the destitute via workhouses, in contrast to the much more generous Speenhamland system which it replaced. With the repeal of the Corn Laws in 1846, England came close to a pure market economy.

These reforms—which facilitated the rapid growth of industry—had their own consequences which in turn provoked an intellectual, political, and policy reaction. The social consequences of unregulated industrialization, in particular, were appalling, in terms of poverty, squalor, and indignities. Labourers were forced to work very lengthy days in dangerous conditions; child labour abounded; and health, sanitation, and housing were all of abysmal standards.[3] In HD terms, this era was one of stagnation if not of

[1] According to Polanyi (1944, 37): 'Enclosures have appropriately been called a revolution of the rich against the poor.'

[2] This was done through the Prescriptions Act, the Inheritance Act, the Fines and Recovery Act, the Real Property Act, and the General Enclosure Act of 1801, as well as subsequent legislation.

[3] Engels was among the first to record conditions of the English working class in detail, publishing his classic on the condition of the working class in England in 1844 (Engels and Kelley 1888). Later in the century, Booth's first study of London's East End was in 1887, and Rowntree's first pioneering survey of poverty in York was in 1899 (Booth 1887, Rowntree 1902). Among many more recent accounts, see, for example, Thompson (1963), Englander (1998), and Nardinelli (1990).

regress. Moreover, there were also economic problems: unhealthy and uneducated workers had low productivity; and the unregulated market was subject to acute fluctuations—the so-called 'business cycle'—with adverse consequences for the owners of capital as well as for workers.

These extreme consequences led to reactions, once again limiting market freedoms. There were numerous intellectual critiques, both liberal and socialist. These included Robert Owen, who initiated the cooperative movement; the writings of Marx and Engels, as well as moderate socialists such as Shaw, Tawney, and Cole; and, in the 1930s, Keynes' powerful critique of the economic model. Collective organizations emerged to resist, reverse, and regulate the changes. Workers brought together in the new factories combined to improve their conditions and the Combination Laws were repealed in the belief that if legalized they would be less threatening (Briggs 1979, Thompson 1963). Political movements also emerged, including the Chartists, the Reform League, the Socialist League, the Fabian Movement in the late nineteenth century, and eventually the Labour Party (whose Constitution required that the state take over the 'commanding heights of the economy') which brought together Fabian socialists and the trade union movement; while in other European countries, powerful Communist movements (and in a few countries, Fascist ones) emerged.

Ultimately, policy reforms regulating the market and improving human conditions resulted from the political pressures exerted by these organizations. The reforms took two forms: on the one hand, piecemeal regulation of markets and the provision of social security in Britain and other countries in Western Europe; and on the other, massive changes in the whole organization of society and the economy following the Marxist and Fascist revolutions.

Focusing on Britain, the reforms which were gradually introduced in response to these critiques and political pressures included a succession of Factory Acts which regulated hours and conditions and banned child labour, and the extension of the franchise to the (male) urban skilled working class in 1867 and to skilled and semi-skilled agricultural labourers and miners in 1884, which increased political pressure to improve working conditions. These were soon followed by the expansion of education to much of the working class and by acts further improving factory conditions. Unemployment insurance and pensions were introduced in the first decade of the twentieth century. Further extensions of the franchise followed the First World War, including extending the vote to women. The reintroduction of tariffs in reaction to the massive unemployment of the 1920s and 1930s represented a further move away from the self-regulating market. Then, during the Second World War, planning and controls basically replaced the market. This was when Polanyi was writing. In the UK, further changes in the same direction occurred in the years immediately after the Second World War, with the Beveridge reforms, the founding of the National Health Service, and the nationalization of basic industries.

This did indeed represent a 'Great Transformation' (the title of Polanyi's book)—from an almost unadulterated market system to a strongly controlled one. In terms of HD policies, the swing to the market was accompanied by policies undermining HD, while the swing towards regulation broadly involved policies promoting HD, as we show in Section 8.3.

A swing-back then occurred in the 1980s, following the basic Polanyi logic: the heavy state control over the market eventually provoked a reverse swing, with a return to the market model. Intellectually, the critique of the Keynesian approach was led by Milton Friedman, who pointed to the inflationary consequences of a Keynesian approach, while Frederich Hayek had long criticized planning for its inefficiencies; others, such as Alan Walters and Arthur Laffer, argued that public sector industries were inefficient, and that high levels of taxation were a disincentive to entrepreneurial activity. There was a strong political reaction, particularly to the increasing power of the trade unions, rising disruptions caused by strikes, and accelerating inflation. Governments were elected espousing monetarism and a market orientation—notably those led by Margaret Thatcher and Ronald Reagan. They soon reversed many of the policies of the 'Great Transformation'. Keynesian macro-policies were discredited. Britain led the way in privatizing previously nationalized industries. Marginal tax rates were reduced and expenditure on social services and social protection restricted. The powers of the trade unions were severely constrained. Financial services were deregulated. The market once again dominated society, albeit a much-regulated market, constrained on most fronts by numerous regulations relating to employment conditions, market structure, trading conditions, etc., while extensive measures of social protection were maintained.

Although Polanyi himself was not analysing developing countries—which, apart from Latin American countries, were mostly colonies when he was writing—since 1950, the Polanyi swings have been echoed in both thought and policy in developing countries, as we traced in Chapter 1. In this context we need to consider two layers of Polanyi-type influences over policymaking and consequent policy swings. First, there are the swings in the developed countries, which obviously influence (and indeed, often determine) what happens in developing countries. Second, there are developments within developing countries themselves which may lead to 'domestic' Polanyi swings.

As pointed out in Chapter 1, from the 1950s during the first decades after developing countries became politically independent, the influence of developed countries over their policies was paramount. Latin American countries, of course, had been independent for much longer but were still strongly influenced by the industrialized countries. The planning and interventionist era which then prevailed was, however, brought to an end from the early 1980s, partly as a result of domestic developments, notably the onset of the debt crisis, but also by the changing philosophy dominating policymaking in developed countries and transmitted to developing countries by the IFIs. A pro-market and anti-state era began, in which human dimensions were given a subordinate role. As argued in Chapter 1, this in turn led to weak HD which provoked an intellectual reaction, including the development of the HD approach itself.

Over time, the intellectual and policy autonomy of developing countries has greatly increased (although with considerable variations among countries). The widespread shift from authoritarian to democratic systems in the 1980s and 1990s meant that popular pressure played a larger role in decision-making, tending to support more HD-type policies. Thought and then policy generally evolved towards a more HD stance, as shown in Chapter 1, leading first to the global agreement on the MDGs in 2000 (and the SDGs in 2015), accompanied by measures to achieve these goals, with increased expenditure on social services and the near-universal introduction of social protection (ODI 2010, Fukuda-Parr 2014). Policy changes from 2000 reversed the apparently inexorable trend towards greater inequality in the majority of Latin American countries, as well as some countries elsewhere (Lopez-Calva and Lustig 2012, Cornia 2014). Yet while social dimensions were given a central role, the dominance of the (now global) market was not challenged.

The Polanyi pendulum (as this is sometimes termed, e.g. Mitchell 2006) provides a powerful overarching framework for understanding changing policy stances, although recent changes have been less extreme—in each direction—than those Polanyi recorded for historical Europe. The reversion to a market model from 1980 left a considerable range of HD-promoting measures in developed countries, while in developing countries, though many HD measures were eliminated or reduced in the 1980s, some policies to promote social developments were adopted from around 1990, with an increasing range in the 2000s even though the economy remained very market-oriented.

8.3. HD Achievements during Polanyi Swings

Can we say which of Polanyi's swings is best for HD? The pure market model tends to mean fewer resources devoted to social security or to investment in human resources, and is likely to increase human *insecurity* generally, through increased market fluctuations;[4] on the other hand, its proponents claim it may lead to a faster growth of market entitlements and of technology and promotes HD through rising incomes.[5] Yet, as shown in Chapter 3, sustained growth in output requires promotion of HD, while analysis suggests that high inequality also threatens the sustainability of growth (Berg et al. 2008, Lansley 2012, Stiglitz 2013).

A broad overview of evidence indicates that HD generally does better in the eras with the more interventionist stance. Yet going back into European history, the HD achievements of the pre-Industrial Revolution regulatory model were extremely poor in terms of life expectancy and of education, although data are deficient:

> In Europe's preindustrial and overwhelmingly agricultural society, people did not in general live long lives. While there were exceptions, by our standards, life expectancy was appallingly low for most and almost inconceivable to a modern audience living in an advanced industrial society where longevity is constantly being revised upwards. (Knapp 1998, 89)

But the market model did not lead to improvements, initially at least. Data for the nineteenth century shows no decline in death rates from 1841 (the first date for which there are statistics) to 1861, and indeed rises for some of the main cities (McKeown and Record 1962, Szreter 1997)—a period at the height of the unregulated market. In the US, '[l]ife expectancy likely reached a high point in the late eighteenth century and then declined until the later nineteenth century' (Haines 2001), from fifty-seven years for white males in 1790–4 to forty-eight years in 1855–9. Similar evidence of worsening conditions in the mid-nineteenth century is shown by the declining heights of army recruits to the US West Point military academy from the 1830s to the 1970s (Haines 2001).

However, there was a definite decline in mortality rates in Britain from 1861 to 1900, although there appears to have been no change in the infant mortality rate throughout the nineteenth century, which remained high, at around 150 per 1,000 live births (McKeown and Record 1962). The improvement in death rates in the last decades of the nineteenth century has been attributed to improved diet (leading to a decline in tuberculosis and typhus) and changes in sanitation (associated with public investment and public

[4] Rodrik (1997) has shown that for developed countries increased fluctuations are associated with globalization and governments' reduced ability to protect people.

[5] For example, Little et al. (1970), arguing for market reforms in 1970, concluded that they would improve income distribution and reduce poverty. This was also what Dollar and Kraay (2002) purported.

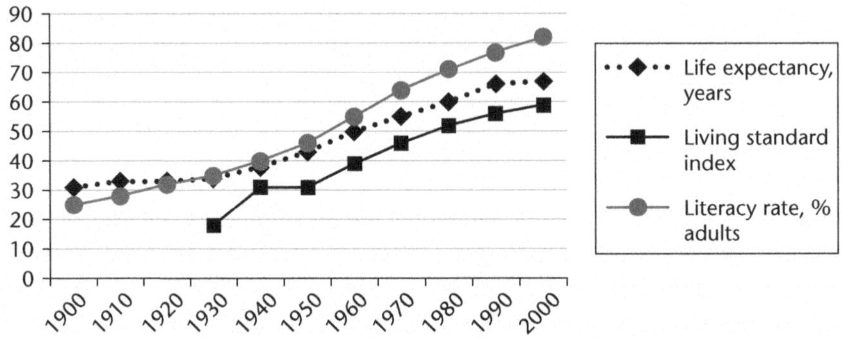

Figure 8.1. Progress in life expectancy, literacy, and living standards in thirteen Latin American countries, 1900–2000

Source: Astorga et al. (2005)

health measures) which led to a reduction in typhus and cholera (McKeown and Record 1962, Szreter 1997). Szreter has argued that public health measures were critical and at least in part due to 'political organisation, particularly the extent to which poorer sections of the community have an effective voice' (Szreter 1997, 717).

A similar picture emerges for the twentieth century for the US and Latin America (see Figure 8.1). The historical living standards index is essentially an estimated HDI, using literacy as the education indicator and 1950 as the base year (Astorga et al 2005). We can see from this that there was some progress in each decade, but the marked acceleration occurred in the interventionist years while there was a slowdown in the pro-market years from 1980 in the Latin American cases.

Examining regional developments from 1960 to 1980, we see a general worsening of performance in the 1980s, with some recovery in the 1990s and better performance in the 2000s almost everywhere (evidence is provided in Figures 1.2 to 1.7 in Chapter 1). There was a slowdown in the improvement in under-five mortality from 1980 and school enrolment, even in the fast-growing region of East Asia (Figures 1.4, 1.5, and 1.6). In sub-Saharan Africa, progress accelerated on under-five mortality and school enrolment in the 2000s. The changes in mortality are partly due to the impact of AIDS and improvements in treatment in the 2000s. Economic growth also slowed significantly in the 1980s everywhere except Asia. Growth improved, however, decade by decade in East Asia, and also improved in the 'market' era in South Asia, both regions where there are strong states that continue to intervene economically; but per capita incomes fell in the 1980s in the regions that were closest to the pure market model—Africa and Latin America—recovering in the 2000s.

In general, this quick review supports the conclusion that market domination is less conducive to progress on HD than more interventionist strategies. State action is needed to advance HD and capabilities. This does not, of course, mean that the market should or need play no role, but rather that it needs to be 'governed', to use Robert Wade's (1990) term, and to be supplemented by public action for promoting HD. Broadly, this is what Drèze and Sen concluded when they argued that one can promote capabilities through 'growth-mediated security', in which the state supplements market-generated entitlements, or through 'support-led security', in which the state takes the lead (Drèze and Sen 1989). The country experience recorded in Chapter 5 illustrates the varying role of the market in 'success' cases.

While Polanyi's swings provide a broad understanding of why policies towards HD change over time, this is at a high level of generality. Actual change takes place because of specific events—movements that develop to support change and responses to these movements by governments. As Piven and Cloward (1979, 36), citing Wolfe (1974), note: 'governments do not change magically through some "historical radical transformation" but only through actual struggles of the time'. In England, changing economic structures gave rise to workers' movements. Extension of the franchise in the nineteenth and early twentieth centuries was an important precondition for social and economic reform. Reform of the electoral franchise—first from the aristocracy to industrialists and property owners and later to working-class males, and eventually women too—was the consequence of pressure from below. As Foot states, the electoral reforms were 'wrung out of Commons and Lords by mass agitation and mass action' (Foot 2005, 169). The first major reform of the franchise (in 1832) occurred against a background of organized peaceful protest and of sporadic violence (Foot 2005, Fraser 2013). Once in place, the reforms changed electoral arithmetic and the complexion of political parties. Protests, mass meetings, petitions, and strikes also contributed to social and economic reforms. Piven and Cloward (1979) detail how movements of the unemployed in the US, involving mass marches, petitions, and occasionally violence, secured enhanced relief, often ad hoc, but eventually through legislation. Similarly, the collective efforts of workers in the 1930s—involving strikes and other mass disruptions—eventually led to major concessions in terms of worker conditions and social relief. Thus, to begin to understand the political conditions for progress on HD, one has to go beyond the general swings of Polanyi, to an analysis of why movements for change emerge and have effect. To do so, it is helpful to draw on the analysis of social movements and of collective protests more generally for understanding pro-HD change at the macro level; and on group formation and group power at the micro level, for understanding how particular groups can improve their position.

8.4. Social Movements and Political Protests

Social movement analysts have developed a framework to help understand when and why people engage in social movements (see especially Tarrow 1998 and Tilly 2004), where social movements are defined as popular (often single-issue) movements, adopting peaceful means, sustained over a reasonable period. As Wilson states, '[a] social movement is a conscious, collective and organised attempt to bring about or resist change in the social order' (Wilson 1973, 8). On the assumption that there is a shared and strongly felt grievance, it is suggested that people initiate such movements when patterns of political opportunities and constraints change; they then employ a repertoire of collective action (e.g. marches, petitions, strikes), which can create new opportunities, which may then be used by others in widening cycles of contention. 'When their struggles revolve round broad cleavages in society; when they bring people together around inherited cultural symbols; and when they can build on—or construct—dense social networks and connective structures, these episodes of contention result in sustained interactions with opponents in social movements' (Tarrow 1998, 1045).

The political opportunity structure consists of the possibilities for (and constraints on) effective action. Countries differ radically in this respect, and in each country there can be major changes in this structure over time. At one extreme, authoritarian and repressive regimes which forbid political protest and collective action of any kind offer very limited opportunities for collective protest. People may be prohibited from holding public meetings, communication may be outlawed, strikes made illegal, etc. Social movements may nonetheless emerge in extreme circumstances or if repression appears to be weakening. For example, wars or financial crises may challenge the power of the authorities, leaving room for public protest, as in Indonesia, for instance, after the financial crisis of the 1990s. With repressive regimes, progress in HD may still occur, generally not as a result of movements from below, but because of the decisions of the regime. In Chile under Pinochet, for example, there was very limited political opportunity, but the dictator did give some priority to education and health although poverty and unemployment increased. Similarly, a strong premium was put on education in South Korea, first by Japanese colonialists and then by the authoritarian generals that acquired power after independence. Communist regimes also allow limited political opportunities, but they give priority to many HD objectives for ideological reasons, and consequently tend to show good performance on the HDI. However, many authoritarian regimes do very poorly on HD, like Burma, North Korea, or Argentina during the dictatorships of the 1930s and 1970s.

This is where the democratizing political reforms of the 1980s and 1990s become relevant. Along with economic reforms, this era saw political reforms in many countries in Latin America and sub-Saharan Africa (Whitehead 2002, UNDP 2002). In Latin America, the military rulers withdrew almost everywhere and ceded to democratic institutions—including allowing universal voting rights among citizens and freedom of association and of the press (Garreton Merino and Newman 2001, UNDP 2002). By 1999, twenty-five out of twenty-six countries in Latin America and the Caribbean had multiparty electoral systems. In Africa, many long-term presidents (in some cases, the same people who had headed the independence movements; in others, rulers who had gained power through war or coups) permitted elections to determine who would govern. In sub-Saharan Africa, twenty-nine out of forty-two countries had multiparty electoral systems by 1999 (UNDP 2002). However, the twenty-first century has seen some retreat from democracy in parts of the world. In some African countries, elected presidents are prolonging their tenure and preventing the democratic transfer of power. While Ghana, Malawi, and Zambia have all allowed government changes through the democratic process, in Uganda and Zimbabwe, among others, such change has been avoided by careful manipulation of the political system. Moreover, in some places organized opposition protests have been followed by coups, displacing the democratically elected government (for example, in Thailand and Egypt).

We noted earlier that electoral reform was an important precondition for social reforms in England in the nineteenth and twentieth centuries. Evidence for other European countries from the eighteenth to the twentieth centuries shows that the introduction of more democratic systems of government was associated with increased expenditures on transfers to the poor and public expenditure on education (Lindert 2004). One reason is that, in principle, democracy allows the preferences of those with incomes below the average to outweigh those with incomes above average since they are more numerous. Moreover, democracy provides the space for collective movements to develop and to influence political parties and democratic decision-making. While democracy provides a favourable environment for social movements to emerge, it does not in itself ensure that such collective action occurs or that social progress is attained, as was illustrated earlier in this book.

First, we should note that not all democracies are equally democratic. The right to vote is just one of a range of conditions required for a full democracy; apart from the vote, the right to form political parties, the fairness of elections, and freedom of the media, are also requirements—many of which are frequently absent in newly formed 'democracies'. As Tarrow (1998) notes, many other conditions besides democracy are necessary for the formation of social movements, and the same is true for political parties favourable to HD. Tarrow suggests that the conditions which favour the development of a social movement include a common cleavage around shared inherited cultural symbols and dense social connections. In nineteenth-century Europe, such dense social connections among workers and common values emerged as a consequence of people working together in factories—in contrast to the feudal isolation of agricultural workers. The trade unions which developed put direct pressure on employers for improved conditions, and eventually helped to form workers' political parties with the explicit objective of improving the conditions of working people. In many developing countries, in contrast, where the modern industrial sector accounts for a small minority of workers, the dense connections permitted by factory work are largely absent. Rural societies involve multiple social and economic relationships across classes which makes it difficult for the poor to organize collectively against the privileged (Scott 1985). Latin American countries seem to be an exception to this tendency, with extensive peasant movements in several countries which have succeeded in making land reform a central political issue (Robles 2001). In addition, there are particular challenges for class or issue-oriented collective organization in multi-ethnic societies, where the inherited cultural symbols and connections tend to be within an ethnic group rather than a class. As a result, political parties tend to be ethnic in nature and to promote the interests of their own cultural group rather than those of the poor as a whole (Posner 2005). Possibly for this reason, empirical investigation shows that multiethnic societies tend to have lower levels of public expenditure (Easterly and Levine 1997, Alesina et al. 1999).

Nonetheless, social movements have developed in many places, including some plural societies, sometimes as single-issue movements (like Right to Food in India), and sometimes class-based ones, like the peasants' and landless workers' movements in Brazil, Ecuador, Colombia, Mexico, Paraguay, and Bolivia. Moreover, alliances between peasants' and workers' movements in Brazil, Bolivia, and Venezuela supported the formation of progressive political parties in these countries, which eventually gained power democratically. Both single-issue and class-based movements have had some success in terms of changing policy towards promoting HD. These are a type of social institution—as defined in Chapter 7—which can help bring about the political conditions for improvements in HD.

The case of the South Korean workers' movement provides an example of how a class-based movement may develop and contribute to an improvement in human conditions. In Korea, the union movement has a long history, dating back to the formation of a union of dockworkers at the end of the nineteenth century, while national-level unions were formed in the 1920s. Their activities were heavily restricted during the period of military rule (1961–79), with union activity confined to the company level and political activity forbidden. However, with the fast growth in factory employment, concentrated in a few industrial centres in the 1970s, working-class consciousness increased and union membership grew rapidly. At the same time, social and political movements developed, based on churches and student organizations. These were united with workers' and peasants' movements in a social movement, *minjung*, which promoted democracy and workers' rights in a similar way to that of the working-class movement in nineteenth-century Britain. Strikes (mainly illegal) occurred throughout the 1980s, culminating in an explosion of industrial unrest in 1987, which was a major factor behind the democratization which followed and which in turn facilitated further unionization. The Korean Confederation of Trade Unions was formed in 1995. The union movement was at first concentrated in light industry, where female workers dominated, but later, reflecting the changes in industrial structure, it became strongest in heavy and chemical industries where men dominated. The union movement pressed for improved work conditions, including wages, and supported the formation of a political party—the Democratic Labor Party—to represent worker interests (Koo 2001, Lee and Lee 2005, Keumsoo n.d.).

In Korea, the advance of democracy and workers' and social movements also led to substantial improvements in well-being. From colonial times onwards, Korean governments had promoted education. But the increasing power of workers' and grassroots movements saw advances in HD in other dimensions, notably real wage share, conditions of work, health care, and pensions. The share of wages in manufacturing rose from around 50 per cent in 1987 to 57 per cent in 1997, but then fell with the financial crisis. However, it remained much higher than in comparable countries with weaker labour movements, including Turkey and Mexico (Onaran 2009). There has been universal health insurance since 1989, while successive acts in the 1980s and 1990s provided for a national pension scheme with universal coverage.

The Brazilian case also provides an instructive illustration of how pro-HD change can result from political change following pressure from peasants' and workers' movements. Historically, Brazil has notoriously had one of the most unequal income and land distributions in the world. Like many other Latin America countries, a dictatorship was replaced by democratic institutions in Brazil in the mid-1980s. Both pre- and post-democratic governments undertook drastic stabilization and adjustment policies in this decade, supported by the IMF. Democratization allowed the Landless Workers' Movement (the *Movimento Sem Terra*, or MST) and the Workers' Party (*Partido dos Trabalhadores*, or PT) to acquire legal status and growing influence. The MST gained a membership of over 1.5 million and was represented in almost all Brazilian states. Besides exerting pressure on government policy in favour of land reform and on environmental issues, it initiated and supported land invasions, providing the land to the landless (Petras and Veltmeyer 2001, Robles 2001, Landertinger 2009). 'Over the course of the MST's twenty-five years of work, it has expropriated some 35 million acres, land that is now occupied by roughly a million families. The settlements, which are cooperatively organized, are home to hundreds of MST-built schools, which have enabled tens of thousands of people to read and write' (Dangl-Znet 2009). The PT was formed out of the 'New Unionism' that emerged in the 1980s, following major strikes by metal workers, led by Lula de Silva (French and Fortes 2005, Hunter 2006).

Lula de Silva was elected president of Brazil in 2002, with the support of both MST and PT, after standing as a candidate for over a decade; his election was partly due to the unpopularity of the adjustment measures. Yet, Lula did not challenge the neoliberal model and continued to follow orthodox economic policy. Moreover, despite strong pressure from the MST, he did little for agricultural workers as his proposed land reforms, initiated as a result of pressure from the MST, were blocked by private agricultural interests. He continued to support agro-business, but he did greatly increase expenditure on basic services and introduced large-scale cash transfer programmes to reduce poverty (*Bolsa Família*), while he raised the minimum wage. Cash transfers reached all of the extremely poor and over three-quarters of the poor (Cornia 2014, 347). Research has shown that these transfers had a significant impact in reducing inequality (Soares et al. 2009). Public spending per child on education doubled during 2000–10 (Cornia 2014, 334), as did expenditure per head on health (World Bank n.d.). Public health expenditure as a proportion of GDP rose from 2.9 per cent to 4.2 per cent, and education from 4.0 per cent to 5.8 per cent, during 2000–10. Average years of education among adults rose by 1.7 years in the 2000s and the educational Gini fell (Cornia 2014, 35). The real minimum wage rose by 59 per cent between 2002 and 2010 (Cornia 2014, 35). Over the years 2001 to 2009, the Gini coefficient measure of inequality of disposable income fell quite sharply, from 0.588 in 2001 to 0.537 in 2009. Between 2001 and 2007, the poorest 60 per cent of the population, which accounted for less than 20 per cent of income in 2001, secured 40 per cent of total growth in income (IPC 2009).

Similar developments in Bolivia again illustrate how peasants' and workers' movements, especially if they form an alliance, can gain power through democratic elections. In Bolivia, a military government was replaced by a democratically elected one in 1982. Bolivia suffered acutely from the debt crisis because of a sharp fall in the price of tin, and was subject to an exceptionally drastic adjustment policy in the early 1980s. This effectively reduced inflation, but at the cost of a major loss of output, high unemployment, and worsening poverty and income distribution. This, together with the policy aiming to eliminate coca production, undertaken by the US and the Bolivian governments, radicalized the population, especially indigenous coca farmers. Evo Morales, himself indigenous, who had been general secretary of the *cocaleros* union (the coca-cultivating peasants) and subsequently leader of the Federation of Unions, was elected president in 2005, with the support of the unions and peasants. A series of social movements were behind this election, including the Peasant Confederation (*Confederación Sindical Única de Trabajadores Campesinas de Bolivia*) and the *Asamblea por la Soberania de los Pueblos*, which together formed the *Movimiento al Socialismo-Unzaguista*, bringing together indigenous peasants and workers (Stefanoni and Alto 2006).

Morales adopted a number of changes likely to promote HD. He nationalized hydrocarbons and retained a greater proportion of the revenue for the state. He introduced a new Constitution giving more power to indigenous people, more state control over natural resources, and greater decentralization—which was endorsed by over 60 per cent of the electorate in January 2009. On the social side, pensions and transfers were extended to one-third of the population, public investment increased sixfold between 2006 and 2011, the minimum wage was raised by 127 per cent, an emergency employment programme was introduced for women, and education programmes were expanded, including policies to eliminate illiteracy. Extreme poverty was reduced from 24 per cent to 14 per cent in urban areas, and from 63 per cent to 43 per cent in rural areas, and there was a small decline in inequality, from a Gini of 0.576 in 2005 to one of 0.556 in 2011 (Crabtree 2009, Molina 2013, Cornia 2014).

In some countries, single-issue mass movements have also brought about significant change in national policy, without gaining political power directly. For example, in India, a mass movement emerged to secure a National Rural Employment Guarantee scheme as part of the Right to Food Campaign, based on a coalition of left-wing parties and involving huge popular marches. An act introducing the scheme was passed in 2005. It potentially revolutionizes opportunities for work and income in rural India, as it guarantees one hundred days of work per household at minimum wages. Although more successful in some areas than others, it has contributed to raising wages generally and reducing rural poverty (Zepeda et al. 2013). Another example from India comes out of the state of Rajasthan where social movements were instrumental in achieving 'Right to Information' legislation which allows citizens to investigate government records (Goetz and Jenkins 1999).

In Morocco, women's organizations united in a *Union de l'Action Feminine* in 1992, and 'launched a grassroots campaign to change the family laws' (Green 2008, 67). Using mass petitions, demonstrations, and lobbying, the movement eventually secured a reformed Family Code which gave women more equality in the law and in marital matters.[6] This was made possible not just by

[6] In his book, Green 'discusses a number of different types of initiative across the world that have enhanced and expanded the powers of the powerless and through that have reduced the unfreedoms that characterise the poverty of the deprived. In bringing about these changes, the state obviously can—and does—have an important role to play, and yet the state is not the only responsible agency that can make a difference, nor is it the only instrument for tackling the general evil that society tends to tolerate and accept. If the evil of poverty and the crime associated with it

a persistent and united movement, but also by a sympathetic government and king—a relatively favourable 'political opportunity structure'.

Overarching identity groups have sometimes been formed, overcoming internal fragmentation, with the intention of forming a united and more powerful lobby for improvement in their conditions. For example:

- The Orang Asli in Malaysia formed a single identity, encompassing eighteen different groups, including different customs and languages, so as to negotiate for improved conditions. The Peninsula Malaysia Orang Asli Association has been formed to help protect Orang Asli culture and their treatment by the state.
- Similarly, the Luhya in Kenya, also constituted by eighteen sub-groups speaking different dialects, united under a single umbrella organization—the Luhya Elders Forum—and identity so as to become an effective force in politics. Together they form about 16 per cent of the Kenyan population and their vote is often decisive in elections.
- Posner (2005) has shown how in Zambia different ethnic groups unite under a common political banner in order to form a majority and secure power democratically.

8.5. What We Learn from the Examples

The examples discussed here fit well with the two theoretical perspectives analysed earlier. In terms of the Polanyi model, these collective movements were an essential element in many places in bringing about policy change favouring HD. The movements developed in reaction to the inequalities and deprivation associated with a model of development that gave a central place to the market while neglecting social dimensions. In England in the nineteenth and twentieth centuries—the case central to Polanyi's analysis—these movements formed a critical part of the politics of change, and of the swing-back of the pendulum, as was also the case in more recent developing country experience.

In terms of the framework presented by social movement theorists, democratization, which was itself in part an outcome of protest and collective movements, was also an important facilitating condition, giving rise to an opportunity structure that allowed such movements to gain formal recognition, develop, and be effective. However, even in the context of democratization, collective organizations and actions face many obstacles, especially in

can come through the actions and inactions of a great many persons, the remedy too can come from the co-operative efforts of people at large' (Green 2008, 67–9).

heterogeneous societies. In many societies, the weak, limited, and uncertain nature of democratization means that collective organization and action is subject to internal restrictions, sometimes outlawing mass meetings or organization, and often limiting press freedom. Second, heterogeneity of class and occupation as well as of identity makes it difficult to form the strong collective identities and loyalty necessary for effective action. Third, elected leaders and parliamentarians are subject to powerful pressure from capitalist interests (local and global), which often finance political parties, so that politicians can be bought in a similar way to the purchase of membership of parliament in the 'rotten' boroughs of early nineteenth-century Britain.[7] In addition, governments themselves face strong constraints resulting from the heavy dependence of many economies on developed country finance, technology, and markets, which, consequently, continue to have considerable power over developing country policies.

While it is not possible to arrive at any simple universal generalizations about the political economy of HD favouring change, we can conclude, first, that democratization provides conditions more favourable to such change than authoritarian regimes, though as noted some authoritarian regimes do promote many of the HD conditions. Second, democracy alone is not enough; 'full' democracy may be needed. Third, collective action is a critical element in supporting progressive policies—including democracy itself. Such collective action can take the form of single-issue advocacy or of the formation of political parties adopting an HD agenda. The challenge is to mobilize collectively, especially in heterogeneous societies where it is especially difficult to form an overarching collective identity that goes beyond a particular ethnicity or religion or occupation. Indeed, Piven and Cloward (1979) have argued that effective mobilization, even of single-identity groups (such as African Americans in the US, or industrial workers), occurs only in exceptional circumstances where there are acute grievances. Yet the history of organized movements among the working class, or by gender or race, suggests that mobilization is less rare than Piven and Cloward (1979) conclude, especially where movements help to form political parties. Yet radical change is rare; piecemeal change is much more frequent. Moreover, continuous pressure may be needed to sustain progress, given the many forces working to undermine it.

[7] The 'rotten' borough of Gatton, Surrey, represented by an MP in England before the 1832 Reform, was a village with 135 inhabitants. In 1830 it was sold for £180,000, approximately £18 million or around US$25 million in 2013 prices (Fraser 2013). In 2012, the amount spent on average by the US Senate winners was estimated at US$11.5 million, <https://www.opensecrets.org/bigpicture/elec_stats.php?cycle=2012>, with the largest expenditure of US$26.7 million in Minnesota, <htpps://www.opensecrts.org/overview/topraces.php>. Evidence of vote-buying in developing countries is quite common (see, for example, Bratton 2008, Chilkoti 2014, Nazeer 2014).

8.6. Politics and the Capabilities Approach

The analysis in this book has shown how important policy choices are in determining HD achievements at a country level, while this chapter has pointed to the political struggles, in particular through collective action, that lie behind policy decisions favourable to HD. Taking a broad historical sweep, the major changes in policy regimes did not come out of the blue, but were generally the outcome of a long history of political movements and struggle. Yet analyses of both capabilities and HD approaches have tended to be 'politics light'. Here we consider how the analysis of political struggle fits with the approach to decision-making in prominent accounts of the capabilities approach.

The two leading proponents of the capabilities approach, Amartya Sen and Martha Nussbaum, have been primarily concerned with defining the approach, and have done much less on the politics of its realization. But each has an implicit view—contained in the way they define the approach—on how to advance HD, although the distinction between the normative (how societies should arrive at their goals) and the political (how they may achieve them) is not totally clear.

Both Sen and Nussbaum point to the need for a 'consensus' to determine the valuable capabilities which a society should seek, in both cases drawing on the ideas of Rawls. Sen argues for a 'reasoned consensus' arising out of deliberative democracy, which should secure societal agreement on the objectives and mechanisms for promoting HD. Deliberative democracy has been defined as a form of democracy that 'asks citizens and officials to justify public policy by giving reasons that can be accepted by those who are bound by it' (Gutman and Thompson 2009, 52), or as Rawls states: 'The definitive idea for deliberative democracy is the idea of deliberation itself. When citizens deliberate, they exchange views and debate their supporting reasons concerning public political questions' (Rawls and Freeman 1999, 579–80). HD priorities at a societal level should then be the outcome of such a deliberative process which presumably should take place in each democratic polity.

The consensus advocated by Nussbaum is an 'overlapping consensus', a concept also derived from Rawls. Rawls defines it as 'a consensus in which it is affirmed by the opposing religious, philosophical and moral doctrines likely to thrive over generations in a more or less just constitutional democracy, where the criterion of justice is that political conception itself' (Rawls 1987, 1). He contrasts this 'moral' conception with a consensus based on 'self- or group interest' (Rawls 1987, 2). Public reason is 'an essential companion conception': that is, 'certain guidelines of enquiry and publicly recognised rules of assessing evidence' (Rawls 1987, 8). It is implicit in Rawls' views that such an overlapping consensus may evolve and may differ across societies. Consequently, it would seem that each society should develop its own concrete interpretation of its overlapping consensus, through a process of democratic deliberation. In this way, the conception is similar to that of Sen's—i.e. a reliance on deliberative democracy and public reasoning—to determine priorities. In contrast, Nussbaum famously has developed a list of valued capabilities that she argues is derived from an overlapping consensus (Nussbaum 2000). She thus goes beyond procedural rules to a specific listing of broadly defined capabilities, and in doing so arguably contradicts the basic idea of an overlapping consensus, which involves reasoned discussions across pluralities in each society.

These conceptions are essentially procedural and normative. They are about the procedures by which HD objectives should be defined and agreed. But would this lead to actual change? The implicit view is that agreement on objectives—what ought to happen—will be followed by agreement on actual policies to achieve such objectives. Yet the nature of deliberative democracy and public reasoning seems very far removed from the messy, conflict-ridden political struggle through which HD has been advanced historically, as analysed in this chapter. Sen's reasoned consensus, achieved through deliberative democratic procedures, is an ideal which democratic societies may strive to attain. But in the political world, where people know their own position and interests (far from a 'veil of ignorance'), progress on HD requires more than this—the underprivileged have to fight for their interests and they cannot expect to make significant progress simply through democratic deliberation. Indeed, without such a struggle democracies can make decisions which worsen HD—for example, by allowing concentration of land and other resources, displacement of peoples, and so on.[8] Moreover, evidence shows many cases of adverse decisions taken in apparently democratic contexts.

What we have seen in the analysis here is that the political underpinning of progress on HD mostly consists of political struggle and conflict rather than consensus. A consensus may eventually be reached but only after decades of political movements, and often there is not a consensus for change, but one side 'wins', as for example with the repeal of the British Poor Law reform of 1834, or the establishment of the welfare state in Europe. As Feldman and Gellert argue:

> The welfare states, which perhaps come closer to providing for the capability(ies) that Sen and Nussbaum advocate, did not emerge in the abstract world in which people decided to 'assign responsibilities' to institutions that promoted social welfare programmes (Nussbaum 2004, 15). Rather, welfare states were historically produced in Western Europe and North America in the early decades of the twentieth century through struggle and negotiation by working-class and women's movements. (Feldman and Gellert 2006, 429)

[8] See the examples in McMichael (2010).

Moreover, as Deneulin (2006) has shown, it is possible to reach an apparent consensus by inclusive discussions, yet not achieve any significant change, as occurred in the Dominican Republic; while in Costa Rica, there was not much consensus (or discussion) but HD-promoting change nevertheless occurred.

Despite his emphasis on public reasoning, Sen too recognizes the need for activism:

> Democratic freedom can certainly be used to enhance social justice and a better and fairer politics. The process, however, is not automatic and requires activism on the part of politically engaged citizens. (Sen 2009, 351)

Much of the literature on the HD approach has also avoided systematic analysis of the politics of change. The UN's Human Development Reports are generally careful to circumvent politics. Most analysis (including much in this book) has classified countries according to their policies (e.g. high social expenditure or low; more or less equal income distribution) but not according to the underlying political systems. There has, nonetheless, long been a recognition that 'political will' is needed to promote an HD approach (Griffin and McKinley 1992, Streeten 1995):

> It is not enough to design programmes which if implemented will increase the well being of the great majority of people, it is also necessary to create the political conditions which make it possible actually to implement human development policies. Thus policy makers intending to introduce a human development strategy cannot afford to neglect the need to create a supporting coalition.
>
> (Griffin and McKinley 1994, 9)

Yet while the analysis presented here supports the view that 'political will' and supporting coalitions are needed, neither outside experts nor domestic policymakers can 'create' a supporting coalition. Coalitions for HD-supporting change come from citizen participation in collective action, in social movements, and in political organizations.

9

Achievements, Challenges, and the Way Forward

The aim of this final chapter is to review achievements and findings on HD, to discuss some problems with the framework, and in so doing, to identify priorities for future research and policy analysis. First, the chapter briefly summarizes major findings from the previous chapters about why some countries have been more successful and others less so in advancing basic HD. Second, moving beyond basic HD, as measured by the HDI, we review progress on many dimensions of HD over the last thirty years. The evidence shows tremendous progress in some, but mixed performance and regress in others. Third, we consider outstanding problems with the framework, coming to conclusions for the way ahead, in the focus of analysis, research, and policymaking.

9.1. Lessons from Country Success and Failure in Basic HD

This book has shown a considerable variation in how well or badly countries have performed on the HDI. Here we review the conditions which make for success and progress, identified in earlier chapters.

An important, if not unexpected, finding is the clear positive relationship between economic growth and progress on basic HD, as analysed in Chapter 3. That chapter showed a chain of causality going from economic growth to HD, and the reverse from HD to economic growth. The chains in both directions are constituted by a set of links that help to determine the relationship between growth and HD. Yet a finding which emerged clearly in Chapter 4, is that growth is neither a necessary nor a sufficient condition for success; some countries experienced good growth but poor progress on HD. For example, Pakistan had above average economic growth from 1980 to 2014 but below average progress on HD, while other countries (e.g. Cuba) had above average HD performance but below average growth.

Looking at country performance as a whole, we found that the elements with a significant positive relationship in the chain from growth to HD were government expenditure on education as a proportion of GDP and educational enrolment. In the reverse relationship from HD to growth, secondary education and the investment ratio were significant factors explaining economic growth besides the level of and change in HD. These were findings derived from the performance of all developing countries over the years 1970–2014. In Chapter 4 we explored the characteristics of particularly successful and unsuccessful countries from 1980 to 2014 in four regions: East and South East Asia, South Asia, Latin America, and the Middle East. We found that the particularly successful countries tended to show higher increases in education and health expenditure, in secondary enrolment, and in the ratio of girls to boys in secondary school, as well as in growth in per capita income. Apart from that we identified three models of success:

1. Countries with good and equitable growth combined with moderate social expenditure—for example, South Korea and Sri Lanka.
2. Countries which had high social expenditure, combined with low or even negative growth and high inequality—for example, Cuba and Mozambique.
3. Countries following an intermediate path, with good but not spectacular growth and a fairly equitable distribution, supported by moderate social expenditure—examples include Nepal and Bangladesh. This third path may be the easiest for other countries to follow as it involves less exceptional performance on any single element.

Deeper analysis of the success stories pointed to the range of actors responsible for success—which varied across countries. The state played an important role in some countries, usually in alliance with other actors. China's success was heavily state-led with support from party ideology and cadres. In Mozambique and Ethiopia, too, the state was responsible for social programmes and economic development, with considerable support from aid donors. In Thailand, there appears to have been an alliance between a populist government and a progressive bureaucracy particularly seeking to advance universal healthcare. In Bangladesh, in contrast, it was civil society and local private business that led to the progress on social services, incomes, and employment. In Nepal, as in Bolivia, community action was important. Aid and remittances also supported well-distributed HD. In several countries, the decentralization of government appears to have made a significant contribution, including in Bolivia, Ethiopia, and Mozambique.

Just as no single policy combination accounts for success, there is no one model of the type of agency that is best suited to advancing valuable goals. Across countries, different actors had the commitment and power to advance basic HD. In terms of the forces of political economy, a broad progressive ideology was shared by the leaders of most successful countries, with perhaps the exception of Bangladesh, the one case where government had a lesser role. Behind the ideology lay political movements: of workers and peasants in the case of Bolivia; of indigenous people in Bolivia and Peru; of the rural and urban poor in Thailand; of communists in Nepal and China; and of civil society in Bangladesh. In Mozambique, Nepal, and Ethiopia, movements and ideology formed during resistance and violent conflict lay behind leaders' and movements' determination to use their power, once acquired, to advance HD. Democratic institutions were in general incidental to the advance of basic HD. Some very successful countries were not democratic at all—such as China and, for a long period, South Korea; for others, democratic institutions provided the essential path for progressive movements to acquire power, such as in Mozambique, Nepal, and Bolivia. Yet democratic freedoms were not always observed once power had been gained.

There is no single story of failure either, but again alternative policy combinations are involved. Some had low social expenditure, negative growth, and unequal distribution—which was the worst combination, shared by a number of countries which experienced conflict, such as the Central African Republic and the Democratic Republic of the Congo. Others had high social expenditure but found this was insufficient to overcome negative growth and unequal distribution, such as in Zimbabwe and Côte d'Ivoire. A third pattern was one in which countries enjoyed moderate growth but had low social expenditure and high inequality, such as Ecuador and Guatemala. For the most part, however, especially poorly performing countries had suffered some political trauma, in the shape of conflict or exceptional mismanagement.

Investigation of the highly successful and exceptionally unsuccessful countries on basic HD confirmed the conclusion that there is no unique relationship between success or failure on basic HD and other dimensions of HD. As already noted, no relationship was found with political rights. Nor did we find any systematic relationship between success on basic HD and good or bad performance on homicides, collective conflict, inequality, or the environment. For example, Brazil, a highly successful country on basic HD, had one of the highest homicide rates, while Nepal—also a successful country—experienced a major conflict. Consequently, we cannot assume that making progress on the HDI will be associated with progress on other dimensions of HD. Section 9.2 therefore reviews global progress on multiple dimensions of HD.

9.2. Aggregate Progress and Regress on the Twelve Dimensions of HD

HD is very broad, encompassing multiple dimensions of human progress. This was clear from the first *Human Development Report* which laid out an extensive agenda: 'Human development is a process of enlarging people's choices. The most critical ones are to lead a long and healthy life, to be educated and to enjoy a decent standard of living. Additional choices include political freedom, guaranteed human rights and self-respect' (UNDP 1990, 9). In Chapter 6, we identified twelve possible dimensions of HD, drawing on philosophical accounts of what constitutes the 'good life'. Although HD is often equated with the HDI, this is a minimal interpretation of HD which we term here 'basic HD', which constitutes just one of our twelve dimensions.

The twelve dimensions were drawn from surveying many approaches towards identifying the characteristics of a full life. While, of course, it is somewhat arbitrary, nonetheless together the dimensions give a broad picture of HD, well beyond the normal identification of HD with the HDI. These are the selected dimensions:

1. Basic HD.
2. Mental well-being (i.e. an individual's psychological state).
3. Empowerment.
4. Political freedom.
5. Social relations.
6. Community well-being.
7. Inequalities.
8. Work conditions.
9. Leisure conditions.
10. Political security (i.e. freedom from political violence or instability).
11. Economic security (i.e. freedom from economic fluctuations).
12. Environmental conditions/sustainability.

Chapter 6 showed generally weak correlations between indicators within and across dimensions at a point in time. Here, we look at changes between 1980 and the present, data permitting. It is difficult to assess change in most of these dimensions both because they are intrinsically difficult to measure and because of lack of data, especially on a global basis. Despite this, in the following sections we make a rough attempt to do so, recognizing that it is on the basis of imperfect indicators and information.

9.2.1. *Basic HD*

There was near-universal progress in basic HD, as measured by the HDI, and illustrated by region in Chapter 4, while Chapter 1 recorded progress by region in under-five mortality, school enrolment, and economic growth, the major elements influencing the HDI. From 1990 to 2015 every country increased its HDI except for Syria and Swaziland. The largest improvements were shown by the countries that started in the low-HDI category. Is the following subsections we focus on the eleven dimensions of HD not included in the HDI. Most of the non-HDI dimensions show a more mixed performance, with some countries showing progress and others regressing.

9.2.2. *Mental Well-being*

We measure *mental well-being* by the suicide rate. However, as is well known, this is not a reliable indicator as it depends on reporting, and under-reporting is likely, especially in some cultures. Moreover, it has shortcomings as an indicator of mental well- or ill-being, since to some extent suicide rates depend on the availability of means, such as poisons or guns. Nonetheless, we use it for lack of any reliable alternative with extensive global coverage over a span of several decades.[1]

The global average of country suicide rates, shown in the WHO database, improved from 1980 to 2014—with a rate of 11.1 per 100,000 people in or around 1980, falling to 8.6 by 2011–14, but regional trends differ.[2] Suicide rates fell in most Western European countries and North America (although the rate almost doubled in Ireland); and it fell substantially in almost all countries from the former Soviet Union and Eastern Europe. However, from relatively low levels, it rose in the majority of Latin American countries, apart from Cuba and Venezuela where it fell significantly. There is a mixed picture in Asia: the rate appears to have fallen in China, especially in the 2000s; it also fell in Sri Lanka, Singapore, and Thailand, but rose somewhat in India and the Philippines. Lack of data prevents us saying anything about African countries.

[1] Another indicator could be the contribution of 'depressive disorders' to the global burden of disease. The global comparison between 2000 and 2012 shows that the incidence has risen (from 1,050 disability-adjusted life years per 100,000 people to 1,081; see WHO 2014). However, this is likely to be equally unreliable since criteria for 'depressive disorders' are likely to vary, and many countries lack comprehensive and reliable health data.

[2] Data from the WHO which includes only eighty-four countries, very few African countries, and limited coverage of other developing regions. It excludes China and India.

The largest proportionate fall was in Hungary, while the biggest increase was in South Korea.[3]

9.2.3. *Empowerment*

'Empowerment' is particularly difficult to define and to measure. We use as indicators the ratio of female to male secondary school enrolment, the poverty rate, the proportion of parliamentary seats held by women, and trade union density. Two of these indicators relate specifically to the position of women, as women generally lack 'empowerment' absolutely and relative to men. On average, each of these indicators improved significantly, except for trade union density which fell:

- The ratio of female to male enrolment improved in every region between 1980 and 2013—from 0.8 to 1 in East Asia, Europe, and Central Asia (developing countries); and from 0.6 to 0.9 in the Middle East, sub-Saharan Africa, and in countries classified as 'fragile'. In Latin America, it started at parity and females slightly exceeded males by 2013. The biggest improvements occurred in Bhutan, Bangladesh, and Nepal. The lowest levels in 2013 were in Afghanistan (a ratio of 0.55), Niger (0.67), Yemen (0.69), and Pakistan (0.73).[4]
- Poverty rates (using the World Bank's international US$1.90 a day standard[5]), between 1981 and 2013,[6] fell in most parts of the world, most dramatically in East Asia and the Pacific from 81 per cent to 3.5 per cent. Poverty fell from 54 per cent to 41 per cent in sub-Saharan Africa. For low-income countries as a whole, it fell from 65 per cent to 46 per cent, and for middle-income countries from 54 per cent to 10 per cent. But among fragile states, the poverty rate remained unchanged at 40 per cent.[7] The largest falls were in China (a fall of eighty-six percentage points), Indonesia (sixty-two percentage points), and Ethiopia (thirty-six percentage points).[8] Nonetheless, some countries continued to show very high rates, such as Madagascar (82 per cent).[9] Moreover, the number of near-poor has been rising, leading to a large 'precariat' (Sumner 2016).

[3] Data are from the WHO (n.d.), apart from Ji et al. (2001) and Wang et al. (2013) for China, and Knipe et al. (2014) for Sri Lanka. For India, see Swanhuyser (2016).

[4] Data are from the World Bank (n.d.), unless otherwise specified.

[5] There are many alternative ways of defining and measuring poverty, and the World Bank international poverty line, used earlier, has many problems (Stewart et al. 2003, Alkire 2015). The MPI of Alkire and Foster (2009) is to be preferred—and is much more in tune with the HD approach. However, systematic historic data for the MPI are not available.

[6] Data are for this period, unless otherwise specified, and are from the World Bank (n.d.).

[7] We should note that data are lacking in many places, especially the poorest countries.

[8] In Indonesia, poverty data are for between 1984 and 2014; in Ethiopia, they span 1981–2010.

[9] The Madagascar figure is for 2012.

- The proportion of parliamentary seats held by women rose in every region and for each HDI category between 1995 (the first year with data) and 2015. The global average was 11 per cent in 1995 and had reached 22 per cent by 2015. The biggest rise was in Rwanda (59.5 percentage points), and the highest ratio was in Rwanda too (63.8 per cent in 2015). However, some countries continued to have very low ratios (below 5 per cent in eleven cases), while only fourteen countries had proportions above 40 per cent, and just two, Rwanda and Bolivia, above 50 per cent.[10]
- Information on trade union density in the years between 1980 and 2013[11] is by no means comprehensive and is confined to high- and middle-income countries. What there is indicates divergent trends. On the one hand, there was an increase in trade union density in a number of middle-income countries, notably South Africa, Taiwan, Turkey, Syria, El Salvador, Hong Kong, and India. But in others there was a decline, including Sri Lanka, Slovakia, the Philippines, and Pakistan. According to Roberts (2014), across sixteen Latin American countries, trade union density fell in every country from peak level to 2005, with an average fall of twelve percentage points. In some countries, like China, Brazil, and Peru, trade union numbers increased substantially, but density decreased. There was a decline in density in most developed countries, substantial in some cases—for example, in the United Kingdom the density fell from 50 per cent of paid employees in 1982 to 19 per cent in 2012, and in the United States from 20 per cent (1983) to 11 per cent (2013). Significant falls also occurred in Denmark, Germany, Ireland, Australia, Japan, the Netherlands, and New Zealand. But a few developed countries saw an increase, including Iceland, Finland, and Portugal. This evidence suggests a mixed picture with respect to trends in worker empowerment, with predominantly declining worker power.[12] Evidence of a positive relationship between trade union density and workers' share in income indicates that where trade union density is declining, wage inequality is likely to increase and wage share to fall (Gordon and Eisenbrey 2012, Jaumotte and Osorio 2015).

Taking these indicators together, there was progress on female empowerment and on poverty, but a much more mixed situation with respect to workers' power.

[10] Data are from the Inter-Parliamentary Union (IPU 2015a, 2015b).

[11] The information here pertains to changes between the first and last date from 1980–2013 for which data are available.

[12] Data are from the ILO and Roberts (2014).

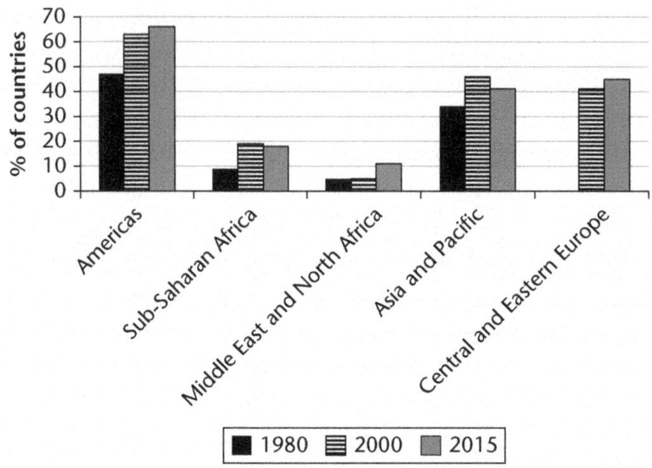

Figure 9.1. Proportion of countries classified as 'free', 1980–2015
Source: Freedom House

9.2.4. *Political Freedoms*

We use Freedom House's measures for political freedom and civil rights. According to these indicators, there was considerable progress in both political rights and civil liberties, which mostly changed in tandem, in every region from 1980 to 2015 (Figure 9.1). The greatest advance was in Eastern and Central Europe and Eurasia, reflecting the end of the Cold War and the fall of Communist regimes. The proportion of countries classified as 'free' according to both indicators in those regions rose from 0 per cent to 45 per cent. Other regions progressed too, but in sub-Saharan Africa and Asia Pacific, there was some regress between 2000 and 2015. For the world as a whole, the proportion of countries classified as 'free' rose from 28 per cent in 1980 to 36 per cent in 2015 and the proportion 'not free' fell from 36 per cent to 32 per cent. Out of 152 countries, 55 per cent showed some improvement in their political and civil rights; 22 per cent experienced worsening rights; and the rest were unchanged. Finland, Iceland, Norway, and Sweden were top ranked globally with a score of 100 per cent in 2016, while among developing countries a number of very small countries in the West Indies (e.g. Dominica and Saint Lucia) scored above 90 per cent; among somewhat larger countries, Ghana and Benin were rated at over 80 per cent. As a region, however, sub-Saharan Africa had the lowest regional 'freedom ratio' (11 per cent) in 2015. The lowest scores (for 2016) were shown by Uzbekistan, North Korea, and Eritrea (3 per cent).[13]

[13] Data are from Freedom House.

9.2.5. *Social Relations*

This is intrinsically difficult to define and measure, and we have to rely on the imperfect indicators available. Three relevant indicators from the World Values Surveys are: the importance of family; the importance of friends; and membership of a sports or recreation group or a music or educational group, or being an active member of a religious organization. These indicators are only available for a subset of countries. Coverage includes countries from most parts of the world but not very poor countries, at least in the earlier waves.

In 80 per cent or more of the countries, the proportion of the population saying that family and friends were very important rose between the surveys covering 1987–93 and the 2010–14 surveys. For the sample as a whole the proportion rose from 84 per cent to 90 per cent for family, and from 36 per cent to 45 per cent for friends. While active membership of recreation or sports groups fell in 60 per cent of the countries, membership of a music or educational group rose in 36 per cent of the countries and fell in 33 per cent; and being an active participant in a religious organization rose in more countries than it fell (45 per cent as against 32 per cent). The Afrobarometer provides information on active participation in a voluntary association or community group for eighteen countries in Africa. For 2008–9 to 2013–14, the number of countries where the proportion rose was about the same as the number where it fell, and in nearly 40 per cent of the countries there was no change. Taking the World Values Surveys and Afrobarometer data together, the biggest rises in associational membership were shown in Taiwan (recreation or sports associations), Colombia (music or educational groups), South Africa (religious membership), and Uganda (participation in community organizations). The biggest falls were in China and Mexico (recreation and sports), Ghana (music or educational groups), Rwanda (religious membership), and Ghana (participation in voluntary or community organizations).[14]

Putting this information together, it would seem that on average there was some improvement in social relations, with the importance of family and friends increasing, and little change overall in associational activities.

9.2.6. *Community Well-being*

As measures of community well-being, we use four indicators: the homicide rate and the rate of deaths by road accidents (negatively), and the rule of law and trust in others (positively).

[14] Data are from the World Values Surveys and Afrobarometer Surveys.

9.2.6.1. HOMICIDE RATE

Using the WHO's deaths by assault as a measure, there was a small worsening from around 1980 to around 2013. Latin American and Caribbean countries had substantially the highest rates over the period and two-thirds of them showed a worsening. Within the region, the biggest reduction was shown by Trinidad and Tobago, and the biggest increase by Jamaica. Data are lacking for other developing regions. The developed countries had much lower rates than the Latin American and Caribbean countries and almost all showed improvement.

9.2.6.2. ROAD ACCIDENT DEATHS

Road accidents account for a rising proportion of deaths—indeed for two-thirds of deaths for those under forty-five years. For 1980 to 2000, deaths from road accidents fell in developed countries, but rose in all other regions, most sharply in Asia (Transport Research Laboratory n.d.), but there was some improvement subsequently. For 2004–13, road deaths per 100,000 of the population fell in 60 per cent of the countries, and rose in a third, with no change in the remainder. However, they rose in the majority of South and East Asian and African countries, and in 40 per cent of Latin American and Middle Eastern countries. They fell universally among developed countries and almost all Eastern European and Central Asian countries. Rates vary hugely from 36.2 per 100,000 people in 2013 in Thailand to 1.9 in Micronesia and 2.8 in Sweden. Ironically, they are highest in the least motorized areas—low-income countries and the African region; and lowest in the most motorized ones—high-income countries. Since they are the product of the number of vehicles per person and the accident rate per vehicle, they tend to increase most (and be highest) in those countries rapidly acquiring vehicles whose safety regulations tend to be relatively weak (WHO 2015).

9.2.6.3. RULE OF LAW

A World Bank indicator which is available from 1996 shows almost no change, on average, between 1996 and 2014, for the world as a whole. The index improved on average in Europe and sub-Saharan Africa, but worsened in South and East Asia, Latin America and the Caribbean, and the Middle East and North Africa. Nonetheless, the aggregate proportion of countries showing an improvement or no change (62 per cent) greatly exceeded the proportion showing a worsening (37 per cent). Finland had the highest index for 2014 and Somalia the lowest; Rwanda showed the greatest improvement over these years, and Nauru the largest deterioration.[15]

[15] The World Justice Project has an independent index of the rule of law, covering one hundred countries for 2014 (see <http://worldjusticeproject.org/sites/default/files/files/wjp_rule_of_law_index_2014_report.pdf>). The ranking is broadly consistent with that of the World Bank, but its coverage is less across time as well as across countries.

9.2.6.4. TRUST IN OTHERS

The World Values and Afrobarometer Surveys include the question: 'Can most people be trusted?' Taken together, fifty-two countries have two surveys which included this question at various times between 1980 and 2014. Of these, the majority in Africa, Latin America, East and South Asia, Eastern Europe, and Central Asia showed reduced trust over time. In contrast, among developed countries (Western Europe, the United States, Australia, New Zealand, and Japan), the majority of countries showed an increase in trust. The developed country group also showed much the highest average level of trust (at over 40 per cent) and Latin American countries the lowest (11.5 per cent).

Hence, overall there is a mixed picture on societal well-being, with considerable variations across countries. The balance of change for developing regions seems to have been negative, with worsening average indices for rule of law (although more countries showed an improvement than a worsening), homicides, deaths by road accidents, and trust. In contrast, there were improvements in all four indicators for most developed countries. However, these averages conceal large variations, and data coverage is very incomplete.

9.2.7. *Inequalities*

We differentiate between four types of inequality: within-country vertical inequality; inter-country inequality; vertical inequality among the world's citizens taken as a whole; and within-country horizontal inequality.

9.2.7.1 WITHIN-COUNTRY VERTICAL INEQUALITY

According to the WIDER (n.d.) dataset for the 124 countries for which there are data, in sixty-two countries, income or consumption inequality increased using the Gini coefficient as the indicator, and in fifteen countries there was no change between 1980 (or nearest date) and 2014 (or nearest date). Breaking this down by region:

- inequality increased in twenty-two out of the twenty-four Eastern European and Central Asian countries, reflecting the transition from socialism;
- in Asia, in two-thirds of countries inequality worsened;
- in both Latin America and the Caribbean and among Western Europe and other developed countries, inequality rose in the majority of countries, but in Western Europe it fell in seven countries and there was no change in four; while
- Sub-Saharan Africa and the Middle East were the only two regions where inequality fell in the majority of countries (in nineteen out of twenty-six African countries; and five out of seven Middle Eastern ones).

The biggest fall in inequality occurred in Senegal (the Gini fell from 0.54 to 0.38, between 1991 and 2011). From 1981 to 2010, Peru had the largest fall, from 0.57 to 0.45. The biggest increases in inequality were experienced by Rwanda, with a rise from 0.29 in 1984 to 0.49 in 2011, and by South Africa, with a rise from 0.49 in 1980 to 0.69 (or 0.77 according to a different estimate) in 2011. For the latest date, the highest inequality was in South Africa and the lowest in Norway (with a Gini of 0.23). However, for all of this we must note that data may be unreliable; often there is more than one estimate for a single date and in some cases, implausible sudden large changes over time. Moreover, it is generally accepted that estimates of household income tend to understate very high incomes, and thus understate the extent of inequality (Lakner and Milanovic 2013).

In contrast, data on education inequality point to marked declines in most countries in the world and, on average, in all regions. The global Gini coefficient for education fell from 0.49 in 1980 to 0.34 in 2010 (Wail et al. 2012). This is probably to be expected, given that there is an upper limit to education coverage at any age (at 100 per cent net enrolment), while there is no upper limit to income.

9.2.7.2. INTER-COUNTRY INEQUALITY

Inter-country inequality, when weighted by population, fell from 1952 to 2011 and particularly sharply from 1990, largely due to the rapid increase in incomes of China and India. This contrasts with non-population weighted income distribution which rose during 1952–2000 but has fallen since (Milanovic 2013). On the basis of data from 1975 to 2004, Ram (2009) shows that the reduction in population weighted inter-country inequality of the HDI between 1975 and 2004 was greater than that of incomes. Again one would expect this, since the income component of the HDI is logged, the education component is subject to an upper limit, and the potential for increasing life expectancy tends to be less the higher the prevailing life expectancy.

9.2.7.3. VERTICAL GLOBAL DISTRIBUTION

This has been estimated for 1988 to 2008 by Lakner and Milanovic (2013), pooling survey data for countries from all over the world. They find a small reduction in the very high inequality of income, with the Gini falling from 0.722 to 0.705. Anand and Segal (2014) supplement the Lakner and Milanovic data which use household surveys with information on the highest incomes, derived from tax information. They find no change in global distribution between 1988 and 2005 once the incomes of the top decile are adjusted by tax data (with a Gini of 0.726 for 1988 and one of 0.727 for 2005). Milanovic

(2016, 123) concludes that 'the evidence suggests that global income inequality is either stable or on a decline'.

9.2.7.4. HORIZONTAL INEQUALITIES

There are no data for global trends in horizontal inequalities along ethnic, racial, or religious categories; indeed, this would be challenging given their context-specificity. Limited evidence on a few countries suggests divergent changes among countries and across different dimensions of inequality. For example, between 2004 and 2012 there was a decline in the poverty levels among both Afro-Brazilians and the white population in Brazil, but almost no change in the probability of being income-poor according to race; 'in both (2004 and 2012), Afro-Brazilians were 1.6 times as likely to be poor than the white population' (Rodríguez Takeuchi and Mariotti 2016, 13). Gaps in non-income dimensions (such as education) point to convergence. In Guatemala, the chances of being poor remained 2.5 times as high for the worst ethnic group as for non-indigenous households between 2000 and 2011, while there was some reduction in inequalities in education and access to sanitation (Rodríguez Takeuchi and Mariotti 2016). But in Vietnam, the relative position of ethnic minorities worsened from 2006 to 2011 (Bhatkal and Mariotti 2016). In Ghana, the income and poverty gap between northerners and the rest of the country widened considerably in the 1990s, but the difference in infant mortality fell; in Côte d'Ivoire, in contrast, during 1985–95 the income gap fell (between the Savannah area and the country as a whole). In Nigeria, North–South inequality fell in relation to female illiteracy but rose in relation to access to electricity (Langer and Stewart 2016). Such divergent trends are probably to be expected. On the one hand, horizontal inequalities are due to specific historical circumstances and economic developments and policy which are likely to differ across countries; on the other hand, there is a tendency for unequalizing access to services initially as a service is first made available, followed by an equalizing movement as a country approaches comprehensive delivery (the Kuznets process). However, inequalities in income are more persistent, since there is no natural equalizing tendency as for service delivery.

9.2.7.5. GENDER INEQUALITY

As shown earlier, the gaps in education between girls and boys have been reduced everywhere and female participation in parliaments has increased. A more general review of gender inequality from 1970 to 2004, investigating education, mortality, political participation, and non-agricultural wage employment, found that:

> Gender inequality is declining in virtually all major domains, that the decline is occurring across diverse religious and cultural traditions, and that population growth is slowing the decline because populations are growing faster in countries where there is the greatest gender inequality. (Dorius and Firebaugh 2010, 1941)

Summarizing the evidence on inequalities, there was worsening of vertical inequality in the majority of countries, especially in Eastern Europe and Central Asia, in the majority of countries in Western Europe and other developed countries, in Asia, and in Latin America taking the period as a whole; but there was reduced inequality for the majority of countries in sub-Saharan Africa and the Middle East, while in Latin America particularly, the 2000s saw an improvement. Inter-country inequality fell, when weighted by population. There was little change in global vertical income distribution when high incomes from tax data are included, suggesting that the effects of reduced inter-country inequalities offset higher within-country inequalities. The limited evidence on horizontal inequalities suggests a mixed performance, while gender inequalities fell almost universally.

9.2.8. *Work Conditions*

The three most important dimensions of work conditions are the quantity and quality of employment and the level of pay.

The *unemployment rate* is one indicator of whether there is enough work, though it is not a good indicator in developing countries without comprehensive unemployment insurance, where people resort to informal employment rather than unemployment if there is not enough 'decent work'. The limited data for the 1980s indicated that the majority of adjusting countries in sub-Saharan Africa and Latin America saw a rise in unemployment (Cornia et al. 1986, Stewart 1995). More comprehensive data available from the 1990s indicate that the unemployment rate rose in most regions in that decade, but fell subsequently. The rate in 2014 was lower than in 1991 in every region other than East Asia and the Pacific, where it remained roughly constant (see Figure 9.2). There appears to have been some rise in Latin America and the Caribbean from 2014 to 2016 (Loungani and An 2016). The proportion of the workforce in *informal employment* is another indicator of the adequacy of quantity of work, and perhaps also an indicator of poor quality of work. Informal employment as a proportion of the total rose in the 1980s in adjusting regions. And in two-thirds of the eleven countries for which there are data, informal employment rose as a proportion of total non-agricultural employment, comparing the average for the 2000s and the 1990s, while it fell in one-third (data from World Bank n.d.). Bacchetta et al. (2009) find a rise in the proportion of informal employment in Latin America between the early 1990s and the 2000s, little change in Asia, and a fall in Africa.

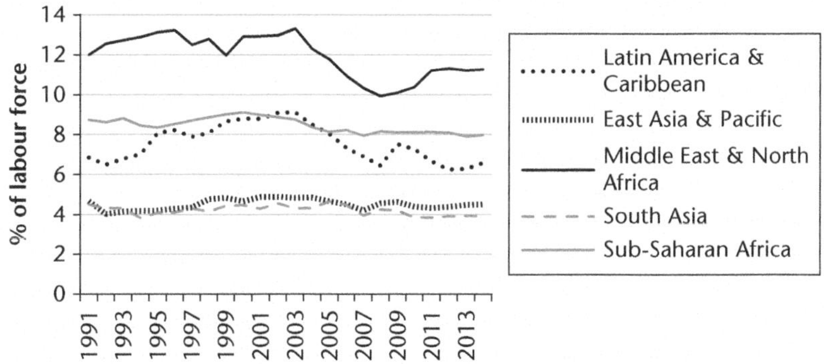

Figure 9.2. Unemployment as % of labour force, 1991–2014
Source: World Bank (n.d.)

There was a fall in *agricultural employment* as a percentage of total employment almost everywhere, which may indicate improved quality of work. For developing countries for which there are data from the 1980s, the average proportion of agricultural employment fell from 26 per cent in the 1980s to 21 per cent in the 2000s. But the overall (relative) rise in informal employment also indicates some worsening in quality of work, while labour market reforms were associated with some decline in formal sector work conditions in terms of job security, especially in developed countries.

A fall in child labour is an indicator of improved quality of work. The ILO records a fall in child labour of one-third during 2000–14, and in children working in hazardous conditions over the same period. There was a greater fall for girls (40 per cent) than for boys (25 per cent).

In high-income countries, there was a general fall in the length of the working week. In twenty-eight of thirty-two high-income countries (Western and Central European countries, plus Australia), between 1997 and 2014, the proportion of the total hours resulting from working weeks of more than forty-nine hours fell; and in twenty-six countries, the proportion from working weeks of more than forty hours decreased (data are from the ILO). Moreover, Sweden is experimenting with a six-hour working day (Alderman 2016).

As far as pay is concerned, the neoliberal reforms of the 1980s involved reducing or abolishing the minimum wage, although this was partially reversed in the 2000s. Reduced minimum wages, together with rising global competition, put downward pressure on the wages of the unskilled. There is growing evidence of a decline in wage share (ILO 2008, Charpe 2011, Stockhammer 2013, Karabarbounis and Neiman 2014, ILO 2015b). Karabarbounis and Neiman (2014) show a clear decline in the wage share of labour as a whole in corporate income from 1975 to 2012 in both developed and developing countries. Most countries (forty-two out of fifty-nine) showed

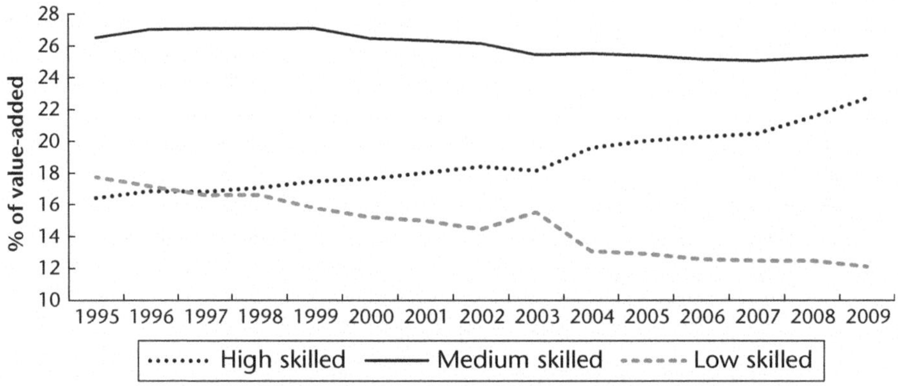

Figure 9.3. Labour's share of corporate income by skill level, 1995–2009
Source: UNDP 2015, HDRO calculations based on data from United Nations Conference on Trade and Development 2015 and Cisco 2015; simple average of forty countries

a decline in labour share; in thirty-seven countries, this fall was statistically significant (at 5 per cent). UNDP (2015) estimates indicate that from 1995 to 2010, the share of the unskilled fell most, the medium skilled share fell a little, while the share of the high skilled rose quite sharply (see Figure 9.3). While there were declines in both developed and developing countries, the absolute share of labour in corporate income is considerably less in developing countries (at less than 40 per cent in 2010), than in developed countries (at around 57 per cent), according to Karabarbounis and Neiman (2014). By region, the declining wage share was most pronounced in Asian countries and least in Latin America (Charpe 2011). The decline in labour share may be partly due to the falling trade union density shown above.[16]

Of course, as with all the other aspects of HD, developments vary across countries, but in general it seems that work conditions worsened in the 1980s, broadly stagnated in the 1990s, and improved somewhat in the 2000s in terms of quantity and quality of work. However, the share of workers in informal employment has increased in some developing regions and the wage share of the unskilled has continued to decline.

9.2.9. *Leisure Conditions*

> Sports, leisure activities... and even paid entertainment allow individuals to manage their free time without constraints. Even in difficult situations, these activities give young people the opportunity to entertain themselves, to relax, to play, and to find cultural enrichment.... [These] activities give

[16] Charpe (2011) shows a statistical relationship between trade union density and wage share, while Gordon and Eisenbrey (2012) show a relationship with inequality.

> young people the possibility of self-expression, personal fulfillment, and personal development as an individual and as a member of a group. In addition, sports and leisure activities can raise awareness in young people that can inspire them to contribute to the improvement of their living conditions through volunteerism. (World Youth Forum 2001, 9, para. 58)

Among factors relevant to leisure conditions are the private consumption of goods likely to be used during leisure, public facilities for leisure activities, and participation in recreational associations, such as sports clubs. Hours available for leisure are relevant in countries where there is enough employment; where people want to do more paid work, the existence of long hours without work may not contribute to good leisure conditions.

As already noted, working hours generally fell in developed countries. No systematic evidence is available for developing countries. There is abundant evidence of rising consumption over and above essentials, which indicates that in most countries there has been an increase in the ability to buy leisure goods. This is also shown by evidence on rising purchases of durable assets (including radios and TVs) in Demographic Health Surveys (Staveteig and Mallick 2014). Figures 9.4, 9.5, and 9.6 show how mobile phone ownership and access to electricity and the internet has increased in every region. Each of these, of course, is an investment as well as a consumption good.

Unfortunately, there is limited evidence on publicly provided facilities or on public expenditures on such facilities at a global level. As is well known, the Chinese built a spate of football stadia across the world in the 2000s, but these are confined to a few major cities and tell us nothing about the totality of local facilities.

The proportion of people who said leisure was very important to them rose from the late 1980s or early 1990s to 2010–14 in most Asian and Latin American

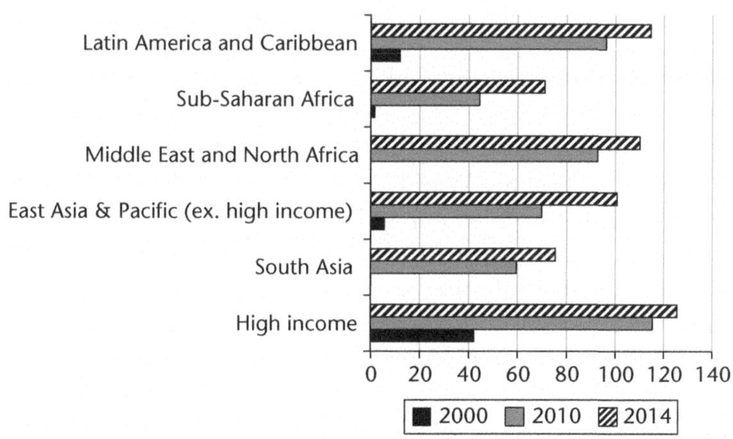

Figure 9.4. Mobile phones per 100 people, 2000–14
Source: World Bank (n.d.)

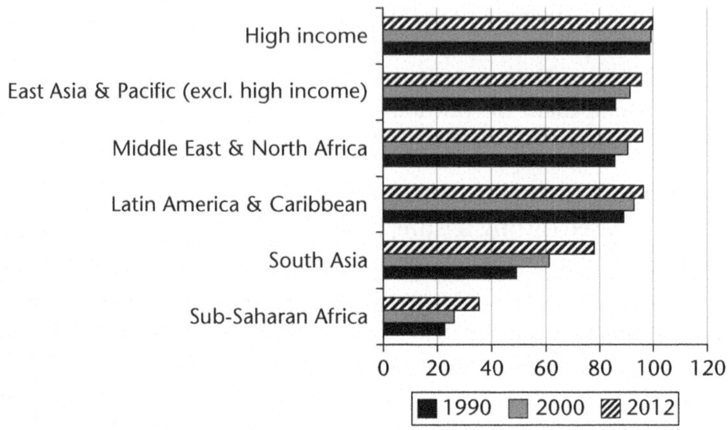

Figure 9.5. % of population with electricity, 1990–2012
Source: World Bank (n.d.)

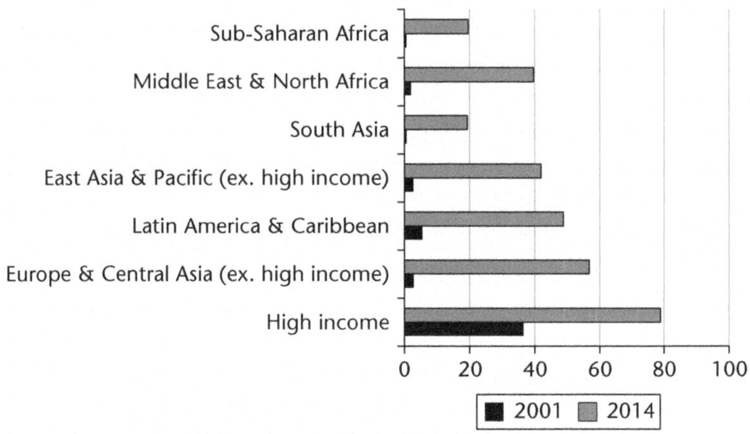

Figure 9.6. % of population with access to internet, 2001 and 2014
Source: World Bank (n.d.)

countries for which there are World Values Survey data, with no discernible trend elsewhere. Active membership of leisure associations (sports/recreation/arts/music) rose in more countries than it fell in Asia and Africa, but fell in the majority of countries in Latin America and among developed countries.[17]

In sum, it seems that the private conditions for leisure improved (more consumer durables, and more time in developed countries), though the

[17] The World Values Survey only has data for more than one period for eight Latin American and Caribbean countries, nine East and South Asian countries, five sub-Saharan African countries, and seven countries in the developed category. The generalizations discussed are based on the earliest and latest period for which there are data, and actual dates vary across countries.

distribution was highly uneven as shown by the data for income inequality. It seems probable that public and voluntary facilities did not keep pace, as indicated by evidence on membership of recreational associations.

9.2.10. *Political Insecurity*

Insecurity arises from a combination of adverse events and a lack of protective mechanisms to help overcome them. There are numerous aspects of human insecurity (UNDP 1994, CHS 2003, UNDP 2014). Sources include ill health, violence, poverty, weak social networks and state safety nets, and economic fluctuations that can lead to loss of employment and income. We have already discussed some relevant trends. The overall improvement in health and the reduction in poverty is likely to have reduced insecurity. On the other hand, the increase in homicide rates in some countries will have worsened it. In addition to these changes, we focus here on political violence and the magnitude of economic fluctuations as additional indicators of insecurity.

As illustrated in Figure 9.7, the number of violent conflicts for the world as a whole rose in the early 1990s, but then declined after 1995. This decline was experienced in every region. But there was a sharp upturn from 2011: battle deaths were less than 25,000 in 2011 and had risen to more than 100,000 by 2014 due to the conflicts in the Middle East, particularly in Syria (Goldstein 2016). Forced displacement—which affected many more people—broadly followed the same pattern, with a decline from the mid-1990s and an upturn in the 2000s, including an especially sharp rise in internal displacement from

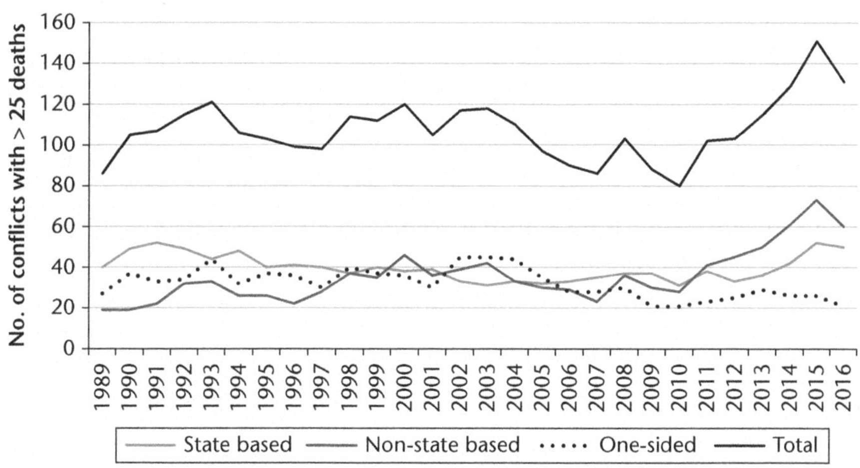

Figure 9.7. Violent conflicts in the world, 1989–2016
Source: Uppsala Conflict Data Program (UCDP)

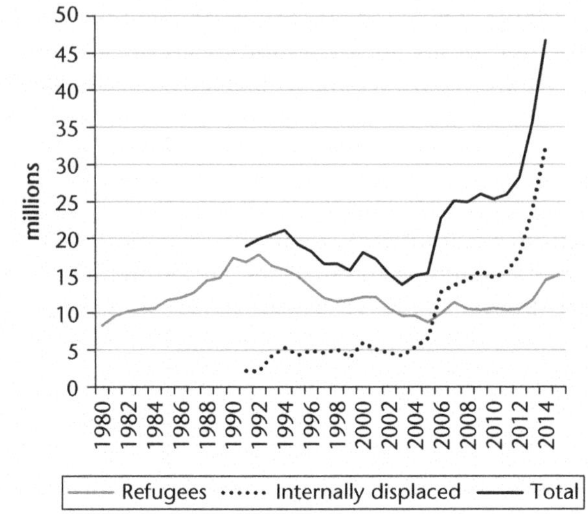

Figure 9.8. Refugees and internally displaced, 1980–2015, millions
Source: UNHCR

2005 (data are not available before 1991) (see Figure 9.8). The flow of refugees rose by one-third between 2011 and 2015.

Global terrorism fell to very low levels between 1980 and 1990, but then rose, especially after 2011. In 2013–14 there were 28,817 incidents compared with 5,248 in 1980–1. The rise was especially fast in the Middle East and in Asia, which accounted for 40 per cent and 41 per cent of the total incidents, respectively, in 2013–14. There was a decline in the Americas. Moreover, mostly the fatalities were quite low; only 4 per cent of incidents involved more than ten fatalities.[18]

Although insecurity from political violence has been rising in recent years, it is, of course, country specific. In most countries and regions of the world, there has been a decline in this type of insecurity. The countries worst affected by major conflicts in 2015 were Syria (accounting for 4.2 million refugees or about 20 per cent of its population, as of mid-2015), Afghanistan (2.6 million), Somalia (1.1 million), then Southern Sudan, the Democratic Republic of the Congo, the Central African Republic, and Burma, each accounting for around half a million refugees.[19] Terrorist incidents have also been rising, particularly in the Middle East (Iraq and Syria) and in Asia (Afghanistan and Pakistan). Terrorist incidents rose dramatically in developed countries in 2015, but globally deaths from terrorism dropped as incidents in Nigeria and Iraq fell.

[18] Information from the Global Terrorism Database, <http://www.start.umd.edu/gtd/>.
[19] Information from UNHCR.

9.2.11. *Economic Insecurity*

Fluctuations in national income are an indicator of national economic insecurity which affects individuals' economic situations. As a measure of this type of insecurity, we have calculated deviations from linear trend growth rates for three periods, as shown in Figure 9.9.[20] In all the developing regions apart from Europe and Central Asia, there was a big reduction in economic insecurity between the 1980s and the 2000s. Europe and Central Asia saw a rise as they went through the transition to a market economy,[21] while high-income countries also saw some rise in insecurity over the period. It could be argued that economic insecurity does not arise from a deviation from a trend if the trend is upward, but is a particular cause of insecurity if per capita income actually falls. Using this as a measure, sub-Saharan Africa, Latin America and the Caribbean, the Middle East and North Africa suffered the worst insecurity in the 1980s—the stabilization and structural adjustment decade—when per capita income fell in most years and for the decade as a whole. For these regions, the later periods were definitely less insecure economically. For developing countries in Europe and Central Asia, falls in incomes occurred for most of the 1990s, associated with the transition from Communism (data are

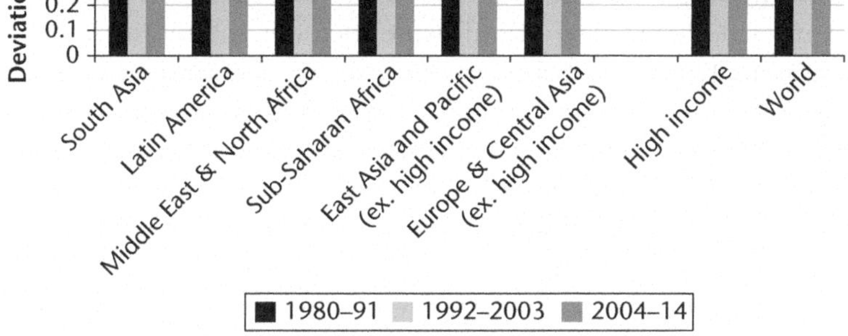

Figure 9.9. A measure of economic insecurity, 1980–2014
Source: World Bank (n.d.)

[20] The deviations relative to the trend are measured by R^2 of the trend line. Figure 9.9 shows deviations as $[1 - R^2]$, so that the higher the column, the more the regional economic insecurity.
[21] For the 1980s, data are only available from 1988.

lacking for the 1980s), but they too saw an improvement in the 2000s. Asia (South and East) saw only one negative dip in per capita income, in 1991, associated with the Asian financial crisis. For high-income countries and the world as a whole, there were two negative periods, 1982 and 2008–9, with the latter involving a much sharper fall in per capita income. Hence, taking a fall in per capita income as the criterion gives much the same picture as the deviations from trend growth.

Economic insecurity of households and individuals depends not only on national fluctuations, but on individual resilience and adaptability, and the availability of safety nets. The increase in education along with diversification of economic activities (indicated by the falling proportion of agricultural employment) make it likely that resilience and adaptability increased over these decades. At the same time, the widespread introduction of cash transfers and other safety nets (such as the Indian National Rural Employment Guarantee Scheme) somewhat abated the hardship caused by economic fluctuations (Rawlings and Rubio 2005, Hanlon et al. 2010). In 2014, 136 countries had social protection floors, although 73 per cent of the world's population were estimated to lack comprehensive coverage (ILO 2015a).

9.2.12. *Environmental Conditions and Sustainability*

The sustainability of achievements on HD is of paramount importance since HD encompasses not just the status of the present generation but that of future generations, too. Measures of resource use and environmental conditions are relevant indicators.

One informative indicator is the material footprint (MF) measure (Wiedmann et al. 2015). The MF measure includes the biomass, fossil fuels, construction materials, and metal ores used in a country's consumption, including in its imports. For the global sustainability of consumption levels supporting HD, it is essential to reduce this MF to avoid rising carbon emissions leading to climate change which are likely to endanger the HD of future generations. The dataset produced by Weidmann et al. (2015), however, shows, on the contrary, a large increase of MF (of 85 per cent) between 1990 and 2008. The increase across nations broadly reflects growth in income, and the Asian increase (led by China) greatly exceeds that of other regions (see Figure 9.10). Nevertheless, while the total MF of China exceeded that of any other country, the MF per person of China was just 18 per cent of that of Singapore—the country with the highest MF per person. Just 7 per cent of the 147 countries for which there are data showed an absolute reduction in MF between 1990 and 2008. Of these, several suffered economic collapse associated with war or mismanagement (such as Iraq, the Democratic Republic of the Congo, Zimbabwe, and North Korea). However, Finland and Taiwan, both

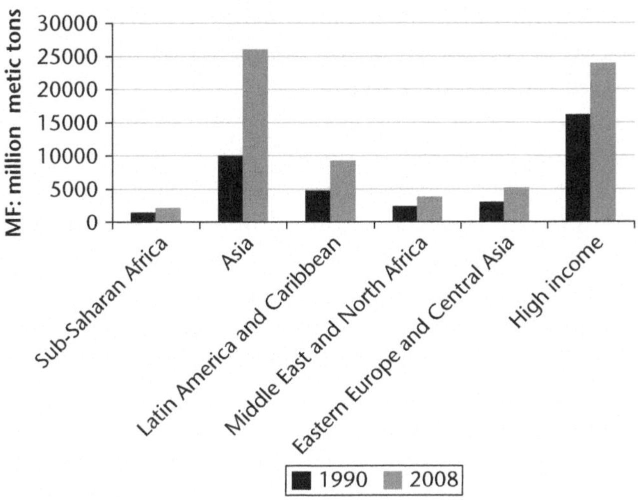

Figure 9.10. Material footprint by region, 1990–2008
Source: Derived from data from Weidmann et al. (2015)

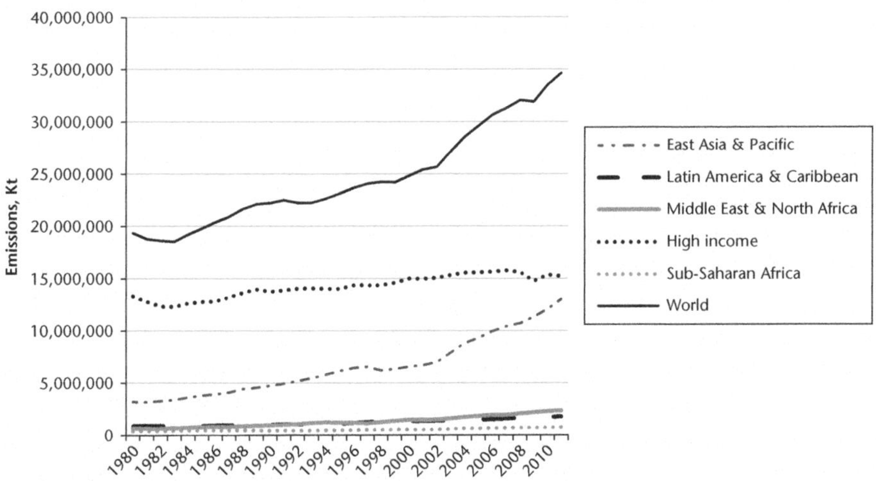

Figure 9.11. CO_2 emissions by region, 1980–2011
Source: World Bank (n.d.)

successful in terms of HD and the economy, showed a significant reduction in MF. The MF of Cuba and South Africa also fell over the period, while their economies grew (but slowly).

An alternative indicator is CO_2 emissions (see Figure 9.11), which differs from the MF, in accounting for the emissions from production, not consumption. This shows a similar picture at a global level, with a worldwide rise of almost 80 per cent between 1980 and 2011, and the sharpest rise in East Asia.

The high-income countries have stabilized their emissions using the CO_2 measure, but this is because they are 'importing' emissions in the form of imported consumption goods, and their MF continues to rise.

Biodiversity is another indicator of environmental conditions. Indices show a marked worsening in species diversity. The Global Living Planet Index shows a decline of 58 per cent in a subset of 3,706 species between 1970 and 2012, with the greatest fall among freshwater species, which fell by three-quarters, while marine systems declined by 36 per cent and terrestrial ones by 38 per cent (WWF Global 2016).

Forestry coverage fell sharply in Latin America and sub-Saharan Africa from 1990 to 2015, but it rose in other regions, and there was a fall of 2–3 per cent in the world as a whole. Despite increasing proportions of primary forests (that particularly support species diversity) which are 'protected', there was an estimated loss of primary forests of 2.5 per cent during 1990–2015, with a much larger loss (10 per cent) in tropical areas (Morales-Hidalgo et al. 2015).

To summarize, in general the sustainability dimension of HD has worsened quite substantially over these years, particularly among countries which were successful in basic HD and economic growth. This represents a very serious defect in the pattern of development adopted, as it threatens the sustainability of HD in the long run.

9.2.13. *Progress and Regress on the Many Dimensions of HD*

This review has shown the great variety in country experience both on twelve dimensions of HD and among countries on each dimension. At a global level, and for most countries, there has been progress on basic HD, on political freedoms (but with progress slowing in the 2000s and being reversed in some places), and on most aspects of empowerment other than workers' power. Social relations appear mostly to have improved, but there is a mixed picture on community well-being, with negative trends among developing countries where almost all indicators saw some worsening, including homicides (data available for Latin America only), road accident deaths, the rule of law, and trust. These indicators mostly improved in developed countries. Inequalities also moved in different directions across countries: global vertical income inequality was broadly unchanged, inter-country inequality reduced, and gender inequalities fell almost everywhere; but vertical within-country income inequality rose in more countries than it fell, and horizontal inequalities showed no systematic tendencies. Economic insecurity seems to have fallen, while political insecurity first rose, then fell, and is once again rising. The clearest negative comes from the environment and sustainability dimension, which deteriorated quite sharply and almost universally according to all indicators. This is a very big negative as it is likely to qualify future progress on all other dimensions. It potentially may threaten food supplies, contribute to rising disease, worsen each type of inequality, reduce community well-being, and heighten political and economic insecurity.

These are broad generalizations covering more than thirty years. Some countries did better than others, and progress was uneven over time. The variation across countries needs to be emphasized as it shows that countries can avoid worsening indicators. For example, a number of African countries experienced reduced inequality, Trinidad and Tobago had a large fall in reported homicides, the rule of law index improved in Rwanda, and South Africa succeeded in 'decoupling' its material footprint—which fell during 1990–2008—from economic growth (Wiedmann et al. 2015).

9.3. Challenges to the HD Framework

The HD approach, which was formally initiated in the *1990 Human Development Report*, is based on two strands of thought, as elucidated in Chapter 1: the basic needs approach and Sen's capability framework. Since then, it has evolved through many contributions embodied in the UNDP global and national Human Development Reports and background papers to the reports, as well as academic literature. The capabilities approach, which has acquired a large academic following, has also evolved in the writings of Sen and Nussbaum and the many others who have adopted and sometimes modified the framework. There is therefore no single work, or body of work, which represents either the HD or the capabilities approach. The discussion here reflects our own view in light of our interpretation of the approach, and not a critical commentary on any particular work. The comments relate to both the HD and capability approaches, which seem to be particularly deficient in three areas: the macro-economy, sustainability, and social as against individual aspects of HD.

9.3.1. *The Economy and HD*

Essentially, the HD approach (and the capabilities framework) has never explored in any depth the implications and requirements of the HD objective for the way the economy is structured and managed. This is odd since who gets income and how (whether from employment or the state) is a hugely important component of the HD outcome. This is not just a question of actual incomes but of their stability and whether people achieve the self-respect and security that arises from obtaining their incomes from employment as against government transfers, whether employment and incomes fluctuate significantly, and the consequences of conditions or quality of work for human flourishing, which is very important since time at work accounts for a large proportion of many people's lives.

Each of these aspects depends on how the economy is organized. Economic history shows that the market system tends to generate considerable periodic fluctuations in output and employment, and often results in a much lower level of employment than that which would secure satisfactory HD. Formal employment greatly lags behind demand for such employment in most developing countries, and in both formal and informal employment, conditions of work—itself an aspect of HD—are poor: employers are able to cut the workforce at short notice, there are many part-time and casual workers, and safety conditions are often deficient, among other elements.[22] These features are not confined to developing countries; in the years following the 2007 financial crisis, Greece, Spain, and Ireland have struggled with massive unemployment rates, especially among young people. The present economic system clearly does not guarantee adequate 'decent' work.[23]

Moreover, globalization and neoliberal policy reforms have led to a decline in the wage share in rich and poor countries, as shown in Section 9.2.8, as well as poor conditions of work. These features threaten progress on HD. A radical redistribution of assets, or new modes of production, such as cooperatives, may be needed to secure truly inclusive growth.

Inegalitarian growth generated by the present economic system could, in principle, be corrected by strongly redistributive taxes and expenditures, as proposed, for example, by Atkinson (2015). Yet the global capitalist system makes it difficult to introduce such progressive taxes. There is a race to the bottom on corporate tax, as countries seek to attract foreign direct investment (Abbas et al. 2012). Similarly, high marginal rates of income tax are discouraged on the grounds that they are deleterious for growth since, it is argued, the most skilled and highly paid will move to where taxes are lower. The IFIs encourage developing countries to move towards greater reliance on indirect taxes relative to the more progressive direct taxes, and indeed this has been the trend. The ratio of direct to indirect taxes fell among developing countries in both the 1980s and from 2000 (data are missing for the 1990s because of reclassification of the database). There was a particularly marked fall in the share of income tax, which is the most progressive tax, with some rise in social security contributions. Regression analysis indicates that the ratio of direct to indirect taxes falls with increased globalization (Martinez-Vazquez et al. 2011). For most developing countries, taxes have only a small redistributive effect, in

[22] The problem was partially acknowledged in UNDP (2015). But links with the economy and its structure were not fully explored.

[23] The term was developed by the ILO (1999): 'The primary goal of the ILO today is to promote opportunities for women and men to obtain decent and productive work, in conditions of freedom, equity, security and human dignity.'

contrast to developed countries where they have a much larger effect (Ostry et al. 2014).

The conventional requirements for macroeconomic management—modest budget deficits combined with pressures to reduce taxation—also affect social expenditures, which we have seen are essential for the promotion of basic HD. Austerity policies typically depress social expenditures, transfers to the poor, and employment, especially where countries have IMF programmes in place (Martorano et al. 2013). A Keynesian approach to macroeconomic policy together with more generous debt write-offs are necessary components of achieving inclusive growth on a sustained basis (Sen 2015). Keynesianism does not imply continuous or rising budget deficits at all times, but rather allows deficits to rise during crises and to be brought towards balance during good times. Where reduced deficits are needed, emphasis is required on raising taxation rather than cutting expenditure, and on protecting and advancing priority social expenditures through a reallocation of government expenditure away from lower-priority elements, such as defence expenditure. Capital expenditure is frequently treated in the same way as current government expenditure in estimating budgetary balances. Yet much capital expenditure contributes to future productivity and can appropriately be financed by borrowing.

Keynesian macro-policies would reduce, if not eliminate, macro-fluctuations, and the provision of comprehensive social protection and unemployment insurance would help protect people during the remaining fluctuations. But these policies, which are not currently adopted in the majority of countries, at best patch up failures, rather than going to the heart of the problem, which is to have an economic system which provides decent work for all (including stability of employment, respect when at work, and good working conditions) and shares out incomes fairly across society. Deep research is needed into the kind of economic system that could achieve this. It would be likely to include a switch from a capitalist system to a 'sharing' economy (i.e. one where resources are owned and controlled by workers, consumers, or the community, and benefits from production shared equitably among them, Mason 2015). Such considerations may become even more essential if robotization threatens employment, as many predict. Yet neither the HD nor capability approaches have generated this type of investigation so far. The market or capitalist consensus remains unquestioned. Since the HD and capability approaches emerged, they have been largely disconnected from economic policymaking—rather, discussions on elucidating, developing, and measuring the HD or capability objective are carried out by HD thinkers, leaving economic policy to mainstream economists.

There is a similar neglect in the SDGs adopted in 2015. In contrast to the MDGs, the SDGs have an explicit economic component in Goal 8: to '[p]romote sustained, inclusive and sustainable growth, full and productive employment and decent work for all'; Goal 9: to '[b]uild resilient infrastructure, promote inclusive and sustainable industrialization and foster innovation'; and Goal 10: to 'reduce inequality within and between countries'. Yet despite the economy's appearance in the goals, the goals and targets do not consider the nature of the economy or the economic management which would be needed to achieve them.

9.3.2. *Sustainability, the Environment, and HD*

The critical importance of environmental considerations was not widely recognized when the HD approach was first developed. Yet although now generally accepted, and 'sustainable HD' is often mentioned, there has not been any revision of the conceptualization or measurement of HD to reflect this. The HDI does not incorporate the HD of future generations but reports on current achievements. There is no explicit time perspective for the HD objective and, as shown in Section 9.2.12, almost every country is contributing to worsening sustainability.

Yet respect for humanity, which is an intrinsic aspect of the HD objective, relates to persons in the future as much as in the present and near present. As Immanuel Kant (quoted in the first *Human Development Report*, UNDP 1990, 9) argues: 'So act as to treat humanity, whether in their own person or in that of any other, in every case as an end withal, never as means only' (2008 [1873], 46). *Every* person implies those of future as well as present generations. Indeed, this is why environment and sustainability is included as one of the twelve dimensions of HD. Yet given the potentially huge cost to future generations of global warming, paying attention only to current HD could be catastrophic for them. This has been accepted in the SDGs: 'Take urgent action to combat climate change and its consequences' is Goal 13.

The HD objective and measurement therefore needs to be revised to include the sustainability objective, bringing into account the costs of current actions and achievements for future generations. There are several ways this could be achieved. A crude short-cut approach would be to discount current HDI by carbon use per person. This has the practical advantage that the HDI of high-income countries would be discounted far more than low-income ones because their carbon emissions are so much larger.

Another approach would be to revise the way income is treated in the HDI to include the negatives of environmental damage, so non-sustainable elements would detract from growth. National accounts were developed in the 1930s before environmental considerations were palpably important. The need to adapt accounts to allow for environmental externalities was recognized by Nordhaus and Tobin in 1972 (Nordhaus and Tobin 1972). Since then numerous efforts have been made to devise green national accounts (Ahmad et al. 1989, Hartwick 1990, Nordhaus and Kokkelenberg 2000). A global initiative—Wealth Accounting and the Valuation of Ecosystem Services (WAVES)[24]—aims to develop a systematic global approach to eco-accounting. Yet, despite some attempts, there have been no serious revisions in the measurement of GDP at operational levels to allow for sustainability. Revising national accounts in this way is an urgent priority since governments, the media, and popular discourse place such emphasis on a country's rate of growth, which encourages a profligate attitude towards sustainability. One way of incorporating sustainability into the HDI would therefore be for 'green income' to replace the current income measures in the HDI. But since the income component is already quite heavily discounted for rich countries given the way income is measured in the HDI, further green discounting would not make much difference for them, and would have more of an effect on the HDI of poor countries. Another possibility would be to incorporate a measure of sustainability into the HDI as a fourth element. But conceptually this is unsatisfactory as sustainability is a condition for continued achievements on HD rather than an aspect of HD itself. The first approach—discounting HDI by carbon use, or a broader measure of environmental costs—is preferable.

Reconceptualizing or 'greening' the HDI is one requirement. Another is to integrate sustainability considerations into policymaking. As previously argued, economic growth, while not a sufficient—or even always a necessary—condition for success on HD, is for the most part important in promoting and sustaining HD. This emerges clearly from the lessons from success and failure on HD discussed in this book. Yet economic growth also leads to increasing carbon use and environmental degradation. The imperative of reducing these adverse effects means that ways need to be found of promoting HD either without economic growth or with a pattern of growth and innovation that reduces the adverse environmental effects.

Here it is helpful to differentiate between low-, medium-, high-, and very high-HD countries. Low-HD countries generally also have very low MF (or carbon emissions) per person and could be permitted to maximize growth without consideration of the adverse environmental issues. Very high-HD countries, which also generally have the highest MF, should aim to increase their HD without further adverse environmental effects, and indeed while reducing their MF; given the advanced stage of their technological capacities, this is a realistic possibility. The high- and medium-HD countries, such as Brazil, India, or China, currently have the highest MF at the margin, both because of their high growth rates and the pattern of that growth. They feel

[24] See WAVES website: <https://www.wavespartnership.org>.

that justice requires that they should be permitted to catch up with the very high-HD countries before restricting carbon use. Yet this is not consistent with global sustainability objectives. Consequently, this group of countries needs to modify their HD-promoting strategies considerably, restricting MF either by reducing growth or by a radical change in technology use. Most of these countries have already achieved quite high basic HD and further improvements need not be very income-intensive. Progress on the other eleven dimensions is not resource-intensive either. The catch-up motive would be lessened if the very high-HD countries moderate their growth and technology use as suggested above, which is a further reason why very high-HD countries should revisit their growth strategies.

The urgency of the sustainability objectives requires an immediate revision of the HD conceptualization to include sustainability in the framework and in measurement.

9.3.3. *The Social and the Individual*

The strongly individualistic basis of the capabilities approach, largely shared by much of the analysis of HD, diverts attention from social or collective well-being, which as shown earlier in this chapter is a dimension of HD which has deteriorated in many developing counties while the HDI has advanced. Yet probably the most important condition for an individual's HD is to be living in a society which is at peace, and one where everyone is treated fairly and with respect. Social cohesion[25] and stability is a hugely important aspect of individual flourishing, and underlying this are social relationships and societal functioning which cannot easily be reduced to individual capabilities because achieving them quintessentially involves relationships among individuals (see Chapter 7). The purist capability advocate would doubtless argue that since a cohesive and stable society is a requirement for individual flourishing, the well-being of the collective derives its value from the progress it allows for the individual.[26] So long as we define 'individuals' to include future generations, it is difficult to disagree with this view. However, the important point remains that the methodological individualism which lies behind the approach tends to mask the importance of groups, collective action, social institutions, and social norms for progress on HD. For this, there is a need for

[25] See definition in Langer et al. (2017) and discussion in Chapter 7.

[26] For example, Nussbaum's (2000, 33–4) famous list of central human capabilities includes 'affiliation', defined as '[b]eing able to live with and toward others, to recognize and show concern for other humans, to engage in various forms of social interaction; to be able to imagine the situation of another' and '[h]aving the social bases of self-respect and non-humiliation; being able to be treated as a dignified being whose worth is equal to that of others'. To achieve this social cohesion is essential, so that the social is included if not emphasized.

an explicit focus on these non-individualistic elements. Avoiding violent conflicts, securing conditions in which the distribution of resources is regarded as broadly fair, and social conditions which prevent social isolation, promote trust among individuals and groups, and so on, should be regarded as essential to the HD agenda. Collective action can have negative effects as well as positive, as powerfully illustrated by the many collectively organized violent conflicts to be observed around the world which undermine most of the conditions for advancing HD. Positively, collective action can be important instrumentally, for example, in generating the political conditions for advancing the circumstances of the deprived. Both positive and negative elements need to be incorporated into the approach, so that achieving good social conditions, institutions, and capacities are firmly embedded in the HD approach.

9.4. Conclusion

The years since HD was first introduced by the UNDP have seen a major shift in development objectives, from a sole focus on economic growth to a broadening to include HD, and more recently sustainable development—goals brought together in the SDGs. These years have seen major and near-universal progress on basic HD, as measured by the HDI. In this book, we have identified the conditions conducive for success on basic HD, and shown that economic growth is not the enemy of HD but an important instrument for its achievement, along with social expenditure and a more equal distribution of resources. However, successes and failures cannot be understood purely by particular policy combinations, but must also be explained in terms of the political economy which led to the policy combinations adopted, as discussed in Chapters 5 and 8. Like the policy combination, the underlying political conditions also varied: success was not always associated with democracy, as illustrated by the experience of non-democratic China; and in some cases, governments were quite weak but civil society was strong, as in Bangladesh. In some, progressive bureaucrats led the process, as in Thailand's health service. Social and political movements also played a critical role, as we observed in Bolivia.

There has also been improvement in many aspects of HD beyond the HDI, as shown earlier in this chapter. Among the broader dimensions, there has been a large increase in the number of countries with generally democratic political systems, and a decline in crime in many countries. Gender gaps in education and earnings have also fallen. Moreover, despite the recent outbreaks of violent conflict in Syria, and the deaths and massive forced migration associated with it, there was little aggregate increase in political violence at a global level since many conflicts ended over this period. But a much more mixed situation occurred for some dimensions—for example, homicides rose and trust fell in many countries. But the most egregious and universal failure concerns environmental sustainability.

When the HD approach was launched in 1990, it was after a neglect of basic HD, such that this demanded urgent attention. 'First things first' pointed to basic HD as an overriding priority—indeed, reflecting this sentiment, this was the title given to one book and one major report on basic needs in the 1980s (ILO 1981, Streeten et al. 1981). As basic HD has advanced, deficiencies at a conceptual level have become apparent, especially in three areas, as discussed earlier. First, there has been a curious neglect of the economy. Despite full acknowledgement that economic growth and HD progress are closely connected (as discussed in Chapter 3), there is much less analysis of the impact of structural characteristics of the modern economy on HD in its multiple dimensions, or of what would be an appropriate macroeconomic approach from an HD perspective. Second, sustainability was not integrated into the framework. Third, the framework neglected social institutions and capacities.

These are clearly major deficiencies in the approach, which have resulted in inadequate attention to critical policy areas. These deficiencies are themselves partly due to strong forces of political economy at a global level, which favour the current system and might make a serious challenge to prevailing views and interests in each of the three areas unacceptable to mainstream thinkers and policymakers. This has to be challenged. These are the priorities for future research, measurement, and policy analysis. Without progress in each, our present achievements on HD may prove to be ephemeral.

References

Abbas, S.M.A., A. Klemm, S. Bedi, and J. Park. 2012. 'A Partial Race to the Bottom: Corporate Tax Developments in Emerging and Developing Economies'. IMF Working Paper WP/12/28. Washington, DC: IMF.

Acemoglu, D. and S. Johnson. 2007. 'Disease and Development: The Effect of Life Expectancy on Economic Growth'. *Journal of Political Economy 115* (6): pp. 925–85.

Adelman, I. and C.T. Morris. 1973. *Economic Growth and Social Equity in Developing Countries*. Stanford: Stanford University Press.

Adler, P.S. and S.-W. Kwon. 2002. 'Social Capital: Prospects For a New Concept'. *The Academy of Management Review 27* (1): pp. 17–40.

Aggrey, N., L. Eliab, and S. Joseph. 2010. 'Human Capital and Labor Productivity in East African Manufacturing Firms'. *Current Research Journal of Economic Theory 2* (2): pp. 48–54.

Aguila, E., A. Kapteyn, and J.P. Smith. 2015. 'Effects of Income Supplementation on Health of the Poor Elderly: The Case of Mexico'. *Proceedings of the National Academy of Sciences 112* (1): pp. 70–5.

Ahmed, N. 2009. 'Sustaining Ready-Made Garment Exports from Bangladesh'. *Journal of Contemporary Asia 39* (4): pp. 597–618.

Ahmad, Y.J., S. El Serafy, and E. Lutz. 1989. *Environmental Accounting for Sustainable Development: A UNEP-World Bank Symposium*. Washington, DC: The World Bank.

Ainsworth, M., K. Beegle, and A. Nyamete. 1996. 'The Impact of Women's Schooling on Fertility and Contraceptive Use: A Study of Fourteen Sub-Saharan African Countries'. *World Bank Economic Review 10* (1): pp. 85–122.

Alderman, H., J. Behrman, D. Ross, S. Khan, and R. Sabot. 1997. 'The Income Gap in Cognitive Skills in Rural Pakistan'. *Economic Development and Cultural Change 46* (1): pp. 97–121.

Alderman, L. 2016. 'In Sweden an Experiment Turns Shorter Workdays Into Bigger Days'. *New York Times*, 20 May. <https://www.nytimes.com/2016/05/21/business/international/in-sweden-an-experiment-turns-shorter-workdays-into-bigger-gains.html>. Accessed 17 June 2017.

Alesina, A., R. Baqir, and W. Easterly. 1999. 'Public Goods and Ethnic Divisions'. *Quarterly Journal of Economics 114* (4): pp. 1243–84.

Alesina, A., R. Di Tella, and R. MacCulloch. 2004. 'Inequality and Happiness: Are Europeans and Americans Different?' *Journal of Public Economics 88* (9–10): pp. 2009–42.

Alesina, A. and D. Rodrik. 1994. 'Distributive Politics and Economic Growth'. *Quarterly Journal of Economics 109* (2): pp. 465–90.

Alkire, S. 2002. *Valuing Freedoms: Sen's Capability Approach and Poverty Reduction*. Oxford: Oxford University Press.

Alkire, S. 2015. *Multidimensional Poverty Measurement and Analysis*. Oxford: Oxford University Press.

Alkire, S. and S. Deneulin. 2002. 'Individual Motivation, Its Nature, Determinants and Consequences for Within Group Behaviour'. In *Group Behaviour and Development: Is the Market Destroying Cooperation?* Edited by J. Heyer, F. Stewart, and R. Thorp, pp. 51–74. Oxford: Oxford University Press.

Alkire, S. and J. Foster. 2009. 'Counting and Multidimensional Poverty Measurement'. OPHI Working Paper 32. Oxford: Oxford Poverty & Human Initiative, Queen Elizabeth House, University of Oxford.

Alston, P. 1987. 'Out of the Abyss: The Challenges Confronting the New UN Committee on Economic, Social and Cultural Rights'. *Human Rights Quarterly 9* (3): pp. 332–81.

Ames, B., E. Connerley, E. Mondlane, D.M. do Rosario, E. Nguenha, and F. Laudemiro. 2010. 'Comparative Assessment of Decentralization in Africa: Mozambique In-Country Assessment Report'. Vermont: USAID.

Amin, S. 1974. 'Accumulation and Development: A Theoretical Model'. *Review of African Political Economy 1* (1): pp. 9–26.

Amsden, A. 1989. *Asia's Next Giant: South Korea and Late Industrialization*. New York: Oxford University Press.

Anand, P., G. Hunter, I. Carter, K. Dowding, F. Guala, and M. van Hees. n.d. 'The Measurement of Capabilities'. The Open University. <https://www.oecd.org/site/worldforum06/38363699.pdf>. Accessed 26 June 2017.

Anand, P., G. Hunter, and R. Smith. 2005. 'Capabilities and Wellbeing: Evidence Based on the Sen-Nussbaum Approach to Welfare'. *Social Indicators Research 74* (1): pp. 9–55.

Anand, S. and P. Segal. 2014. 'The Global Distribution of Income'. In *Handbook of Income Distribution, Volume 2A–2B*, edited by A. Atkinson and F. Bourgiugnon, pp. 937–80. Amsterdam: Elsevier.

Anderson, E.S. 1999. 'What is the Point of Equality?' *Ethics 109* (2): pp. 287–337.

Argawal, B. 2010. *Gender and Green Governance: The Political Economy of Women's Presence Within and Beyond Community Forestry*. New York: Oxford University Press.

Aristotle [and R. Crisp]. 2014. *Nicomachean Ethics*. Cambridge: Cambridge University Press.

Asian Development Bank. 2009. 'Developing Nepal's Social Protection Strategy'. <http://www.adb.org/publications/developing-nepals-social-protection-strategy>. Manila: Asian Development Bank.

Astorga, P., A.R. Berges, and V. Fitzgerald. 2005. 'The Standard of Living in Latin America during the Twentieth Century'. *Economic History Review 58* (4): pp. 765–96.

Atkinson, A.B. 2015. *Inequality: What can be Done?* Cambridge, MA: Harvard University Press.

Bacchetta, M., E. Ernst, J.P. Bustamante, International Labour Organization, and World Trade Organization. 2009. 'Globalization and Informal Jobs in Developing Countries'. Geneva: International Labour Organization and World Trade Organization.

Balassa, B. 1971. *The Structure of Protection in Developing Countries*. Baltimore: Johns Hopkins Press.

Baldacci, E., B. Clements, S. Gupta, and Q. Cui. 2008. 'Social Spending, Human Capital, and Growth in Developing Countries'. *World Development 36* (8): pp. 1317–41.

Ball, L., D. Furceri, D. Leigh, and P. Loungani. 2013. 'The Distributional Effects of Fiscal Consolidation'. IMF Working Paper 13/151. Washington, DC: IMF.

Banerjee, A., E. Duflo, R. Glennerster, and K. Cynthia. 2014. *The Miracle of Microfinance? Evidence from a Randomized Evaluation*. Cambridge, MA: MIT Poverty Action Lab.

Banerjee, A. V. and E. Duflo. 2012. *Poor Economics: Barefoot Hedge-fund Managers, DIY Doctors and the Surprising Truth about Life on Less than $1 a Day*. London: Penguin.

Bardhan, P.K. and D. Mookherjee. 2006. *Decentralization and Local Governance in Developing Countries: A Comparative Perspective*. Cambridge, MA: Massachusetts Institute of Technology Press.

Barrientos, A. and D. Hulme. 2008. *Social Protection for the Poor and Poorest: Concepts, Policies and Politics*. Basingstoke and New York: Palgrave Macmillan.

Barro, R.J. 2001. 'Human Capital and Economic Growth'. *American Economic Review 91* (2): pp. 12–17.

Barro, R.J. 2013. 'Education and Economic Growth'. *Annals of Economics and Finance 14* (2): pp. 301–28.

Bécares, L., M. Stafford, J. Laurence, and J. Nazroo. 2011. 'Composition, Concentration and Deprivation: Exploring their Association with Social Cohesion among Different Ethnic Groups in the UK'. *Urban Studies 48* (13): pp. 2771–87.

Beezy, N. 2008. *Income Distribution in Venezuela Post Hugo Chavez*. Pomona: California Polytechnic University Press.

Behrman, J. and S. Parker 2013. 'Is Health of the Aging Improved by Conditional Cash Transfer Programs? Evidence From Mexico'. *Demography 50* (4): pp. 1363–8.

Behrman, J. and B.L. Wolfe. 1987. 'Investments in Schooling in Two Generations in Pre-Revolutionary Nicaragua: The Roles of Family Background and School Supply'. *Journal of Development Economics 27* (1–2): pp. 395–419.

Behrman, J.R. 1990. 'The Action of Human Resources and Poverty on One Another: What We Have Yet to Learn'. Living Standards Measurement Surveys (LSMS), Working Paper 74. Washington, DC: World Bank.

Behrman, J.R. 1993. 'The Economic Rationale for Investing in Nutrition in Developing Countries'. *World Development 21* (11): pp. 1749–71.

Behrman, J.R. 1996. 'Impact of Health and Nutrition on Education'. *World Bank Research Observer 11* (1): pp. 23–37.

Behrman, J.R. and A.B. Deolalikar. 1987. 'Will Developing Country Nutrition Improve with Income? A Case Study for Rural South India'. *Journal of Political Economy 95* (3): pp. 492–507.

Behrman, J.R. and A.B. Deolalikar. 1988. 'Nutrition and Labor Productivity in Agriculture: Estimates for Rural South India'. *Review of Economics and Statistics 70* (3): pp. 406–13.

Bennell, P. 1996. 'Rates of Return to Education: Does the Conventional Pattern Prevail in Sub-Saharan Africa?' *World Development 24* (1): pp. 183–99.

Bentham, J. 1776. 'A Fragment on Government being an Examination of what is Delivered, on the Subject of Government in General'. In *The Introduction to Commentaries on the Laws of England, with a Preface, in which is Given a Critique on the Work at Large, by Sir William Blackstone*. Dublin: Printed for J. Sheppard.

Bentham, J. [and J. Bowring]. 1838. *The Works of Jeremy Bentham*. Edinburgh: Published under the superintendence of J. Bowring.

Berg, A., J.D. Ostry, and J. Zettelmeyer. 2008. 'What Makes Growth Sustained?' IMF Working Paper WP/08/59. Washington, DC: International Monetary Fund.

Beugelsdijk, S., H.L.F. de Groot, and A.B.T.M. van Schaik. 2004. 'Trust and Economic Growth: A Robustness Analysis'. *Oxford Economic Papers 56* (1): pp. 118–34.

Bhasin, K. 1979. 'Breaking Barriers: A South Asian Experience of Training for Participatory Development'. Hunger Campaign/Action for Development, Regional Change Agents' Programme, Bangkok, Food and Agricultural Organization (FAO) (March–May 1978) <http://www.fao.org/docrep/006/T7838E/T7838E11.htm>.

Bhatkal, T. and P. Lucci. 2015. *Community-Driven Development in the Slums: Thailand's Experience*. Case Study Report: Urban Poverty. London: Overseas Development Institute.

Bhatkal, T. and C. Mariotti. 2016. *Who is Being Left Behind in Asia? An Illustration in Bangladesh and Vietnam*. London: Overseas Development Institute.

Birdsall, N. 1985. 'Public Inputs and Child Schooling in Brazil'. *Journal of Development Economics 18* (1): pp. 67–86.

Birdsall, N. 1993. 'Social Development is Economic Development'. World Bank Policy Research Working Paper 1158. Washington, DC: World Bank.

Birdsall, N., R. Ross, and R. Sabot. 1995. 'Inequality and Growth Reconsidered: Lessons from East Asia'. *World Bank Economic Review 9* (3): pp. 477–508.

Birdsall, N. and R. Sabot. 1994. 'Inequality as a Constraint on Growth in Latin America'. *Development Policy Review*. Washington, DC: Inter-American Development Bank.

Blanchflower, D.G. and A. Oswald. 2004. 'Wellbeing over Time in Britain and the USA'. *Journal of Public Economics 88* (7–8): pp. 1359–87.

Bledsoe, C., F. Banja, and A.G. Hill. 1998. 'Reproductive Mishaps and Western Contraception: An African Challenge to Fertility Theory'. *Population and Development Review 24* (1): pp. 15–57.

Bloom, D.E. and D. Canning. 2005. 'Health and Economic Growth: Reconciling Micro and Macro Evidence'. CDDRL Working Paper 42. Stanford: Center on Democracy, Development and the Rule of Law.

Bloom, D.E., D. Canning, and G. Fink. 2014. 'Disease and Development Revisited'. *Journal of Political Economy 122* (6): pp. 1355–66.

Bloom, D.E., D. Canning, and J. Sevilla. 2004. 'The Effect of Health on Economic Growth: A Production Function Approach'. *World Development 32* (1): pp. 1–13.

Bloor, K. 2010. *The Definitive Guide to Political Ideologies*. Milton Keynes: Authorhouse.

Bongaarts, J. and J. Casterline. 2013. 'Fertility Transition: Is Sub-Saharan Africa Different?' *Population and Development Review 38* (1): pp. 153–68.

Booth, C. 1887. 'The Inhabitants of Tower Hamlets (school board division), Their Condition and Occupations'. *Journal of the Royal Statistical Society 50*: pp. 326–40.

Bornstein, D. 2005. *The Price of a Dream: The Story of the Grameen Bank*. Oxford: Oxford University Press.

Bostock, D. 2000. *Aristotle's Ethics*. Oxford: Oxford University Press.

Bourguignon, F. 2003. 'The Growth Elasticity of Poverty Reduction: Explaining Heterogeneity across Countries and Time Periods'. In *Inequality and Growth: Theory and Policy Implications*, edited by T.S. Eicher and S.J. Turnovsky, pp. 2–26. Cambridge, MA: Massachusetts Institute of Technology Press.

Bratton, M. 2008. 'Vote Buying and Violence in Nigerian Election Campaigns'. *Electoral Studies 27* (4): pp. 621–32.

Briggs, A. 1979. *The Age of Improvement, 1783–1867*. London, Longman.

Brown, G. 2012. 'Nepal: First Steps Towards Redressing HIs?' In *Horizontal Inequalities and Post-Conflict Development*, edited by A. Langer, F. Stewart, and R. Venugopal, pp. 256–96. London: Palgrave.

Bruck, T. 2001. 'Mozambique: The Economic Effects of War'. In *War and Underdevelopment Volume 2: Country Experiences*, F. Stewart, E.V.K. FitzGerald, and Associates, pp. 89–118. Oxford: Oxford University Press.

Bruno, M., M. Ravallion, and L. Squire. 1999. 'Equity and Growth in Developing Countries: Old and New Perspectives on the Policy Issues'. Policy Research Working Paper 1563. Washington, DC: World Bank.

Burchardt, T. and J. Le Grand. 2002. 'Constraint and Opportunity: Assessing Employment Capability'. CASE Paper 55. London: Centre for the Analysis of Social Exclusion, London School of Economics.

Burchardt, T. and P. Vizard. 2011. '"Operationalizing" the Capabilities Approach as a Basis for Equality and Human Rights Monitoring in Twenty-first Century Britain'. *Journal of Human Development and Capabilities 12* (1): pp. 91–119.

Burger, R.P. and F.J. Teal. 2014. 'The Effect of Schooling on Worker Productivity: Evidence from a South African Industry Panel'. CSAE Working Paper 2014–10. Oxford: The Centre for the Study of African Economies.

Bush, George. 1999. 'A Distinctly American Internationalism'. Ronald Reagan Presidential Library, Simi Valley, California, 19 November. <https://www.mtholyoke.edu/acad/intrel/bush/wspeech.htm>. Accessed 28 May 2017.

Camdessus, M. 1990. Speech to the US Chamber of Commerce, 26 March.

Camfield, L. 2005. 'Researching Quality of Life in Developing Countries'. *ESRC Research Group on Well-Being in Developing Countries Newsletter 3* (1).

Camfield, L. 2006. 'The Why and How of Understanding "Subjective" Wellbeing: Exploratory Work by the WeD Group in Four Developing Countries'. WeD Working Paper 26. Bath: ESRC Research Group on Well-being in Developing Countries.

Caprio, G., P. Honohan, and J.E. Stiglitz (2001). *Financial Liberalization: How Far, How Fast?* Cambridge: Cambridge University Press.

Card, D. 2001. 'Estimating the Return to Schooling: Progress on Some Persistent Econometric Problems'. *Econometrica 69* (5): pp. 1127–60.

Cederman, L.-E., N.B. Weidmann, and K.S. Gleditsch. 2011. 'Horizontal Inequalities and Ethno-Nationalist Civil War: A Global Comparison'. *American Political Science Review 105* (3): pp. 478–95.

Chakrangi, L. and R. Ram. 2010. 'Growth Elasticity of Poverty: Estimates from New Data'. *International Journal of Social Economics 37* (12): pp. 923–32.

Chambers, R. 1997. *Whose Reality Counts? Putting the First Last.* London: Intermediate Technology Publications.

Charpe, M. 2011. 'The Labour Share of Income: Determinants and Potential Contribution to Exiting the Financial Crisis'. *World of Work Report 1*: pp. 55–73.

Checchi, D. 2003. 'Inequality in Incomes and Access to Education: A Cross-Country Analysis (1960–95)'. *Labour 17*: pp. 153–201.

Chen, M.A. 1983. *A Quiet Revolution: Women in Transition in Rural Bangladesh.* Cambridge: Schenkman.

Chenery, H., M.S. Ahluwalia, C.L.G. Bell, J.H. Duloy, and R. Jolly. 1979. *Redistribution with Growth: Policies to Improve Income Distribution in Developing Countries in the Context of Economic Growth.* London: Oxford University Press.

Chevalier, A., C. Harmon, and I. Walker. 2004. 'Does Education Raise Productivity, or Just Reflect It?' *Economic Journal 114* (499): pp. F499–F511.

Chilkoti, A. 2014. 'Indian Elections: A Festival of Vote Buying'. *Financial Times blogs,* beyond brics, 6 May 2014. <http://blogs.ft.com/beyond-brics/2014/05/06/india-elections-as-festival-of-vote-buying/?mhq5j=e3>. Accessed 2 October 2014.

Chingono, M. 2001. 'War, Economic Change and Development in Manica Province, 1982–1992'. In *War and Underdevelopment, Vol. 2 Country Experiences,* edited by F. Stewart, E.V.K. FitzGerald, and Associates, pp. 89–118. Oxford: Oxford University Press.

Chowdhury, A. 2009. 'Microfinance as a Poverty Reduction Tool: A Critical Assessment'. DESA Working Paper 89 ST/ESA/2009/DWP/89. New York: United Nations.

CHS (Commission on Human Security). 2003. *Human Security Now.* New York: United Nations.

Claridge, T. 2012. 'Social Capital Research'. <http://www.socialcapitalresearch.com/definition.html>. Accessed 15 February 2012.

Clark, A. and A. Oswald. 1994. 'Unhappiness and Unemployment'. *Economic Journal 104* (424): pp. 648–59.

Clark, G. 2014. *The Son Also Rises: Surnames and the History of Social Mobility.* Princeton: Princeton University Press.

Clay, J.W. and B.K. Holcomb. 1986. *Politics and the Ethiopian Famine 1984–1985.* Cambridge, MA: Cultural Survival.

Cole, J.S. 1988. 'Social Capital in the Creation of Human Capital'. *American Journal of Sociology 94,* Supplement: pp. S95–S120.

Cooper, K. and K. Stewart. 2013. 'Does Money Affect Children's Outcomes: A Systematic Review'. Joseph Rowntree Foundation. <https://www.jrf.org.uk/reports>.

Cornia, G.A. 2004. *Inequality, Growth, and Poverty in an Era of Liberalization and Globalization.* Oxford: Oxford University Press.

Cornia, G.A. 2011. 'The New Macro Fundamentals and Income Inequality'. Florence: University of Florence.

Cornia, G.A. 2014. *Falling Inequality in Latin America: Policy Changes and Lessons.* Oxford: Oxford University Press.

Cornia, G.A., R. Jolly, and F. Stewart. 1986. *Adjustment with a Human Face.* Oxford: Oxford University Press.

Council of Europe. 2007. 'Report of High-Level Task Force on Social Cohesion in the 21st Century: Towards an Active, Fair and Socially Cohesive Europe'. Brussels: Council of Europe.

Cowell, F.A. and E. Flachaire. 2017. 'Inequality with Ordinal Data'. *Economica 84*: pp. 290–321.

Crabtree, J. 2009. 'Bolivia: New Constitution, New Definition'. *Open Democracy*. <https://www.opendemocracy.net/article/bolivia-new-constitution-new-definition>. Accessed 10 January 2016.

Crocker, D. 2006. 'Sen and Deliberative Democracy'. In *Capabilities Equality*, edited by A. Kaufman, pp. 155–96. London: Routledge.

Dangl-Znet, B. 2009. 'Common Ground: Learning from Latin American Social Movements'. Venezuelaanalysis.com. 6 July 2009. <https://venezuelanalysis.com/analysis/4661>. Accessed 26 June 2017.

Dean, J., S. Desai, and J. Riedel. 1994. 'Trade Policy in Developing Countries since 1985: A Review of the Evidence'. World Bank Discussion Papers 267. Washington, DC: World Bank.

Deininger, K. and P. Olinto. 2000. 'Asset Inequality, Inequality and Growth'. Policy Research Working Paper 2375. Washington, DC: World Bank.

De Maio, I., F. Stewart, and R. van der Hoeven. 1999. 'Computable General Equilibrium Models, Adjustment and the Poor in Africa'. *World Development 27* (3): pp. 453–70.

Deneulin, S. 2006. *The Capability Approach and the Praxis of Development*. Basingstoke: Palgrave Macmillan.

Deolalikar, A.B. 1993. 'Gender Differences in the Returns to Schooling and School Enrollment Rates in Indonesia'. *Journal of Human Resources 28* (4): pp. 899–932.

Deraniyagala, S. 1995. 'Technical Change and Efficiency in Sri Lanka's Manufacturing Industry'. DPhil thesis, University of Oxford.

de Waal, A. 1991. *Evil Days: Thirty Years of War and Famine in Ethiopia*. New York and London: Human Rights Watch.

Dillon, A., J. Friedman, and P.H. Serneels. 2014. 'Health Information, Treatment, and Worker Productivity: Experimental Evidence from Malaria Testing and Treatment among Nigerian Sugarcane Cutters'. CSAE Working Paper 2014–13. Oxford: Centre for the Study of African Economies.

Djankov, S., R. La Porta, F. Lopez-de-Silanes, and A. Schleifer. 2002. 'The Regulation of Entry'. *Quarterly Journal of Economics 117* (1): pp. 1–37.

Dolan, P. 2014. *Happiness by Design: Finding Pleasure and Purpose in Everyday Life*. London: Allen Lane.

Dolfsma, W. and C. Dannreuther. 2003. 'Subjects and Boundaries: Contesting Social Capital-Based Policies'. *Journal of Economic Issues 37* (2): pp. 405–13.

Dollar, D. and A. Kraay. 2002. 'Growth is Good for the Poor'. *Journal of Economic Growth 7* (3): pp. 195–225.

Dorius, S.F. and G. Firebaugh. 2010. 'Trends in Global Gender Inequality'. *Social Forces 88* (5): pp. 1941–68.

Dorosh, P.A. and S. Rashid. 2015. 'Ethiopia's 2015 Drought: No Reason for a Famine'. IFPRI Research Blog, 14 December 2015. <http://www.ifpri.org/blog/ethiopias-2015-drought-no-reason-famine>. Accessed 18 January 2016.

Doyal, L. and I. Gough. 1991. *A Theory of Human Need.* Basingstoke: Macmillan Education.

Drèze, J. and A.K. Sen. 1989. *Hunger and Public Action.* Oxford: Clarendon Press.

Drèze, J. and A.K. Sen. 2013. *An Uncertain Glory: India and its Contradictions.* London: Allen Lane.

Easterlin, R.A. 1974. 'Does Economic Growth Improve the Human Lot? Some Empirical Evidence'. In *Nations and Households in Economic Growth*, edited by P. David and M. Reder, pp. 89–125. New York: Academic Press.

Easterlin, R.A. 2001. *Subjective Well-Being and Economic Analysis.* Amsterdam: Elsevier.

Easterly, W. and R. Levine. 1997. 'Africa's Growth Tragedy: Policies and Ethnic Divisions'. *Quarterly Journal of Economics 112* (4): pp. 1203–50.

Edwards, M. 2004. *Civil Society.* London: Polity.

Edwards, S. 1993. 'Openness, Trade Liberalization and Growth in Developing Countries'. *Journal of Economic Literature 31* (3): pp. 1358–93.

Engels, F. [and F. Kelley]. 1888. *The Condition of the Working Class in England in 1844: With Appendix Written 1886, and Preface 1887.* London: William Reeves.

Englander, D. 1998. *Poverty and Poor Law Reform in Britain: From Chadwick to Booth, 1834–1914.* London: Longman.

Erfan, A. 2004. 'The Rise of the Bangladesh Garment Industry: Globalization, Women Workers, and Voice'. *NWSA Journal 16* (2): pp. 34–45.

Etzioni, A. 1993. 'Liberals, Communitarians and Choices'. In *Socio-Economics: Towards a New Synthesis*, edited by A. Etzioni and P. Lawrence, pp. 347–52. Armonk, NY: M.E. Sharpe.

Faguet, J.-P. 2003. 'Decentralization and Local Government in Bolivia: An Overview from the Bottom Up'. Crisis States Working Paper 29. London: London School of Economics.

Faguet, J.-P. 2012. *Decentralization and Popular Democracy: Governance from Below in Bolivia.* Ann Arbor: University of Michigan Press.

Fei, J. and G. Ranis. 1964. *Development of the Labor Surplus Economy: Theory and Policy.* Homewood, IL: R.D. Irwin.

Fei, J., G. Ranis, and F. Stewart. 1985. 'A Macroeconomic Framework'. In F. Stewart, *Planning to Meet Basic Needs*, pp. 14–34. London: Macmillan.

Feldman, S. and P. Gellert. 2006. 'The Seductive Quality of Central Human Capabilities: Sociological Insights into Nussbaum and Sen's Disagreement'. *Economy & Society 35* (3): pp. 423–52.

Fernquest, J. 2013. 'Thailand's New Health Care Policy: A Threat to the Poor?' *Bangkok Post,* 6 June.

Fillenbaum, G.G., S.L. Blay, C.F. Pieper, K.E. King, S.B. Andreoli, and F.L. Gastal. 2013. 'The Association of Health and Income in the Elderly: Experience from a Southern State of Brazil'. *PLoS ONE 8* (9): p. e73930.

Finnis, J. 1980. *Natural Law and Natural Rights.* Oxford: Clarendon Press.

Finnis, J., J.M. Boyle, and G. Grisez. 1987. *Nuclear Deterrence, Morality and Realism.* Oxford: Clarendon Press.

FitzGerald, V. 1999. 'Global Capital Market Volatility and the Developing Countries: Lessons from the East Asian Crisis'. *IDS Bulletin 30* (1): pp. 19–32.

Foley, M. and B. Edwards. 1999. 'Is it Time to Disinvest in Social Capital?' *Journal of Public Policy 19* (2): pp. 141–73.

Foot, P. 2005. *The Vote: How it was Won and How it was Undermined.* London: Penguin Viking.

Forrest, R. and A. Kearns. 2001. 'Social Cohesion, Social Capital and the Neighbourhood'. *Urban Studies 38* (12): pp. 2125–43.

Foster, A.D. and M.R. Rosenzweig. 1996. 'Technical Change and Human Resources and Investments: Consequences of the Green Revolution'. *American Economic Journal 86* (4): pp. 931–53.

Frank, A.G. 1969. *Capitalism and Underdevelopment in Latin America: Historical Studies of Chile and Brazil.* New York: Monthly Review Press.

Franklin, S.S. 2010. *The Psychology of Happiness: A Good Human Life.* Cambridge: Cambridge University Press.

Fraser, A. 2013. *Perilous Question: The Drama of the Great Reform Bill 1832.* London: Weidenfeld & Nicolson.

Frazer, G. n.d. 'Firm Productivity, Worker Ability, and Returns to Education'. University of Toronto. <http://web.ceu.hu/labor/cost/Papers/Frazer.pdf>. Accessed 8 March 2015.

French, J.D. and A. Fortes. 2005. 'Another World is Possible: The Rise of the Brazilian Workers' Party and the Prospects for Lula's Government'. *Contemporary Affairs 2* (3): pp. 13–31.

Frey, B. and A. Stutzer. 2002. *Happiness and Economics.* Princeton: Princeton University Press.

Friedman, M. 1969. *The Optimum Quantity of Money and Other Essays.* London: Macmillan.

Fukuda-Parr, S. 2014. 'Global Goals as a Policy Tool: Intended and Unintended Consequences'. *Journal of Human Development and Capabilities 15* (2/3): pp. 118–31.

Furtado, C. 1985. *La Nueva Dependencia: Deuda Externa y Monetarismo.* Buenos Aires: Centro Editor de America Latina.

Gambetta, D. 1988. *Trust: Making and Breaking Cooperative Relations.* Oxford: Basil Blackwell.

Garcia, M. 1990. 'Resource Allocation and Household Welfare: A Study of Personal Sources of Income on Food Consumption, Nutrition and Health in the Philippines'. PhD thesis. Institute of Social Studies, The Hague.

Garreton Merino, M.A. and E. Newman. 2001. *Democracy in Latin America: (Re)constructing Political Society.* New York and London: United Nations University Press.

Gay, J. 1731 [1978 with W. King]. *An Essay on the Origin of Evil.* New York: Garland.

Gebreeyesus, M. 2016. 'Industrial Policy and Development in Ethiopia: Evolution and Present Experimentation'. Learning to Compete Working Paper 6. Washington, DC: Brookings Institution.

Ghai, D. and A. Rahman. 1981. 'Rural Poverty and the Small Farmers Development Programme in Nepal'. Geneva: International Labour Organization.

Ghosh, P. 2014. 'Despite Low Pay, Poor Work Conditions, Garment Factories Empowering Millions of Bangladesh Women'. *International Business Times*, 25 March. <http://www.ibtimes.com/despite-low-pay-poor-work-conditions-garment-factories-empowering-millions-bangladeshi-women-1563419>.

Goetz, A.M. and R. Jenkins. 1999. 'Accounts and Accountability: Theoretical Implications of the Right to Information Movement in India'. *Third World Quarterly 20* (3): pp. 603–22.

Goldstein, J.S. 2016. 'World Backsliding on Peace'. *The World Post*. <http://www.huffingtonpost.com/joshua-s-goldstein/world-backsliding-on-peace_b_7924964.html>. Accessed 25 April 2016.

Gooptu, N. 2002. 'Sex Workers in Calcutta and the Dynamics of Collective Action: Political Activism, Community Identity and Group Behaviour'. In *Group Behaviour and Development: Is the Market Destroying Cooperation*, edited by J. Heyer, F. Stewart, and R. Thorp, pp. 227–52. Oxford: Oxford University Press.

Gordon, C. and R. Eisenbrey. 2012. 'As Unions Decline, Inequality Rises'. Economic Policy Institute. <http://www.epi.org/press/unions-decline-inequality-rises/>. Accessed 3 April 2016.

Government of Nepal and UNDP. 2014. *Human Development Report Nepal 2014: Beyond Geography, Unlocking Human Potential*. Kathmandu: UNDP.

Graham, C. 2009. *Happiness around the World: The Paradox of Happy Peasants and Miserable Millionaires*. Oxford, New York: Oxford University Press.

Graham, C. 2011. *The Pursuit of Happiness: An Economy of Wellbeing*. Washington, DC: Brookings Institution Press.

Graham, C. and A. Felton. 2006. 'Does Inequality Matter to Individual Welfare: An Exploration Based on Happiness Surveys in Latin America'. *Journal of Economic Inequality 4* (1): pp. 107–22.

Graham, C. and M. Hoover. 2007. 'Optimism and Poverty in Africa: Adaptation or a Means to Survival'. Afrobarometer Working Paper 76. <http://afrobarometer.org/publications/>.

Graham, C. and S. Pettinato. 2002. *Happiness and Hardship: Opportunity and Insecurity in New Market Economies*. Washington, DC: Brookings Institution Press.

Green, D. 2008. *From Poverty to Power: How Active Citizens and Effective States can Change the World*. Oxford: Oxfam International.

Griffin, K. and T. McKinley. 1992. 'Towards a Human Development Strategy'. HDRO Occasional Paper 6. New York: HDRO, UNDP.

Griffin, K. and T. McKinley. 1994. *Implementing a Human Development Strategy*. Basingstoke: Macmillan.

Gutman, A. and D. Thompson. 2009. *Democracy and Disagreement*. Cambridge, MA: Harvard University Press.

Guzmán, J.C., A.R. Morrison, and M. Sjöblom. 2008. 'The Impact of Remittances and Gender on Household Expenditure Patterns: Evidence from Ghana'. In *The International Migration of Women*, edited by A. Morrison, M. Schiff, and A. Sjöblom, pp. 125–52. Washington, DC and London: World Bank and Palgrave Macmillan.

Haddad, L. and H.E. Bouis. 1991. 'The Impact of Nutritional Status on Agricultural Productivity: Wage Evidence from the Philippines'. *Oxford Bulletin of Economics and Statistics 53* (1): pp. 45–69.

Haines, M. 2001. 'Life Expectancy'. In *The Oxford Companion to United States History*, edited by P. Boyer, M. Dubofsky, E. Monkkonen, R. Number, D. Oshinsky, and E. Rosenberg, pp. 444–5. Oxford: Oxford University Press.

Hanlon, J., A. Barrientos, and D. Hulme. 2010. *Just Give Money to the Poor: The Development Revolution from the Global South*. Sterling, VA: Kumarian Press.

Hardoon, D., S. Ayele, and R. Fuentes-Nieva. 2016. 'An Economy for the 1%: How Privilege and Power in the Economy Drive Extreme Inequality and How This Can Be Stopped'. Oxfam Briefing Paper 210. Oxford: OXFAM.

Harris, J. 2015. '"Developmental Capture" of the State: Explaining Thailand's Universal Coverage Policy'. *Journal of Health Politics, Policy & Law 40* (1): pp. 165–93.

Harris, J.R. and M.P. Todaro. 1970. 'Migration, Unemployment and Development: A Two-Sector Analysis'. *American Economic Review 60* (1): pp. 126–42.

Hartwick, J.M. 1990. 'Natural Resources, National Accounting, and Economic Depreciation'. *Journal of Public Economics 43* (3): pp. 291–304.

Helliwell, J.F., R. Layard, and J.D. Sachs, eds. 2012. *World Happiness Report 2012*. New York: Sustainable Development Solutions Network.

Helliwell, J.F., R. Layard, and J.D. Sachs, eds. 2013. *World Happiness Report 2013*. New York: Sustainable Development Solutions Network.

Helliwell, J.F. and S. Wang. 2013. 'World Happiness: Trends, Explanations and Distribution'. In *World Happiness Report 2013*, edited by J.F. Helliwell, R. Layard, and J.D. Sachs, pp. 19–38. New York: Sustainable Development Solutions Network.

Helpman, E. and P. Krugman. 1986. *Market Structure and Foreign Trade: Increasing Returns, Imperfect Competition and the International Economy*. Cambridge, MA: Massachusetts Institute of Technology Press.

Heyer, J., F. Stewart, and R. Thorp, eds. 2002. *Group Behaviour and Development: Is the Market Destroying Cooperation?* Oxford: Oxford University Press.

Hicks, N. and P.P. Streeten. 1979. 'Indicators of Development: The Search for a Basic Needs Yardstick'. *World Development 7* (6): pp. 567–80.

Hirschman, A.O. 1958. *The Strategy of Economic Development*. New Haven: Yale University Press.

Hoddinott, J., H. Alderman, J.R. Behrman, L.J. Haddad, and S. Horton. 2013. 'The Economic Rationale for Investing in Stunting Reduction'. *Maternal and Child Nutrition 9*, Supplement 2: pp. 69–82.

Hoddinott, J. and L. Haddad. 1995. 'Does Female Income Share Influence Household Expenditures? Evidence from Côte d'Ivoire'. *Oxford Bulletin of Economics and Statistics 57* (1): pp. 77–96.

Holcomb, S. 1995. *Managing to Empower: The Grameen Bank's Experience of Poverty Alleviation*. Dhaka: University Press; London: Zed Books.

Hooghe, M. 2012. 'Social Cohesion in Contemporary Societies: An Update of Theoretical Approaches'. In *Contemporary Theoretical Perspectives on the Study of Social Cohesion and Social Capital*, edited by M. Hooghe: pp. 1–7. Brussels: Konlinkelijke Vlaamse Academie van Belgie voor Wetenscheppen en Kunsten.

Hotchkiss, D.R., N.B. Mock, and E.E. Seiber. 2002. 'The Effect of the Health Care Supply Environment on Children's Nutritional Status in Rural Nepal'. *Journal of Biosocial Science 34* (2): pp. 173–92.

Hsiao, F.S.T. and M.-C.W. Hsiao. 2006. 'FDI, Exports, and GDP in East and Southeast Asia: Panel Data versus Time-Series Causality Analyses'. *Journal of Asian Economics 17* (6): pp. 1082–106.

Hulme, D. 2008. 'The Story of the Grameen Bank'. BWPI Working Paper 60. Manchester: BWPI.

Hume, D. 1751. *An Enquiry Concerning the Principles of Morals*. London: A. Millar.

Humphries, D.L., K.A. Dearden, B.T. Crookston, T. Woldehanna, M.E. Penny, and J.R. Behrman. 2017. 'Household Food Group Expenditure Patterns are Associated with Child Anthropometry at Ages 5, 8 and 12 years in Ethiopia, India, Peru and Vietnam'. *Economics and Human Biology 26*: pp. 34–41.

Hunter, W. 2006. 'Growth and Transformation of the Workers' Party in Brazil, 1989–2002'. Working Paper 326. Notre Dame: Kellogg Institute for International Studies.

Hutcheson, F. 1726. *An Inquiry into the Original of our Ideas of Beauty and Virtue in Two Treatises: I. Concerning Beauty, Order, Harmony, Design. II. Concerning Moral Good and Evil*. London: Printed for J. Darby, A. Bettesworth, F. Fayram, J. Pemberton, C. Rivington, J. Hooke, F. Clay, J. Batley, and E. Symon.

Hyder, S. 2009. 'Women's Financial Independence amongst Garment Workers in Bangladesh: Summary of Research'. <https://www.law.berkeley.edu/files/shaina_hyder–summary_of_research(2).pdf>. Accessed 25 November 2015.

Ibrahim, S.S. 2006. 'From Individual to Collective Capabilities: The Capability Approach as a Conceptual Framework for Self-Help'. *Journal of Human Development 7* (3): pp. 397–416.

ILO. 1970. *Towards Full Employment*. Geneva: ILO.

ILO. 1972. *Employment, Incomes and Equality*. Geneva: ILO.

ILO. 1976. *Employment, Growth and Basic Needs: A One-World Problem*. Geneva: ILO.

ILO. 1981. 'First Things First: Meeting the Basic Needs of the People of Nigeria'. Report to the Government of Nigeria by a JASPA Basic Needs Mission. ILO: Addis Ababa.

ILO. 1999. 'Report of the Director-General: Decent Work'. <http://www.ilo.org/public/english/standards/relm/ilc/ilc87/rep-i.htm>. Geneva: ILO.

ILO. 2000. 'Measuring Decent Work with Statistical Indicators'. Geneva: ILO.

ILO. 2008. *Global Wage Report 2008–09: Minimum Wages and Collective Bargaining: Towards Policy Coherence*. Geneva: International Labour Office.

ILO. 2013. 'Social Protection Assessment-Based National Dialogue: Towards a Nationally Defined Social Protection Floor in Thailand'. <http://www.ilo.org/secsoc/information-resources/publications-and-tools/.../index.htm>. Accessed 18 June 2017.

ILO. 2015a. *World Social Protection Report 2014–15*. Geneva: ILO.

ILO. 2015b. *Global Wage Report 2014–15: Wages and Income Inequality*. Geneva: ILO.

Immink, M. and F. Viterri. 1981. 'Energy Intake and Productivity of Guatemalan Sugarcane Cutters: An Empirical Test of the Efficiency Wage Hypothesis'. *Journal of Development Economics 9* (2): pp. 273–87.

International Covenant on Economic, Social and Cultural Rights. 1966. G.A. Res. 2200a, UN Doc A/63/6.

IPC. 2009. 'What Explains the Decline in Brazil's Inequality?' *One Pager 89*. International Policy Centre for Inclusive Growth.

IPU. 2015a. *Women in Parliament: 20 Years in Review*. Geneva: IPU.

IPU. 2015b. *Women in National Parliaments, Situation as of 1 December 2015*. <http://www.ipu.org/wmn-e/arc/classif011215.htm>.

Islam, S. 2001. *The Textile and Clothing Industry of Bangladesh in a Changing World Economy*. Dhaka: Centre For Policy Dialogue, University Press Limited.

Jackson-Han, S. 2013. 'HDR 2013 Public Forum at the World Bank'. Blog report. <http://www.hdr.undp.org/en/content/blog-report-hdr-2013-public-forum-world-bank>. Accessed 28 May 2017.

Jamison, D. and P. Moock. 1984. 'Farmer Education and Farm Efficiency in Nepal: The Role of Schooling, Extension Services and Cognitive Skills'. *World Development 12* (1): pp. 67–86.

Jaumotte, F. and C. Osorio. 2015. 'Inequality and Labor Market Institutions'. IMF Discussion Note SDN/15/14. Washington, DC: IMF.

Ji, J., A. Kleinman, and A.E. Becker. 2001. 'Suicide in Contemporary China: A Review of China's Distinctive Suicide Demographics in their Sociocultural Context'. *Harvard Review of Psychiatry 9* (1): pp. 1–12.

Jobin, W.R. 2014. 'Increased Economic Productivity after Suppressing Malaria Transmission in 14 African Countries'. *The Africa Policy Journal 11*, posted on 25 April 2014. <https://apj.fas.harvard.edu/increased-economic-productivity-after-suppressing-malaria-transmission>.

Johnes, G. 2006. 'Education and Economic Growth'. 12th Lecture in the Eric John Hanson Memorial Lecture Series, University of Alberta.

Jones, P. 2001. 'Are Educated Workers Really More Efficient?' *Journal of Development Economics 64* (1): pp. 64–79.

Jones, S. and F. Tarp. 2015. 'Understanding Mozambique's Growth Experience through an Employment Lens'. WIDER Working Paper 2015/109. Helsinki: UNU-WIDER.

Jütting, J., C. Kauffmann, I. McDonnell, H. Osterrieder, N. Pinaud, and L. Wegner. 2004. 'Decentralisation and Poverty in Developing Countries: Exploring the Impact'. OECD Development Centre Working Paper. Paris: OECD Development Centre.

Kabir, B. 1999. *Politics of Military Rule and the Dilemmas of Democratization in Bangladesh*. New Delhi: South Asian Publishers.

Kahneman, D. 2003. 'A Psychological Perspective on Economics'. *American Economic Review 93* (1): pp. 162–8.

Kahneman, D., A. Krueger, D. Schkade, N. Schwartz, and A. Stone. 2004. 'A Survey Method for Characterising Daily Life Experience: The Day Reconstruction Method (DRM)'. *Science 306* (5702): pp. 1776–80.

Kakwani, N. 1995. 'Structural Adjustment and Performance in Living Standards in Developing Countries'. *Development and Change 26* (3): pp. 469–502.

Kant, I. 2008 [1873]. *Fundamental Principles of the Metaphysics of Morals*, translated by Thomas Kingsmill. New York: Cosimo Classics.

Kaplan, T. 1997. *Crazy for Democracy: Women in Grassroots Movements*. New York and London: Routledge.

Karabarbounis, L. and B. Neiman. 2014. 'The Global Decline of the Labor Share'. *Quarterly Journal of Economics 129* (1): pp. 61–103.

Kearns, A. and R. Forrest. 2000. 'Social Cohesion and Multilevel Urban Governance'. *Urban Studies 37* (5–6): pp. 995–1017.

Keumsoo, K. n.d. 'History of Labor Movement in Korea'. <https://icemmncindonesia.files.wordpress.com/ . . . /history-of-labor-movement-in-korea>. Accessed 22 September 2014.

Khan, M.S. 1990. 'Relative Price Changes and the Growth of the Public Sector'. World Bank Policy, Research, and External Affairs Working Paper 423. Washington, DC: World Bank.

Khan, M.S. and M.D. Knight. 1985. 'Fund-Supported Programs and Economic Growth'. IMF Occasional Papers 41. Washington, DC: IMF.

Khanal, D.R. 2012. 'Social Security/Social Protection in Nepal: Situation Analysis'. Kathmandu: ILO.

Killick, T. 1976. 'The Possibilities of Development Planning'. *Oxford Economic Papers 41* (4): pp. 161–84.

Killick, T. and M. Malik. 1995. 'Country Experiences with IMF Programmes in the 1980s'. *World Economy 15* (4): pp. 599–632.

King, E.M. and L.A. Lilliard. 1987. 'Education Policy and Schooling Attainment in Malaysia and the Philippines'. *Economics of Education Review 6* (2): pp. 167–81.

Kingdon, G. and J. Knight. 2007. 'Community Comparisons and Subjective Wellbeing in a Divided Society'. *Journal of Economic Behavior and Organization 64* (1): pp. 669–90.

Klein, H. 1993. *Historia de Bolivia*. La Paz: Libreria-Editorial Juventud.

Kleynhans, E.P.J. and J.R. Labuschagne. 2012. 'Human Capital Constraints in South Africa: A Firm-Level Analysis'. *Managing Global Transitions 10* (1): pp. 69–86.

Knack, S. and P. Keefer. 1997. 'Does Social Capital have an Economic Payoff? A Cross-country Investigation'. *Quarterly Journal of Economics 112* (4): pp. 1251–88.

Knapp, V.J. 1998. 'Life Expectancy, Infant Mortality and Malnutrition in Preindustrial Europe: A Contemporary Explanation'. *Nutrition and Health 12* (2): pp. 89–95.

Knight, J.B. and R. Gunatilaka. 2011. 'Does Economic Growth Raise Happiness in China?' *Oxford Development Studies 39* (1): pp. 1–24.

Knight, J.B. and R.H. Sabot. 1990. *Education, Productivity, and Inequality: The East African Natural Experiment*. New York: Oxford University Press, published for the World Bank.

Knipe, D.W., C. Metcalfe, R. Fernando, M. Pearson, F. Konradsen, M. Eddleston, and D. Gunnell. 2014. 'Suicide in Sri Lanka 1975–2012: Age, Period and Cohort Analysis of Police and Hospital Data'. *BMC Public Health 14* (1): pp. 1–13.

Kondo, N. 2012. 'Socioeconomic Disparities and Health: Impacts and Pathways'. *Journal of Epidemiology 22* (1): pp. 2–6.

Koo, H. 2001. *Korean Workers: The Culture and Politics of Class Formation*. Ithaca, NY: Cornell University Press.

Kroll, C. 2013. 'Global Development and Happiness: How can Data on Subjective Wellbeing Inform Development Theory and Practice'. IDS Working Paper 432. Sussex: Institute of Development Studies.

Krueger, A.O. 1974. 'The Political Economy of the Rent-Seeking Society'. *American Economic Review 64* (3): pp. 291–303.

Kumar, N. and A. Quisumbing. 2010. 'Does Social Capital Build Women's Assets? The Long-Term Impacts of Group-Based and Individual Dissemination of Agricultural

Technology in Bangladesh'. CAPRI Working Paper 97. Washington, DC: Collective Action and Property Rights, IFPRI.

Kurlantzick, J. 2011. 'Thailand: A Democratic Failure and its Lessons for the Middle East'. Council on Foreign Relations, Expert Brief, 24 March. <https://www.cfr.org/expert-brief/thailand-democratic-failure-and-its-lessons-middle-east>. Accessed 10 January 2015.

Kymlika, W. 1995. *Multicultural Citizenship: A Liberal Theory of Minority Rights*. Oxford: Oxford University Press.

Lakner, C. and B. Milanovic. 2013. 'Global Income Distribution: From the Fall of the Berlin Wall to the Great Recession'. Policy Research Working Paper 6719. Washington, DC: World Bank.

Lal, D. 1983. *Poverty of Development Economics*. London: Institute of Economic Affairs.

Lall, S. 1994. 'The East Asia Miracle Study: Does the Bell Toll for Industrial Strategy?' *World Development 22* (4): pp. 645–54.

Landertinger, L. 2009. 'Brazil's Landless Workers' Movement (MST)'. Baptista Prizewinning Essay. York: Department of Sociology and Philosophy, University of York.

Langer, A. and S. Mikami. 2011. 'The Relationship between Objective and Subjective Horizontal Inequalities: Evidence from Five African Countries'. In *Preventing Violent Conflict in Africa*, edited by Y. Mine, F. Stewart, S. Fukuda-Parr, and P.T. Mkandawire, pp. 208–51. London: Palgrave.

Langer, A. and F. Stewart, 2016. 'Regional Imbalances, Horizontal Inequalities, and Violent Conflicts: Insights from Four West African Countries'. <http://documents.worldbank.org/curated/en/768071468191326719/Regional-imbalances-horizontal-inequalities-and-violent-conflicts-insights-from-four-West-African-countries>. Washington, DC: World Bank Group.

Langer, A., F. Stewart, K. Smedts, and L. Demarest. 2017. 'Conceptualising and Measuring Social Cohesion in Africa: Towards a Perceptions-Based Index'. *Social Indicators Research 131* (1): pp. 321–43.

Lansley, S. 2012. *The Cost of Inequality: Why Equality is Essential for Recovery*. London: Gibson Square.

Lavy, V., J. Strauss, D. Thomas, and P. Vreyer. 1996. 'Quality of Health Care, Survival and Health Outcomes in Ghana'. *Journal of Health Economics 15* (3): pp. 333–57.

Layard, R. 2011. *Happiness*, revised edition. London: Penguin.

Layard, R., D. Chisolm, V. Patel, and S. Saxena. 2013. 'Mental Illness and Unhappiness'. In *World Happiness Report 2013*, edited by J.F. Helliwell, R. Layard, and J. Sachs, pp. 39–54. New York: Sustainable Development Solutions Network.

Leamer, E. 1993. 'Factor Supply Differences as a Source of Comparative Advantage'. *American Economic Review 83* (2): pp. 436–9.

Lebedinski, L. and V. Vandenberghe. 2013. 'Assessing Education's Contribution to Productivity using Firm-Level Evidence'. IRES Discussion Papers No. 2013017. Institut de Recherches Economiques et Sociales (IRES).

Lee, Y.-M. and M.B. Lee. 2005. 'The Development of the Industrial Relations Field in Korea'. In *Advances in Industrial and Labor Relations Volume 14*, edited by D. Lewin and B. Kaufman, pp. 279–99. Bingley: Emerald Publishing House.

Leturque, H. and S. Wiggins. 2010. 'Thailand's Story: Thailand's Progress in Agricultural Transition and Sustained Productivity Growth'. London: Overseas Development Institute.

Lewis, A. 1954. 'Economic Development with Unlimited Supplies of Labour'. *Manchester School of Economic and Social Studies 22* (2): pp. 139–91.

Leys, C. 1975. *Underdevelopment in Kenya: The Political Economy of Neo-Colonialism*. London: Heinemann.

Li, H. and H.-F. Zou. 1998. 'Income Inequality is Not Harmful for Growth: Theory and Evidence'. *Review of Development Economics 2* (3): pp. 318–34.

Lindert, P.H. 2004. *Growing Public: Social Spending and Economic Growth since the Eighteenth Century*. Cambridge: Cambridge University Press.

Lipton, M. 1977. *Why Poor People Stay Poor: A Study of Urban Bias in World Development*. London: Temple Smith.

Lipton, M. and M. Ravallion. 1995. 'Poverty and Policy'. In *Handbook of Development Economics Volume 3*, edited by J. Behrman and T.N. Srinivasan, pp. 2251–658. Amsterdam: North Holland.

Little, I.M.D. 1982. *Economic Development: Theory, Policy, and International Relations*. New York: Basic Books.

Little, I.M.D, T. Scitovsky, and M. Scott. 1970. *Industry and Trade in Some Developing Countries*. Oxford: Oxford University Press.

Locke, J. 1773. *An Essay Concerning the True Original, Extent and End of Civil Government*. Boston: Edes and Gill.

Lopez-Acevedo, G. 2006. 'Mexico: Two Decades of the Evolution of Education and Inequality'. World Bank Policy Research Working Paper No. 3919. Washington, DC: World Bank.

Lopez-Calva, L.F. and N. Lustig. 2012. *Decline in Inequality in Latin America: Technology Change, Educational Upgrading and Democracy*. Washington, DC: Brookings Institution.

Loungani, P. and Z. An. 2016. 'Unemployment Troubles Ahead for Emerging Markets'. IMF Direct. <https://blogs.imf.org/2016/05/03/unemployment-troubles-ahead-for-emerging-markets/>. Accessed 4 May 2016.

Lovell, C. 1992. *Breaking the Cycle of Poverty: The BRAC Strategy*. Dhaka: University Press.

Lucas, R.E. 1988. 'On the Mechanics of Economic Development'. *Journal of Monetary Economics 22* (1): pp. 3–42.

Lykken, D. and A. Tellegen. 1996. 'Happiness is a Stochastic Phenomenon'. *Psychological Science 7* (3): pp. 186–9.

Mahalanobis, P.C. 1953. 'Some Observations on the Process of Growth in National Income'. *Sankya 12* (4): pp. 307–12.

Mahmud, S. 2002. 'Informal Women's Groups in Rural Bangladesh: Operation and Outcomes'. In *Group Behaviour and Development: Is the Market Destroying Cooperation?* Edited by J. Heyer, F. Stewart, and R. Thorp, pp. 209–26. Oxford: Oxford University Press.

Majumdar, M. and J. Mooij. 2011. *Education and Inequality in India: A Classroom View*. London: Routledge.

Malhotra, T.C. 2006. 'Bangladesh: A Growing Textile Economy'. *Textile World Asia*, 1 January. <http://textileworldasia.com/textile-world-asia/twa-features/2006/01/bangladesh-a-growing-textile-economy/>. Accessed 15 November 2015.

Mancini, L., F. Stewart, and G. Brown. 2008. 'Approaches to the Measurement of Horizontal Inequalities'. In *Horizontal Inequalities and Conflict: Understanding Group Violence in Multiethnic Societies*, edited by F. Stewart, pp. 85–105. London: Palgrave Macmillan.

Marshall, M.G. 2002. 'Global Terrorism: An Overview and Systematic Analysis', Center for Systemic Peace Occasional Paper 3, University of Maryland.

Marshall, M.G. 2005. 'Major Episodes of Political Violence, 1946–2004'. Center for Systemic Peace, University of Maryland.

Martinez-Vazquez, J., V. Vulovic, and Y. Liu. 2011. 'Direct versus Indirect Taxation: Trends, Theory and Economic Significance'. Economics Faculty Publications. <https://pdfs.semanticscholar.org/f22e/58f504f3b7dc1742c4fe5e54937033602ee9.pdf>. Atlanta: Department of Economics, Georgia State University.

Martorano, B., G.A. Cornia, and F. Stewart. 2013. 'Human Development and Fiscal Policy: Comparing the Crises of 1982–85 and 2008–11'. In *Towards Human Development: New Approaches to Macroeconomics and Inequality*, edited by G.A. Cornia and F. Stewart, pp. 221–4. Oxford: Oxford University Press.

Mason, P. 2015. *PostCapitalism: A Guide to Our Future*. London: Allen Lane.

Masud-All-Kamal, M. and C.K. Saha. 2014. 'Targeting Social Policy and Poverty Reduction: The Case of Social Safety Nets in Bangladesh'. *Poverty & Public Policy 6* (2): pp. 195–211.

McGuire, J. 2010. *Wealth, Health and Democracy in East Asia and Latin America*. Cambridge: Cambridge University Press.

McKeown, T. and R.G. Record. 1962. 'Reasons for the Decline of Mortality in England and Wales during the Nineteenth Century'. *Population Studies 16* (2): pp. 94–122.

McMichael, P., ed. 2010. *Contesting Development*. London: Routledge.

Medina, M. 1998. 'Scavenger Cooperatives in Developing Countries'. *Biocycle International: Gaining Momentum 39* (6): pp. 70–3.

Menon, G.A. 2010. 'Recoveries of Space and Subjectivity in the Shadow of Violence: The Clandestine Politics of Pavement Dwellers in Mumbai'. In *Contesting Development*, edited by P. McMichael, pp. 151–64. London: Routledge.

Milanovic, B. 2013. 'Global Inequality in Numbers: In History and Now'. *Global Policy 4* (2): pp. 198–208.

Milanovic, B. 2016. *Global Inequality: A New Approach for the Age of Globalization*. Cambridge, MA: Belknap Press.

Mill, J.S. [R. Crisp and NetLibrary Inc.] 1998. *Utilitarianism*. Oxford: Oxford University Press.

Miller, D. 1976. *Social Justice*. Oxford: Oxford University Press.

Ming, L., C. Zhao, and W. Guanghua. 2005. 'Equality for the Sake of Growth: The Nexus of Inequality, Investment, Education and Growth in China'. *Economic Research Journal 12*.

Mitchell, M.T. 2006. *Michael Polanyi: The Art of Knowing*. Wilmington: ISI Books.

Moestue, H. and S. Huttly. 2008. 'Adult Education and Child Nutrition: The Role of Family and Community'. *Journal of Epidemiology and Community Health 62* (2): pp. 152–9.

Molina, F. 2013. 'Why is Evo Morales Still Popular? Strengths of the MAS in the Creation of a New Order'. *Nueva Sociedad 245*. <http://lifeonleft.blogspot.co.uk/2013/07/why-is-evo-morales-still-popular.html>. Accessed 30 July 2014.

Molina, G.G. and M. Purser. 2010. 'Human Development since 1970: A Social Convergence Story'. Human Development Research Paper 2010/02. New York: HDRO/UNDP.

Morales-Hidalgo, D., S.N. Oswalt, and E. Somanathan. 2015. 'Status and Trends in Global Primary Forest, Protected Areas, and Areas Designated for Conservation of Biodiversity from the Global Forest Resources Assessment 2015'. *Forest Ecology and Management 352*: pp. 68–77.

Morley, S. 2000. 'The Effect of Growth and Economic Reform on the Distribution of Income in Latin America'. *CEPAL Review 71*: pp. 23–40.

Morris, D.M. 1977. *The PQLI: Measuring Progress in Meeting Human Needs*. Washington, DC: Overseas Development Council.

Mosley, P., J. Harrigan, and J.F.J. Toye. 1991. *Aid and Power: The World Bank and Policy-Based Lending in the 1980s. Volume 2: Case Studies*. London: Routledge.

Mughal, M. and B. Diawara. 2011. 'Explaining Income Inequalities in Developing Countries: The Role of Human Capital'. CATT Working Paper No. 2011–2012_2. Pau France, Centre d'Analyse Théorique et de Traitement des données économiques.

Muñoz, I., M. Paredes, and R. Thorp. 2006. 'Collective Action, Conflict and Ethnicity in Peru'. CRISE Working Paper 24. Oxford: Centre for Research on Inequality, Human Security and Ethnicity.

Murshed, S.M. and S. Gates. 2005. 'Spatial-Horizontal Inequality and the Maoist Insurgency in Nepal'. *Review of Development Economics 9* (1): pp. 121–34.

Mutua, M.W. 2001. 'Savages, Victims, and Saviors: The Metaphor of Human Rights'. *Harvard International Law Journal 42* (1): pp. 201–45.

Mveyange, A. 2015. 'On the Fertility Transition in Africa: Income, Child Mortality, or Education?' WIDER Working Paper 2015/089. Helsinki: UNU-WIDER.

Najera, J.A. and J. Hempel. 1996. 'The Burden of Malaria'. Geneva: World Health Organization.

Narayan-Parker, D. with R. Patel, K. Schafft, A. Rademacher, and S. Koch-Schulte. 2000. *Crying Out for Change: Voices of the Poor*. Oxford and New York: Oxford University Press for the World Bank.

Nardinelli, C. 1990. *Child Labor and the Industrial Revolution*. Bloomington: Indiana University Press.

Nath, S. 1997. 'The Impact of BRAC's Education Programme on Raising Basic Education Levels for the Children of Rural Bangladesh' MSc Development Economics Thesis. Oxford: University of Oxford.

Nazeer, Z. 2014. 'Banned, but Vote-Buying Still Plagues Indonesia's Election Process'. *The Jakarta Post*, 17 March. <http://www.thejakartapost.com/news/business>. Accessed 18 June 2017.

Nee, M. 1996. *Towards Restoring Life: Cambodian Villages*. Sydney: Overseas Service Bureau.

Nordhaus, W. and E. Kokkelenberg. 2000. *Nature's Numbers: Expanding the National Account to Include the Environment.* New York: National Academy Press.

Nordhaus, W. and J. Tobin. 1972. 'Is Growth Obsolete?' *Economic Research: Retrospect and Prospect. Volume 5: Economic Growth*, pp. 1–80. New York: National Bureau of Economic Research.

North, D.C. 1991. 'Institutions'. *Journal of Economic Perspectives 5* (1): pp. 97–112.

Nozick, R. 1974. *Anarchy, State, and Utopia.* Oxford: Blackwell.

Nur, E. 1993. 'The Impact of Malaria on Labor Use and Efficiency in the Sudan'. *Social Science and Medicine 37* (9): pp. 1115–19.

Nurkse, R. 1953. *Problems of Capital Formation in Underdeveloped Countries.* Oxford: Blackwell.

Nussbaum, M. 2000. *Women and Human Development: A Study in Human Capabilities.* Cambridge: Cambridge University Press.

Nussbaum, M. 2004. 'Beyond the Social Contract: Capabilities and Social Justice'. *Oxford Development Studies 32* (1): pp. 3–18.

ODI. 2010. *Millennium Development Goals: Report Card. Measuring Progress Across Goals.* London: Overseas Development Institute.

ODI. 2015. 'Ethiopia's Remarkable Development Progress'. <https://www.odi.org/opinion/9885-ethiopias-remarkable-development-progress>. Accessed 18 January 2016.

OECD. 2011. Background Document to OECD Conference on Social Cohesion and Development, 20–21 January 2011. <http://www.oecd.org/dev/pgd/internationalconferenceonsocialcohesionanddevelopment.htm>. Accessed 18 January 2017.

Oman, C. and G. Wignaraja. 1991. *The Postwar Evolution of Development Thinking.* Paris: OECD.

Onaran, O. 2009. 'Wage Share, Globalization and Crisis: The Case of Manufacturing Industry in Korea, Mexico and Turkey'. *International Review of Applied Economics 23* (2): pp. 113–34.

Orihuela, J.C. 2012. 'Post-Conflict Economic Policy and Group Inequalities in Peru'. In *Horizontal Inequalities in a Post-Conflict Context*, edited by A. Langer, F. Stewart, and R. Venugopal, pp. 186–208. London: Palgrave.

Ostry, J.D., A. Berg, and C.G. Tsangarides. 2014. 'Redistribution, Inequality and Growth'. IMF Staff Discussion Note SDN/14/02. Washington, DC: IMF Research Department.

Oxhorn, P., A.D. Selee, and J.S. Tulchin, eds. 2004. *Decentralization, Democratic Governance, and Civil Society in Comparative Perspective: Africa, Asia, and Latin America.* Baltimore, MD: Johns Hopkins University Press.

Pack, H. and L. Westphal. 1986. 'Industrial Strategy and Technological Change'. *Journal of Development Economics 22* (1): pp. 87–128.

Palma, G. 1978. 'Dependency: A Formal Theory of Underdevelopment or a Methodology for the Analysis of Concrete Situations of Underdevelopment'. *World Development 6* (7–8): pp. 881–924.

Parker, S.W., L. Rubalcava, and G. Teruel. 2008. 'Evaluating Conditional Schooling and Health Programs'. In *Handbook of Development Economics Volume 4*, edited by T.P. Schultz and J.A. Strauss, pp. 3963–4035. Amsterdam: Elsevier.

Patel, V. 2001. 'Inequality and Mental Health in Developing Countries'. In *Poverty, Inequality and Health*, edited by D. Leon and G. Walt, pp. 247–62. Oxford: Oxford University Press.

Perotti, R. 1993. 'Political Equilibrium Income Distribution and Growth'. *Review of Economic Studies 60* (4): pp. 755–76.

Persson, T. and G. Tabellini. 1994. 'Is Inequality Harmful for Growth?' *American Economic Review 84* (3): pp. 600–21.

Petras, J. and H. Veltmeyer. 2001. 'Are Latin American Peasant Movements a Force for Change? Some New Paradigms Revisited'. *Journal of Peasant Studies 28* (2): pp. 83–118.

Picard, J. and A. Mills. 1992. 'The Effect of Malaria on Work Time: Analysis of Data from Two Nepali Districts'. *The Journal of Tropical Medicine and Hygiene 95* (6): pp. 382–9.

Pigou, A.C. 1932. *The Economics of Welfare*. London: Macmillan.

Piketty, T. 2014. *Capital in the Twenty-First Century*. Cambridge, MA: Belknap Press.

Pitt, M.M., S.R. Khandker, and J. Cartwright. 2006. 'Empowering Women with Micro Finance: Evidence from Bangladesh'. *Economic Development and Cultural Change 54* (4): pp. 791–831.

Pitt, M.M., M.R. Rosenzweig, and M.N. Hassan. 1990. 'Productivity, Health and Inequality in the Intrahousehold Distribution of Food in Low-Income Countries'. *American Economic Review 80* (5): pp. 1139–56.

Piven, F.F. and R.A. Cloward. 1979. *Poor People's Movements: Why They Succeed, How They Fail*. New York: Vintage books.

Polanyi, K. 1944. *The Great Transformation*. Boston: Beacon Press.

Popper, K.R. 2002. *The Open Society and Its Enemies*. London: Routledge.

Porter, M., K. Schwab, X. Sala-i-Martin, and A. López-Claros, eds. 2004. *The Global Competitiveness Report 2004–2005*. London: Palgrave, Macmillan.

Posner, D.N. 2005. *Institutions and Ethnic Politics in Africa*. New York: Cambridge University Press.

Prebisch, R. 1950. *The Economic Development of Latin America and its Principal Problems*. New York: United Nations.

Preston, Lewis T. 1992. 'Address to the Board of Governors'. 22 September 1992. Washington, DC: World Bank.

Priestley, J. 1768. *An Essay on the First Principles of Government, and on the Nature of Political, Civil, and Religious Liberty*. Dublin: James Williams.

Przeworski, A., M. Alvarez, J.-A. Cheibub, and F. Limongi. 2000. *Democracy and Development: Political Institutions and Well-Being in the World, 1950–1990*. Cambridge: Cambridge University Press.

Psacharopolous, G., S. Morley, A. Fiszbein, J. Lee, and B. Wood. 1992. 'Poverty and Income Distribution in Latin America: The Story of the 1980s'. World Bank Technical Paper 351. Washington, DC: World Bank.

Psacharopoulos, G. and H.A. Patrinos. 2004. 'Returns to Investment in Education: A Further Update'. *Education Economics 12* (2): pp. 111–34.

Putnam, R.D. 2000. *Bowling Alone: The Collapse and Revival of American Community*. New York: Simon & Schuster.

Putnam, R.D., R. Leonardi, and R. Nanetti. 1993. *Making Democracy Work: Civic Traditions in Modern Italy*. Princeton, NJ and Chichester: Princeton University Press.

Quddus, M. and S. Rashid. 2000. *Entrepreneurs and Economic Development: The Remarkable Story of Garment Export from Bangladesh*. Dhaka: The University Press.

Quisumbing, A. and J.A. Maluccio. 2000. 'Intrahousehold Allocation and Gender Relations: New Empirical Evidence from Four Developing Countries'. Discussion Paper 86. Washington, DC: International Food Policy Research Institute (IFPRI).

Rahim, A. 1997. *Politics and National Formation in Bangladesh*. Dhaka: University Press.

Ram, R. 1985. 'Exports and Economic Growth: Some Additional Evidence'. *Economic Development and Cultural Change 33* (2): pp. 415–25.

Ram, R. 2009. 'Intercountry Inequality in Human Development: A 30-Year Perspective'. *Journal of Economic Studies 36* (5): pp. 481–9.

Ranci, C. 2011. 'Competitiveness and Social Cohesion in Western European Cities'. *Urban Studies 48* (13): pp. 2789–804.

Ranis, G. and F. Stewart. 1994. 'Decentralisation in Indonesia'. *Bulletin of Indonesian Economic Studies 30* (3): pp. 41–72.

Ranis, G. and F. Stewart. 2000. 'Strategies for Success in Human Development'. *Journal of Human Development 1* (1): pp. 49–70.

Ranis, G. and F. Stewart. 2012. 'Success and Failure on Human Development, 1970–2007'. *Journal of Human Development and Capabilities 13* (2): pp. 167–96.

Ranis, G., F. Stewart, and A. Ramirez. 2000. 'Economic Growth and Human Development'. *World Development 28* (2): pp. 197–220.

Ranis, G., F. Stewart, and E. Samman. 2006. 'Human Development: Beyond the Human Development Index'. *Journal of Human Development 7* (3): pp. 323–58.

Ranis, G., F. Stewart, and E. Samman. 2009. 'Country Patterns of Behavior on Broader Dimensions of Human Development'. In *Arguments for a Better World. Volume II: Society, Institutions and Development*, edited by K. Basu and R. Kanbur, pp. 119–28. Oxford: Oxford University Press.

Rashid, S. 2014. 'If Finance Works, Microfinance Works: Contextual Evaluation and the Irrelevance of Randomized Controlled Trials'. *Journal of Poverty Alleviation & International Development 5* (2): pp. 117–43.

Ravallion, M. 2009. 'A Comparative Perspective on Poverty Reduction in China, Brazil and India'. World Bank Policy Research Working Paper 5080. Washington, DC: World Bank.

Rawlings, L.B. and G.M. Rubio. 2005. 'Evaluating the Impact of Conditional Cash Transfer Programs'. *The World Bank Research Observer 20* (1): pp. 29–55.

Rawls, J. 1971. *A Theory of Justice*. Cambridge, MA: Belknap Press.

Rawls, J. 1987. 'The Idea of Overlapping Consensus'. *Oxford Journal of Legal Studies 7* (1): pp. 1–25.

Rawls, J. 1993. *Political Liberalism*. New York: Columbia University Press.

Rawls, J. [and S.R. Freeman]. 1999 [1972]. *Collected Papers*. Cambridge, MA and London: Harvard University Press.

Reimers, M. and S. Klasen. 2013. 'Revisiting the Role of Education for Agricultural Productivity'. *American Journal of Agricultural Economics 95* (1): pp. 131–52.

Rienks, S.L. and M.E. Wadsworth. 2012. 'Stress as a Mechanism of Poverty's Ill Effects on Children'. *CYF News*, July. American Psychological Association. <http://www.apa.org/pi/families/resources/newsletter/2012/07/stress-mechanism.aspx>. Accessed 10 June 2017.

Robbins, L.R.B. 1945. *An Essay on the Nature and Significance of Economic Science*, 2nd edition. London: Macmillan.

Roberts, K.M. 2014. 'The Politics of Inequality and Redistribution in Latin America's Post-Adjustment Era'. In *Falling Inequality in Latin America: Policy Changes and Lessons*, edited by G.A. Cornia, pp. 49–69. Oxford: Oxford University Press.

Robison, L.J., A.A. Schmid, and M.E. Siles. 2002. 'Is Social Capital Really Capital?' *Review of Social Economy 60* (1): pp. 1–24.

Robles, W. 2001. 'The Landless Rural Workers' Movement (MST) in Brazil'. *Journal of Peasant Studies 28* (2): pp. 146–61.

Rodríguez Takeuchi, L.R. and C. Mariotti. 2016. 'Who is Being Left Behind in Latin America? An Illustration in Brazil and Guatemala'. London: Overseas Development Institute.

Rodríguez Takeuchi, L. and E. Samman. 2015. 'Patterns of Progress on the MDGs and Implications for Target Setting Post-2015'. Development Progress Research Report 1. London: Overseas Development Institute.

Rodrik, D. 1997. *Has Globalization Gone Too Far?* Washington, DC: Institute for International Economics.

Roemer, P.M. 1986. 'Increasing Returns and Long Run Growth'. *Journal of Political Economy 94* (5): pp. 1002–37.

Rohde, J. 2005. *Learning to Reach Health for All: Thirty Years of Instructive Experience at BRAC*. Dhaka: University Press.

Romer, D. 1990. 'Endogenous Technological Change'. *Journal of Political Economy 98* (5, Part 2): pp. S71–S102.

Rosenstein-Rodan, P. 1943. 'Problems of Industrialisation of Eastern and South-Eastern Europe'. *Economic Journal 53* (210/211): pp. 202–11.

Rosenzweig, M.R. 1995. 'Why are there Returns in Schooling?' *American Economic Review 85* (2): pp. 153–8.

Roser, M. 2017. Our World in Data. <https://ourworldindata.org/>. Accessed 6 June 2017.

Rostow, W.W. 1960. *The Stages of Economic Growth: A Non-Communist Manifesto*. Cambridge: Cambridge University Press.

Rousseau, J.-J. 1968 [1762]. *The Social Contract*. London: Penguin.

Rowntree, B.S. 1902. *Poverty: A Study of Town* Life, 2nd edition. London: Macmillan and co.

Roy, I. 2012. 'Capable Subjects: Power and Politics in Eastern India'. DPhil thesis, University of Oxford.

Sah, J., ed. 2003. 'Social Mobilization and Mapping of Social Mobilization in Nepal'. Kathmandu: National Planning Commission.

Sahn, D.E., P.A. Dorosh, and S.D. Younger. 1997. *Structural Adjustment Reconsidered: Economic Policy and Poverty in Africa*. Cambridge: Cambridge University Press.

Sampson, R.J. and J.D. Morenoff. 2006. 'Durable Inequality. Spatial Dynamics, Social Processes and the Persistence of Poverty in Chicago Neighbourhoods'. In *Poverty Traps*, edited by S. Bowles, S.N. Durlauf, and K.R. Hoff, pp. 176–203. Princeton, NJ: Sage Russell Foundation and Princeton University Press.

Savedoff, W.D. and T.P. Schultz. 2000. 'Wealth from Health'. Washington, DC: Inter-American Development Bank.

Schäferhoff, M., D. Evans, N. Burnett, P. Komaromi, J. Kraus, A. Levin, C. Dayo Obure, E. Pradhan, C.S. Sutherland, E. Suzuki, and D.T. Jamison. 2015. 'Estimating the Costs and Benefits of Education from a Health Perspective'. Background paper for the Oslo Summit on Education for Development. Executive Summary. Berlin: SEEK Development. <http://www.r4d.org/wp-content/uploads/SEEK-EstimatingCostsBenefitsEducationHealthPerspective.pdf>. Accessed 8 September 2017.

Schneewind, J.B. 2003. *Moral Philosophy from Montaigne to Kant: An Anthology*. Cambridge: Cambridge University Press.

Schokkaert, E. and L. van Ootegem. 1990. 'Sen's Concept of the Living Standard Applied to the Belgium Unemployed'. Recherches Economiques de Louvain. Louvain: IRES.

Schultz, T.P. 2002. 'Wage Gains Associated with Height as a Form of Human Capital'. *American Economic Review Papers and Proceedings 92* (2): pp. 349–53.

Schultz, T.P. 2007. 'Population Policies, Fertility, Women's Human Capital, and Child Quality'. In *Handbook of Development Economics, Volume 4*, edited by T. Schultz and J. Strauss, pp. 3249–303. Amsterdam: Elsevier.

Scott, J.C. 1985. *Weapons of the Weak: Everyday Forms of Peasant Resistance*. New Haven and London: Yale University Press.

Seers, D. 1962. 'Why Visiting Economists Fail'. *Journal of Political Economy 70* (4): pp. 325–38.

Seers, D. 1969. 'The Meaning of Development'. *International Development Review 11* (4): pp. 3–4.

Seers, D. 1972. 'What are we Trying to Measure?' *Journal of Development Studies 8* (3): pp. 21–36.

Selowsky, M. 1981. 'Nutrition, Health and Education: The Economic Significance of Complementarities at an Early Age'. *Journal of Development Economics 9* (3): pp. 331–46.

Sen, A.K. 1975. *Employment, Technology and Development*. Oxford: Clarendon Press.

Sen, A.K. 1977. 'Rational Fools: A Critique of the Behavioral Foundations of Economic Theory'. *Philosophy and Public Affairs 6* (4): pp. 317–44.

Sen, A.K. 1980. 'Equality of What?' In *Tanner Lectures on Human Values*, pp. 197–220. Cambridge: Cambridge University Press.

Sen, A.K. 1992. *Inequality Reexamined*. Oxford: Clarendon Press.

Sen, A.K. 1997. 'Human Rights and Asian Values'. Sixteenth Morgenthau Memorial Lecture on Ethics and Foreign Policy, New York: Carnegie Council. <https://www.carnegiecouncil.org/publications/archive/morgenthau/ . . . /254_sen.pdf>.

Sen, A.K. 1999a. *Development as Freedom*. Oxford: Oxford University Press.

Sen, A.K. 1999b. 'Democracy as a Universal Value'. *Journal of Democracy 10* (3): pp. 3–17.

Sen, A.K. 2002. 'Health Perception versus Observation'. *British Medical Journal 324*: pp. 860–21.

Sen, A.K. 2009. *The Idea of Justice*. London: Allen Lane.

Sen, A.K. 2015. 'The Economic Consequences of Austerity'. *New Statesman*, 4 June. <http://www.newstatesman.com/politics/2015/06/amartya-sen-economic-consequences-austerity>. Accessed 30 June 2015.

Shelley, P.B. 1932. *The Masque of Anarchy: A Poem*. London: Edward Moxon.

Singer, H.W. 1950. 'The Distribution of Gains between Investing and Borrowing Countries'. *American Economic Review Papers and Proceedings 40* (2): pp. 473–85.

Smart, R.N. 1958. 'Negative Utilitarianism'. *Mind 67* (268): pp. 542–3.

Soares, S., R.G. Osório, M. Medeiros, and E. Zepeda. 2009. 'Conditional Cash Transfers in Brazil, Chile and Mexico: Impacts upon Inequality'. *Estudios Economicos*, Numero Extraordinaire: pp. 207–24.

Sobhan, R. 2002. 'The Political Economy of the State and Market in Bangladesh'. Centre for Policy Dialogue, Dhakar.

Söderbom, M.M. and F.J. Teal. 2004. 'Size and Efficiency in African Manufacturing Firms: Evidence from Firm-Level Panel Data'. *Journal of Development Economics 73* (1): pp. 369–94.

Sohn, B. 2000. *How Much has Health Improvement Contributed to the Korean Economic Growth?* Providence, RI: Brown University.

Spence, R. 1999. 'The Centrality of Community-Led Recovery'. In *Recovery from Armed Conflict in Developing Countries: An Economic and Political Analysis*, edited by G. Harris, pp. 204–22. London: Routledge.

Staveteig, S. and L. Mallick. 2014. 'Intertemporal Comparisons of Poverty and Wealth with DHS Data: A Harmonized Asset Index Approach'. DHS Methodological Reports 15. Rockville, MD: ICF International.

Stefanoni, P. and H.D. Alto. 2006. *Evo Morales, de la Coca al Palacio: Una Opportunidad para la Izquierda Indígena*. La Paz: Malatesta.

Stewart, F. 1977. *Technology and Underdevelopment*. London: Macmillan.

Stewart, F. 1985. *Planning to Meet Basic Needs*. London: Macmillan.

Stewart, F. 1989. 'Basic Needs Strategies, Human Rights and the Right to Development'. *Human Rights Quarterly 11* (3): pp. 347–74.

Stewart, F. 1995. *Adjustment and Poverty: Options and Choices*. London: Routledge.

Stewart, F. 2006. 'The Evolution of Economic Ideas: From Import Substitution to Human Development'. In *Economic Doctrines in Latin America*, edited by E. V. K. FitzGerald and R. Thorp, pp. 48–71. London: Palgrave Macmillan.

Stewart, F., ed. 2008. *Horizontal Inequalities and Conflict: Understanding Group Violence in Multiethnic Societies*. London: Palgrave.

Stewart, F. 2010. 'Power and Progress: The Swing of the Pendulum'. *Journal of Human Development and Capabilities 11* (3): pp. 371–95.

Stewart, F. 2012a. 'Employment Policies and Horizontal Inequalities in Post-Conflict Situations'. In *Horizontal Inequalities and Post-Conflict Development: Laying the Foundations for Durable Peace*, edited by A. Langer, F. Stewart, and R. Venugopal, pp. 61–83. London: Palgrave.

Stewart, F. 2012b. 'The Impact of Global Economic Crises on the Poor: Comparing the 1980s and 2000s'. *Journal of Human Development and Capabilities 13* (1): pp. 83–106.

Stewart, F. 2013a. 'Approaches towards Inequality and Inequity'. Office of Research Working Paper. Florence: UNICEF.

Stewart, F. 2013b. 'Capabilities and Human Development: Beyond the Individual. The Critical Role of Social Institutions and Social Competencies'. Human Development Occasional Paper 2013/03. <http://hdr.undp.org/en/reports/global/hdr2013/occasional-papers/>.

Stewart, F. 2014. 'Against Happiness: A Critical Appraisal of the Use of Measures of Happiness for Evaluating Progress in Development'. *Journal of Human Development and Capabilities 15* (4): pp. 293–307.

Stewart, F. and A. Langer. 2008. 'Horizontal Inequalities: Explaining Persistence and Change'. In *Horizontal Inequalities and Conflict: Understanding Group Violence in Multi-ethnic Societies*, edited by F. Stewart, pp. 54–78. London: Palgrave.

Stewart, F., C. Ruggeri Laderchi, and R. Saith. 2003. 'Does it Matter that we Don't Agree on the Definition of Poverty? A Comparison of Four Approaches'. *Oxford Development Studies 31* (3): pp. 243–74.

Stewart, F. and E. Samman. 2001. 'Food Aid during Civil War: Conflicting Conclusions from Alternative Approaches'. In *War and Underdevelopment, Volume One, The Economic and Social Consequences of Conflict*, F. Stewart, E.V.K. FitzGerald, and Associates, pp. 169–204. Oxford: Oxford University Press.

Stewart, F., W. Van der Geest, and International Labour Office Employment Department. 1995. 'Adjustment and Social Funds: Political Panacea or Effective Poverty Reduction?' Geneva: International Labour Office.

Stiglitz, J.E. 1994. *Whither Socialism?* Cambridge, MA and London: Massachusetts Institute of Technology Press.

Stiglitz, J.E. 2013. *The Price of Inequality*. London: Penguin Books.

Stiglitz, J.E., A. Sen, and J.-P. Fitoussi. 2010. *Mismeasuring Our Lives: Why GDP Doesn't Add Up*. New York: The New Press.

Stiglitz, J.E. and A. Weiss. 1981. 'Credit Rationing in Markets with Imperfect Information'. *American Economic Review 71* (3): pp. 393–410.

St John, R.B. 2010. *Toledo's Peru Vision and Reality*. Gainesville: University Press of Florida.

Stockhammer, E. 2013. 'Why Have Wage Shares Fallen? A Panel Analysis of the Determinants of Functional Income Distribution'. Conditions of Work and Employment Series 35. Geneva: ILO.

Stone, A.A. and C. Mackie, eds. 2014. *Subjective Wellbeing: Measuring Happiness, Suffering and Other Dimensions of Experience*. <http://www.nap.edu>. Washington, DC: National Research Council, National Academies Press.

Strauss, J. 1986. 'Does Better Nutrition Raise Farm Productivity?' *Journal of Political Economy 94* (2): pp. 297–320.

Strauss, J. and D. Thomas. 1995. 'Human Resources: Empirical Modeling of Household and Family Decisions'. In *Handbook of Development Economics Volume 3*, edited by J.R. Behrman and T.N. Srinivasan, pp. 1883–2023. Amsterdam: North Holland.

Strauss, J. and D. Thomas. 1997. 'Health and Wages: Evidence on Men and Women in Urban Brazil'. *Journal of Econometrics 77* (1): pp. 159–85.

Streeten, P. 1995. *Thinking about Development*. Cambridge: Cambridge University Press.

Streeten, P.P., S.J. Burki, M. ul Haq, N. Hicks, and F. Stewart. 1981. *First Things First: Meeting Basic Human Needs in Developing Countries*. New York: Oxford University Press.

Sumner, A. 2016. 'The World's Two New Middles: Growth, Precarity, Structural Change, and the Limitations of the Special Case'. WIDER Working Paper 2016/34. Helsinki: WIDER/UNU.

Sunkel, O. 1969. 'National Development Policy and External Dependence in Latin America'. *Journal of Development Studies 6* (1): pp. 23–48.

Suri, T., M. Boozer, G. Ranis, and F. Stewart. 2011. 'Paths to Success: The Relationship between Human Development and Economic Growth'. *World Development 39* (4): pp. 506–22.

Swanhuyser, E. 2016. 'Suicide Deaths in India Increasing at an Alarming Rate'. *Humanosphere*. <http://www.humanosphere.org/global-health/2016/08/suicide-deaths-india-increasing-alarming-rate/>. Accessed 10 May 2017.

Szreter, S. 1997. 'Economic Growth, Disruption, Deprivation, Disease, and Death: On the Importance of the Politics of Public Health for Development'. *Population and Development Review 23* (4): pp. 693–728.

Tarrow, S.G. 1998. *Power in Movement: Social Movements, Collective Action and Politics*. Cambridge: Cambridge University Press.

Thailand Government. 2007. 'Health Policy in Thailand 2007'. Bangkok: Bureau of Policy and Strategy, Ministry of Public Health.

Thomas, D., J. Strauss, and M.H. Henriques. 1991. 'How Does Mother's Education Affect Child Height?' *Journal of Human Resources 26* (2): pp. 183–211.

Thompson, E.P. 1963. *The Making of the English Working Class*. London: Victor Gollancz.

Thorp, R. and M. Paredes. 2010. *Ethnicity and the Persistence of Inequality: The Case of Peru*. New York: Palgrave Macmillan.

Thorp, R., F. Stewart, and A. Heyer. 2005. 'When and How Far is Group Formation a Route out of Chronic Poverty?' *World Development 33* (6): pp. 907–20.

Tilly, C. 2004. *Social Movements 1768–2004*. Boulder: Paradigm Publishers.

Transport Research Laboratory. n.d. 'Road Safety in Developed and Developing Countries'. <http://www.transport-links.org/crse/Section 2/2.2–Global trends.pdf>.

Truman, H. 1949. Inaugural Address, 20 January. <https://www.trumanlibrary.org/whistlestop/50yr_archive/inagural20jan1949.htm>. Accessed 28 May 2017.

Tsai, M.-C. 2006. 'Does Political Democracy Enhance Human Development in Developing Countries? A Cross-national Analysis'. *American Journal of Economics and Sociology 65* (2): pp. 233–68.

Tuladhar, R., C. Sapkota, and N. Adhikar. 2014. 'Effects of Migration and Remittance Income on Nepal's Agricultural Yield'. ADB South Asia Working Paper Series 27.

Ul Haq, M., I. Kaul, and I. Grunberg. 1996. *The Tobin Tax: Coping with Financial Volatility*. New York: Oxford University Press.

UNDESA-WHO. 2010. 'UNDESA-WHO Policy Analysis: Mental Health and Development: Integrating Mental Health into All Development Efforts including MDGs'. 12 September 2010. <http://www.who.int/mental_health/policy/mhtargeting/mh_policyanalysis_who_undesa.pdf>. Accessed 2 October 2013.

UNDP. 1990. *Human Development Report 1990*. New York: Oxford University Press.

UNDP. 1991. *Human Development Report 1991*. New York: UNDP.

UNDP. 1993. *Human Development Report: People's Participation*. Oxford: Oxford University Press.

UNDP. 1994. *Human Development Report 1994*. Oxford: Oxford University Press.

UNDP. 1996. *Human Development Report 1996*. New York: Oxford University Press.

UNDP. 2002. *Human Development Report 2002*. New York: Oxford University Press.

UNDP. 2004a. *Survey of Socially Mobilised Communities (SMCs)*. Kathmandu: Institute for Integrated Development Studies.

UNDP. 2004b. *Human Development Report 2004*. New York: Oxford University Press.

UNDP. 2006. *Human Development Report 2006, Beyond Scarcity: Power, Poverty and the Global Water Crisis*. London: Palgrave Macmillan.

UNDP. 2007. *Human Development Report 2007/8, Fighting Climate Change: Human Solidarity in a Divided World*. London: Palgrave Macmillan.

UNDP. 2008. *Informe sobre Desarrollo Humano República Dominicana 2008: Desarrollo Humano, Una Cuestión de Poder*. Dominican Republic: UNDP.

UNDP. 2009. *Nepal Human Development Report 2009, State Transformation and Human Development*. Katmandu: UNDP.

UNDP. 2011. *Sustainability and Equity: A Better Future for All*. New York: UNDP.

UNDP. 2013. *Human Development Report 2013, The Rise of the South: Human Progress in a Diverse World*. New York: UNDP.

UNDP. 2014. *Human Development Report 2014, Sustaining Human Progress: Reducing Vulnerabilities and Building Resilience*. New York: UNDP.

UNDP. 2015. *Human Development Report 2015: Work for Human Development*. New York: UNDP.

UNDP. 2016. *Human Development Report 2016: Human Development for Everyone*. New York: UNDP.

Ungpakorn, G.J. 2013. 'Thailand: The Bloody Civil War in Patani and the Way to Achieve Peace'. *Links International Journal of Socialist Renewal*, 24 November. <http://links.org.au/taxonomy/term/296?page=1>. Accessed 12 February 2017.

Ungpakorn, G.J. 2015. 'The Role of Thai Social Movements in Democratisation'. International Conference on Human Rights and Education.

UNHCR. 2002. *UNHCR Yearbook 2002*. <http://www.unhcr.org/uk/statistics/unhcrstats/4a07e87d6/unhcr-statistical-yearbook-2002.html>. Accessed November1st 2016.

UNICEF. 2004. *State of the World's Children 2004*. New York: UNICEF.

United Nations. 2015. *Transforming our World: The 2030 Agenda for Sustainable Development*. New York: United Nations.

UNODC. n.d. International Homicide Statistics. <http://www.unodc.org/documents/data-and-analysis/IHS%20methodology.pdf>. Accessed 18 September 2016.

UNSD. 2016. UNdata. United Nations Statistical Division, Department of Economic and Social Affairs, United Nations. <http://data.un.org/>.

Uphoff, E.P., K.E. Pickett, B. Cabieses, N. Small, and J. Wright. 2013. 'A Systematic Review of the Relationships between Social Capital and Socioeconomic Inequalities in Health: A Contribution to Understanding the Psychosocial Pathway of Health Inequalities'. *International Journal for Equity in Health 12* (54).

Ura, K., S. Alkire, T. Zangmo, and K. Wangdi. 2010. 'A Short Guide to Gross National Happiness Index'. Thimphu, Bhutan: The Centre for Bhutan Studies.

Uslaner, E.M. 2008. *Corruption, Inequality, and the Rule of Law: The Bulging Pocket Makes the Easy Life*. Cambridge and New York: Cambridge University Press.

van Deurzen, I., W. van Oorschot, and E. van Ingen. 2014. 'The Link between Inequality and Population Health in Low and Middle Income Countries: Policy Myth or Social Reality?' *PLoS ONE 9* (12): p. e115109.

Vapattanawong, P., M.C. Hogan, P. Hanvoravongchai, E. Gakidou, T. Vos, A.D. Lopez, and S.S. Li. 2007. 'Reductions in Child Mortality Levels and Inequalities in Thailand: Analysis of Two Censuses'. *The Lancet 369* (9564): pp. 850–5.

Vizard, P. 2006. *Poverty and Human Rights: Sen's 'Capability Perspective' Explored*. Oxford: Oxford University Press.

von Braun, J. 1988. 'Effects of Technological Change in Agriculture on Food Consumption and Nutrition: Rice in a West African Setting'. *World Development 16* (9): pp. 1083–98.

Wade, R. 1990. *Governing the Market: Economic Theory and the Role of Government in East Asian Industrialization*. Princeton, NJ: Princeton University Press.

Wagstaff, A. and W. Manachotphong. 2012a. 'The Health Effects of Universal Healthcare: Evidence from Thailand'. World Bank Research Policy Working Paper 6119. Washington, DC: World Bank.

Wagstaff, A. and W. Manachotphong. 2012b. 'Universal Healthcare and Informal Labor Markets: The Case of Thailand'. World Bank Policy Research Working Paper 6116. Washington, DC: World Bank.

Wail, B., H. Said, and K. Abdelhak. 2012. 'A New Data Set of Educational Inequality in the World, 1950–2010: Gini Index of Education by Age Group'. Document de Travail, AMSE WP No. 2012–09. Aix-Marseilles School of Economics (AMSE).

Wang, C.W., C.L. Chan, and P.S. Yip. 2013. 'Suicide Rates in China from 2002 to 2011: An Update'. *Social Psychiatry & Psychiatric Epidemiology 49* (6): pp. 929–41.

Warren, B. 1980. *Imperialism: Pioneer of Capitalism*. London: New Left Books.

Warren, K. 1999. *The Violence Within: Cultural and Political Opposition in Divided Nations*. Boulder, CO: Westview Press.

Weiss, K. 2014. 'Bangladesh Women Find Liberty in Hard Labour'. *Los Angeles Times*. <http://www.latimes.com/world/asia/la-fg-c1-bangladesh-garment-workers-20140313-m-story.html>.

Westerveen, G. 1984. 'Towards a System for Supervising States' Compliance with the Right to Food'. In *The Right to Food*, edited by P. Alston and K. Tomasevski, pp. 119–24. Dordrecht: Netherlands Institute of Human Rights.

Whitehead, L. 2002. *Democratization: Theory and Experience*. Oxford: Oxford University Press.

WHO. 2004. WHO Global Status Report on Alcohol 2004. Geneva: WHO. <http://www.who.int/substance_abuse/publications/globalstatusreportalcoholchapters/en/>.

WHO. 2015. *Global Status Report on Road Safety*. Geneva: WHO.

WHO. 2014. *Global Health Estimates 2014 Summary Tables: DALY by Cause, Age and Sex, 2000–2012*. Geneva: WHO. <http://www.who.int/healthinfo/global_burden_disease/en/>.

WHO. n.d. 'Health Statistics and Information Systems: Estimates for 2000–2015'. <http://www.who.int/healthinfo/global_burden_disease/estimates/en/index1.html>. Accessed November 2016.

Wibulpolprasert, S. and P. Pengpaibon. 2003. 'Integrated Strategies to Tackle the Inequitable Distribution of Doctors in Thailand: Four Decades of Experience'. *Human Resources for Health 1*: pp. 1–12.

WIDER. n.d. World Income Inequality Database (WIID). World Institute for Development Economics Research. <https://www.wider.unu.edu/project/wiid-world-income-inequality-database>.

Wiedmann, T.O., H. Schandl, M. Lenzen, D. Moran, S. Suh, J. West, and K. Kanemoto. 2015. 'The Material Footprint of Nations'. *Proceedings of the National Academy of Sciences 112* (20): pp. 6271–6.

Wilkinson, R.G. and K.E. Pickett. 2006. 'Income Inequality and Population Health: A Review and Explanation of the Evidence'. *Social Science and Medicine 62* (7): pp. 1768–84.

Wilkinson, R.G. and K.E. Pickett. 2008. 'Income Inequality and Socioeconomic Gradients in Mortality'. *American Journal of Public Health 98* (4): pp. 699–704.

Williamson, J. 1989. 'What Washington Means by Policy Reform'. In *Latin American Readjustment: How Much has Happened*, edited by J. Williamson. Washington, DC: Institute for International Economics.

Williamson, J. 1990. *The Progress of Policy Reform in Latin America*. Washington, DC: Institute for International Economics.

Williamson, J. 1997. 'The Washington Consensus Revisited'. In *Economic and Social Development into the XXI Century*, edited by L. Emmerij. Washington, DC: Inter-American Development Bank.

Wilson, J. 1973. *Introduction to Social Movements*. New York: Basic Books.

Wolfe, A. 1974. 'New Directions in the Marxist Theory of Politics'. *Politics and Society 4* (2): pp. 131–59.

Wolgemuth, J.C., M.C. Latham, A. Hall, and D. Crompton. 1982. 'Worker Productivity and Nutritional Status of Kenyan Road Construction Laborers'. *American Journal of Clinical Nutrition 36* (1): pp. 68–78.

Wood, A. 1994. *North-South Trade, Employment, and Inequality Changing Fortunes in a Skill-Driven World*. IDS Development Studies Series. Oxford: Oxford University Press.

World Bank. 1990. *World Development Report 1990: Poverty*. New York: Oxford University Press.

World Bank. 2007. Project Information Document, Concept Stage. Project Name: Nepal, Post-Conflict Emergency Program. Washington, DC: World Bank.

World Bank. 2012. 'Thailand: Sustaining Health Protection for All'. <http://www.worldbank.org/en/news/feature/2012/08/20/thailand-sustaining-health-protection-for-all>. Accessed 10 January 2016.

World Bank. 2015. *World Development Report 2015: Mind, Society and Behavior*. Washington, DC: World Bank.

World Bank. 2016. 'Development Goals in an Era of Demographic Change'. Global Monitoring Report 2015/16. Washington, DC: World Bank.

World Bank and UNDP. 1989. *Africa's Adjustment and Growth in the 1980s*. Washington, DC: World Bank.

World Bank. n.d. World Development Indicators. <http://databank.worldbank.org/data/reports.aspx?source=world-development-indicators>.

WWF Global. 2016. *Living Planet Report 2016*. <http://wwf.panda.org/about_our_earth/all_publications/lpr_2016/>. Accessed 4 December 2016.

World Youth Forum. 2001. 'Dhaka Youth Empowerment Strategy'. <http://www.cinu.org.mx/temas/desarrollo/dessocial/integracion/dakar2001.doc>. Accessed 15 May 2016.

Yang, W. and P. Kanavos. 2012. 'The Less Healthy Urban Population: Income-Related Health Inequality in China'. *BMC Public Health 12* (804).

Zak, P.J. and S. Knack. 2001. 'Trust and Growth'. *The Economic Journal 111* (470): pp. 295–321.

Zepeda, E., S. McDonald, M. Panda, G. Kumar, with C. Sapkota. 2013. 'Employing India: Guaranteeing Jobs for the Rural Poor'. Washington, DC: Carnegie Endowment for International Peace. <http://carnegieendowment.org/2013/02/11/employing-india-guaranteeing-jobs-for-rural-poor/ff2s?reloadFlag=1>. Accessed 30 July 2014.

Index of Names

Note: Tables are indicated by an italic *t* following the page number.

Abbas, S.M.A. 230
Acemoglu, D. 56
Adelman, I. 45n2
Adler, P.S. 174n7
Aggrey, N. 54
Aguila, E. 48
Ahmad, Y.J. 233
Ahmed, N. 98
Ainsworth, M. 57
Alderman, H. 219
Alderman, L. 48
Alesina, A. 32, 57, 196
Alkire, S. 19n14, 21, 124, 170, 210n5
Alston, P. 14
Alto, H.D. 199
Ames, B. 112
Amin, S. 12
Amsden, A. 18n13
An, Z. 218
Anand, P. 159
Anand, S. 216
Anderson, E.S. 34
Argawal, B. 169
Aristotle 26, 27, 30, 124, 127
Asian Development Bank 101
Astorga, P. 192
Atkinson, A.B. 230

Bacchetta, M. 218
Balassa, B. 12
Baldacci, E. 50
Ball, L. 24
Banerjee, A.V. 98, 166
Bardhan, P.K. 49
Barrientos, A. 24
Barro, R.J. 55, 62
Bécares, L. 175
Behrman, J.R. 48, 51, 55, 56, 78
Bennell, P. 53
Bentham, J. 28
Berg, A. 57, 191
Beugelsdijk, S. 177
Bhasin, K. 170
Bhatkal, T. 104, 105, 217
Birdsall, N. 48, 54, 57
Blanchflower, D.G. 31, 31n5
Bledsoe, C. 57
Bloom, D.E. 55–6
Bloor, K. 177
Bongaarts, J. 57
Booth, C. 187n4
Bornstein, D. 98
Bostock, D. 124
Bouis, H.E. 56
Bourguignon, F. 47
Bowring, J. 28
Bratton, M. 201n8
Briggs, A. 188
Brown, G. 101
Bruck, T. 110
Bruno, M. 47n3
Burchardt, T. 125–6*t*, 127, 159
Burger, R.P. 54
Bush, G.W. 4n2

Camdessus, M. 20
Camfield, L. 125–6*t*, 127, 130
Canning, D. 55
Caprio, G. 19
Card, D. 53
Casterline, J. 57
Cederman, L.-E. 176, 181
Chakrangi, L. 47
Chambers, R. 167
Charpe, M. 219, 220, 220n16
Checchi, D. 48
Chen, M.A. 169
Chenery, H. 13, 29, 33
Chevalier, A. 53
Chilkoti, A. 201n8
Chingono, M. 110
Chowdhury, A. 98
CHS (Commission on Human Security) 87n6, 223

Claridge, T. 174n7
Clark, A. 29
Clark, G. 174
Clay, J.W. 107
Cloward, R.A. 193, 201
Cole, J.S. 176
Cooper, K. 48
Cornia, G.A. 18, 19, 24, 25, 56, 190, 198, 199, 218
Council of Europe 175
Cowell, F.A. 32n6
Crabtree, J. 199
Crocker, D. 167

Dangl-Znet, B. 169, 198
Dannreuther, C. 174n7
Dean, J. 17n11
Deininger, K. 57
De Maio, I. 18n12
Deneulin, S. 19n14, 204
Deolalikar, A.B. 48, 55, 56
Deraniyagala, S. 54
de Waal, A. 107
Diawara, B. 56
Dillon, A. 55
Djankov, S. 153
Dolan, P. 29–30
Dolfsma, W. 174n7
Dollar, D. 191n6
Dorius, S.F. 218
Dorosh, P.A. 109
Doyal, L. 125–6*t*, 127, 128
Drèze, J. 159, 193
Duflo, E. 166

Easterlin, R.A. 22, 26, 29
Easterly, W. 196
Edwards, B. 174n7
Edwards, M. 162n4
Edwards, S. 55
Eisenbrey, R. 211, 220n16
Engels, F. 187n4
Englander, D. 187n4
Erfan, A. 98
Etzioni, A. 159

Faguet, J.-P. 113n9, 114
Fei, J. 7, 8, 21
Feldman, S. 203
Felton, A. 32
Fernquest, J. 105n8
Fillenbaum, G.G. 48
Finnis, J. 125–6*t*, 127
Firebaugh, G. 218
FitzGerald, V. 19
Flachaire, E. 32n6
Foley, M. 174n7
Foot, P. 187, 193
Forrest, R. 175, 176
Fortes, A. 198
Foster, A.D. 54, 54n8
Foster, J. 21, 210n5
Frank, A.G. 12
Franklin, S.S. 31
Fraser, A. 187, 193
Frazer, G. 54
Freeman, S.R. 202
French, J.D. 198
Frey, B. 29
Friedman, M. 16
Fukuda-Parr, S. 24, 190
Furtado, C. 12

Gambetta, D. 177
Garcia, M. 49
Garreton Merino, M.A. 195
Gates, S. 100
Gay, J. 28, 28n3
Gebreeyesus, M. 107, 109
Gellert, P. 203
Ghai, D. 171
Ghosh, P. 98
Gleditsch, K.S. 89
Goetz, A.M. 199
Goldstein, J.S. 223
Gooptu, N. 169
Gordon, C. 211, 220n16
Gough, I. 125–6*t*, 127, 128
Government of Nepal 102
Graham, C. 26, 30, 31, 32, 36, 37, 38
Green, D. 199, 199–200n7
Griffin, K. 202, 204
Gunatilaka, R. 32, 36
Gutman, A. 202
Guzmán, J.C. 48

Haddad, L. 49, 56
Haines, M. 191
Hanlon, J. 226
Hardoon, D. 24
Harris, J.R. 8n4, 105, 105n7, 108
Hartwick, J.M. 233
Helliwell, J.F. 26, 37n9
Helpman, E. 19
Hempel, J. 55
Henriques, M.H. 51
Heyer, J. 168, 185n1
Hicks, N. 33
Hirschman, A.O. 7
Hoddinott, J. 49, 56
Holcomb, B.K. 107
Holcomb, S. 98
Hooghe, M. 175
Hoover, M. 37

Hotchkiss, D.R. 51
Hsiaoa, F.S.T. 55
Hsiaob, M.-C.W. 55
Hulme, D. 24, 98
Hume, D. 28
Humphries, D.L. 48
Hunter, W. 198
Hutcheson, F. 28
Huttly, S. 51
Hyder, S. 98

Ibrahim, S.S. 160n3
ILO (International Labour Organization) 9–10, 13, 13nn6–7, 14, 20, 104, 211n12, 219, 226, 230n23, 236
Immink, M. 56
Integrated Network for Societal Conflict Research 143
IPC (International Policy Centre for Inclusive Growth) 198
IPF (Inter-Parliamentary Union) 211n10
Islam, S. 98

Jackson-Han, S. 4n1
Jamison, D. 54
Jaumotte, F. 211
Jenkins, R. 199
Ji, J. 210n3
Jobin, W.R. 55
Johnes, G. 55
Johnson, S. 56
Jones, P. 54
Jones, S. 110
Jütting, J. 49

Kabir, B. 97
Kahneman, D. 26, 29, 31
Kakwani, N. 18n12
Kanavos, P. 48
Kant, I. 232
Kaplan, T. 169
Karabarbounis, L. 219, 220
Kearns, A. 175, 176
Keefer, P. 177
Kelley, F. 187n4
Keumsoo, K. 197
Khan, M.S. 18n12
Khanal, D.R. 101
Killick, T. 8, 18n12
King, E.M. 48
King, W. 28
Kingdon, G. 32, 36
Klasen, S. 54
Klein, H. 113n9
Kleynhans, E.P.J. 54
Knack, S. 177
Knapp, V.J. 191
Knight, J.B. 32, 36, 53
Knight, M.D. 18n12
Knipe, D.W. 210n3
Kokkelenberg, E. 233
Kondo, N. 48
Koo, H. 197
Kraay, A. 191n6
Kroll, C. 41, 42
Krueger, A.O. 12
Krugman, P. 19
Kumar, N. 169
Kurlantzick, J. 106
Kwon, S.-W. 174n7
Kymlika, W. 177

Labuschagne, J.R. 54
Lakner, C. 216
Lal, D. 17
Lall, S. 18n13
Landertinger, L. 197
Langer, A. 174, 175n8, 178, 179, 217, 234n25
Lansley, S. 191
Lavy, V. 51
Layard, R. 22, 26, 29, 30, 31, 32, 35, 40, 42
Leamer, E. 55
Lebedinski, L. 54
Lee, M.B. 197
Lee, Y.-M. 197
Le Grand, J. 159
Leturque, H. 104
Levine, R. 196
Lewis, A. 7
Leys, C. 12n5
Li, H. 57
Lilliard, L.A. 48
Lindert, P.H. 195
Lipton, M. 47
Little, I.M.D. 12, 17, 19, 191n6
Locke, J. 34
Lopez-Acevedo, G. 48n4
Lopez-Calva, L.F. 190
Loungani, P. 218
Lovell, C. 98
Lucas, R.E. 19, 54
Lucci, P. 104, 105
Lustig, N. 190
Lykken, D. 38, 38n10

Mackie, C. 31
Mahalanobis, P.C. 7
Mahmud, S. 98, 169
Majumdar, M. 48n4
Malhotra, T.C. 98
Malik, M. 18n12
Mallick, L. 221
Maluccio, J.A. 48
Manachotphong, W. 105n8

Mancini, L. 179
Mariotti, C. 217
Marshall, M.G. 154*t*
Martinez-Vazquez, J. 230
Martorano, B. 24, 231
Mason, P. 231
Masud-All-Kamal, M. 97
McGuire, J. 78, 86
McKeown, T. 191, 192
McKinley, T. 204
McMichael, P. 203n8
Medina, M. 169
Menon, G.A. 169
Mikami, S. 179
Milanovic, B. 216–17
Mill, J.S. 26, 30, 31
Miller, D. 127
Mills, A. 55
Ming, L. 48n4
Mitchell, M.T. 190
Moestue, H. 51
Molina, F. 199
Molina, G.G. 78
Moock, P. 54
Mooij, J. 48n4
Mookherjee, D. 49
Morales-Hidalgo, D. 228
Morenoff, J.D. 174
Morley, S. 24
Morris, C.T. 45n2
Morris, D.M. 20, 33
Mosley, P. 18n12
Mughal, M. 56
Muñoz, I. 170
Murshed, S.M. 100
Mutua, M.W. 167
Mveyange, A. 57

Najera, J.A. 55
Narayan-Parker, D. 125–6*t*, 127, 128, 167
Nardinelli, C. 187n4
Nath, S. 98
Nazeer, Z. 201n8
Nee, M. 177n9
Neiman, B. 219, 220
Newman, E. 195
Nordhaus, W. 233
North, D.C. 160
Nozick, R. 34
Nur, E. 55
Nurkse, R. 7
Nussbaum, M. 125–6*t*, 127, 127n4, 158, 167, 202, 203, 234n26

ODI (Overseas Development Institute) 108, 109, 190
OECD (Organisation for Economic Co-operation and Development) 175
Olinto, P. 57
Oman, C. 12
Onaran, O. 197
Orihuela, J.C. 116, 119
Osorio, C. 211
Ostry, J.D. 231
Oswald, A. 29, 31, 31n5
Oxhorn, P. 162n4

Pack, H. 18n13, 55
Palma, G. 12
Paredes, M. 115, 119
Parker, S.W. 51
Patel, V. 40
Patrinos, H.A. 53
Pengpaibon, P. 105
Perotti, R. 55
Persson, T. 57
Petras, J. 197
Pettinato, S. 30
Picard, J. 55
Pickett, K.E. 48
Pigou, A.C. 28–9n4
Piketty, T. 24
Pitt, M.M. 56, 98
Piven, F.F. 193, 201
Polanyi, K. 185–9, 187n2, 193
Popper, K.R. 43n12
Porter, M. 151*t*, 152*t*, 153*t*
Posner, D.N. 196, 200
Prebisch, R. 7
Preston, L.T. 20
Priestley, J. 28
Przeworski, A. 86
Psacharopolous, G. 53, 56
Purser, M. 78
Putnam, R.D. 174n, 176

Quddus, M. 98
Quisumbing, A. 48, 169

Rahim, A. 97
Rahman, A. 171
Ram, R. 47, 55, 216
Ranci, C. 175
Ranis, G. v, 7, 8, 49, 74n1, 78, 123n1, 164, 182, 183n11
Rashid, S. 98, 109
Ravallion, M. 47
Rawlings, L.B. 226
Rawls, J. 34, 124, 125–6*t*, 127, 127nn3–4, 128, 202
Record, R.G. 191, 192
Reimers, M. 54
Rienks, S.L. 40

Robbins, L.R.B. 29
Roberts, K.M. 211, 211n12
Robison, L.J. 174n7
Robles, W. 196, 197
Rodríguez-Takeuchi, L. 59n9
Rodrik, D. 57, 191n5
Roemer, P.M. 19
Rohde, J. 98
Romer, D. 55
Rosenstein-Rodan, P. 7
Rosenzweig, M.R. 54, 54n8
Roser, M. 75
Rostow, W.W. 7
Rousseau, J.-J. 34
Rowntree, B.S. 187n4
Roy, I. 160n3
Rubio, G.M. 226

Sabot, R.H. 53, 57
Sah, J. 101
Saha, C.K. 97
Sahn, D.E. 18n12
Samman, E. 59n9, 110
Sampson, R.J. 174
Savedoff, W.D. 55
Schäferhoff, M. 51
Schneewind, J.B. 28n3
Schokkaert, E. 159
Schultz, T.P. 55, 56
Scott, J.C. 196
Seers, D. 3, 13, 29, 33
Segal, P. 216
Selowsky, M. 56
Sen, A.K. 13, 20, 21, 27, 29, 33, 36, 41, 42, 124, 158, 159–60, 159n2, 162, 167, 193, 202, 203, 204, 231
Shelley, P.B. 184
Singer, H.W. 7
Smart, R.N. 43n12
Soares, S. 198
Sobhan, R. 97
Söderbom, M.M. 54
Sohn, B. 55, 56
Spence, R. 177n9
Staveteig, S. 221
Stefanoni, P. 199
Stewart, F. v, 14, 14n8, 20, 21, 24, 26n1, 34n8, 47, 49, 74n1, 78, 86, 101, 110, 113, 115, 116, 158n1, 174, 176, 210n5, 217, 218
Stewart, K. 48
Stiglitz, J.E. 19, 22, 26, 41, 191
St John, R.B. 117
Stockhammer, E. 219
Stone, A.A. 31
Strauss, J. 47, 56
Streeten, P.P. 14, 20, 33, 204, 236
Stutzer, A. 29
Sumner, A. 210
Sunkel, O. 12
Suri, T. v, 62, 63, 78
Swanhuyser, E. 210n3
Szreter, S. 191, 192

Tabellini, G. 57
Takeuchi, L.R. 217
Tarp, F. 110
Tarrow, S.G. 194, 195
Teal, F.J. 54
Tellegen, A. 38, 38n10
Thailand Government 105
Thomas, D. 47, 51, 56
Thompson, D. 202
Thompson, E.P. 187, 187n4, 188
Thorp, R. 115, 119, 168, 170, 185n1
Tilly, C. 194
Tobin, J. 233
Todaro, M.P. 8n4
Transport Research Laboratory 214
Truman, H. 6
Tsai, M.-C. 86
Tuladhar, R. 102

ul Haq, M. 19
UNDESA-WHO 40
UNDP (United Nations Development Programme) 1, 17n11, 20, 21, 22, 27, 33, 45, 49, 50, 87n6, 99, 100, 101, 102, 102n3, 123, 149*t*, 150*t*, 151*t*, 152*t*, 158n1, 159, 168, 168n6, 195, 208, 220, 223, 230n22, 232
Ungpakorn 106
UNHCR (United Nations High Commission for Refugees) 154*t*
UNICEF (United Nations Children's Fund) 62, 151*t*
United Nations 22
UNODC 87n7
Uphoff, E.P. 48n5
Ura, K. 42
Uslaner, E.M. 176

Vandenberghe, V. 54
van Deurzen, I. 48n6
van Ootegem, L. 159
Vapattanawong, P. 48, 104
Veltmeyer, H. 197
Viterri, F. 56
Vizard, P. 125–6*t*, 127, 167
von Braun, J. 48

Wade, R. 18n13, 193
Wadsworth, M.E. 40
Wagstaff, A. 105n8
Wail, B. 216
Wang, C.W. 210n3

Wang, S. 37n9
Warren, B. 12n5
Warren, K. 177n9
Weiss, A. 19
Weiss, K. 99
Westerveen, G. 14
Westphal, L. 18n13, 55
Whitehead, L. 195
WHO (World Health Organization) 151*t*, 209n1, 210nn3–4, 6, 214
Wibulpolprasert, S. 105
WIDER 109, 115, 215
Wiedmann, T. O. 226, 227, 229
Wiggins, S. 104
Wignaraja, G. 12
Wilkinson, R.G. 48
Williamson, J. 17, 17n11, 20
Wilson, J. 194
Wolfe, A. 184, 193
Wolfe, B.L. 48, 51
Wolgemuth, J.C. 56
Wood, A. 43, 55
World Bank 17n11, 19n14, 20, 24, 101, 102, 105n8, 114, 198, 218
World Youth Forum 221
WWF Global 228

Yang, W. 48

Zak, P.J. 177
Zepeda, E. 199
Zou, H.-F. 57

Index of Subjects

Note: Tables and figures are indicated by an italic *t* and *f* following the page number.

Afghanistan 38*t*, 210, 224
Africa
  community well-being 214
  economic growth and human development, relationship between 56–7, 60–1, 62, 63, 64, 68*f*
  education expenditure 79
  evolution of development thought 8, 18, 19
  Human Development Index 76
  leisure conditions 222
  life expectancy 74–5
  Polanyi swings 192
  political opportunity structure 195
  secondary enrolment rates 80
  suicide rate 209
  work conditions 218
agency 33, 34–5, 40, 44, 121, 207
agriculture 196, 219, 226
  Brazil 198
  economic growth and human development, relationship between 54
  Ethiopia 107–9, 119
  Europe 191
  evolution of development thought 7
  Great Britain 188
  Mozambique 110, 119
  Nepal 100
  Peru 115, 116
  Thailand 102–4, 106
aid 118
  agencies 15, 17
  Ethiopia 107, 108*f*, 109
  Mozambique 110, 112
  Nepal 101
  positive transition 206
  to social sectors,1970–2010 15, 16*f*
AIDS/HIV 75, 76, 192
  deaths from
    as community well-being indicator 137–8*t*, 139, 151*t*
    and HDI, correlation between 144*t*
    and income, correlation between 146, 156*t*
  economic growth and human development, relationship between 61
  evolution of development thought 24
alcohol consumption 137–8*t*, 144*t*, 151*t*, 156*t*
Algeria
  carbon emissions 91*f*
  economic growth and human development, relationship between 66
  education expenditure 79*f*
  female secondary education enrolment 81*f*
  Gender Inequality Index 87*f*
  health expenditure 80*f*
  homicides 88*f*, 88
  income 82*f*
  inequality 83*f*
  negative transition 78, 94, 95*f*, 96, 119–20, 120*f*
  political freedom index 86*f*
  poverty 84*f*
  secondary enrolment rates 80*f*
  violent conflict 89*f*
Andean Pact countries 15
Arab countries *see* Middle East
Argentina 194
Aristotle 27, 30, 124
Asia
  community well-being 214, 215
  economic growth and human development, relationship between 61, 63, 64, 68*f*
  environmental conditions 226, 227*f*
  evolution of development thought 17, 19
  Human Development Index 76
  inequalities 215, 218
  leisure conditions 221
  life expectancy 75
  political freedom 212*f*, 212
  political violence 224
  scavengers 169
  secondary enrolment rates 80
  work conditions 218, 220

austerity policies 231
Australia 211, 215, 219
autonomy 17, 35, 133, 164–7, 181–2, 190

Bangladesh
  Building Resources across Communities (BRAC) 50, 98
  carbon emissions 91*f*
  economic growth and human development, relationship between 50–1, 56, 60
  education expenditure 79, 79*f*
  empowerment 210
  Environmental Progress Index 90*f*
  female secondary education enrolment 81*f*
  Gender Inequality Index 87*f*
  Grameen Bank 50, 98
  health expenditure 80*f*, 80
  homicides 88*f*, 88
  income 81, 82*f*
  inequality 83*f*
  political economy 207
  political freedom index 86*f*
  positive transition 84–5, 92, 95*f*, 96–9, 118–19, 206, 235
  poverty 84*f*
  secondary enrolment rates 80*f*
  violent conflict 89*f*
basic needs 127
  challenges 229
  evolution of development thought 13–14, 15, 17, 20–1
  and happiness 33
Basu, Kaushik 4n1
Bechtel 169
behavioural economics 19n14
Belaúnde, Fernando 115
Belgium 54
Benin 212
Bentham, Jeremy 28, 187
Bhutan
  empowerment 210
  Gross National Happiness Index 26, 30, 41, 42*t*, 42
biodiversity 228
Bolivia
  carbon emissions 91*f*
  Constitution 113, 199
  economic growth and human development, relationship between 47, 66
  education expenditure 79*f*
  empowerment 211
  female secondary education enrolment 81*f*
  Gender Inequality Index 87*f*
  health expenditure 80*f*
  homicides 88*f*
  income 82*f*
  independence 112
  inequality 83*f*
  political economy 207
  political freedom index 86*f*
  positive transition 76, 95*f*, 95, 112–14, 118, 206, 235
  poverty 84*f*
  secondary enrolment rates 80*f*
  social institutions and capabilities 169
  social movements 196, 198–9
  violent conflict 89*f*
  water rights movement 169
Brazil
  economic growth and human development, relationship between 47, 48, 56
  empowerment 211
  environmental conditions 233
  inequalities 216–17
  Landless Workers' Movement (MST) 197–8
  social movements 196–7
  successful transition 207
  Workers' Party (PT) 197–8
Building Resources across Communities (BRAC) 50, 98
Burkina Faso 60, 66
Burma 224
  carbon emissions 91*f*
  education expenditure 79*f*
  female secondary education enrolment 81*f*
  Gender Inequality Index 87*f*
  health expenditure 80*f*
  homicides 88*f*, 88
  political freedom index 86, 86*f*
  political opportunity structure 194
  poverty 84*f*
  secondary enrolment rates 80*f*
  success and failure in human development 77–8, 85, 90
  violent conflict 89*f*
business cycle 188

Cambodia 60
capabilities 124, 158–83, 234–5, 236
  analysis 173–9
    as essential for human development 161–73
  challenges 229, 231, 234
  classifying 173–4
  definitions 160–1
  economic growth and human development, relationship between 52, 54, 67
  effects on capabilities and human development approaches 179–81
  evolution of development thought 18, 19, 20–1, 22
  and happiness 27, 29, 31–4, 38–9, 41–2
  impact on individual capabilities 162–4, 163*t*
  and individual autonomy 164–7

and individual capabilities, relationship between 171–3, 172*f*
individualism 158–60, 234
macro and micro aspects 174–9
Polanyi swings 193
political economy 184–5, 202–4
power 169–71
capital formation
1960–2014 9*f*
Bolivia 96
economic growth and human development, relationship between 61, 62
negative transitions 120*f*
Thailand 103
carbon emissions 89–90, 91*f*, 91, 227*f*, 227–8, 232–4
Caribbean
community well-being 214
economic growth and human development, relationship between 62, 68*f*
economic insecurity 225
environmental conditions 227*f*
Human Development Index 75*f*
inequalities 215
leisure conditions 221–2*f*
political opportunity structure 195
success and failure in human development 77*t*
work conditions 218, 219*f*
Central African Republic 207, 224
Central Asia
community well-being 214, 215
country classification according to human development, economic, political, and social performance 182*t*
economic insecurity 225, 225*f*
empowerment 210
environmental conditions 227*f*
happiness 38*t*
inequalities 215, 218
Central Europe 212*f*, 212, 219
challenges to the human development framework 229–35
child labour
and HDI, correlation between 144*t*
and income, correlation between 156*t*
social norms 165
as work conditions indicator 139, 140*t*, 153*t*, 219
children's height for age 48
Chile 32, 47, 48, 194
China
carbon emissions 91*f*
economic growth and human development, relationship between 47, 48, 66
education expenditure 79*f*
empowerment 210, 211
environmental conditions 226, 233
female secondary education enrolment 81*f*
Gender Inequality Index 87*f*
happiness 36
health expenditure 80*f*
homicides 88*f*, 88
income 82*f*
inequalities 83*f*, 216
leisure conditions 221
political economy 207
political freedom index 86, 86*f*
positive transition 76, 84, 90, 206, 235
poverty 83, 84*f*
secondary enrolment rates 80*f*
social relations 213
suicide rate 209
violent conflict 89*f*
Chissano, Joaquim 112
cinema attendance 141, 141*t*, 144*t*, 153*t*, 156*t*
civic work, participation in 136, 137–8*t*, 151*t*, 213
civil society 47, 50, 105, 129, 206, 207, 235
civil war 24, 118
Mozambique 110
Nepal 99, 100, 101
class-ridden society 174
climate change 22, 24, 232
collective protests 185, 193–201, 235
collective violence 142–3, 143*t*, 154*t*
collective well-being 234
Colombia 56, 169, 196, 213
colonialism 6
Communism 186, 188, 194
community well-being 128, 129, 136–9, 213–15, 228
high-income countries 157*t*
and income, correlation between 146
indicators 131*t*, 137–8*t*, 145*t*, 151–2*t*
conflict
Bangladesh 96
Central African Republic 207
civil war 24, 99, 100, 101, 110, 118
Congo 121, 207
Côte d'Ivoire 121
environmental conditions 226
Ethiopia 90, 107, 207
incidence 85, 87–9, 89*f*
Mozambique 110, 112, 207
negative transitions 121, 207
Nepal 99, 100, 101, 102, 118, 207
Peru 116, 117, 118
political struggle 203
social institutions and capabilities 167, 169, 173, 175–8
Sri Lanka 90
successful transitions 118, 119, 207

conflict (*cont.*)
  Zimbabwe 90
  see also political violence; violence
Congo, Democratic Republic of the
  capital formation 120*f*
  carbon emissions 91*f*
  economic growth 120*f*
    and human development, relationship between 56, 65
  education expenditure 121
  environmental conditions 226
  female secondary education enrolment 81*f*
  Gender Inequality Index 87*f*
  health expenditure 80*f*
  homicides 88*f*
  Human Development Index 209
  income 82*f*
  inequality 83*f*
  negative transition 78, 85, 92, 95*f*, 96
  political freedom index 86*f*, 90
  political violence 121, 207, 224
  poverty 84*f*, 121
  secondary enrolment rates 80*f*
  violent conflict 89*f*
contraception, availability of 134*t*, 135, 144*t*, 150*t*, 156*t*
corruption 137–8*t*, 139, 151*t*
  Bangladesh 97
Costa Rica 204
Côte d'Ivoire
  capital formation 120*f*
  carbon emissions 91*f*
  economic growth 120*f*, 120, 121
    and human development, relationship between 47, 48, 49, 50
  education expenditure 79*f*
  Environmental Progress Index 90*f*
  female secondary education enrolment 81*f*
  Gender Inequality Index 87*f*
  health expenditure 80*f*
  homicides 88*f*
  income 82*f*
  inequalities 83*f*, 217
  negative transition 78, 85, 91–2, 95*f*, 96, 207
  political freedom index 86*f*, 90
  poverty 83, 84*f*
  secondary enrolment rates 80*f*
  violent conflict 89*f*, 89
CPI cycle 142*t*, 144*t*, 153*t*, 156*t*
crime rate 136, 137–8*t*, 151*t*
  and happiness 37, 39
Cuba
  carbon emissions 91*f*
  economic growth and human development, relationship between 206
  education expenditure 79*f*
  environmental conditions 227
  Environmental Progress Index 90*f*
  female secondary education enrolment 81*f*
  Gender Inequality Index 87*f*
  health expenditure 80*f*, 80
  homicides 88*f*
  income 81, 82*f*
  inequalities 81–3, 83*f*
  political freedom index 86, 86*f*
  poverty 84*f*
  secondary enrolment rates 80*f*
  successful transition 76, 84, 90, 92, 206
  suicide rate 209
  violent conflict 89*f*

decentralization 49
deliberative democracy 167, 184, 202, 203
deliberative rationality 124, 127
democracy 86, 121, 165, 190, 204
  Bangladesh 97
  Bolivia 114, 198
  deliberative 167, 184, 202, 203
  Ethiopia 107
  Mozambique 112, 118
  Nepal 99, 101, 102
  Peru 115, 117, 118
  political opportunity structure 194–5, 196, 197, 200–1
  successful transition 207, 235
  Thailand 106, 118
Democratic Labour Party (South Korea) 197
Denmark 211
dependency school 12, 14, 15
depressive disorders 209n1
developed countries
  community well-being 215
  economic growth and human development, relationship between 48
  economic insecurity 225, 225*f*, 226
  empowerment 211
  environmental conditions 227*f*
  evolution of development thought 2–3, 6–7, 12–13, 16–17, 22
  happiness 29–30
  human development indicators 147, 157*t*
  leisure conditions 221, 221–2*f*
  Polanyi swings 189–90
  tax systems 231
  work conditions 220
developing countries
  economic growth and human development, relationship between 206
  evolution of development thought 2, 6, 10–18, 22, 24–5
  happiness 30
  leisure conditions 221
  Polanyi swings 189–90
  political opportunity structure 196

success and failure in human development 74–6
tax systems 230–1
work conditions 219, 220
dirigisme 17
divorce rate 136, 136*t*, 144*t*, 151*t*, 156*t*
Dominica 212
Dominican Republic 66, 204
droughts 107, 109

East Asia
carbon emissions 89–90
community well-being 214, 215
country classification according to human development, economic, political, and social performance 182*t*
economic growth and human development, relationship between 55, 65
economic insecurity 225*f*, 226
education expenditure 79
empowerment 210
environmental conditions 227*f*, 227
evolution of development thought 12, 18–19
financial crisis 103
Human Development Index 75*f*
leisure conditions 221–2*f*
manufactured exports from 55
Polanyi swings 192
success and failure in human development 77*t*, 91–2
work conditions 218, 219*f*
Eastern Europe
community well-being 214, 215
environmental conditions 227*f*
economic growth and human development, relationship between 57
inequalities 215, 218
Polanyi swings 186
political freedom 212*f*, 212
suicide rate 209
economic growth
Bangladesh 96, 97
Bolivia 113, 114
environmental considerations 233–4
Ethiopia 107, 108*f*
evolution of development thought 6–7, 8, 13, 14, 15, 19
and happiness 39
and human development, relationship between 45–73, 205–6
Chain A 46*f*, 47–52, 59–61
Chain B 46*f*, 52–8, 61–3
cross-country empirical analysis 58–64
virtuous and vicious cycles and lopsided development 64–6
Nepal 100
Peru 116, 117
Polanyi swings 191, 192
success and failure in human development 76, 81, 82*f*, 84–5, 92, 119, 120–1
see also transitions: negative; transitions: positive
Thailand 103
see also gross domestic product (GDP)
economic security 129, 141–2, 225–6, 225*f*, 228
high-income countries 157*t*
indicators 131*t*, 142*t*, 145*t*, 153–4*t*
economy, as challenge to the human development framework 229–32, 236
Ecuador
capital formation 120*f*
carbon emissions 91*f*
economic growth 92, 94, 119, 120*f*, 120
education expenditure 79*f*
female secondary education enrolment 81*f*
Gender Inequality Index 87*f*
health expenditure 80*f*
homicides 88*f*
income 82*f*
inequalities 83*f*, 83, 121
negative transition 78, 85, 95*f*, 96, 207
political freedom index 86*f*
political turbulence 121
poverty 83, 84*f*, 84, 121
secondary enrolment rates 80*f*
social movements 196
violent conflict 89*f*
education
Bangladesh 98–9
Bolivia 199
Brazil 198
East Asia 192
economic growth and human development, relationship between 48–58, 66, 67, 206
cross-country empirical analysis 59–62, 70*t*
and economic security 226
Ethiopia 107–8, 109
evolution of development thought 18
expenditure *see* education expenditure
and exports 55
female *see* female education
and fertility rates 56–7
and happiness 37, 41, 42–3
and income 48, 52–4, 56–7, 59, 60
inequalities 216
and infant health 51
and life expectancy 61
Mozambique 110–11, 112
Nepal 99, 100, 102
Peru 117
pre-industrial Europe 191
and productivity 53–5

education (*cont.*)
 pro-planning pro-industrialization policies 8
 social institutions and capabilities 161, 166, 167
 South Korea 197
 sub-Saharan Africa 192
 success and failure in human development 78, 92
 Thailand 103, 104, 106
 see also primary school enrolment; secondary school enrolment
education expenditure
 1980–2010 23*f*
 Bangladesh 96, 97
 Bolivia 113–14
 Brazil 198
 economic growth and human development, relationship between 50, 59, 60, 206
 Ethiopia 107
 Mozambique 111
 negative transitions 121
 Nepal 100
 Peru 115, 117
 success and failure in human development 78–9, 79*f*, 83–4, 92
 Thailand 103
Egypt
 carbon emissions 91*f*
 economic growth and human development, relationship between 66
 education expenditure 79*f*
 Environmental Progress Index 90*f*
 female secondary education enrolment 81*f*
 Gender Inequality Index 87*f*
 health expenditure 80*f*
 homicides 88*f*, 88
 income 82*f*
 inequalities 83*f*, 83
 political freedom index 86*f*
 political opportunity structure 195
 positive transition 77
 poverty 84*f*
 secondary enrolment rates 80*f*
 violent conflict 89*f*
electricity 116, 221, 222*f*
El Salvador 211
Emergency Social Fund, Bolivia 113
emigration 101, 110
employment
 Bolivia 199
 challenge to the human development framework 230, 231
 conditions 139, 140*t*, 141, 153*t*
  and HDI, correlation between 144*t*
  and income, correlation between 156*t*
 economic growth and human development, relationship between 47
 evolution of development thought 8, 13, 15
 and happiness 36
 India 199
 Nepal 101
empowerment 129, 133–5, 210–11, 228
 high-income countries 157*t*
 indicators 131*t*, 134*t*, 145*t*, 149–50*t*
Engels, Friedrich 188
England 186–8, 193, 195, 200
environmental conditions 129, 143, 226–9, 227*f*
 high-income countries 157*t*
 indicators 131*t*, 145*t*, 155*t*
Environmental Progress Index (EPI) 89, 90*f*, 90
environmental sustainability 144*t*, 226–8, 236
 challenge to the human development framework 232–4
 as environmental conditions indicator 143, 155*t*
 evolution of development thought 22–3, 24
 and happiness 40
 and income, correlation between 156*t*
equality *see* inequality/equality
Eritrea 212
Ethiopia
 agriculture 119
 carbon emissions 91*f*, 91
 economic growth and human development, relationship between 50, 51
 education expenditure 79*f*
 empowerment 210
 female secondary education enrolment 81*f*
 Gender Inequality Index 87*f*
 health expenditure 80*f*
 homicides 88*f*
 inequalities 83*f*
 political economy 207
 political freedom index 86*f*, 118
 positive transition 76, 95*f*, 95, 107–9, 206
 poverty 83, 84*f*
 Productive Safety Net Programme (PSNP) 109
 public expenditure 118
 secondary enrolment rates 80*f*
 violent conflict 88, 89*f*, 90
evolution of development thought 1–25
 1950s to 1990s 6–21
 1990s onwards 21–4
 framework 2–3, 4*f*
 overview of major changes 4–6, 5*t*
exports
 from Bangladesh 98
 and education 55
 from Ethiopia 107, 109
 manufacturing 141, 142*t*, 142, 154*t*
 from Mozambique 110, 111*f*
 from Nepal 100, 101
 from Thailand 103

family, value placed on 136, 136*t*, 144*t*, 151*t*, 156*t*, 213
famine 107
Fascism 188
female control over household income 47, 48–9
female education
  Bangladesh 99
  economic growth and human development, relationship between 48, 51–2, 56–7, 66, 206
    cross-country empirical analysis 59, 60, 61, 62–3, 68*f*
  Ethiopia 108
  and fertility rates 56–7
  and inequality 48
  and infant health 51
  and life expectancy 61
  Nepal 102
  and poverty 48, 59
  success and failure in human development 78, 81*f*, 81, 83, 84, 92
  Thailand 103
  see also secondary school enrolment: female/male ratio
female employment
  Bangladesh 98
  Bolivia 199
female empowerment 210, 211
  Bangladesh 97, 98–9, 119
  women's groups 169
female literacy rate 96, 99
female suicide 133*t*, 133, 149*t*
fertility rates 56–7
Finland 211, 212, 214, 226–7
food expenditure 48–9
food production 110, 111*f*, 115, 116*f*
food security 109
foreign direct investment (FDI)
  corporate tax 230
  economic growth and human development, relationship between 54, 57
  evolution of development thought 8, 15
  Mozambique 110
  Peru 116
forestry coverage 228
France 7, 33
freedom of worship 135, 135*t*, 150*t*
free press 135, 135*t*, 136, 151*t*
FRELIMO 110, 112
Friedman, Milton 189
friends, value placed on 136, 136*t*, 144*t*, 151*t*, 156*t*, 213
Fujimori, Albert 116, 118
'full life', defining the 124–30
functionings 21, 41, 127n4
  social institutions and capabilities 162, 234
G77 15
Gambia 48
Garcia, Alan 115, 117
garment industry, Bangladesh 97, 98
Gender Development Index (GDI)
  and Human Development Index, correlation between 144*t*
  and income, correlation between 156*t*
  as inequality indicator 139, 140*t*, 152*t*
  Nepal 102
  Thailand 103
Gender Empowerment Measure (GEM)
  as empowerment indicator 133, 134*t*, 135, 150*t*
  and Human Development Index, correlation between 144*t*
  and income, correlation between 156*t*
  Nepal 102
gender factors
  child labour 219
  inequality 217–18, 228
  see also female control over household income; female education; female employment; female empowerment; female literacy rate; female suicide; male literacy rate; male suicide; women
Gender Inequality Index (GII) 87*f*, 87, 91, 92
  Nepal 102
Germany 211
Ghana
  economic growth and human development, relationship between 47, 51, 54, 66
  inequalities 217
  political freedom 212
  political opportunity structure 195
  social relations 213
Gini coefficient 103, 215–16
  Bangladesh 97
  Bolivia 114, 199
  Brazil 198
  economic growth and human development, relationship between 59, 61, 62, 63, 66
  Ethiopia 109
  happiness 32
  and Human Development Index, correlation between 144*t*
  and income, correlation between 156*t*
  as inequality indicator 139, 140*t*, 152*t*
  Mozambique 111
  negative transitions 121
  Nepal 100
  Peru 115, 117
  see also income distribution; inequality/equality
Global Barometer Surveys 181
globalization 191n5, 230

Global Living Planet Index 228
global warming *see* climate change
Grameen Bank 50, 98
Great Britain
  Bill of Rights 33
  Combination Laws (1799,1800) and repeal 187, 188
  Corn Laws repeal (1846) 187
  Factory Acts (1867,1884) 188
  human rights 33
  Labour Party 188
  Polanyi swings 185–9, 191
  Poor Law reform (1834) 187, 203
  Reform Act (1832) 187
  'rotten' boroughs 201
  see also England; United Kingdom
Greece 230
green accounting 232–3
gross domestic product (GDP)
  1961–2010 11*f*
  business cycle 141, 142*t*, 144*t*, 153*t*, 156*t*
  economic growth and human development, relationship between 60, 61, 62, 66, 68*f*, 71*t*
  evolution of development thought 18
  green 232–3
  negative transitions 120*f*
  Peru 116*f*
  success and failure in human development 75, 82*f*
  Thailand 103
  see also economic growth
gross national product (GNP)
  evolution of development thought 13, 21, 22
  happiness 26–7, 29, 44
  and human development, relationship between 46*f*, 47, 49, 57, 58
growth *see* economic growth
Guatemala
  carbon emissions 91*f*
  economic growth and human development, relationship between 56, 66
  education expenditure 79*f*
  Environmental Progress Index 90*f*
  female secondary education enrolment 81*f*
  Gender Inequality Index 87*f*
  health expenditure 80*f*
  homicides 88*f*, 88
  income 82*f*
  inequalities 81, 83*f*, 83, 217
  negative transition 78, 85, 92, 94, 95*f*, 96, 120*f*, 120, 121, 207
  political freedom index 86*f*
  poverty 84*f*
  secondary enrolment rates 80*f*
  violent conflict 89*f*, 89
Guebeza, Armando 112
Guinea 60
Guyana 50

Haiti 81*f*
happiness 26–44
  alternative approaches 33–6
  classic utilitarians 27–9
  correlates 38*t*
  definitions and measurement 30–2
  evolution of development thought 22
  and Human Development Index, relationship between 35–6, 35*t*, 36*f*
  inequality 139, 140*t*, 152*t*
  neo-utilitarians 29–30
  possible adverse policy implications 38–41
  problems as a guide to development policy 36–8
  subjective evaluations, role of 41–3
  see also life satisfaction
Hayek, Friedrich 189
health expenditure
  Bangladesh 96–7
  Bolivia 113–14
  Brazil 198
  economic growth and human development, relationship between 50–1, 54, 59, 60, 63, 206
  Ethiopia 107
  Human Development Index 78–80, 81, 83, 84
  Mozambique 111
  Nepal 100
  Peru 115–16, 117
  success and failure in human development 80*f*, 92
  Thailand 103, 105
health/ill health
  Bangladesh 98
  Bolivia 114
  economic growth and human development, relationship between 48, 52, 53, 55–6, 67
  Ethiopia 107, 109
  and happiness 36, 37, 39, 40
  health-promoting behaviours 166, 167
  inequalities 139, 140*t*, 153*t*
    and Human Development Index, correlation between 144*t*
    and income, correlation between 156*t*
  life expectancy 192
  Mozambique 112
  Peru 117
  and security 223
  Thailand 103–4, 105–6
Heckscher–Ohlin model 55
historical context *see* evolution of development thought

HIV *see* AIDS/HIV
homicide rate 228, 229, 236
as community well-being indicator 214, 215
and insecurity 223
success and failure in human development 87–8, 88*f*
Honduras 32
Hong Kong 211
horizontal inequalities 140*t*, 152*t*, 217, 218, 228
and Human Development Index, correlation between 144*t*
and income, correlation between 156*t*
social cohesion 176, 177, 179
social exclusion 179
human development allocation ratio 49
human development improvement function (HDIF) 51–2
Human Development Index (HDI) 21, 123–4
Bangladesh 96
basic human development 208, 209, 235
in broader definition of human development 129
as core indicator of human development 130, 132, 149*t*
correlation with human development indicators 143–7, 144*t*, 146*t*, 148
high-income countries 147
and economic growth, relationship between 45
environmental sustainability 23, 232, 233
and happiness, relationship between 29, 32, 35–6, 35*t*, 36*f*, 41
inter-country inequality 216
Nepal 99
success and failure 74–6, 75*f*, 78–9, 91–2
economic performance 81–5
social indicators 79–81
Thailand 103
human development priority ratio 49
Human Development Reports 229
1990 229
Kant 232
objectives of human development 1, 21, 123
process of human development 33, 159, 208
Basu on 4n1
capabilities 21
Multidimensional Poverty Index 22
political economy 204
Human Poverty Index (HPI) 133, 134*t*, 150*t*
human rights (HR) 14
and happiness 27, 33–4, 37, 39, 41, 42, 44
social institutions and capabilities 167
Hungary 210

Iceland 211, 212
identity, national 177
ill health *see* health expenditure; health/ill health
illiteracy *see* literacy/illiteracy
immunization rate 107, 108, 114, 116
import-substituting industrialization (ISI)
Bolivia 113
evolution of development thought 8, 12, 15
negative transitions 119
Peru 115
income
Bangladesh 96
Bolivia 113
as core indicator of human development 130, 132, 149*t*
correlation with human development indicators 143, 146*t*, 146–7, 148, 156*t*
distribution *see* income distribution
economic growth and human development, relationship between 47–8, 53, 56, 60, 206
and education 48, 52–4, 56–7, 59, 60
environmental considerations 232
Ethiopia 107, 108*f*
evolution of development thought 1, 4, 6, 13, 20–1, 22
and happiness 37, 39
Mozambique 110, 111*f*
Peru 115, 117
success and failure in human development 75, 81, 82*f*, 84
income distribution
economic growth and human development, relationship between 52, 57
evolution of development thought 18, 24, 25
happiness 28–9, 32
Polanyi swings 191n6
see also Gini coefficient; inequality/equality
income tax 230
Independent Committee of Experts on Economic, Social and Cultural Rights 20
India
economic growth and human development, relationship between 47, 48, 50, 54n8, 56
empowerment 211
environmental conditions 233
evolution of development thought 8, 15
Green Revolution 54n8
independence 74n2
inequalities 216
mental ill health among the poor 40
National Dairy Cooperative Federation 169, 171
National Rural Employment Guarantee scheme 199, 226
Self Employed Women's Association 50, 169–70
sex workers 169
slum and pavement dwellers 169
social institutions and capabilities 169–70, 171

India (*cont.*)
social movements 196, 199
suicide rate 209
individualism 158–60, 234
Indonesia 47, 56, 66, 194, 210
industrialization 6, 7, 8–12
inequality/equality 129, 139, 215–18, 228, 229
Bangladesh 96, 97
Bolivia 114
Brazil 198
economic growth and human development, relationship between 48, 56, 57, 58
evolution of development thought 13, 24
gender inequality 217–18, 228
happiness 32
high-income countries 157*t*
indicators 131*t*, 140*t*, 145*t*, 152–3*t*
negative transitions 121
Nepal 100
Peru 115, 117
Polanyi swings 191
social cohesion 176
success and failure in human development 78, 81–3, 83*f*, 84, 85, 92
Thailand 102
see also Gini coefficient; horizontal inequalities; income distribution; rural–urban inequalities; vertical inequalities
infant mortality rate
correlation with human development indicators 146*t*
economic growth and human development, relationship between 51, 59–61, 62, 63, 68*f*, 70*t*
Ethiopia 108
evolution of development thought 8
Great Britain 191
Mozambique 110, 112
as physical well-being indicators 149*t*
success and failure in human development 76
Thailand 104
see also under-five mortality rate
inflation 115
informal employment
evolution of development thought 8
and Human Development Index, correlation between 144*t*
and income, correlation between 156*t*
as work conditions indicator 139, 140*t*, 141, 153*t*, 218, 219
insecurity *see* economic security; political security
interest rates 16
International Covenant on Civil and Political Rights 34
International Covenant on Economic, Social and Cultural Rights 14, 15, 34
international financial institutions (IFIs)
evolution of development thought 2, 13, 17–18, 20
Polanyi swings 190
tax systems 230
International Labour Organization (ILO) 13, 14, 15, 105
International Monetary Fund (IMF)
austerity policies 231
Bolivia 113
Brazil 197
evolution of development thought 17, 18n12, 20
Peru 115, 116
international poverty rate
as empowerment indicator 133, 134*t*, 149*t*, 210
and Human Development Index, correlation between 144*t*
and income, correlation between 156*t*
internet use 141, 141*t*, 153*t*, 221, 222*f*
investment
Bangladesh 96
Bolivia 113
economic growth and human development, relationship between 54, 57, 58, 64, 66, 206
Ethiopia 108
evolution of development thought 8, 18, 19
Mozambique 110
Nepal 100, 102
Peru 117
Thailand 103
see also foreign direct investment (FDI)
Iran 54
Iraq
carbon emissions 91*f*
economic growth and human development, relationship between 66
environmental conditions 226
Environmental Progress Index 90*f*
Gender Inequality Index 87*f*
health expenditure 80*f*
homicides 88*f*, 88
income 81, 82*f*
inequalities 83*f*
negative transition 78, 91, 95*f*, 96, 119, 120*f*, 120–1
political freedom index 86*f*
political violence 224
poverty 83, 84*f*
violent conflict 89*f*
Ireland 209, 211, 230
Islamic Salvation Front (Algeria) 119

Jamaica 214
Japan 211, 215
Jefferson, Thomas 27, 33
Jolly, Richard 13
juridical independence
  and Human Development Index, correlation between 144*t*
  and income, correlation between 156*t*
  as political freedom indicator 135, 135*t*, 136, 151*t*

Kenya
  economic growth and human development, relationship between 49–50, 53, 54, 56
  evolution of development thought 13
  Harambee Schools 50
  Luhya Elders Forum 200
  social movements 200
Keynes, John Maynard 188
Keynesianism 7, 16, 186, 189, 231
Korea, Democratic People's Republic of *see* North Korea
Korea, Republic of *see* South Korea

Labour Party (Great Britain) 188
labour share of corporate income 219–20, 220*f*
Laffer, Arthur 189
Latin America
  community well-being 214, 215
  country classification according to human development, economic, political, and social performance 182*t*
  economic growth and human development, relationship between 56, 62, 63, 64, 65, 68*f*
  economic insecurity 225, 225*f*
  education expenditure 79
  empowerment 210, 211
  environmental conditions 227*f*, 228
  evolution of development thought 6, 8, 17, 18, 19, 25
  happiness 32, 38*t*
  Human Development Index 75*f*
  inequalities 215, 218
  leisure conditions 221–2, 221–2*f*
  life expectancy 75, 192*f*
  literacy rate 192*f*
  living standards 192*f*
  Polanyi swings 190, 192
  political opportunity structure 195, 196
  scavengers 169
  secondary enrolment rates 80–1
  success and failure in human development 77*t*, 92
  suicide rate 209
  work conditions 218, 219*f*, 220
leisure conditions 141, 220–3
  high-income countries 157*t*
  indicators 131*t*, 141*t*, 145*t*, 153*t*
Leontief paradox 55
Lewis, A. 7, 8
life expectancy
  Bangladesh 96
  correlation with human development indicators 146*t*
  economic growth and human development, relationship between 56, 59–61, 63, 68*f*, 69*t*
  Latin America 192*f*
  Nepal 99, 102
  as physical well-being indicators 149*t*
  Polanyi swings 191
  pre-industrial Europe 191
  success and failure in human development 74–5
  US 191
life satisfaction
  and Human Development Index, correlation between 144*t*, 147
  and income, correlation between 146, 156*t*
  as mental well-being indicator 133*t*, 133, 149*t* *see also* happiness
literacy/illiteracy
  Bolivia 199
  correlation with human development indicators 146*t*
  female 96, 99
  Latin America 192*f*
  male 96, 99
  Nepal 99
  as physical well-being indicators 149*t*
  see also female literacy rate; male literacy rate
living standards 192*f*
Lula da Silva, Luiz Inácio 198

Madagascar 66, 210
Mahalanobis, P.C. 7, 8
malaria 55, 166
Malawi 49–50, 60, 195
Malaysia 47, 48, 66, 174, 200
male literacy rate 96, 99
male suicide 132–3, 133*t*, 144*t*, 146, 149*t*, 156*t*
Mali 60
malnutrition 18, 96, 116
manufacturing exports 141, 142*t*, 142, 154*t*
Marx, Karl 188
Marxism 12
material footprint (MF) 226–7, 227*f*, 228, 229, 233–4
maternal mortality rate
  Bolivia 114
  correlation with human development indicators 146*t*
  Ethiopia 108, 109

maternal mortality rate (*cont.*)
Mozambique 112
as physical well-being indicator 149*t*
Thailand 104
mental well-being 132–3, 209–10
high-income countries 157*t*
and income, correlation between 146
indicators 130, 131*t*, 133*t*, 145*t*, 149*t*
Mexico 19, 48, 196, 197, 213
Micronesia 214
Middle East
carbon emissions 90
community well-being 214
country classification according to human development, economic, political, and social performance 182*t*
economic insecurity 225, 225*f*
education expenditure 79
empowerment 210
environmental conditions 227*f*
health expenditure 79
Human Development Index 75*f*
inequalities 215, 218
leisure conditions 221–2*f*
political freedom 212*f*
political violence 223, 224
secondary enrolment rates 80
success and failure in human development 77*t*, 92
work conditions 219*f*
Mill, J.S. 31
Millennium Development Goals (MDGs) 5–6, 21–2, 24, 190
minimum wage policy
Bolivia 199
Brazil 198
evolution of development thought 8
and Human Development Indicator, correlation between 144*t*
and income, correlation between 156*t*
India 199
as work conditions indicator 139, 140*t*, 141, 153*t*, 218
mobile phones *see* phone availability
monetarism 12, 17, 189
Morales, Evo 113, 114, 198–9
Morocco 199–200
Mozambique
carbon emissions 91*f*
civil war 110
decentralization 118
economic growth 84, 119
education expenditure 79*f*
Environmental Progress Index 90*f*, 90
female secondary education enrolment 81*f*
Gender Inequality Index 87*f*
health expenditure 80*f*
homicides 88*f*
income 81, 82*f*
independence 110
inequalities 83*f*, 84
political economy 207
political freedom index 86*f*, 118
positive transition 76, 95*f*, 95, 110–12, 206
poverty 84*f*
secondary enrolment rates 80*f*
violent conflict 88, 89*f*
multiculturalism 177
Multidimensional Poverty Index (MPI) 21, 210n5
Bolivia 114
Mozambique 111
Nepal 100
Peru 117
Multi Fibre Agreement 98

national accounts 232–3
national poverty rate 133, 134*t*, 149*t*
natural disasters
as community well-being indicator 137–8*t*, 139, 152*t*
evolution of development thought 24
and Human Development Index, correlation between 144*t*
and income, correlation between 156*t*
Nauru 214
needs *see* basic needs
negative transitions *see* transitions: negative
neighbours, tolerance of
as community well-being indicator 137–8*t*, 139, 152*t*
and Human Development Index, correlation between 144*t*
and income, correlation between 156*t*
as social relations indicator 136, 136*t*, 151*t*
neoclassical economics 12, 18–19
neoliberalism 14–15, 16–17, 19, 230
neo-utilitarians 29–30, 31, 44
Nepal
carbon emissions 91*f*
civil war 99, 100, 101
Constitution 99–100
economic growth 92
and human development, relationship between 51, 54, 60, 66
education expenditure 79*f*
empowerment 210
female secondary education enrolment 81*f*
Gender Inequality Index 87*f*
health expenditure 80*f*
homicides 88*f*, 88
income 81, 82*f*
inequalities 83*f*
political economy 207

political freedom index 86*f*, 90
positive transition 85, 95*f*, 95, 99–102, 118, 206, 207
poverty 83, 84*f*
secondary enrolment rates 80*f*
Small Farmer Development Programme 101
social institutions and capabilities 170
violent conflict 89*f*
Netherlands 211
new growth theories 54
New International Economic Order (NIEO) 15
newspaper use 141, 141*t*, 153*t*
New Zealand 211, 215
Nicaragua 47, 48, 50
Niger 66, 210
Nigeria 217, 224
non-governmental organizations (NGOs) 50
North Africa
community well-being 214
economic insecurity 225, 225*f*
environmental conditions 227*f*
leisure conditions 221–2*f*
political freedom 212*f*
success and failure in human development 77*t*
work conditions 219*f*
North Korea 194, 212, 226
Norway 212, 216
nutrition 52, 55, 56, 57, 67
malnutrition 18, 96, 116

oil prices 15–16
Organisation for Economic Co-operation and Development (OECD) 12
Organization of Petroleum Exporting Countries (OPEC) 15–16
orphans, incidence of 137–8*t*, 139, 151*t*
Owen, Robert 188

Pacific
economic insecurity 225*f*
empowerment 210
environmental conditions 227*f*
Human Development Index 75*f*
leisure conditions 222*f*
political freedom 212*f*, 212
work conditions 218, 219*f*
Pakistan
Bangladesh's independence from 96, 97
carbon emissions 91*f*
economic growth and human development, relationship between 47, 53, 205–6
education expenditure 79, 79*f*
empowerment 210, 211
Environmental Progress Index 90*f*
female secondary education enrolment 81*f*
Gender Inequality Index 87*f*
health expenditure 80*f*, 80
homicides 88*f*
income 82*f*
inequalities 83*f*
negative transition 77, 91
political freedom index 86*f*
political violence 224
poverty 84*f*
secondary enrolment rates 80*f*
social institutions and capabilities 170
violent conflict 89*f*
Papua New Guinea
carbon emissions 91*f*
Environmental Progress Index 90*f*
female secondary education enrolment 81*f*
Gender Inequality Index 87*f*
health expenditure 80*f*
homicides 88*f*
income 82*f*
negative transition 77
political freedom index 86*f*
poverty 84*f*
secondary enrolment rates 80*f*
violent conflict 89*f*
Paraguay 196
pavement dwellers 169
Peasants Confederation (Peru) 115
pensions 101, 113, 199
People's Revolutionary Democratic Front (Ethiopia) 107
Peru
carbon emissions 91*f*
economic growth and human development, relationship between 48, 66
education expenditure 79*f*
empowerment 211
female secondary education enrolment 81*f*
FONCODES Project 116
Gender Inequality Index 87*f*
health expenditure 80*f*
homicides 88*f*
income 82*f*
inequalities 83*f*, 216
political economy 207
political freedom index 86*f*
positive transition 76, 95*f*, 95, 114–17, 118, 119
poverty 84*f*
secondary enrolment rates 80*f*
social institutions and capabilities 170
violent conflict 89*f*
Philippines 47, 49, 56, 209, 211
phone availability
and Human Development Index, correlation between 144*t*
income, correlation between 156*t*

phone availability (*cont.*)
as leisure conditions indicator 141, 141*t*, 153*t*, 221, 221*f*
physical quality of life index (PQLI) 20
physical well-being 149*t*
Pinochet, Augusto 194
planning 7, 8–12, 15
Polanyi swings 185–93, 200
political economy 184–204, 207
capabilities approach 202–4
lessons from the examples 200–1
Polanyi swings 185–93
social movements and political protests 194–200
political freedom 129, 133, 135–6, 212*f*, 212, 228
Bangladesh 97
high-income countries 157*t*
index 86, 86*f*, 90
indicators 131*t*, 135*t*, 145*t*, 150–1*t*
Mozambique 112
positive transition 118
political protests 185, 193–201
political rights and civil liberties 212
and Human Development Index, correlation between 144*t*
and income, correlation between 156*t*
as political freedom indicator 135–6, 135*t*, 150*t*
political security 129–30, 142–3, 223–4, 228
high-income countries 157*t*
indicators 131*t*, 143*t*, 145*t*, 154*t*
political stability/instability 57, 142, 143*t*, 143, 154*t*
political terror
and Human Development Index, correlation between 144*t*
and income, correlation between 156*t*
as political freedom indicator 135, 135*t*, 136, 150*t*
political violence 223–4, 223–4*f*, 235–6
and Human Development Index, correlation between 144*t*
and income, correlation between 156*t*
as political security indicator 143*t*, 143, 154*t*
Polynesian Islands 212
population growth 8, 56–7
portfolio share of investment 141, 142*t*, 144*t*, 154*t*, 156*t*
Portugal 211
positive transitions *see* transitions: positive
poverty
Bangladesh 97
Bolivia 114, 199
Brazil 198
economic growth and human development, relationship between 47–8, 52, 56, 59
as empowerment indicator 210, 211
Ethiopia 107, 109
evolution of development thought 8, 12–13, 17–22, 24
and happiness 36, 39–40
and Human Development Index, correlation between 147
and insecurity 223
India 199
Mozambique 111
MPI *see* Multidimensional Poverty Index
needs of the poor 127
negative transitions 121
Nepal 100, 101, 102
Peru 115, 116, 117
Polanyi swings 191n6
social institutions and capabilities 166, 168–71
success and failure in human development 78, 83, 84*f*, 84
Thailand 103, 104, 105, 106
see also international poverty rate; national poverty rate
Prebisch, R. 7, 8
primary school enrolment
1970–2014 10*f*
Bangladesh 99
Bolivia 114
Ethiopia 107–8
Mozambique 110, 111
Nepal 99
Peru 116
success and failure in human development 75
Thailand 103
prison population
and Human Development Index, correlation between 144*t*
and income, correlation between 146, 156*t*
as mental well-being indicator 132–3, 133*t*, 149*t*
Pua Thai Party 106
public expenditure
Bangladesh 96–7
Bolivia 113–14, 199
challenge to the human development framework 231
economic growth and human development, relationship between 49–52, 63–4, 66
evolution of development thought 18, 23–4
multi-ethnic societies 196
Peru 115–16
success and failure in human development 78, 85, 92
see also education expenditure; health expenditure
public health 192

public institutions index 137–8*t*, 152*t*
public reasoning 202–3, 204

radio use 141, 141*t*, 153*t*
Reagan, Ronald 16, 189
redistribution 13, 15, 28–9, 32
refugees 224*f*, 224
  and Human Development Index, correlation between 144*t*
  and income, correlation between 156*t*
  as political security indicator 142, 143*t*, 154*t*
remittances 101–2, 206
RENAMO 110, 112
research and development (R&D) 54–5
Revolutionary Vanguard (Peru) 115
road accident deaths 214, 215, 228
rule of law 228, 229
  as community well-being indicator 137–8*t*, 139, 152*t*, 214, 215
  and Human Development Index, correlation between 144*t*
  and income, correlation between 156*t*
rural–urban inequalities
  and Human Development Index, correlation between 144*t*
  and income, correlation between 156*t*
  as inequality indicator 139, 140*t*, 152*t*
rural–urban migration 8
Russia 38*t*
Rwanda
  carbon emissions 91*f*
  community well-being 214
  education expenditure 79*f*
  empowerment 211
  female secondary education enrolment 81*f*
  Gender Inequality Index 87*f*
  health expenditure 80*f*
  homicides 88*f*
  income 82*f*
  inequalities 81–3, 83*f*, 216
  political freedom index 86*f*
  positive transition 76
  poverty 84*f*
  rule of law 229
  secondary enrolment rates 80*f*
  social relations 213
  violent conflict 89*f*

Sachs, Jeffrey 113
Saint Lucia 212
sanitation 103, 106, 114, 116, 191–2
Sarkozy Commission 22, 26, 41, 42
Saudi Arabia
  carbon emissions 90, 91*f*
  economic growth and human development, relationship between 66
  education expenditure 79*f*
  female secondary education enrolment 81*f*
  Gender Inequality Index 87*f*
  health expenditure 80*f*
  homicides 88*f*
  negative transition 78, 84, 91
  political freedom index 86, 86*f*
  secondary enrolment rates 80*f*
  violent conflict 89*f*
savings 8, 19, 57, 58
scavengers 169, 170
school *see* education; primary school enrolment; secondary school enrolment
secondary school enrolment
  1970–2014 11*f*
  Bangladesh 99
  Bolivia 114
  economic growth and human development, relationship between 59–63, 68*f*, 206
  Ethiopia 107–8
  female/male ratio
    economic growth and human development, relationship between 206
    as empowerment indicator 134*t*, 135, 150*t*, 210
    and HDI, correlation between 144*t*
    and income, correlation between 156*t*
  Mozambique 110, 111–12
  Nepal 99
  Peru 116, 117
  success and failure in human development 75, 78, 80*f*, 80–1, 83, 84, 92
  Thailand 103
security *see* economic security; political security
Seers, Dudley 8, 13, 20
Selassie, Haile 107
Sen, Amartya 13, 20, 21, 27, 29, 33, 36, 41, 42, 124, 158, 159–60, 159n2, 162, 167, 193, 202, 203, 204, 231
Senegal 216
sex workers 169
Shinawatra, Thaksin 104, 105–6, 118
Shinawatra, Yingluk 106
Shining Path movement 115, 116, 170
Sierra Leone 56, 65n11
Singapore 209, 226
Singer, Hans 7n3, 13
skilled birth attendance 107, 108
Slovakia 211
slum dwellers 169
Smith, Adam 187
social capital 48n5, 52, 174, 176
social cohesion 172, 173, 174–9, 234
  components 176–7
  domains 176*t*
  high vs low 178*f*
  triangle 178*f*
social expenditure *see* public expenditure

social inclusivity 172, 173, 174, 178–9
social institutions and capabilities 158–83, 234–5, 236
  analysis 173–9
    as essential for human development 161–73
  classifying 173–4
  definitions 160–1
  effects on capabilities and human development approaches 179–81
  impact on individual capabilities 162–4, 163*t*
  and individual autonomy 164–7
  and individual capabilities, relationship between 171–3, 172*f*
  macro and micro aspects 174–9
  power 169–71
social integration 175
socially mobilized communities (SMCs), Nepal 101, 102
social movements 185, 193–200
social norms 160, 161–2
  analysing 174
  impact on individual capabilities 163*t*, 163
  and individual autonomy 164–7
  and individual capabilities 171
social relations 129, 136, 213, 228
  high-income countries 157*t*
  indicators 131*t*, 136*t*, 145*t*, 151*t*
social security 231
  contributions 230
  as economic security indicator 142*t*, 142, 154*t*
  and Human Development Index, correlation between 144*t*
  and income, correlation between 156*t*
  Nepal 100–1
  Thailand 104, 106
social solidarity 175
social spending *see* public expenditure
social well-being 234
Somalia 214, 224
South Africa
  economic growth and human development, relationship between 54
  empowerment 211
  environmental conditions 227, 229
  happiness 36
  inequalities 216
  social institutions and capabilities 169
  social relations 213
  squatter community 169
South Asia
  community well-being 214, 215
  country classification according to human development, economic, political, and social performance 182*t*
  economic insecurity 225*f*, 226
  education expenditure 79
  Human Development Index 75*f*
  leisure conditions 221–2*f*
  Polanyi swings 192
  political freedom 212
  success and failure in human development 77*t*, 92
  work conditions 219*f*
South East Asia
  carbon emissions 89–90
  country classification according to human development, economic, political, and social performance 182*t*
  economic growth and human development, relationship between 65
  education expenditure 79
  success and failure in human development 77*t*, 91–2
Southern Sudan 224
South Korea
  carbon emissions 91*f*
  economic growth and human development, relationship between 56, 66
  education expenditure 79*f*
  Environmental Progress Index 90*f*
  evolution of development thought 8, 18–19
  female secondary education enrolment 81*f*
  Gender Inequality Index 87*f*
  health expenditure 80*f*
  homicides 88*f*, 88
  income 82*f*
  inequalities 83*f*, 83
  political freedom index 86*f*
  political opportunity structure 194
  positive transition 76, 84, 90, 91, 206
  poverty 84*f*
  secondary enrolment rates 80*f*
  social movements 196–7
  suicide rate 210
  violent conflict 89*f*
Soviet Union 186, 209
Spain 230
spiritual well-being 129
Sri Lanka
  carbon emissions 91*f*
  economic growth and human development, relationship between 54, 56, 66
  education expenditure 79, 79*f*
  empowerment 211
  Environmental Progress Index 90*f*
  female secondary education enrolment 81*f*
  Gender Inequality Index 87*f*
  health expenditure 80*f*
  homicides 88*f*
  income 82*f*
  inequality 83*f*
  Movement of Thrift and Credit Cooperative Societies (SANASA) 170

political freedom index 86*f*
positive transition 76, 84, 90, 206
poverty 84*f*
secondary enrolment rates 80*f*
social institutions and capabilities 170
suicide rate 209
violent conflict 88, 89*f*
stabilization and adjustment policies 17–18
structural adjustment loans 17–18
structuralism 12
sub-Saharan Africa
community well-being 214
country classification according to human development, economic, political, and social performance 182*t*
economic growth and human development, relationship between 55, 65
economic insecurity 225, 225*f*
empowerment 210
environmental conditions 227*f*, 228
evolution of development thought 17
Human Development Index 75*f*, 76
income 81
inequalities 215, 218
leisure conditions 221–2*f*
malaria 55
Polanyi swings 192
political freedom 212*f*, 212
political opportunity structure 195
poverty 83
success and failure in human development 77*t*, 92
work conditions 218, 219*f*
substance abuse 166, 167
success and failure in human development 74–93
aggregate achievements 74–8
economic performance 81–5
environment 89–91
gender empowerment 87
homicides/violent conflict 87–9
political rights index 86
social indicators 79–81
Sudan 66
suicide 209–10
female 133*t*, 133, 149*t*
male 132–3, 133*t*, 144*t*, 146, 149*t*, 156*t*
sustainability *see* environmental sustainability
Sustainable Development Goals (SDGs) 22, 190, 231–2, 235
Swaziland 209
Sweden 212, 214, 219
Syria 209, 211, 223, 224, 235

Taiwan 8, 18–19, 211, 213, 226–7
Tanzania 53, 54
taxation 110, 230–1
technology transfers 15
telephone availability *see* phone availability
television ownership 141, 141*t*, 153*t*
terms of trade
Bolivia 113
as economic security indicator 141, 142*t*, 142, 154*t*
and Human Development Index, correlation between 144*t*
and income, correlation between 156*t*
Mozambique 110–11, 112
negative transitions 119, 121
neoliberalism 17
Peru 115, 117
positive transitions 119
terrorism 224
Thailand
Baan Mankong programme 105
carbon emissions 91*f*
community well-being 214
economic growth and human development, relationship between 48, 54
education expenditure 79*f*
Farmers' Federation 170–1
female secondary education enrolment 81*f*
Gender Inequality Index 87*f*
health expenditure 80*f*
homicides 88*f*
income 82*f*
inequality 81, 83*f*, 83
political economy 207
political freedom index 86*f*
political opportunity structure 195
positive transition 76, 95*f*, 96, 102–6, 117–19, 206, 235
poverty 84*f*
Rural Doctors' Society 105, 106
secondary enrolment rates 80*f*
social institutions and capabilities 170–1
suicide rate 209
violent conflict 89*f*
Thai Rak Thai Party (TRT) 104, 106, 118
Thatcher, Margaret 16, 189
Togo 65
Toledo, Alejandro 116–17
trade unions
political opportunity structure 196, 197
union density
as empowerment indicator 134*t*, 135, 150*t*, 210, 211
and Human Development Index, correlation between 144*t*
and income, correlation between 156*t*
labour share of corporate income 220
transitions, negative 94, 95*f*, 96, 119–22, 207
transitions, positive 94–119, 95*f*, 121–2, 206–7
Bangladesh 96–9

transitions, positive (*cont.*)
Bolivia 112–14
common features 117–19
Ethiopia 107–9
Mozambique 110–12
Nepal 99–102
Peru 114–17
Thailand 102–6
Trinidad and Tobago 214, 229
trust in others 228, 236
as community well-being indicator 136, 137–8*t*, 152*t*, 215
social cohesion 176–7
Tunisia
carbon emissions 91*f*
economic growth and human development, relationship between 66
education expenditure 79*f*
female secondary education enrolment 81*f*
Gender Inequality Index 87*f*
health expenditure 80*f*
homicides 88*f*
income 82*f*
inequalities 81, 83*f*, 83
political freedom index 86*f*
positive transition 77
poverty 84*f*
secondary enrolment rates 80*f*
violent conflict 89*f*
Turkey 197, 211

Uganda 50, 54, 195, 213
underemployment 8, 58
under-five mortality rate
1960–2014 10*f*
Bangladesh 96
as core indicator of human development 130, 132, 149*t*
correlation with human development indicators 143, 146*t*, 146, 148
high-income countries 147
East Asia 192
Ethiopia 109*f*, 109
Nepal 99
public expenditure 50
sub-Saharan Africa 192
Thailand 104
see also infant mortality rate
unemployment
challenge to the human development framework 230
economic growth and human development, relationship between 58
evolution of development thought 8, 13
and happiness 36–7, 39
and Human Development Index, correlation between 144*t*
and income, correlation between 156*t*
as work conditions indicator 139, 140*t*, 141, 153*t*, 218, 219*f*
union density *see* trade unions: union density
United Kingdom
Department for International Development 101
economic growth and human development, relationship between 53
empowerment 211
evolution of development thought 7, 16
happiness 30
see also England; Great Britain
United Nations (UN)
Convention on the Rights of the Child 20
evolution of development thought 15
Right to Development 20
United States
Agency for International Development 101
collective protests 193
community well-being 215
Constitution 27, 33, 34n7
Declaration of Independence 33
empowerment 211
evolution of development thought 16
happiness 27–8, 32, 34n7, 38*t*
human rights 33
life expectancy 191
Polanyi swings 191
Senate winners, electoral spend of 201n8
social institutions and capabilities 161
Universal Declaration of Human Rights (UDHR) 14, 34
utilitarianism 27–30, 43–4, 159
Uzbekistan 212

value-added (1960–2014) 9*f*
Velasco, Juan 114–15
Venezuela 196, 209
vertical inequalities 215–17, 218, 228
social cohesion 176
social exclusion 179
Vietnam 48, 217
violence
collective 142–3, 143*t*, 154*t*
political *see* political violence
success and failure in human development 87, 88–9, 89*f*, 90, 91

wages
Bangladesh 98
evolution of development thought 8
minimum *see* minimum wage policy
Walters, Alan 189
Washington consensus 17–18, 20
water
Bolivia 114, 169

environmental sustainability 22
Peru 116
Thailand 103, 106
Wealth Accounting and the Valuation of Ecosystem Services (WAVES) 23, 233
welfare economics 28
welfare state 203
well-being
evolution of development thought 22
see also community well-being; happiness; mental well-being; physical well-being; social well-being; spiritual well-being
Western Europe
community well-being 215
inequalities 215, 218
Polanyi swings 186
work conditions 219
women
education *see* female education
employment *see* female employment
empowerment *see* female empowerment
equal opportunities 166, 167
literacy *see* female literacy rate
married teenagers 133, 134*t*, 150*t*
micro-credit 98, 99
parliamentarians 133, 134*t*, 150*t*, 210, 211
socially mobilized communities (Nepal) 101
suicide *see* female suicide
women's groups 169, 170, 199–200
work conditions 139–41, 218–20
high-income countries 157*t*
indicators 131*t*, 145*t*, 153*t*
working hours 219, 221
World Bank
Bolivia 113
evolution of development thought 12, 14, 15, 17, 18n12, 20
Nepal 101
Thailand 105
Wealth Accounting and the Valuation of Ecosystem Services (WAVES) 233
World Development Report (1990) 20
World Health Organization (WHO) 105
World Values Survey 181, 213, 215, 222

Yemen 210

Zambia 65n11, 195, 200
Zimbabwe
carbon emissions 91*f*
education expenditure 79*f*
environmental conditions 226
female secondary education enrolment 81*f*
Gender Inequality Index 87*f*
health expenditure 80*f*
homicides 88*f*
income 82*f*
inequalities 83*f*
negative transition 78, 85, 90, 92, 121, 207
political freedom index 86*f*
political opportunity structure 195
poverty 83, 84*f*
secondary enrolment rates 80*f*
violent conflict 88, 89*f*

The manufacturer's authorised representative in the EU for product safety is Oxford University Press España S.A. of El Parque Empresarial San Fernando de Henares, Avenida de Castilla, 2 - 28830 Madrid (www.oup.es/en or product.safety@oup.com). OUP España S.A. also acts as importer into Spain of products made by the manufacturer.
Printed and bound by CPI Group (UK) Ltd, Croydon, CR0 4YY
14/09/2026
02216290-0004